STALEMATE

STALEMATE

Autonomy and Insurgency
on the China-Myanmar Border

Andrew Ong

CORNELL UNIVERSITY PRESS   ITHACA AND LONDON

Copyright © 2023 by Cornell University

All rights reserved. Except for brief quotations in a review, this book, or parts thereof, must not be reproduced in any form without permission in writing from the publisher. For information, address Cornell University Press, Sage House, 512 East State Street, Ithaca, New York 14850. Visit our website at cornellpress.cornell.edu.

First published 2023 by Cornell University Press

Library of Congress Cataloging-in-Publication Data

Names: Ong, Andrew, 1983– author.
Title: Stalemate : autonomy and insurgency on the China-Myanmar border / Andrew Ong.
Description: Ithaca : Cornell University Press, 2023. | Includes bibliographical references and index.
Identifiers: LCCN 2022036219 (print) | LCCN 2022036220 (ebook) | ISBN 9781501769139 (hardcover) | ISBN 9781501770715 (paperback) | ISBN 9781501769146 (pdf) | ISBN 9781501769153 (epub)
Subjects: LCSH: United Wa State Army (Burma) | Government, Resistance to—BurmaHistory—21st century. | Burma—Politics and government—1988– | Burma—History—Autonomy and independence movements
Classification: LCC DS530.65 .O524 2023 (print) | LCC DS530.65 (ebook) | DDC 959.105—dc23/eng/20220823
LC record available at https://lccn.loc.gov/2022036219
LC ebook record available at https://lccn.loc.gov/2022036220

For my parents
With gratitude for their grace, love, and patience

Contents

Preface	ix
Acknowledgments	xv
List of Abbreviations	xvii
Note on Transliterations	xix
Introduction	1
1. Peripheral Cosmopolitanisms	29
2. Topographies of Power	64
3. Oscillations and Incongruities	98
4. Frontier Accumulations	130
5. Gestures of Governance	162
Epilogue	196
Notes	205
References	231
Index	249

Preface

On February 1, 2021, the Myanmar military (Tatmadaw) launched a coup to take power in the country, imprisoning lawfully elected members of Parliament and the leader of the victorious National League for Democracy (NLD) party, Aung San Suu Kyi. The Tatmadaw created the State Administration Council (SAC) to govern Myanmar, as key NLD leaders either fled the country or were detained. A widespread Civil Disobedience Movement (CDM) emerged to protest the takeover and was quickly met with violent repression, with thousands of civilian deaths at the hands of security forces. Coming in the midst of the world's longest-running civil war of over seventy years, and the wake of the military's mass atrocities against the Rohingya people in Western Myanmar, the political landscape of the country was increasingly militarized and politically divided.

Widespread condemnation of the Tatmadaw, however, brought large parts of the country together. In the months that followed, NLD parliamentarians formed a parallel National Unity Government (NUG) from exile, bringing on board ethnic minority representatives. Any hopes of external humanitarian or "Responsibility to Protect" interventions quickly faded—the international community had little resolve to act. Together with Burmese civil society leaders, the NUG called for the twenty or so of the country's Ethnic Armed Organizations (EAOs) to join forces to defeat the Tatmadaw. These EAOs had been sporadically battling the Tatmadaw over the seventy years of civil war, yet only the Karen National Union (KNU), Karenni National Progressive Party (KNPP), and the Kachin Independence Organization (KIO) responded in any notable way. Most other groups remained silent or issued hollow condemnations of the Tatmadaw which were not backed up with military action.

The United Wa State Army (UWSA) was one group that remained outside the fray. With thirty thousand troops and a self-governed region of its own, the UWSA is by far Myanmar's largest EAO. In Wa Region, located on the border with China, the Chinese currency, language, and mobile networks are predominantly used, and the polity is far closer economically and politically to China than to Myanmar. The UWSA's military arsenal of artillery pieces, armored vehicles, anti-aircraft weapons, sniper rifles, and even armed drones would give any coalition against the Tatmadaw a significant boost should it get involved. But the UWSA has had a strangely ambivalent history of political relations with its neighbors. It wasn't clear which side it might back, if at all. The UWSA was a "spoiler" in the peace process, perpetually refusing to sign the Nationwide Ceasefire Agreement (NCA) of 2015, and even creating a political alliance opposing it. The UWSA repeatedly scuttled peace talks with the Tatmadaw and exchanged threatening statements over the last two decades. Most of its political demands had been ignored by the Myanmar government since its formation in 1989. But post-coup calls for the UWSA to join the fight against the Myanmar military fell on deaf ears. It was not a simple case of allyship over a common enemy.

In the years prior to the coup, there had been much talk about Myanmar as Western China's gateway to the Indian Ocean, and a strategic partner in China's Belt and Road Initiative (BRI) that would facilitate the projection of Chinese economic and military power westwards. "The New Silk Road" overland into Central Asia and the "String of Pearls" in the Indian Ocean were all stops in this ambitious geostrategic project to find political allies and economic partners across the globe. Sitting on the border of Yunnan Province in Southwestern China, Wa Region was a key piece of the puzzle for both Myanmar's territorial sovereignty and China's infrastructural ambitions. The planned China Myanmar Economic Corridor and an operational oil and gas pipeline running to the Indian Ocean ran only miles to the northwest of Wa Region. Wa Region was not just in a place to affect the geostrategic calculations of any Myanmar government but also well located to extract premiums of its own from trade and infrastructure corridors into the rest of Myanmar. Stability in and around the peripheral highlands of Myanmar, it seemed, was increasingly crucial to the ambitions and prosperity of the lowland giants.

The UWSA's refusal to throw its lot in with other anti-Tatmadaw forces across the country led to a whole slew of different explanations. Some observers described leaders of the UWSA as narrow-minded ethnonationalists who saw the coup as a Burmese problem rather than an issue for the entire country. Others asserted that the UWSA was a Chinese proxy, and China had not granted permission for it to be involved. Or that UWSA did not like NLD leader Aung San Suu Kyi and preferred to deal with the Myanmar military commanders they knew best. Or that UWSA members were only interested in making money through business deals and illicit economy, and the chaos across the country suited their goals of self-interested accumulation. None of these explanations were right, though each contained some elements of truth.

A closer look, however, suggests that the UWSA's lack of involvement was entirely in line with its political positions of the past two decades.

This book was written years before the coup, but its findings and descriptions of Wa Region and the UWSA and its worldview are extremely salient to Myanmar's post-coup political environment. It offers insights into how Wa Region maintains its autonomy and imagines its political future within the Union of

Myanmar, a perspective that yet remains unchanged. Understanding how power, capital, and governance operate in Wa Region hints at the types of arrangements and relations that it might take to accommodate the region within the country at some time in the future.

This is the story of how the UWSA and the people of Wa Region see the world from their peripheral highland. Through ethnographic accounts of interactions with ordinary people and officials and through firsthand descriptions of events that occurred between 2014 and 2015, this book depicts the values, practices, and relations in Wa Region that shape and enact its relational autonomy. By looking at both logics of authority in political culture, practices of governance, mobility, and commerce and political history and relations with China, Myanmar, and international organizations, this book depicts a process of region-making perpetually ongoing.

One key point I make is that the study of armed insurgents and their politics cannot be limited to deciphering their intent and explicit political demands in peace negotiations or their successes or failures in effecting governance of their areas. Such study also requires an understanding of their political culture—how they imagine their counterparts and navigate relations with them. These are shaped by social values and logics, one of which in Wa Region is a commitment to self-reliance and autonomy. Another point I argue is that while many of the movements and relationships that create autonomy in the highlands appear disorderly, unlawful, and subversive to the nation-state, these very same movements and relationships have produced an ongoing stability and limited the outbreak of armed conflict.

"Stalemate" is an empirical descriptor of the relationship between the UWSA and the Myanmar state, one that appears stalled, or at an impasse. Yet on closer scrutiny, a political dynamism unfolds. The absence of fighting yet lack of progress in peace talks is not a static deadlock of incompatible political demands but a fitful process of maneuvers and counterpostures: steps back and forward, left and right, a circuitous path to no teleological end, often with an appearance of political hiatus. The limited news coming from or produced about Wa Region is filled with stories of dynamic disorder—new weapons, drugs, secret talks, shifting alliances, illicit extractive industries, and troop movements. Few emphasize the somewhat paradoxical stability amid these tales of supposed chaos: Wa Region has not seen an outbreak of fighting against the Myanmar state for thirty years.

This paradox complicates the exhortations of political observers who call for more negotiations, the signing of peace agreements, and the implementation of federal solutions, while simultaneously pressing for the eradication of conflict economies and shadow trades. This causal-type analysis—that a lack of formal peace opens spaces for drug production, arms trafficking, and unsustainable resource exploitation, which in turn leads to more conflict—is too simplistic. But this does not necessarily call for "holistic" approaches to "conflict transformation." A dynamic stalemate recognizes the intersections of these issues and the impossibility of granting one primacy over the other, whether in priority or "sequencing," to adopt the language of peacebuilding. The notion of stalemate also suggests that political opportunism is always possible, that the absence of fighting is never guaranteed. The UWSA's current disengagement from the post-coup politics of Myanmar is not a given.

This book engages at least two problematics in political anthropology. It shows how peripheral polities at the edges of states have maintained their autonomy past the 1950s, past the period that James C. Scott suggested was almost impossible, given the expanding reach of lowland states. One quick answer often assumed in Myanmar studies is that the UWSA has profited off the drug trade, armed itself to the teeth with weapons from China and the black market, and then served as China's threatening proxy in Myanmar's civil war. China then uses its influence over the UWSA to bargain with the Myanmar government: "Accede to our political or economic requests, and we will send the Wa to the peace talks." This explanation, however, denigrates the autonomy, maneuvering, and agency of the UWSA.

The second problematic engages the difficulty of imagining political polities through lenses other than those of statehood or "stateness." We struggle with a tendency to view "nonstate" insurgent actors as pathological forms of states, failing, but always aspiring to "proper" or "fuller" statehood—whether in status or governance. The UWSA seems anomalous in this metric: why does it not, with its full control of its territory, strong military, and administrative apparatus, attempt to secede or declare independence? What does it really "want", and what is the "end state"? What are the benefits to maintaining a liminal, autonomous polity? What other logics of governance and autonomy are at play in Wa Region? Is the case of Wa Region an "unresolved conflict," and what might resolution look like?

Perhaps Wa Region is not as anomalous as it seems. Other autonomous regions—labeled "de facto states" or "states-within-states"—display similar forms of durability and stability. Nagorno-Karabakh, Transnistria, Abkhazia, South Ossetia, the Luhansk People's Republic, Zapatista areas in Chiapas, Tigray, Somaliland, Puntland, the Turkish Republic of Northern Cyprus, and other unfolding areas in Syria and Yemen have often been able to shift in and out of open armed conflict by maintaining ceasefires and order. Statehood is not necessarily temporarily deferred but often is left beyond the horizon, a distant possibility. These autonomous zones might offer lessons on how to stabilize conflict and avoid the onset of violence or its escalation, questioning our assumptions about the necessity of recognized statehood and state-like governance. Rather than being seen as unresolved conflicts, they could be seen as forms of stability and compromise outside the registers of "stateness." This book offers an insight into how one such region in highland Southeast Asia has managed to be just that.

There are no answers to the durability of Wa autonomy. Following the 2021 coup, Myanmar's faltering peace process is now dead in the water. The chasm between the NUG and the SAC positions has created a wait-and-see attitude among many of the EAOs. China continues to assert itself in its southern neighbor, previously brandishing the peace process, and now post-coup influence, as leverage. The Rohingya crisis (now almost forgotten) has destroyed channels between the international community and the Tatmadaw; Western mediation and facilitation are now barely feasible. Solidarities between the armed groups wax and wane; tin resources are running out in the Wa Region. The older generation of Wa leaders are moving on in age. What becomes of unity within each EAO and the ties between their future generations of leaders? This book offers stories and insights for the long term, as Wa Region's prominence in Myanmar's politics ebbs and flows.

Acknowledgments

This project first owes its conception and completion to the many friends and hosts I met in the field, in Wa Region, and in the neighboring Yunnan Province of China. I am deeply grateful for the hospitality and friendship shown by companions, officials, people in Pangkham, football teammates, and hosts in villages, who gave me a chance to understand a far-flung part of the world. They remain unnamed, but I recall their faces and demeanors fondly. I hope they see in this book a reflection of the world they showed me.

Colleagues at the World Food Programme gave me an opportunity to contribute, had patience with my mistakes, offered their friendship, and showed me an image of professionalism and commitment under many constraints. These include Domenico Scalpelli, Guillaume Foliot, Jean-Luc Kohler, Simon Hacker, Ayuka Ibe, Arsen Sahakyan, and Silja Lehtinen. In Pangkham, the WFP team treated me like family and provided warmth and companionship; much of the knowledge in this book I learned from their decades of living and operating in the region, in particular, SNM and AKL. My predecessor and mentor, SB, who looked out for me like a son—much gratitude for his vast experience and perseverance.

My professors and advisers at Harvard: the late Paul Farmer, who inspired the directions of the research and made it possible; the late Mary Steedly, for her encouragement and care; Ajantha Subramaniam, for her sharp wit and kindness; Arthur Kleinman, for his unwavering support and dedication to students; and Byron Good and Mary-Jo Delvecchio Good, whose care for my well-being extended far beyond academics. Also, Asad Ahmed, Steven Caton, and Nick Harkness for kindness in engaging with my work. Fellow students saw me through the research and writing periods: Marty Alexander, Vivien Chung, Margaret Czerwienski, Ofer Dynes, Shuang Frost, Sam Hawkins, Abbas Jaffer, Andrew Littlejohn, Jared McCormick, Benny Shaffer, and Dilan Yildirim. Naor Ben-Yehoyada, Namita Dharia, Veronika Kusumaryati, and Ramyar Rossoukh have all had significant input in shaping the ideas and writing of this book. I received funding from GSAS and the Asia Center at Harvard. I am deeply grateful for Tessa Montague, Annie Spokes, Will Frost, Marc Warner, Lauren Forbes, and Ilya Feige, who were indispensable parts of my time in Cambridge and supported me through difficult periods.

Colleagues at the Asia Research Institute (ARI) in Singapore were gracious and welcoming, giving me a space to begin rethinking my PhD dissertation. I thank

Maitrii Aung-Thwin, Michelle Miller, Shiori Shakuto, Sharlene Anthony, and Tim Bunnell in particular. ARI funded an invaluable book workshop where Maitrii, Louisa Lombard, Michael Gilsenan, John Buchanan, Courtney Wittekind, and Elliott Prasse-Freeman pored over an initial manuscript draft and made it much better. I also thank Michael Montesano, Moe Thuzar, and Terence Chong at ISEAS-Yusof Ishak Institute, who provided a place to continue my research and writing. This book was finally completed at Nanyang Technological University with the indispensable space and resources granted by Joseph Liow and Khong Yuen Foong. Much gratitude to two anonymous manuscript reviewers, and Jim Lance, Clare Jones, and Karen Laun of Cornell University Press, for their kind guidance in the editorial process. Also, Anne Jones and the copyediting team. I thank Steve Tickner for allowing me the use of his photograph of the UWSA's Thirtieth Anniversary celebration.

Much gratitude also to friends in Yangon—Max Belleri, Narcisco Rosa-Berlanga, Julia Stricker, and Margherita Pedroni. I would like to thank seven other Burmese friends and interlocutors for the wonderful conversations and insights we exchanged when I arrived in Yangon. I wish them grace, strength, and justice in this dire time. And other friends in Myanmar studies—John Buchannan, Stephen Campbell, Charlie Carstens, Chang Wen-Chin, Amy Doffegnies, Enze Han, Masao Imamura, Bertil Lintner, David Mathieson, Kevin MacLeod, and Hans Steinmüller—for their generosity, insights, and camaraderie. Magnus Fiskesjö at Cornell for his kind input and support. Elliott Prasse-Freeman for being my cheerleader and close reader of my work.

Finally, this book owes much to my family—Rachel and Joel and their beautiful children for their unconditional love; my parents, who dealt with anxiety and uncertainty repeatedly, showing great grace and unwavering care. And to my partner, for keeping us together and me grounded, and making me a better person.

Abbreviations

AFPFL	Anti-Fascist People's Freedom League
ASEAN	Association of Southeast Asian Nations
BGF	Border Guard Force
BRI	Belt and Road Initiative
CCP	Chinese Communist Party
CNY	Chinese yuan
CPB	Communist Party of Burma
EAO	Ethnic Armed Organization
FACE	Frontier Areas Committee of Enquiry
FPNCC	Federal Political Negotiation and Consultative Committee
INGO	International Non-Governmental Organization
KIO	Kachin Independence Organization
KKY	Ka Kwe Ye militia
KMT	Kuomintang
KNPP	Karenni National Progressive Party
KNU	Karen National Union
MI	Burmese Military Intelligence
MMK	Myanmar kyat
MNDAA	Myanmar National Democratic Alliance Army (Kokang Army)
MTA	Mong Tai Army
NCA	Nationwide Ceasefire Agreement
NDAA	National Democratic Alliance Army (Monglar Army)
NDF	National Democratic Front
NGO	Non-Governmental Organization
NLD	National League for Democracy
NRPC	National Reconciliation and Peace Center
NUG	National Unity Government
PLA	People's Liberation Army
PMF	People's Militia Force
SAC	State Administration Council
SAD	Self-Administered Division
UN	United Nations
UNFC	United Nationalities Federal Council
UNODC	United Nations Office on Drugs and Crime

USD	United States dollar
UWSA	United Wa State Army
UWSP	United Wa State Party
WFP	World Food Programme
WNA	Wa National Army
WNC	Wa National Council

Note on Transliterations

This book uses the Hanyu Pinyin system to romanize Chinese words. I use the notation "Chn" for both Chinese and Yunnanese terms, the notation "Bse" for Burmese terms, and the notation "Wa" for Wa terms. I use Hanyu Pinyin for place names in China, and the closest local romanization for place names in Myanmar and Wa Region, cognizant that a variety of spellings are used for the same place depending on the language of reference (e.g., Mong Pawk, Minepauk, and Mengbo are accepted romanizations for the same town in Wa, Burmese, and Hanyu Pinyin, respectively).

Given the potential sensitivity of research in Wa Region, I change all names of individuals except for the UWSA's chairman and well-known Myanmar political figures. These pseudonyms are kept consistent throughout the book. While I keep the names of townships and districts true, I create fictitious names for villages outside Pangkham. I also omit the specific positions or departments of Wa officials and other individuals but represent the general social profiles and status of these individuals accurately.

STALEMATE

INTRODUCTION

This is a book about insurgent autonomy: of region-making in a highland periphery controlled by Myanmar's largest insurgent armed group. A tale of a thirty-year traverse of a border landscape amid mutable political relations, competing narratives, and capricious shadow economies. This book tells a story of how an autonomous polity is constructed—through political military maneuvers and the intermittent excursions of people and capital at the edges of the state. Autonomy in the highlands is an assertion of self-reliance, dignity, and survival: it is not running away or merely keeping others out; it is about navigating relations and engagements with the outside. Here, border cosmopolitanisms and local logics of authority interact with regional geopolitics. This book is a view of these processes—values, practices, and relations—from the periphery, an account of elites and ordinary people inhabiting an insurgent zone between Myanmar and China, enacting the extraordinary political project of Wa Region.

The unrelenting road meandered around the knolls, descending first into the valley and past the small hydroelectric dam, then made a slow, steady climb in treacherous loops around spur lines, roads once carved into the hillsides with painstaking grit. Scattered rockfall lent clues as to the recency of road renovation. We were four hours into this journey, leaving far behind the gaudy hustle of Pangkham, the "capital" of Wa Region (see figure 1), where I had arrived a week earlier to work in the World Food Programme's (WFP) suboffice. My appointment, implementing food security programs in the hills, overlapped with

FIGURE 1. Town of Pangkham, the "capital" of Wa Region, May 2015. The pagoda to the right was renovated with funds provided by the Myanmar government.

that of my predecessor by several weeks: "I will make the introductions, you will learn to engage the leaders, and then you will continue this task on your own." These introductions entailed a road trip northward to another key town of the Wa hills, to greet a top-ranking official. It was part of paying respect and "reporting" (Chn: *bao*) to leaders whenever one arrived in their jurisdictions.

Outside the main town, Wa and Shan villages of anywhere between twenty and fifty households were spread across the remote hills, clustered houses with zinc roofs and thatched walls (see figure 2). Heading north, we passed light green fields of terraced paddy, dotted with trees and occasional rocks. We passed smallholder tea and pine plantations, sugarcane grown on slopes far off in the distance. Herds of tenacious black goats trotted roadside marshaled by young children. We passed through five of the twenty-four small townships that made up Wa Region, spaced roughly an hour's drive apart; their five-day markets drew in people of the surrounding remote villages, hours' walk from the main road. The towns were small settlements of concrete buildings lining the road, some partially demolished; one centered around a Shan monastery, another around a ramshackle market, and yet another around a spanking new township office. Sizable plateaus were hard to come by in these hills, and where they were found, small towns and old trading routes formed.

FIGURE 2. The road north from Pangkham runs through a Wa village, September 2015.

The insurgent group ruling Wa Region, the United Wa State Army (UWSA), is just over thirty years old. Wa Region itself is a part of Shan State in Myanmar and on the border with China. In 1989, ethnic Wa commanders and troops mutinied against the Communist Party of Burma (CPB), which had set up its bases in Wa Region. They drove the CPB leaders across the border into China, ending twenty years of CPB occupation. They had grown tired of the enlistment of Wa soldiers into the CPB's revolutionary struggle against the Myanmar state, which brought thousands of battle deaths for little in return. The fledgling UWSA quickly agreed to a bilateral ceasefire with the Myanmar government, one that has held for thirty years without open conflict. During this time, the UWSA established Wa Region (Wa: *Meung Vax*) as an autonomous territory, consolidated the Wa army, established an administrative apparatus, and maintained careful external relations with both China and Myanmar. The working language in towns and in the administration is Chinese, and Chinese mobile networks are predominantly used. The UWSA developed an economy initially built on opium, then rubber, casinos, and tin, completely adopting the Chinese currency (CNY). Segments of this economy materialized repeatedly along the road from Pangkham: a quiet gold mine with pits covered by a large, corrugated zinc roof, sprawling dark green rubber plantations reaching into the valleys, and fields of upland paddy where opium poppy once proliferated. The roads (old and new) were a historical repository, a mode of seeing, their trajectories curating a visitor's knowledge of the region.

The UWSA is Myanmar's and Southeast Asia's largest insurgent group, with a military of about thirty thousand today, governing four hundred fifty thousand mainly rural inhabitants across two noncontiguous swathes of territory.[1] Wa Region (Chn: *wabang*) is the primary territory on the border with China, the other being South Wa (Chn: *nanwa*), or the 171 military command, on the border with Thailand. These two areas are roughly twenty-seven thousand square kilometers in total, the size of Belgium.[2] The limited representations of Wa Region and its inhabitants in gossip and news reports make them infamous for three things: headhunting, drug production, and belligerent "spoiler" behavior. Media articles and books wove together their sordid past of highland headhunting and isolated "primitiveness," crafting the image of "Asia's Deadliest Drug Cartel" embedded in the narco-economy of the Golden Triangle, a group of reclusive and heavily armed warlords obstructing progress in nationwide peace talks.[3] Top Wa leaders were blacklisted by the US Treasury Department with million-dollar rewards for their capture; these media reports had put them third on the "wanted list" just behind Osama bin Laden and Saddam Hussein. Yet the lack of visitor access to the region and the drowning out of other narratives by rumors about weapons and narcotics production left the UWSA as one of the most poorly understood armed groups in Southeast Asia.[4]

The UWSA is an anomalous polity in the ambit of "nonstate" armed actors—unlike many of the armed groups across the country and beyond, it eschews secession and independence, committed to staying within the Republic of the Union of Myanmar—all this despite controlling its own territory and running its border crossings with China, with no Myanmar government presence. The UWSA leadership rejects being branded "rebels," defined as those who seek "either to capture the state or secede from it."[5] Insurgency remains the best descriptor: armed actors beyond state control who refuse to disarm. Polite allegiances to the country are periodically reaffirmed, and the ceasefire has held for thirty years, yet the UWSA is nowhere close to any form of political settlement. Its commander in chief, Bao Youxiang, was said by an interlocutor of mine to have remarked in 2015, "Why can't we just go back to the way it was before, when nobody bothered us?"

James Scott's 2009 highly influential thesis on state evasion posited that highland societies were shaped by their preoccupation with an escape from state capture. They developed particular social and political structures and used geographical distance and mountainous terrain to make it difficult for lowland states to incorporate them. Scott suggests, however, that this evasion was nearly impossible after the 1950s, when technological innovations and state legibility projects reduced the "friction of terrain." But Wa Region presents itself as a puzzle that drags Scott's theory on into the present day. How is it that this highland polity, while part of the Myanmar state's sovereign territory, has managed to remain almost completely beyond its grasp?

This book is not simply a history of the Wa polity's struggle in warding off encroachments by nation-states but an ethnographic account of its leadership who buttress their authority through capital accumulation and of ordinary people eking out livelihoods in the inhospitable mountains. How did a group of Wa guerrilla leaders establish an administration, build an economy, equip an army, and keep the Tatmadaw at bay up to the present day, where other groups slipped in and out of skirmishes and conflict? How has the militarized Myanmar state, described as simultaneously rapacious and indifferent,[6] come to tolerate these shows of defiance from a peripheral ethnic minority? And how should we understand the UWSA, too easily reduced to "rebels," "ethnonationalists," "warlords," "a de facto independent state," or "spoilers" in peace talks?[7] Answers to these inquiries lead us to reflect on the preponderance of state-centric assumptions that privilege institutions and order, and conformity to the global order of governance through nation-states.

We arrived in the northern town just as the sun's rays swept pleasantly in, a gentle basin high in the hills, flanked by a large mountain to the south. Even at an altitude over two thousand meters, it was strangely chilly for summer. Small knolls inundated with manicured tea bushes ring the eastern approach; the three roads that enter the town—north, southeast, and west—converge on its main market. A grand, red brick building sits amid one of the inner knolls, surrounded by a band of greenery, then rice fields at its base. Skirting the edge of the basin feels like peering down into a grassy bowl, thousands of small houses clustered within the catchment of green and orange.

WFP's role in Wa Region involved providing rice rations for schoolchildren, building water systems, and developing farmland assets. Food security in the hills was an extensive logistical enterprise of transporting and distributing food, a system thankfully set in place long before I arrived. My role was effectively one of relations management—reporting to Yangon headquarters and donors while maintaining good terms with Wa leaders for continued access and monitoring. This involved translation (language as well as procedures) and connection building, a challenge for all visitors adapting to new knowledges and dispositions, as I was to learn that evening.

We drove into the courtyard of the mansion, past the young armed guard: "Their rifles are taller than them," the common sneer went. Lined up on the basketball court and garages were all manner of vehicles—Humvees, Land Cruisers, pickups, and Lexus SUVs—others hidden under tarpaulins. Cars marked presence, their plates identifying who had arrived, who was leaving, and who visited frequently with whom.[8] No one who was anyone walked; it would embarrass all. This mansion was perched on the side of the mountain, with polished marble floors, patios, gazebos for sitting, koi ponds, and frangipani-lined pebbled pathways. Inside, a central staircase and dozens of rooms, surprisingly modest and somewhat dated aesthetics for Wa leaders' standards. The architecture was Chinese grandeur, brown marbled columns bearing a large mahogany-framed façade overlooking town, with pine trees and palms marking the extent of the property. Authority was made manifest in both scale and detail.

The leader had just woken up from his afternoon nap, walking slowly out to the veranda with the help of a soldier. An entourage quickly materialized. A young soldier brought the herbal medicines, another brought a lighter and cigarettes, and another helped the leader into his long coat. This was the leader's late afternoon routine—waking, greeting visitors and friends who awaited him, playing cards, snacking, smoking, and proceeding to dinner just as dusk arrived. With him that day were a series of Chinese and Wa visitors, some of whom were just passing through and others, I would later learn, who were regular fixtures.

My companion greeted him with a slight bow. A warm grin spread across his face as they embraced and exchanged pleasantries in Chinese. "You are back! The Burmese haven't gotten you yet!" I was briefly introduced but not made the center stage; old friends would catch up first. And old friends there were many—it would be an anxious and disorienting evening for me, distinguishing the visitors, conversations, ranks, and motives. I used Mandarin early on in my stay, but within months I became accustomed hearing and speaking the Yunnanese dialect, which helped greatly in engagements.

We sat across the veranda waiting for others to arrive. Visiting and dining were often all-male affairs, with nearly twenty men present that evening, taking turns to approach the leader. Some were his relatives, others close friends, and others officials informally reporting from the districts we had just passed. The UWSA runs an administration with seven "ministries" or departments ranging from finance to political works, overseen by a politburo and central committee, working primarily in the Chinese language. Despite breaking free from CPB rule and Communist ideology, the UWSA perpetuates the language and nomenclature of Chinese political structures. The Wa administration is headed by Chairman Bao Youxiang, also the commander in chief of the army.[9] The UWSA and the Wa administration run in parallel with the political wing, the United Wa State Party (UWSP; Bao is also its head), and the lack of civilian-military distinction leaves a seemingly authoritarian ethos; there is nothing approaching separation of powers.

We were ushered by the entourage to the dining room, where a plate of raw sashimi materialized astonishingly in the middle of the Wa hills, alongside a spread of other dishes. Blanched prawns were arranged on an adjacent dish, each critter an alarming bright orange. "We just brought it in from Mengding," the leader explained, referring to a Chinese border town in neighboring Yunnan Province. I cautiously disguised my lack of enthusiasm for raw seafood thousands of kilometers from the ocean. Dinner was a performance. Each time the leader reached for a pork bone, all nearby to sprung to their feet to assist him in this acquisition. This care and attention were partly due to age and unease of movement but largely from the importance of bodily displays of reverence and familiarity. Uniformed soldiers were ever attendant, providing sheets of tissue, filling rice bowls, pouring rice wine, and changing plates.

The toasts, a key part of dinner, began right from the start. Guests from other tables would approach the main table, toasting the leader first, and then the other occupants at the table, in order of perceived rank. Toasting practices were a complex domain through which respect could be given or denied—one-handed, two-handed, with or without bow, gulping the shot down, or sipping halfheartedly.[10] The visitors were all here to accompany, not necessarily to discuss any specific business, but to be present. Their backgrounds were a microcosm of Wa Region's political and economic world. One present was a Chinese businessman courting permission to work a mine, another an ethnic Wa personal accountant of the leader from China, another a member of a Wa cultural association from Myanmar seeking funds; others were Chinese former officials whose designations were unclear. And yet others had positions I would establish only long after the fact. This was but the first of many dinners to come.

Sashimi and prawns safely tucked away, the leader retired to an adjacent pavilion with a lounge area. More visitors arrived, sitting on the sofas or stools, smoking cigarettes. The flat-screen TV was always tuned in to the Chinese news or programs about military innovation and weaponry. By this stage of the evening everyone was boisterous and tipsy, the effects of the relentless dinner toasts wearing in. My companion sat next to the leader, whispering into his ear. Late in the evening came the quiet kind word and the vouching for so integral to the building of relationships. "He's a good guy, from a good school," "He's here to work and will write a book," "Take care of him," "He will work hard," and so on. The leader called a district official over and instructed him to exchange numbers with me: "Call him if there's any trouble."

These hospitality encounters were the myriad everyday events of region-making. They were the interfaces that unremittingly churned out business deals, traveling peoples, political agreements, security strategies, and patronage relations. Out in the remote Wa peripheries were a cosmopolitan mix of hustlers, agents, and big men tangling paths—navigating power, and reworking histories at all scales. And despite stories of chaos and disorder, a set of rules and norms were decidedly present, shaping these cross-boundary interactions. People built impressions, pushed national agendas, and exchanged commercial opportunities. Their ties scaled up to regional geopolitics—relations between Wa and Chinese businessmen, between townships and districts, between Wa leaders and representatives of international organizations, and between UWSA leaders and Myanmar commanders. These were the sites and encounters that produced Wa Region, smoothed over its edges, and kept its equilibrium for decades.

Relational Autonomy

This book is an ethnography of autonomy, an exploration of a highland polity staving off the engulfment of lowland states. It is about the articulation of a political project—neither state nor nonstate, neither separated from nor incorporated into Myanmar. Wa Region's autonomy, as this book demonstrates through five chapters of ethnography and history, is constituted through political maneuvers, capital accumulation, traveling and dwelling inhabitants, power relations, and forms of governance. This autonomy, I argue, is best understood as a *relational autonomy*, enacted through engaging with the "outside" by creating intermittent, oscillating political relations and managing porosity. Relational autonomy is also informed by an incongruity between local political culture and social values—how Wa actors understand autonomy—and the imposed expectations of statehood, territorial sovereignty, and governance of the modern world. Wa Region becomes illustrative: a fluid border zone where capitalism and forms of state formation come together to shed light on the ideologies of statehood. As Madeleine Reeves writes of the Ferghana Valley, another such liminal zone, these spaces "should be deemed neither exceptional, nor marginal, but *diagnostic*. They are sites that expose with particular clarity the contestation over the limits of the state—spatial, institutional and personal."[11]

I regard Wa Region as an autonomous polity to avoid linking it too narrowly with sovereign territory, even as boundaries of control are obviously meaningful to its military.[12] "Polity" also eschews state-centric thinking that incarcerates a potentially broad range of political projects in antagonistic ("nonstate"), pathological ("quasi-state"), or evolutionary ("proto/parastate") terms. Armed groups and insurgents are too quickly seen as a diminished mimicry of statehood: using "the language of failed states or bastard forms of belonging."[13] As Louisa Lombard argues in the Central African Republic, notions of diminished statehood are negative expressions of an ideal-type that poorly address empirical realities: "Yet rather than re-centering analysis away from the ideal-type state model to better align with the empirical context, people often end up sticking with the old state-based labels and categories. This ideal-type state form is a kind of phantom limb, albeit one the patient never had in the first place."[14]

I also refer to the polity as "Wa Region" to avoid premature assumptions about status and to conjure a place that is larger in the imaginary than a specific political entity (see figure 3). It is a place continually in the making, rather than the aspirational entity "Wa State" claimed by the UWSA. The Myanmar government has repeatedly denied the UWSA's request to elevate the status of their area to a "State" level, like that of Shan and Kachin States. I also refer to the "Wa State Government" (Chn: *wabang zhengfu*) as the "Wa administration," to better capture a sense of unrecognized governance that does not often operate according to state logics.

I have three objectives in this book. First, I intend to depict region-making and the enactment of relational autonomy—through an ethnographic story of the values, practices, and relations that make up Wa Region, the UWSA, and its inhabitants. The narrative of this book sees the world from the hills, turning the gaze back on the state from the peripheries through the schemes of elites and aspirations of ordinary people alike. Second, I unpack the constitution of this autonomy through a frame of *tactical dissonance*, a descriptor of the *oscillations* of political and economic relations, and the *incongruity* between the logics of local political culture and the commonplace understandings of what a sovereign state or modern government should look like. Third, I hope to provoke a rethinking of the relationship between *disorder* and *stability*. Relations and practices seen as disorderly and dangerous—the conflict economy, the arms and wildlife trade, the "bad" governance of the UWSA, and failed peace negotiations—turn out to be part of the long-standing and durable stalemate between the UWSA and the Myanmar military. They cannot simply be regarded as developmental or conflict resolution issues to be tackled individually or sequentially. I ask, in conclusion, what implications does this stability have for mediators and insurgent actors in Myanmar and beyond?

Autonomy, Region-making, and State Evasion

Autonomy in the Wa hills is a lived assertion of dignity and self-reliance—from the polity, from the leadership, from its inhabitants. On closer inspection, autonomy turns out to be extremely reliant on relations and connections, entangled

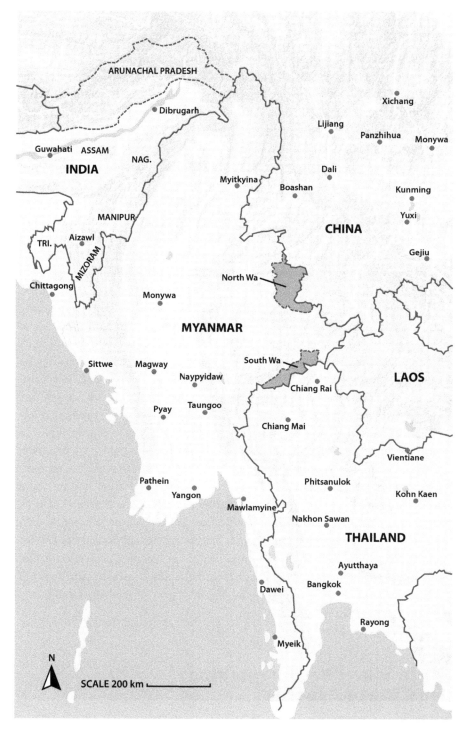

FIGURE 3. Map of Wa Region (shaded) as located within Myanmar and the wider Southeast Asian region. Note the UWSA controls a region on the Thai border as well, known as "South Wa."

with and susceptible to wider political and economic flows of the region. It does not exist in a vacuum, nor is it isolated in "zones of refuge" distanced from external influence, nor does it depend on external recognition bestowed by neighboring states or supranational organizations, based on registers of formal statehood in the international order. It continues amid the world's longest-running civil war in Myanmar. While autonomy may appear to be primarily de facto, based on the threat of armed violence protecting it from external aggression, it is never total, impinged on by neighboring economic and geopolitical constraints. Autonomy cannot be an essentialized freedom and noninterference. It is both a social value and a qualified empirical condition.

Highland autonomy has been famously framed by James C. Scott through the registers of evasion, an escape from the state into the shatter zones of "Zomia." In the *Art of Not Being Governed*, he dubbed Southeast Asian highlanders "maroon communities" or "state evaders," settling in "zones of refuge" populated by peoples fleeing the conscription, taxation, and enslavement of lowland states.[15] They adapted their cultural forms and political organization—"escape agriculture," egalitarian social orders, and oral instead of written histories—to resist incorporation into the lowland states. Scott caveated this, however, suggesting that Zomian autonomy was on the decline, that technological overcoming of the "friction of terrain" would render such autonomy impossible past the 1950s. States would ultimately gain a foothold and subsume these spaces into territorial and governing boundaries.

Scott's account triggered intense debate. It was criticized for historical and conceptual inaccuracies, most notably for creating simplistic binary between state evasion and state co-optation, or freedom and oppression. It purportedly effaced the possibilities for negotiation, leaving little else but "political paralysis" in between.[16] It also gave little credit to state projects, too quickly underplayed the benefits of their governance, and lumped a variety of state formations together.[17] Jonsson, in particular, accused Scott of romanticizing freedom and valorizing Zomians: "Western readers are offered goggles through which to see a binary of freedom and oppression; not inequality, contradictions, complexity, pleasure, or negotiation."[18]

But Scott never dismissed engagement between lowland and upland; acknowledgments of negotiated autonomy appear throughout Scott's account: "The process of positioning and mutual adaptation is, to a large degree, the leitmotif of hill politics."[19] Autonomy is not a binary divide between detached highland and lowland regions or states enabled by the friction of terrain but one constructed through relations of mutual engagement and negotiation. In this book, I offer a contemporary account of what highland-lowland or state-periphery negotiations look like at the level of elites and ordinary people. While there may no longer be room for running away, careful negotiation maintains possibilities for autonomous political projects.

Here, Iris Marion Young's conceptualization of relational autonomy as based on a self-determination through *non-domination* is instructive.[20] She contrasts relational autonomy against models of state sovereignty that are premised on noninterference and an impossible separation between inside and outside. Rather than noninterference and isolation, Young suggests that relational autonomy is the absence of domination. Cross-boundary relations continue but are as unmarked by injustice and oppression as possible. The Wa political project has long recognized this: it has never been about keeping outsiders out but seeking relations with neighbors characterized by respect and dignity. Nevertheless, as we shall see, questions of justice, nondomination, and inequality are contradictory once the gaze is turned inward within Wa Region.

Discussions of Scott's state evasion and residual autonomy in "zones of refuge" resonate with themes of sovereignty. Here, debates have emerged interrogating sovereignty's increasingly fragmented and interdependent nature.[21] To qualify the spatiotemporal dimensions of sovereignty borne and exercised by different actors, scholars have crafted a slew of prefixes: "graduated," "micro-," "disaggregated," and "lateralized," emphasizing contestations between state apparatuses, subnational actors, and global networks.[22] Debates about sovereignty have instead moved toward an appreciation of entanglement and relationality, as the political philosopher Wendy Brown argues: "[Sovereignty] has no internal essence, but rather is completely dependent and relational, even as it stands for autonomy, self-presence, and self-sufficiency."[23] Autonomy is a careful maneuvering to avoid domination, a condition effected by myriad practices and relations.[24] Like sovereignty, it is entangled and interdependent, defined by encounters and interactions at its boundaries. Wa Region's autonomy, though guarded by fortified knolls and bunkers, comes less from keeping intruders out than from managing their flows into and through it. This is the core of relational autonomy—not mere political arrangements or prescribed legal geographies, aspirationally codified in constitutions and ceasefires. Relations, rather than recognizable institutions, have primacy in this "nonstate" space.

It is autonomy, rather than the Western-centric, theoretically laden concept of sovereignty, that has been central for the Wa people.[25] A Mon-Khmer group numbering around a million spread across the hills of today's China-Myanmar border, the Wa consider themselves autochthonous to the area, acknowledged by neighbors to be among the oldest indigenous peoples of the region.[26] Warfare, constant raiding, and headhunting between neighboring Wa realms and villages created fortified villages as autonomous polities, resisting unification under a single chieftain or king, or the emergence of hierarchical political structures.[27] Wa society was egalitarian, without an elite stratification. The key anthropologist of the Wa, Magnus Fiskesjö, describes them as an "anti-state," a "predatory periphery" not evading surrounding states but engaging, extracting tribute, and often preying on them.[28] Consequently, the Wa language has diverse dialects within a small geographical area, the most prolific being Parauk of the Cangyuan and Kunma areas in the central Wa hills.[29] Chinese historians divided them into "tame" and "wild" Wa, based on practices of headhunting and the nature of their ties with surrounding states.[30] Many remain subsistence agriculturalists today, growing upland rice, millet, maize, poppy, and other crops, dependent on rainfall without irrigation systems (see figures 4 and 5).

The long-standing autonomy of the Wa hills has seen its ups and downs. It was disrupted in the 1950s with the arrival of Kuomintang (KMT) armies, searching for staging areas from which to launch counterattacks against the Chinese Communists. Wa chieftains formed guerrilla bands to defend themselves from outsiders, while raiding one another. Some allied with Burmese military garrisons at the perimeters of the Wa hills. In 1960, the China-Burma border was finalized following decades of negotiations between the Chinese and British; a line cleaved the historical Wa realms in two, without any prior consultation of indigenous Wa. On the ground, of course, it had little effect. The CPB arrived in the late 1960s, building alliances with several Wa guerrilla leaders in 1969 and incorporating their people and strongholds into ideological struggle against the Burmese state. The formation of the UWSA following the mutiny of 1989, however, ejected the CPB, creating an immediate ceasefire between Wa Region and the Myanmar state. April 17, 1989, now stands as the official date of the formation of Wa "statehood," the beginning of a journey that has now entered its fourth decade.

As spaces for idealized autonomy inevitably shrank, lowland states projected political and economic power into their peripheries. In Myanmar, many highland groups repelling the state turned to armed insurgency in the 1950s, and continue to today, navigating geopolitical relations in a region packed with state powers and cross-border extractive interests.[31] Armed groups were drawn into decades of co-optation and conflict: proxy CIA-Communist battles, land struggles, and narcotics trafficking and other shadow economies.[32] Autonomy had to be defended from a widening variety of actors: from the threat and occupation of the Myanmar military (Tatmadaw), from an overdependence on China for political support and economic markets, from the vicissitudes of frontier markets and commodity prices, from physical and legal restrictions on mobility through border crossings, and from the expectations and demands of the international community to eradicate narcotics and illicit economies. Qualified engagement, then, rather than evasion, was the name of the game.

FIGURE 4. Terraced farmland with paddy just prior to harvest in the Wa hills, August 2015.

FIGURE 5. Village on a spur line in the center of Wa Region, October 2015.

Tactical Dissonance: Constituting Relational Autonomy

My second objective is to illustrate *how* this relational autonomy is maintained through what I call *tactical dissonance*.[33] Tactical dissonance involves two elements—*oscillations* in political ties shifting between affinity to and distance from the Myanmar state, and an *incongruity* between Wa elites' understanding of autonomy and the modes and registers of statehood and sovereignty promulgated by the community of nation-states. Oscillation combines a sense of intermittence in tempo, fluctuation in degree, and ambivalence of direction.[34] This is most clearly seen in the fluctuating political relations between Wa Region and the Myanmar state, described in chapter 3. UWSA postures of opposition are complemented with acts of subordination, through strategies of making relations and then breaking them. This maintains an ambiguous position that widens space for maneuver. But the notion of oscillation also extends to the erratic mobilities of people, capital, and commodities, both controlled and facilitated by the UWSA. I detail these stories in chapters 1 and 4, with focus on moving people and capital, respectively.

The notion of incongruity reflects how Wa conceptions of autonomy do not conform easily to external expectations of effective governance or inviolable sovereignty. Instead, the Wa Region has only partially adopted state logics, raising a standing army and creating a government apparatus yet not fully developing services or investing in legibility projects to govern its subjects. Chapters 2 and 5 use ethnographic accounts of power, authority, and forms of governance to demonstrate the incongruities between Wa and external understandings of what a state or government should do for its people. In short, because governance in Wa Region is predicated on different logics and values, it often appears as bad governance to outsiders.

A curious military spectacle unfolded in Pangkham on April 17, 2019, three years after I had left. The "Grand Celebration of the Thirtieth Anniversary of the Establishment of Peace" saw contingents of stern-faced soldiers marching in salute around a new stadium, brandishing automatic rifles and rocket-propelled grenades. Next came antiaircraft guns towed behind trucks, and more white-gloved soldiers hoisting mobile surface-to-air missiles on their shoulders. Later, four armed drones mounted on the back of armored jeeps, ordnance attached to their pylons; then, a sniper platoon clad menacingly in bandanas and full ghillie suits, long-barreled rifles at the ready. Synchronized bootsteps echoed across the field, and starched olive-green uniforms bore the UWSA insignia.

But armed force was also punctuated by celebration—villagers in traditional Wa, Lahu, and Shan dress followed, baskets slung from foreheads, stooping as they advanced rhythmically to cut imaginary rice stalks with their sickles. Performers in colorful outfits represented all ethnic groups, the ardors of dance etched on their faces as they stepped left and right in concert, palms open to the sky. Students in tracksuits waved flags, a fluttering sea of primary colors, stars, and hills, matched by thousands more spectators lining the edges of the stadium and grandstand. The people and the military, it suggested, moved as one.

The insurgent parade was a spectacularly curated assertion of armed autonomy, interlaced with key gestures of deference and protocol. Chairman Bao entered the track in a military jeep, half-waving, half-saluting to the crowds. Photographers scrambled for the best shots as he took his place regally at the center of the grandstand. The flag of Myanmar and the flag of "Wa State," borne by two uniformed soldiers, were slow-marched onto the field. The crowd stood in silence as Myanmar's national anthem, "Kaba Ma Kyei" (Till the End of the World), was played—a song unfamiliar to most present. In a symbolic (almost hollow, given the weapons on display) gesture of subordination to the Myanmar state, the Myanmar flag was carefully hoisted higher than the Wa State flag (see figure 6).

"We do not push for separation, or agitate for secession" (Chn: *bugao fenlie, bunao duli*, lit. make noise about independence), Chairman Bao began his speech, reaffirming the stance of nonsecession, reiterating a commitment to the Union

FIGURE 6. Flag raising at the Thirtieth Anniversary Celebration, Pangkham, April 2019. Photo Credit: Steve Tickner.

of Myanmar. He reminded all present that the UWSA had in the past "defended" the sovereignty of the nation, coming to the aid of the Myanmar government against other armed militias. Yet the speech was laced with a latent threat: "With one hand we raise high the banner of peace and democracy, with the other, the banner of armed self-defense." Indeed, the fearsome weaponry on display seemed somewhat inharmonious with lofty pronouncements of the "establishment of peace" (Chn: *heping jianshe*).

This stalemate of "no war, no peace" between the UWSA and the Myanmar military has led to political observers of Myanmar's long-running civil war constantly trying to figure out their political position. Of the twenty or so Ethnic Armed Organizations (EAOs), none have the political and military clout of the UWSA. Their significance to Myanmar's conflict map stems from two aspects: the lack of claims for independence or secession, and their close ties with China, which veteran journalist Bertil Lintner describes as "giving Beijing leverage inside Burma."[35] Nonsecession and close relations with China mean the UWSA's allegiance to Myanmar is always suspect. Unlike other EAOs like the Kachin and Karen armies, they have almost no ties to the West. Rumors fluctuate between them either signing onto the Twenty-First Century Panglong Peace Conference (the nationwide peace process) or hindering it by enforcing an oppositional alliance. Rather than trying to uncover the specific UWSA political strategy, this book offers an insight into the UWSA's political culture, from values to relations to political practices, giving a sense of how the UWSA might view these political arrangements.

Indeed, the thirtieth anniversary celebration presented a microcosm of contemporary insurgent politics in Myanmar—marked by the presence of various distinguished guests in the grandstand front row. Seated directly to the left of Chairman Bao was China's Special Envoy for Asian Affairs Sun Guoxiang, who had spent the previous four years scurrying between the various EAOs of Myanmar, cajoling and advising their leaderships to participate in Myanmar's peace process. Chinese overt involvement in Myanmar's peace process began around 2016, despite declarations of nonintervention and respect for Myanmar's sovereignty. China hosted meetings in Kunming between the northern EAOs and government negotiators, acted as a go-between with the Tatmadaw, provided logistical support to ensure EAO presence at peace talks, and through Special Envoy Sun, visited EAO areas to listen and provide counsel.[36] None of this, of course, was solely in the service of world peace.

Following Myanmar's realignment of foreign policy toward reintegration into the international community from 2011, China moved to ensure it retained influence over its southwestern neighbor. Myanmar is crucial to China's geostrategic interests—for access to the Indian ocean, its wealth of natural resources, and its role in the ambitious infrastructural Belt and Road Initiative (BRI). China's state-owned and private companies invested heavily in hydroelectric projects, oil and gas exploration, plantations, and extractive industries across northern Myanmar.[37] Sun's presence in Pangkham was an expression of China's close relationship with the UWSA and its intentions to facilitate peace in exchange for a continuation of its "most-favored nation" status. As Lintner observed, "The UWSA is an effective bargaining chip when [China] wants to put pressure on the Myanmar government not to stray too close to the West.... Sending even more arms to the UWSA is what China would do if its strategic and economic interests in Myanmar are under threat."[38] The Myanmar delegation on Chairman Bao's right was even more revealing for the absences. Myanmar state counselor Daw Aung San Suu Kyi from the National League for Democracy (NLD) government had been invited, as had Tatmadaw commander in chief General Min Aung Hlaing, but neither accepted. Which heads of a sovereign state would show up to observe an insurgent parade of troops and equipment so defiantly displayed?[39] Accepting an invitation from the "Wa State People's Government" might bestow acknowledgment of its status, yet ignoring it completely was not an option, given their centrality to the ongoing peace process. Instead, the Myanmar government was represented by a Union minister and the vice-chair of the government's Peace Commission, retaining a degree of cordial acknowledgment.[40] Relations were lukewarm—the UWSA had refused to sign the Nationwide Ceasefire Agreement in 2015, leading other EAOs to also refrain from participation in the Tatmadaw's landmark quest for international legitimacy. Months later, the Tatmadaw would lodge a protest against the UWSA celebrations: "We can see that they acted like a parallel government and parallel army. I would say the Tatmadaw has shown the greatest possible tolerance in that regard ... because it wants peace."[41] In response, the UWSA reiterated its stance of nonsecession and pointed to military parades being par for the course in Myanmar celebrations, dismissing accusations of a challenge to the state as the work of agitators.

Farther to the sides of the Myanmar and China representatives were other UWSA politburo leaders, flanked by leaders of EAO allies in a show of armed solidarity. The UWSA had since 2015 emerged as the leader of the northern EAOs, organizing summits in its territory for discussions of joint negotiating positions against the Myanmar state. Despite having a bilateral ceasefire of its own, the UWSA allegedly provided arms, shelter, and training to other EAOs engaged in skirmishes with the Tatmadaw. These leaders visited Pangkham with increasing frequency; the commander of the burgeoning Arakan Army, which called for the autonomy of the Rakhine people, spoke enviously of the UWSA governing a territory of its own.[42] But solidarity had its limits: a coalition formed in 2017 was all but in tatters by 2019, some members engaged in fighting with the Myanmar while others kept the peace. It was difficult to keep a unified stance when circumstances varied greatly from one group to the next.

Missing from the grandstand were any representatives of the international community. Despite the excitement of having been invited to Pangkham by the UWSA for their maiden visits, they were ultimately denied travel authorization from the Myanmar government. "Don't say that we are not open to the outside; we have invited diplomats, heads of development agencies, and journalists, but it is up to the Myanmar government to decide whether they can come," a senior Wa official told me. Most international press watched from afar: only local journalists were allowed. Media sensationalized the event as "a show of force," how the Wa "flexed their muscles" in an "impressive display of power," the "big stick diplomacy" of a "de facto independent state."[43]

To the Burmese media, coming from lower Myanmar, several things were striking: primarily, the clear influence of China, with the use of Chinese signage, architecture, and currency in Pangkham, the Chinese mobile coverage networks, the speeches and everyday conversations in Chinese. Also evident was the stark progress in development compared with other places in Shan and Kachin States—Pangkham was filled with concrete high-rise buildings and paved roads, a sparkling new conference hall and stadium, glittering restaurants and clubs, neon glows radiating into the night sky. Finally, reporters were intrigued by the overt degree of autonomy and even defiance of this show of military force, the administrative ministries, and the hierarchy of UWSA officials. Some compared them in organization and strength to Hezbollah, others to the Tamil Tigers of old. Was this not a showcase of the prosperity that autonomy brought, an aspirational model for other armed groups?

These different visitors and the entities they represented were all involved in the political theater of Myanmar's ethnic politics over the last seventy years. They were part of the making of alliances, breaking of agreements, and declaration of political demands—oscillating between affinity and distance. Chapter 3 covers these intermittent histories in more detail. Across the political negotiations between the UWSA and the Tatmadaw from 2009 onward, the UWSA has never sought fully any of the possible political models on offer—of independence or territorial sovereignty, of federalism and confederation, of secession and rebellion. It struggles to articulate its understanding of autonomy to external actors. In fact, remaining slippery and refusing to have its identity reified—as separatists, rebel governors, drug lords, ethnonationalists, or a parallel state—is essential to the Wa project of dissonance.

Rethinking Disorder and Stability

Highland autonomy is a history of navigation—actors of the Myanmar-China highlands have for centuries extracted an economic premium from flows of people and things across their domains—Qing rebels, opium, salt, and minerals, the Burma Road of World War II, Kuomintang armies, and now timber and jade. Highland insurgents modulate flows by taxing, facilitating trade, building roads, establishing checkpoints, and threatening networks. In the last decade, as China's BRI projects have driven southward to the Indian Ocean, pipelines and transport corridors bisecting the Myanmar-China highlands have become central to geopolitics. Insurgents' premiums now make them valuable allies and strategic bargaining chips: they can create instability, threatening projects and holding Myanmar's reputation and international standing hostage. They also have their uses: as conduits for the billion-dollar jade trade, narcotics, and other extractive and plantation sectors, or as justification for continued Tatmadaw militarization. Leveraging their role as gatekeepers and facilitators along these corridors, insurgents buttress their prospects of survival through rent-seeking.

Yet while Wa Region threatens the Myanmar state's sacrosanct notion of national sovereignty, the relationship is not solely antagonistic. The Myanmar state has often co-opted peripheral insurgents through what Kevin Woods calls "ceasefire capitalism":[44] ceasefires in exchange for economic or extractive concessions. Taking the form of mining enclaves, jade concessions, plantations, and casino towns, these commercial relations have both expanded and fragmented the reach of the Myanmar state. Ken MacLean calls this the "entrepreneurial turn," a mode of governance through informal concessions (and competition with other militia groups), extending the Myanmar state's reach while paradoxically undermining its authority.[45] These illicit economies of the unruly borderlands have contributed to the maintenance of the thirty-year ceasefire between Wa Region and the Myanmar state.

Some relations with the Myanmar state could even be described as collusion. The UWSA ran an entire repertoire of illicit businesses through affiliated entrepreneurs and companies in the 1990s, utilizing commercial concessions granted by their good ties with Tatmadaw Senior General Khin Nyunt. The UWSA's reputation rapidly centered around the narcotics trade by the 2000s, with Golden Triangle opium central to its early economy. By 2002, *Time* magazine declared the UWSA a "Speed Tribe," an iconic photograph of a child soldier adorning its cover.[46] Despite a headline opium ban in 2005, the UWSA remained involved in heroin and methamphetamine production and trafficking, accusations lent weight by the sheer amounts of wealth accrued by the Wa leadership.[47] An impressive portfolio of property, plantations, extractive industries, and other investments in Myanmar and overseas now supplies the Wa apparatus and infrastructure projects. Wa businessmen and their affiliates are allegedly now key mafia-like players in the billion-dollar jade industry in Kachin State, using Chinese networks to monopolize cross-border flows.[48] The shadow economy included arms trafficking, narcotics, and even wildlife parts and online gambling, creating connectivity across autonomous regions. Central to this were personal networks and economic incentives for cooperation and the suspension of hostilities. Disorder, it seemed, somehow lent itself to stability.

In this sense, the enactment of Wa relational autonomy was also a story of highland frontier arbitrage. Standing between Myanmar and China, not merely geographically but also commercially, Wa Region was well positioned to extract surplus or favor through brokerage—of gems, jade, construction projects, and timber. The challenge, as Welker notes in her study of the "enactment" of the corporation in Indonesia, "is not simply to take such entities apart but to understand how in everyday life ordinary actors put them together."[49] This book, then, lays out the myriad economic processes, geographical affordances, political constraints, and everyday mobilities that conspire to produce an autonomous region at the margins of the state.

This paradox between disorder and stability challenges many of our basic assumptions underpinning policy work in conflict economies, state building, and peace formation. These policies seek to mitigate disorder by "addressing" root causes, seeking resolution and strengthening institutions. But if disorder is key to stability, then not treating it as pathology opens new modes of analysis. In Myanmar (and beyond), for instance, approaches that propose resource management and the equitable distribution of revenues or the regulation of shadow and illicit economies to avoid "fueling" conflict might have missed a key point.[50] The seeming disorder of conflict economies and extractive or commercial concessions are not only "business deals in lieu of politics . . . that do not address key political demands," as a political observer puts it. Instead, they are themselves integral forms of politics in Myanmar, central to the forging of relations, compromise, and possibly even peace.[51]

This book deals with a second theme, in addition to sovereignty, that of borderland studies. It is informed by the work of Southeast Asian scholars on how highland societies and agrarian principalities gradually came to terms with the reach of the modern state.[52] Previously cast as mandala systems of power and influence radiating outward from centers in the highland peripheries, these "interpenetrating political systems" gradually transited to a delineation of a geo-body of the territorial state, where nation-state boundaries were drawn through their lands.[53] Instead of focusing on territorial sovereignties of bounded nation-states, I follow border studies scholars who adopt process geographies—examining how economic networks and political relations construct regions and how economies exploit their locations as nodes along cosmopolitan pathways of circulations of Southeast Asia.[54] Agency and creativity of people and leaders are central to this tale of autonomy. Despite its reputation for reclusiveness and isolation, Wa Region is inextricably enmeshed in the borderland shadow economy; it is unclear where center ends and periphery begins, an autonomy of entanglement.

The third theme this book addresses is that of governance. Conversations in the burgeoning literature on rebel governance explore how rebel groups' governance techniques seek to optimize recruitment, buttress legitimacy, and accumulate resources for military ends. Such analyses often set state bureaucratic and technocratic logics as the benchmark for measuring effective governance. These assumptions often render governance instrumental. This book builds on the work of other writers in this field, who turn also to ethnicity, political culture, and custom, to examine political logics that shape the forms that governance takes. The negotiations and encounters between UWSA officials and developmental actors from the outside, which I describe in chapter 5, highlight the incongruities between a state developmentalist logic and logics of governance in Wa Region. It is these incongruities that accentuate the UWSA as "bad governors," or failing to provide for their people, "ruthless warlords" who turn a blind eye to the long-suffering peasantry. Governance, instead, becomes an arena in which political relations are negotiated, maintaining the relational autonomy of Wa Region.

Relational autonomy, then, gives us an alternate lens to some insurgent groups. If we regard insurgent groups like the UWSA as autonomous polities engaged in a political project of region-making, we focus instead on practices and relations. These practices are not necessarily rational pursuit of a political agenda or seeking to profit and accumulate but carving out a space in the world for themselves and their people. Autonomy avoids assumptions of rebellion and antagonism, of secession or ethnonationalism, which bring with them impetuses for certain types of intervention. Engaging such insurgent groups might seek not to buttress state building or capacity building, or address presumed underlying grievances but instead to first build relations across boundaries. Thinking of autonomy as dignity and nondomination, a project of the polity to manage its own flows, rather than evasion and freedom, might expand our possibilities and modes of engagement.

Access and Personhood

My entry to Wa Region came as the head of the WFP suboffice, a small outfit of twenty-four staffers implementing food security projects across the Wa hills. WFP had worked in Wa Region since 2004, initially engaged in opium-substitution programs to cover food gaps and cash shortfalls. Interventions gradually shifted to school feeding, nutrition, and the building of schools and water supply systems within villages. When I arrived in 2014, the number of nongovernmental organizations (NGOs) had dropped to three, from a previous high of nine, as donor interest flagged and access for outsiders became difficult. The Tatmadaw regulated NGOs' access by denying travel authorizations, using it as a tool, albeit ineffectively, to increase pressure on the UWSA. While the Wa authorities officially welcomed all forms of development assistance, making periodic appeals for support in agriculture and healthcare, new organizations found it difficult in practice to work at township levels, where a lack of prior personal relationships made officials suspicious of their intentions (see chapter 5).[55]

My research was an engaged anthropology—examining how political culture and logics shaped relations with external actors.[56] Project management in Wa Region—keeping logistics and relations smooth with UWSA authorities, ensuring access to villages, townships, and warehouses—and advocating for assistance from headquarters and donors down in Yangon positioned me as a broker of sorts. This was in fact a work of anthropological translation—explaining the nature of UN procedures and interventions to the Wa authorities while simultaneously conveying field nuances down to heads in Yangon. Translation failed as often as it worked. My engaged perspective colored the lenses with which I saw Wa Region, sometimes as a series of conflict and developmental problems to be tackled, sometimes as a hopelessly entrenched marginality almost insurmountable under the political and economic constraints.

The intermediary role made clear to me just how poorly the Wa political project and its practices fit with the registers of many outsiders. Many of the messages in this book are implicitly shaped by the task of explaining how things in the field operated to Yangon audiences. The combination of fieldwork and employment was a valuable point of entry; it positioned me as an inside-outsider, someone present with a job, a "work unit" (Chn: *danwei*) of my own, engaged in the collective endeavor of providing services. The UN was hosted with care but in no way adulated; officials would often say, "We appreciate your help, but after the UN leaves, we are still here." Wa officials were resigned when faced with what they saw as misunderstanding by outsiders: "By this time, if you UN people still cannot understand what is happening here, how can we explain further?"

The partial "insiderness" shaped my fieldwork in important ways—officials and friends rarely stopped to explain things to me or assumed I needed clarifications; instead, their interactions were largely candid and lacked additional layers of commentary. There were propaganda parades, interviews, and festivals, but mostly UWSA officials were surprisingly frank, perhaps also having a self-assuredness engendered by autonomy. Many stories I heard were not recounted directly for me but performed for an audience present at the dinner table or gathered at an official's house. This relative forthrightness allowed me to get an unmediated sense of the issues that mattered in town.

Being male gave me easier access to leadership circles but being unmarried in my early thirties undermined social status. Nor did I possess the portly gut of middle-aged business success. There were no kinship ties that bound me to any leaders; I relied on the strong ethic of hospitality of particular patrons, who made possible my liberties and access to others. I was viewed as a Singaporean (from the region), young, unthreatening, and inexperienced, possibly sympathetic, and willing to learn. I spoke Mandarin and within months had picked up the Yunnanese dialect, though the occasional regional accent remained beyond comprehension. The process of initiation was fraught with anxiety—figuring out how to navigate and position myself in the political landscape of Wa Region—exerting the right level of authority befitting my role, yet not overstepping the limitations of my age. This anxiety comes across through the ethnographic renderings.[57]

My research was, to a large part, the difficult task of "studying up."[58] The WFP role gave me access to UWSA officials and community leaders at all levels, and I was often invited to formal and informal meetings with visiting outside representatives in Pangkham, during a period of ongoing negotiations with the Myanmar government and other EAOs.[59] When I explained to top-ranking leaders early on that I was writing a book, some were indifferent, others encouraging: "Ask me anything; I will tell you and you can write it." Others were far more careful: "After you leave, do not spread falsehoods about this place" (Chn: *buyao luanchuan*, implying also, "Do not spread certain things to people it should not be spread to"). The fuller meanings of consent would have to be carefully navigated in both data gathering and representation. What interlocutors might not fully grasp were the implications of their statements, or how outsiders might interpret them, even as they remained unconcerned about possible repercussions. Factual stories about mining, weapons, casinos, drugs, politics, or the wildlife trade could too easily be sensationalized to the detriment of Wa Region. My initial writing was far more cautious, but in the years since I left the field, the political position of the UWSA has become even more assured, the passage of time offering me some leeway and freedom in divulgence. What to tell and how to tell it remain a key part of an anthropological responsibility.

A key element of navigating the politics of knowledge in the borderlands was knowing how to evaluate speakers and sources. People often spoke freely but also exaggerated and gossiped; it was less a question of hearing stories and more of learning who knew what and who could be believed. In a militarized masculine frontier society, few admitted ignorance; answers would almost always be given to questions. Much of the hearsay and gossip circulating in media reports could possibly have originated in such ways—eager inquirers asking questions that received confirmation from equally eager sources.[60] Indeed, Andrew Selth described knowledge production in Myanmar as a "mass of misleading chaff constantly floating around Rangoon."[61] Uncertainty might be an object of study in itself. This book deliberately disappoints readers searching for details about the narcotics trade or weapons and even details about political factionalism or the who's who of business conglomerates that investigative journalism tries to uncover.[62]

Despite being about insurgency, this book is not about armies and militarization. I did not have reliable access to the military elements of the UWSA, nor did I visit barracks or camps. Even though the green military fatigue is ubiquitous across the region, it is often used as durable farming attire, circulated by demobilized soldiers or militia. This leads the uninitiated to draw misimpressions that Wa Region is teeming with soldiers, ploughshares into swords on command. Of course, there are brigades cloistered in their camps up in the hills, down roads blocked off to prying eyes, and conscription and the reserve militia remain part of social life.[63] Videos posted to YouTube and Facebook, however, show UWSA military training and troop capacity, giving a sense of how sensitive (or not) these issues are.

Nor is this book about the narco-economy or arms trade; there are already a number of these texts, and reports, with varying degrees of reliability.[64] I refrained from asking directly about weapons, drugs, and other illicit trades, though stories were forthcoming in everyday conversations. My curiosity was constrained partly by an embodied caution but also by a sense of what I did not want to become, the type of person who asked questions wantonly (Chn: *dongwenxiwen*, lit. asking east and west), a reckless, indiscreet outsider with a sense of entitlement to receiving answers.[65] Fiskesjö writes of his time conducting research in Wa areas: "The question of propriety was a highly important issue: people reminisced about 'small things,' like how I had brought liquor and cigarettes to funerals."[66] Referrals and being vouched for by others were crucial to building social personhood; this created expectations, and I could not diminish the standing of those who spoke well for me. I tried my best not to succumb to the gratification that comes with being "in the know," peddling soundbites and intrigue, a constant temptation for those working in difficult areas.

This book deals with male leaders and officials and not with female leaders. There was only one woman holding a deputy bureau head role, and several heads of the Wa Women's Association (out of roughly eighty similar-level appointments). Leadership positions in this militarized setting were overwhelmingly male, even though the rank and file included many women. My social circles were also largely male—UWSA officials, business affiliates, footballing friends, village leaders, and WFP colleagues—and there were social limitations to my ability to spend extended periods of time with female acquaintances, especially those married. Future research will hopefully tell the stories of women in Wa Region, of gender in Wa households.[67]

Instead, this book is about how relational autonomy and region-making unfold, how political sensibilities and economic flows shape present geopolitical relations, and how the UWSA adapts its responses and tactics. Storytelling becomes a key mode of uncovering how the polity engages the world around it, far more revealing than interpreting official political statements. I tell stories of interactions, travels, contextualized utterances, material exchanges, and political culture. This is sense-making of what is starkly unfamiliar—illicit trades, children in military uniforms, the carrying of weapons, hierarchies and power relations, the poverty and long-suffering of ordinary people. To inhabitants these were simply part of the everyday: a dismissive wave of the hand and "This is not strange" (Chn: *buqiguai*) were common responses to my expressions of surprise. Wa officials were aware of how their practices appeared to outsiders—one advised me early on in my stay, "Well, at least you are here for a while. A place like this, I would say, you need two years to understand."

Outline

This book explores this tale over five chapters. Chapter 1 begins by uncovering the cosmopolitan nature of a seemingly peripheral Wa Region, examining its socioeconomic world and what it means to be an inhabitant of the region, a transitory blend of dwelling and traveling. Autonomy behaves as a bold assertion of self-reliance and independence, yet it is highly reliant on markets and regulation from the outside. Managing the porosity of the boundaries is central to the Wa polity. I explore the social worlds of urban and rural people, as they struggle to harness the promise of the borderlands, working different arenas to eke out livelihoods. But as much as mobility shapes the region, others often find their lives detached from the linguistic, employment, and educational structures of the wider country. Autonomy turns out not to be a form of separation and isolation or an enforced marginality in a self-perpetuating system, but selectively curtailing, permitting, and facilitating porosity and movement.

Chapter 2 examines the political culture of Wa Region, and the logics of authority that enable political relations. It depicts the meanings, sensibilities, and lived experiences of being powerful in Wa Region. Authority is based on values of autonomy—demonstrated through wealth, strength, and ability—but also the building of relations. This sense of autonomy is a continuation and adaptation rather than rupture with a Wa highland past; not simply a replacement of it with the militarized authoritarianism of the UWSA. These values and practices—what makes someone powerful, and how should he behave?—not only shape contemporary politics between and among elites and ordinary people but also scale upward onto Wa Region's relations with the outside. They form the cultural lenses through which UWSA leaders engage with Myanmar and Chinese counterparts. Through accounts of interactions, contestations, and events, I show how the ability to make sense of topographies of power and manipulate relations, and adequately performing hospitality and generosity, are central to successful political relationships in Wa Region. These ultimately have implications for relations between Wa Region and the outside. I hope these portrayals show more similarities than differences between Wa political society and other societies. The supposedly disorderly borderland is governed by recognizable rules and values of social propriety.

Chapter 3 scales logics of authority and political culture up to Wa Region's political relations with China, Myanmar, and other EAO counterparts. Stalemate is not stasis but the dynamic negotiation and maneuvering between actors and organizations. Tracing the longer history of the borderlands through the life history of a Wa official, it details the oscillations of armed politics and relations in the Myanmar-China borderlands (1950s–2000s). The chapter also narrates the incongruities between how autonomy is imagined and expressed by the UWSA leadership and by the Myanmar state in the peace negotiations (2012–2019). The government demands the preservation of sovereignty and an indivisibility of the Union, while the UWSA seeks to demarcate the front lines in practical terms to avoid skirmishes. Promises of solidarity and unity have their limits; mistrust is bred in the detail. I suggest that the history of the UWSA began as a project of autonomy that was gradually channeled into an ethnonationalist endeavor through what Lombard calls "conventionalization," forcing claim-making into established and recognizable modes and registers. Yet throughout the disorderly relations and failed peace negotiations, stability holds in the form of the absence of fighting.

Chapter 4 focuses on borderland figures and five types of accumulation that rely on cross-border movement, examining how accumulation and capital flows constitute Wa Region's autonomy. The frontier attracts capital to its spaces beyond the reach of state regulation, drawing on figures like the trickster, businessman, and entrepreneur, who exploit surpluses across boundaries to make a profit. Despite the image of disorder, the frontier has a culture and norms of its own, a mix of daring, spectacle, and vigilance: the five types of accumulation here take place through fraud, logistics, and the creation of spectacles. Wa Region's relational autonomy is premised on a receptivity to economic flows, yet this comes with a price, a precarious dependence on surrounding markets and prices. Autonomy is never without its constraints. Chapter 4 is a tale of the illicit, of improvisation, and of the hustle.

Chapter 5 focuses on governance as a field through which the authority of Wa leaders is performed and political relations with the outside are managed. Through stories of festivals, UN projects, discussions about development assistance, and the self-critiques of leaders, the chapter shows how logics of governance in Wa Region are incongruous with those of the bureaucratized, rationalized national state apparatus, contrary to the expectations of the "international community." Rather, they are deeply intertwined with local political culture and logics of authority. The chapter shows up the incongruities between the expectations of governance by NGOs, UWSA officials, and ordinary people. Commonplace critiques of the UWSA administration failing to adhere to "good governance" standards, perpetuating great economic inequalities and failing to provide healthcare and education services to their people, are not solely due to incompetence or "primitiveness"; they are also based on a different understanding of authority. Governance for the UWSA is not about effective provision of services or legitimacy building but gesturing toward providing for subjects, acknowledging and discharging the expectations that come with authority. Obligations end prior to material provision. Further, governance is an arena in which political relations are navigated with the outside. Development assistance is not regarded as a gift that Wa leaders need to boost their region but rather a conduit through which relations are managed with Myanmar, China, and the international community.

Louisa Lombard argues in the Central African Republic that the knowledge structures of international intervention and its optics are the larger problem, rather than a faith that more information or "context" about the political situation will help problem resolution ("people already have a lot of information").[68] Yet while I agree wholeheartedly, it seems that misconceptions about the UWSA are so ingrained, and information so scarce, that "context" seems still the first step in a struggling peace process. Fundamentally, more context and more information must also run parallel to an attempt to understand the political logics and practices of Myanmar's many insurgent polities on their own terms. This might lend itself to a truer renegotiation of state-periphery relations in Myanmar.

1

PERIPHERAL COSMOPOLITANISMS

> The goal is not so much to replace the cultural figure "native" with the intercultural figure "traveler." . . . What is at stake is a comparative cultural studies approach to specific histories, tactics, everyday practices of dwelling *and* travelling: traveling-in-dwelling, dwelling-in-traveling.
>
> —James Clifford, *Routes*

Landslide up ahead. Huge rocks, large enough to crush a person, have covered the entire asphalt road twice over. The air is hot and heavy; clouds fill the valley below. Vehicles have already begun to detour, skirting the obstacle through thick mud at the edge of the precipice. Hitting a large, submerged rock could roll a vehicle over the edge, to plummet into the gray mist below. Men stand at the sides, sleeves and trousers folded, throwing flatter rocks into the mud to help vehicles build traction. An unwitting minibus becomes trapped. Exasperated hollering and raised hands admonish the driver, who has now blocked the only remaining pass. We shut off the engine and wait. Passengers disembark, and a military truck, fortuitously in the queue behind, ambles forward. Ropes are tied, men shout orders, and the truck drags the hapless bus out of the mud. The driver parks it; he will not try again. The oncoming cars start now, and this time a Chinese-made pickup. My companion disparages the Chinese-made vehicles: "They are not strong enough for this area." As predicted, a defeated and bedraggled driver soon trundles over to plead for assistance. A Toyota Hilux in full reverse drags it out (see figure 7). Travel in these hills is a communal affair.

It is especially nightmarish in the rainy season, morale-sapping weather that halted Communist or Tatmadaw campaigns for months during the 1970s. Every year just prior to the rainy season is a quick military rush to gain ground before the hiatus. Dirt congeals into relentless mud or large ponds, bogging down vehicles, impassable in many areas. Large tracts of the road network in Wa Region are still awaiting sealing and tarring, in time for the 2019 thirtieth anniversary of the UWSA. For now, a good road is a wide road, where one does

FIGURE 7. A pickup stuck in the mud with a tow being organized on the road north from Pangkham, August 2014.

not fear slipping off the edge. Thick fog at night deflects vehicle headlights downward, reducing visibility to mere meters. Roving livestock add to the perils, and hardened ruts under the mud throw the vehicle from side to side as it advances.

Rain is friend and enemy; it prevents military advance but provides tactical barriers and impediments against the opposition. It nourishes crops yet eats away the farmland slopes for upland paddy. Water undercuts the dirt roads that villagers rely on for access to markets; road repairs of all kinds must be carried out after every season. One spots these work parties in drier Decembers maintaining preordained stretches, mobilized by local Wa authorities at one member per household, chipping away at slopes and filling the deep furrows.[1]

But travel was often a visual delight—the stunning beauty of the highlands unfolded in a horizontal sliver of bluish green in the distance, segments where hilltops emerge above the layer of low cloud. During the rainy season, a medium blue-gray canopy blankets Wa Region, and the sun absconds for weeks. Yellow-green rice fields fan out across the hills, punctuated by dark green clumps of bamboo, sprouting from cleared slopes like fraying shuttlecocks. Shrubbery or pine trees from smallholder plantations line the edges of the highway, their seedlings purchased in bundles from the market. Roads are framed by the high sloping walls of exposed orange dirt from large, stepped terraces cut into sides of the hills by the voracious diggers of the road-building companies.

A Tale of Two Crossings

Wa Region's roads span two different boundaries—one east, one west—both borders of securitized states, each with particular forms and feels of permissiveness. Roads channel the vision of the traveler, making legible the expanse of terrain, yet concealing others, forcing shadow acts to flee beyond. The routes in and out of Wa Region are weathered by decades of traversal from peoples and things. Roads and their affordances—vision, capacity, speed, porosity—become the makers of place, creating a blend of freedom, refuge, distance, and containment.

Boundary 1: West

The road to Pangkham from Myanmar areas begins in the Shan town of Lashio, turning southward headlong onto the old Burma Road. Diverting east across the Shan plateau, gray concrete roadside dwellings become sparser, potholes appear, and roads narrow, their edges eaten away by impatient overtaking drivers. Past the dusty petrol stations, past old silver mines, past sand and rock quarries. We are still in Myanmar government-controlled territory.

"This is owned by Wa Region," my companion says, implying the polity's capacity to take ownership, as he gestures at a vast walnut plantation. In people's imaginaries and everyday speak, there is much overlap between the political entity and parallel commercial enterprises, between public and private. The land is reportedly leased for a price to one of the UWSA's affiliated companies by local Tatmadaw commanders. In fact, many of the roads running from Myanmar areas to peripheries like Wa Region were built by conglomerates owned by insurgent leaders or their kin.[2] Lucrative contracts and asphalt smoothed over past rifts.

We pass Dangyan, a "garrison town" on the way to the Wa hills, scarred by the fighting of the *Ka Kwe Ye* militia (KKY; see chapter 3) and Communist Party of Burma (CPB) periods. Dangyan, initially an amalgamation of small Shan villages, then bolstered by Yunannese refugees from the 1950s, has a centuries-long history of trade connections through the Wa hills. Chang Wen-chin describes it as a black-market hub for opium and silver trading in the 1960s, when its population was 80 percent Chinese.[3] Several figures in this chapter were born here, outside of Wa Region proper; it is now little more than small streets of houses bisected by two main thoroughfares. Police checkpoints guard both routes into town, with faded mugshot lists of wanted criminals in tattered plastic nailed to their wooden posts.

Uphill on the approach are at least two Tatmadaw bases. Farther from Myanmar state control, the odd militia (*pyithusit*) checkpoint appears, and a scruffy guard emerges to lift the gantry. We scamper through with a wave of the hand before he can ask questions.

A view of the Tar Gaw Et Bridge, completed in 1997 and spanning the Salween River below, emerges. It is still another forty minutes' drive down the winding road to the river, through the luxuriant vegetation that engulfs both sides of the deep gorge. Large trucks make five-point turns to get around the tight corners. The Salween is *the* river of Shan State, a barrier, a conduit, a source of biodiversity and nourishment, an emblem of identity. On one bank, a series of nondescript wooden structures with zinc roofs house the Myanmar Immigration, Customs, Military Intelligence, and Border Affairs officials, whose sole task seems to be collecting paperwork (one stack each). The wait here can take up to an hour if tensions are high—on one occasion in 2015, Wa vehicles were delayed for hours in a tit-for-tat reprisal for the UWSA's refusal to grant Tatmadaw officials passage to China. Tar Gaw Et is the only official crossing point to Wa Region over the Salween (see figure 8), but at least two other informal barge crossings are used where the river

FIGURE 8. Crossing Tar Gaw Et Bridge into Wa Region, September 2014.

eases into flatter terrain. Timber, cars, cattle, minerals, and other commodities cross there to evade official taxation. Crossing the Salween is crossing the threshold.[4]

Intriguingly, the spur line on the opposite bank is also Myanmar-controlled, fortified with Tatmadaw outposts, protecting the eastern flank of the bridge. This sliver of land, Man Kan subtownship, seems the wrong side of the Salween, vulnerable, and surrounded by Wa army outposts to the north and south. Up the ridge is a Shan village, thatched houses around an old Banyan tree, the ground inundated with a nauseating layer of pig feces. Beyond this, a breathtaking pagoda is perched on a large boulder on the edge of the hill, a proper tourist attraction were it not for its precarious frontline location. Two more sets of Tatmadaw gates where unfamiliar travelers are interrogated—*why ever would they want to enter Wa Region?*

The no man's land between the front lines sees a winding saddle between two knolls, dominated by several UWSA bunkers. When tensions rose over skirmishes in South Wa in 2015, the overgrowth was burned to clear a field of fire. The Wa boundary gates are surprisingly lax with passage: a barbed wire fencing (demarcating minefields?) creates a channel through which bright yellow dump trucks and private taxis cross sporadically, as do petty laborers on motorbike. Fortifications are foot-wide wooden logs piled into a barrier and packed with earth, covered with a zinc sheet, with little attempts at camouflage. These have been the boundaries since 1989, and everyone knows where everyone else is.

From this boundary crossing, the road winds downhill into Man Xiang township and the rest of Wa Region proper, with the newly built thoroughfare still showing signs of collapse and fragility (see figure 9). Connectivity is not a given.

Boundary 2: East

To the east, the Nam Kha River marks the international border between China and Myanmar. Nestled in the dark green foliage of the rubber plantations are a series of makeshift bamboo huts, temporary shelters for the waiting porters and boatmen on the banks of the river. For 100 CNY (16 USD), rubber dinghies and bamboo rafts readily materialize from the shrubbery to transport people or goods into the slower eddies on the opposite bank, bypassing customs checks or border inspection. There is a boatman for the crossing, fee collectors on arrival, motorcycle riders for transport to the bus station, and porters to help with goods. This mini-industry is manned by the Dai inhabitants of Menga Village of China—"In the past they used to call the police when strangers appeared in their village. Now they warn everyone whenever the police emerge from the station. They even hide crossers in their village if a patrol passes," a friend says, chuckling. This informal crossing, tolerated by the Chinese security apparatus, occurs in full view of the official border bridge several hundred meters upriver.

FIGURE 9. A road collapse in the hills on the road north, September 2015. Road repairs are needed after every rainy season.

Over the past six years the illicit crossings have moved farther downstream, as Chinese authorities fortify the riverbank to prevent erosion, inscribing material authority in the process. Simple fencing and a paved track run along the embankments on the Chinese side, both a park for evening jaunts and a possible route for border patrols, a delineated field of vision for surveillance cameras. But dirt trails always find their way through the plantations down to the water. Travelers wait in the small eateries lining the main road a few hundred meters away, whisked down to the river by motorbike when the coast is clear. Rubber dinghies, big enough for six people lying down plus a boatman balancing precariously at the edge, harness the current to drift into the opposite bank. Clients include tourists from Yunnan trying their luck at the casino in Pangkham, casual construction laborers from Sichuan, entrepreneurs from as far as the eastern Chinese cities, and groups of miners from all over. Wa Region is practically open—a tent is set up on the Wa side of the riverbank where "registration" occurs with a young soldier on duty. Any form of documentation will suffice. The fee is paid, and the migrant ambles down into town.

The Chinese authorities did make some attempt to control this crossing, with border police occasionally patrolling the banks of the river and increased video surveillance. A tired barbed wire fence and signboard warnings were part of the obstacles that border crossers nonchalantly sidestepped. Checks increased when numbers became too blatant, if security campaigns were launched at the provincial level, or if a dignitary was visiting nearby. Or if a changeover of border guard unit required a stern first impression. Other friends told me stories of warning shots being fired to stop border crossers in their tracks, but never with a sense of heavy-handedness, since these were mainly ordinary Chinese citizens. Many were let off after questioning in police stations, and others fined token sums of money depending on their status. This was a porosity that was discretionary and unpredictable.

A Wa official laughed at my surprise over such blatant contravention of immigration law, challenging one's impression of the totalitarian disciplinary Chinese state. "This does not count as illegal crossing [Chn: *toudu*]," he said; "illegal crossing is when you travel to America hidden in the back of a container. Here, this happens by the hundreds every day and it does not worry either side, since most are locals [Chinese or Myanmar nationals]." Others dismissed it with bravado—"I have been back and forth more times than I can count. Everybody does it. I just show them my ID if stopped; anyway, they know I am not up to no good; they are reasonable. What can they do? People need to make a living."

Upriver, the official bridge to China is the "Menglian Port Joint Inspection Station" on the Chinese side, its Wa counterpart a large white building with blue roofs, adorned with the horns of the Wa totemic water buffalo. The bridge was built in 2007, and as a Chinese Provincial Level Crossing Point, Chinese locals cross to Wa Region with either a Border Pass (Chn: *bianminzheng*) or an Exit and Entry Permit issued by the Chinese police (Chn: *churujingzheng*). A Wa visitor traveling in the opposite direction would have his Wa Identity Card (Chn: *wabang shenfenzheng*) checked and be issued a pass in return for leaving his household registration document at the checkpoint.[5] This, of course, was subject to change, depending on the political winds.

A distinct division of space in the entire cross-border transport industry gives clues to commodities on the move—heavy dump trucks or large, twelve-ton cattle trucks with double rear axles sit on the outsides of the roundabout. Smaller trucks for household products have open tops with metal bars. A hefty, orange construction digger perches on a flatbed truck at the opposite end. Inside the roundabout are short queues of three-wheeler taxis waiting for passengers and their wares. Groups of men congregate here in the morning sun for daily labor, rushing to offer their services whenever a pickup pulls up. Toiling middle-aged women flog hotel brochures to new Chinese arrivals. Sedans and motorbikes arrive to drop off friends, customers, and goods. Some Wa-registered cars return from China, with dozens of people crossing on foot in either direction. Pickups with Chinese plates have just come over the border; bags of carrots and leafy vegetables have passed the inspections. Another is full of heavy-duty tires for trucks. Sand, stone, bags of cement, rice, PVC pipes, meat, and electronics. Everything waits, waits, and then moves.

Cosmopolitanism, Porosity, and Relational Autonomy

Borders, we are told, are not impermeable bisections; they are sites of creativity and innovation, where people find ways to breach, to infiltrate, to bypass.[6] "Secret trades," "illicit flows," "shadow economies," "porous borders" highlight the informality of boundaries, inhabitants indifferent to the territoriality of the state.[7] The state is also implicated in its own transgression, what Carolyn Nordstrom calls the "extra-state" harnesses state apparatuses to facilitate movement for profit and survival—bribing, coercing, co-opting, and evading state agents.[8] Here, the bridging of borders and frontiers is valorized, ordinary people drawn to discrepancies in prices and legalities created by borders and states, exploiting rent gaps produced by different regulatory regimes. There are ethnic Wa, Chinese, Burmese, Shan, and Lahu; some from other urban centers, many from rural villages—now all residents of Pangkham. They extract premiums through this movement across borders, subverting the state yet profiting off the limits of its laws and markets.[9] These are the enterprises, the transactions and circulations that enact a region.

This chapter charts out the social world of Wa Region, beginning with the complex relations between people: ethnic Wa people (*wazu*), "local people" (*bendiren*), "borderlanders" (*bianmin*), Myanmar nationals (*miandianren*), migrants (*waidiren*), visitors, villagers (*nongmin*), ordinary people (*laobaixing*), or entrepreneurs. Many consider themselves, and others, "inhabitants" of Wa Region: the "*wabangren*," or a person from or of Wa Region. *Wabangren* is limited neither to the ethnic Wa people (but also Chinese, Shan, Lahu, even Burmese), nor to nationals of Myanmar (but also China, and those who have never registered with any authority), nor to those born here. Instead, it describes a borderland belonging to the region as a whole. The "inhabitant" challenges meanings of local and outsider, migrant and native. It breaks down histories of indigeneity. Belonging becomes region-making.

And yet many of these inhabitants, particularly those in Pangkham, are on the move. James Clifford's notion of *discrepant cosmopolitanisms* reminds us that not all people and commodities move with equal ease and success.[10] Clifford attends to the overlaps between *dwelling* and *traveling* as modes for cultural comparison, rejecting simple distinctions between cosmopolitan travelers and local sedentarist "natives." Instead, "cultures of displacement and transplantation are inseparable from specific, often violent, histories of economic, political, and cultural interaction."[11] Much movement is marked by impermanence, without the prospect of settling or safety, without security of life and livelihood. Nor does movement in and of itself guarantee progress or flourishing, contra some of the romanticized claims of the "mobilities turn."[12] Political histories and socioeconomic structures shape the possibilities and constraints of movement for varied peoples. Mobility, as Julie Chu reminds us, is a quality that manifests in varied forms—traveling business class or stowed away in a cargo container—each form valued differently by audiences and bundled with other qualities such as speed, comfort, lightness, and privilege.[13]

A sense of frontier liberty pervaded Pangkham. Despite the touted authoritarianism of the UWSA leadership, some inhabitants spoke of a personal freedom beyond the surveillance of the Chinese and Myanmar states, "We are free here; you can go wherever you want." "Everyone here from China has something wrong with them—they come here to evade the law," another friend mused; "here they do whatever they want." There were few to no identity checks to arrive and move within Wa Region; the price of this freedom was a heightened susceptibility to the whims of the borderland political economy and "security situation." There were frequent arrests and returns of alleged criminals to China, while ethnic Burmese people were sometimes treated with suspicion, needing a local patron to anchor them in town society. Pangkham and the other smaller towns at the edges of Wa Region—Nam Tit and Mong Phen—fluctuated in size, receiving travelers fleeing conflict or crackdowns or seeking opportunities. The border world for many was marked less by a concern for relations with the metropoles, but relations with other frontier towns—all nodes in the political economy of the China-Myanmar border, temporary destinations of travel and dwelling (see figure 10).

Governing this region called for a Foucauldian security apparatus of semi-regulated flows—permitting circulation and attracting capital so that value could be extracted or retained but stepping in when limits of tolerance were approached.[14] Chinese-supplied CCTV cameras cropped up at key road intersections in Pangkham, and observation posts loomed ominously over the town from cliffs on the Chinese side. It was not clear who was on the other side of these screens, what they might be looking for, and what conduct was deviance. Flexibility and ambiguity remain the order of the day for frontier authorities—harsh laws scare away businesses and capital that flourish in partial legality; lax laws give little security to person and property, discouraging enterprise.

In this chapter, I show how porosity and movement are central to socioeconomic relations and the making of the autonomous polity. Relational autonomy required compromise and adaptation to the prevailing constraints of regional

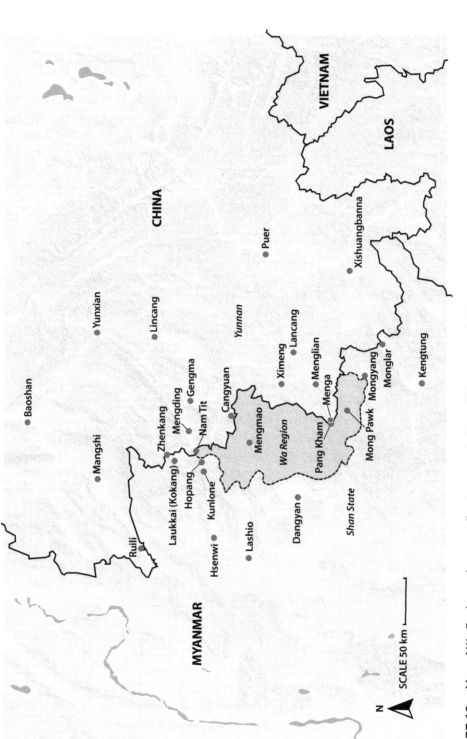

FIGURE 10. Map of Wa Region and surrounding towns and cities of Myanmar and China.

politics and markets: rather than enforcing borders or keeping out intruders, it was the management of porosity and movement. Movement is inherently intermittent—halted by weather, security, or economic or political conditions. While ordinary people and Wa officials spoke of freedom in Pangkham, they were acutely aware that this autonomy hinged on an ability to navigate political relations and local forms of authority (see chapter 2). Freedom had limits. It did not exist in a vacuum. Personal or political projects might transgress borders but were bounded by norms and social expectations. The aggregate sum of these resulting relations, "dwelling-in-traveling" and "traveling-in-dwelling" of ordinary travelers and political leaders alike, constituted autonomy, both proud assertion of self-reliance and the regulation of vulnerabilities.[15]

Cows were a simple example of this cosmopolitanism, leveraging border disparities to extract premiums. Large cattle trucks pile toward the Chinese border crossing, their captive bovine the true boundary crossers. They had first been marched from areas surrounding Dangyan west of Wa Region, where they had been grazed to maturity on the flatter lands of the Shan plateau. Then, floated on barges across the Salween into Wa Region, they are tethered in sixes with bamboo poles, lumbering along the roads, heavy hooves kicking up dust amid the gravel. Weary men trudge alongside their charges; the cows, strapped with rice, pots, clothes, and other supplies, are goods-bearing goods themselves. They camp out along the roads in the evenings, on journeys that take up to two weeks. The convoy lumbers through Pangyang before arriving on the outskirts of Pangkham, sold there to Chinese businessmen. Large, caged trucks take them across the Chinese border and into Chinese cattle markets, where a single cow (Chn: *huangniu*) fetches between 8,000 and 11,000 CNY (between 1,330 and 1,830 USD). Deducting taxes, earned profit was half the total sale price (i.e., six to eight cows brought profit of between 30,000 and 45,000 CNY [between 5,000 and 7,500 USD]). From this, of course, the costs of one to two years of rearing were deducted. By contrast, a cow sold locally in Wa Region might earn 4,000 to 6,000 CNY. Pigs, on the other hand, were banned from sale into China for fear of cross-border disease.

Arbitrage had become increasingly difficult in recent years. Cattle herders were under pressure from both Myanmar military and Shan militias to pass through their checkpoints, paying them dues. This competitive taxation was destroying profits through double charging. If herders traveled through Shan checkpoints and ran into a Burmese checkpoint later on, they would be reprimanded or fined for having evaded the earlier Burmese checkpoints (unable to produce the requisite receipts) or accused of supporting the Shan militia. This happened in the converse manner as well. Similar cattle trade routes from Eastern Shan State to

Thailand had completely ceased for these reasons by mid-2015; the route to China was still viable, albeit with greatly reduced profits.[16] Taxes on the Wa side were more stable—a "registration fee" (Chn: *dengjifei*), a Salween River–crossing fee, regular road checkpoint levies, and finally the official government registration and vaccination charges.[17] There were simply too many actors involved along the way, and ad hoc checkpoints made cost estimation nearly impossible. The porosity of travel in the borderlands invited the caprice of rent-seeking along the way.

Dwelling-in-Traveling, Traveling-in-Dwelling

Ah Yong is back in town today. He shifts between Pangkham and Mong Yang, his small hometown in Myanmar government–controlled eastern Shan State, a three-hour drive across muddy roads beyond Wa Region. A stocky thirty-one-year-old ethnic Chinese man, he quickly recruited me into his football faction when I first arrived. Evenings with him are routine—a quick shower after the game, and back out to one of the little roadside barbecue joints for skewered meat and copious amounts of cheap Chinese beer. His elder brother Ji joins us on evenings when there are no European football matches. Otherwise, he remains glued to screens at the casino hoping bets cash in. Kyi, his portly Aini friend (described by Ah Yong as someone who plies "his routes"), shows up as well.[18] The borderlands are full of itinerants like them, who cross boundaries on a weekly basis in search of money.

Ah Yong's younger sister married a chief aide of a Wa Politburo leader and has been living in Pangkham for several years. Officially "unemployed" but always laboring, Ah Yong helps take care of his sister's children, and his brother-in-law often gives him money for expenses. His parents run a medium-sized provision store back in Mong Yang. Haphazard stacks of plastic buckets, incense sticks, and packs of toilet paper swamp the storefront of the family shophouse on the market street. In his twenties he drove a tractor cart ("trawlergy") across the boundary into Mong Phen in Wa Region, selling Burmese and Thai goods there. "What did you sell?" "*What didn't I sell?*" Thai products add variety to those from China—Western household names like Danish Butter Cookies, Oreos, or Dettol reach Wa Region from the Thai border via Tachilek and then Kengtung, subject to customs duties and informal taxes along the way. By late 2015, tolls had become so high that it was no longer worth importing them, and Pangkham stocks ran low. For mercantile people like Ah Yong, livelihoods often meant trading and moving tangible things, buying and reselling (among the younger generation e-commerce over the Chinese social networking app WeChat has emerged, with varying success). Over the years he has been all over eastern Shan State, Wa Region, and into China, fluent in Chinese, Burmese, and Shan.

Ah Yong's mobility between Wa and Myanmar areas is facilitated by possession of both an official Myanmar ID and a Wa identity card. On the former his ethnicity is given as Lahu, one of Shan State's minorities—"It is not easy to make an identity card as a Chinese," he explains. When conflict sparked between the Tatmadaw, UWSA, and Shan EAOs and militias in the 1990s and 2000s, he ran to the relative safety of Kengtung, afraid of being recruited as an ammunition porter by armed groups. He hates officials, soldiers, and the police: "They are greedy; they take from the people; they are all the same. But the Tatmadaw particularly is full of drunkards and criminals, enlisted as long as they have arms and legs." He has no allegiance to any side: "It is the people who suffer. When they want to fight, we run to wherever is safe. If here is chaotic we run there. If there is chaotic we run back here." Inhabitants like Ah Yong call into question presumed links between population, territory, and identity.

But the informalities that permit his supposedly seamless travel are precisely what makes sustaining livelihoods difficult. Detached from land and formal labor, employment is based on fleeting personal connections. More recently, Ah Yong found work as a foreman for a hotel construction project, a hotel owned by another of our football friends. The work lasted no more than a couple of months. As we down glasses of weak beer and chew sunflower seeds amid card games, Ah Yong talks about the difficulties of looking for work: "I would like to travel out to find work, but I have no education; it is always hard to find work outside." "Is it hard to get a job as an ethnic Chinese?" He claims no, there is no discrimination in Myanmar, contrasting it favorably with America's past of slavery. "Here, people generally get along and it's the government and military that they don't like. The military abuses everyone, Burmans included."

As we drop Ah Yong's sister off later that evening, she prompts me: "Is there a job in your office? Can you find a role for him?"—a request he has been too shy to make himself. But he has only been in school up to Grade 4, before the instabilities of Eastern Shan State forced him to move. Because he is without basic English or mathematics skills, the UN has no place for him, even as a driver. His list of daily appointments instead includes watching local cockfights, football, massages, karaoke evenings, chewing on skewers of barbecued meat with friends. Ah Yong sends me voice notes when he is back in Mong Yang (he can read but finds typing into the phone slow) and video clips of himself lounging on a friend's porch in front of paddy fields. His other WeChat Moments show visits to a Shan temple, the scores and results from a football tournament, scenes from travel on roads. Shopkeeping and allowances from his elder sister cover most of his daily costs, but there is little in the way of longer-term employment. He is not struggling to survive, but he is not able to raise a family. Ah Yong's mobility is stagnant, transitions without accumulation. What might autonomy mean to inhabitants without material provision?

Transitions and Circulations

After jumping the railings into the football field at the People's Park in Pangkham, giving a quick glance across the field reveals the extent of today's attendees. There is Ah Liu, a Chinese officer in the UWSA transport unit based in Pangkham, and Lei, a skinny, hard-running Wa-Burmese man from Dangyan who works odd jobs on construction sites in town. Ah Chit, a short, portly Wa from Dangyan, has a big man complex validated by a crew of Burmese sidekicks employed in his construction firm; he has some lesser ties to the leaders here. Nyi Du, a sinewy Burmese car mechanic whose talents include chewing betelnut while chasing the ball, relentlessly distributes its dark red stain all across the field. Xian, Burmese, has an excellent left foot. Aung, a tall, bulky Kachin man from the Kachin liaison office in Pangkham, drives the Kachin Independence Organization (KIO) representative around town. Ai Nyi, Rong, and Sam Rong, all young Wa men in different administrative units of the UWSA (including the commercial tax bureau), I have met off-field in their uniform on several occasions. Shwe, a menacing hothead with fading tattoos and supposed links to Shan militia, plies the road down to Kengtung and Tachilek. Tun is a burly Shan driver for one of the deputy ministers of finance; Saw, the Karen building contractor who works on Ah Chit's hotel properties; and Ah Hong, a Wa driver for the wife of a UWSA leader. Htun, supposedly a highly skilled Burmese carpenter, makes furniture for Pangkham's wealthy.

I have been playing here for more than a year now, several evenings a week. I can tell friends from a great distance by the way each one runs and moves. Football, through its recurrent micro-tests of composure and solidarity, reveals a great deal about one's personality. Most are in their early twenties, the older players in mid-thirties. I do not always understand their names—real names or nicknames—or exactly what they do ("I'm with this-and-that commander"). I learn more when I run into them off the field, at an event, part of a minister's entourage, or running errands, and observing their company and how they carry themselves. I run into Ai Nyi on the road traveling to Lashio, Lei at a construction site up in Ai Cheng, Rong at a New Harvest festival in Wein Kao, Saw buying nails at the hardware shop in Pangkham market, Dee at a gathering with his KIO boss. Shwe pays for my meal as he leaves the restaurant. Tun went missing for several months, allegedly running into trouble at a Myanmar checkpoint outside of Monglar for smuggling. He turned up months later. This is a transitory community, always on the move.

My basic Burmese and accented Chinese cast doubt on my origins—they had taken to calling me "Sing-ga-paw" for the longest time, unable to figure out my name or whether it was appropriate to address me by it. We chat about the latest occurrences in town ("Didn't you hear the grenade accident last night? So loud!"), and about football, where a wide range of allegiances to European football teams are on display—PSG, Atletico Madrid, Chelsea, and Dortmund—all imitation jerseys from Thailand. Someone is always sporting the latest Predator or F50 boots.

The field is a melting pot, a diagnostic site for exploring social relations among young men this side of the Salween River, men from diverse ethnic backgrounds. Especially the fights. The fights throw up simmering disputes and antipathies, hierarchies—who gets bullied, who defends others, and why. Ah Chit tells me about a fight that broke out several months ago. "A group of Shans from outside came to play one evening and tackled and hit Du hard. They thought that they could bully him because he was Burmese in the Shan State, but we don't do this here. A big brawl broke out; Rong fought them. We take care of our own." "Our own" never seemed to include locals of South Asian heritage who had moved to Pangkham from lower Myanmar to escape communal tensions in 2013—they had no names, only the derogatory label "kalar."[19]

At the borders, social relations were not as divided along ethnic lines as one might imagine given the long-running civil war. Instead, they were based on factionalisms around individuals. "It's gotten much better now. In the past if the entourage of some junior Wa leaders came to play, they would send soldiers to chase and beat up anyone who angered them," another friend explained. Social hierarchies and rules are apparent, too. You could not tackle hard someone of higher social status, or fight him, you could only vent on his teammates. Factions formed. In the red mist boundaries were stretched. Players crossed identity lines and in so doing, made themselves conspicuous.

On the sidelines one evening, a man in his mid-twenties sauntered over to speak with me. A spectator in red-checked dress shirt and jeans, Shaw heard I was from Singapore and working in the UN: "How much are your wages?" He suggested a figure. I nodded, as I always did with whatever figure was suggested, unless too blatantly off the mark. We spoke, our eyes fixated on the football game in front of us. When I did scrutinize Shaw, he was surprisingly fair-skinned but sported the customary betel-stained palate. He was Hui Muslim from Dangyan, he said. His wife was Wa, but now Hui after marriage. He learned his fluent Chinese just from selling clothes in the Dangyan market. He had met his Wa wife in Man Xiang, the Wa township bordering the Myanmar areas, when he crossed the Salween to start a motorbike repair shop. He moved to Wa Region after marriage and had three children with her, the daughter of a military man in Man Xiang.

Through these connections, Shaw now ran a business selling cars from Thailand to Myanmar. He did this by bringing them up through Wa and Monglar regions, then smuggling them across the Salween to Myanmar areas, a somewhat circuitous route to avoid duties. It was early enough in my stay that I was puzzled by Shaw—a smuggler?—speaking so loosely and without caution. He also dealt in secondhand cars, bringing them all to Man Tun, a crossing point over the Salween where barges shipped timber and goods back and forth. There an official Wa checkpoint collects taxes, he explained, but the Myanmar side is unofficial, run by the Tatmadaw, who collect their own taxes independent of higher authority. Taxes there are lower than if they came officially across the bridge at Tar Gaw Et. Once in Myanmar, the cars are sold and given fake number plates. "You can choose—YGN or MDY or SHN." He uses a computer, presumably for getting into some database, to select car numbers. With Myanmar licenses, cars can be sold for nearly double their previous worth in Wa Region. Indiscreet or entrepreneurial, trader or smuggler, these categories possessed their own situational definitions. I made a mental note to sell him my car when I left, but never saw him again.

Almost a year later, I traveled this route in Man Tun, right down to the banks of the river, searching for a colleague of mine we had temporarily lost contact with. The road leaving the market wound through the hills past newly planted rubber, past workers' housing—purple zinc roofs over neatly laid-out terraced houses. The tepid Salween flowed southward down below, its banks wide and silted up as it slowed around four consecutive bends. A tributary joined at the bottom of the spur, centuries of erosion leveling the other banks. It was an ideal crossing point: only a few kilometers downriver, the Salween narrowed back into a rocky gorge with steep forested banks on either side of the river.

The Wa customs checkpoint here comprised a group of soldiers playing cards outside a building with a gantry barrier. A soldier gestured to the back of our pickup, and the young guide sent by the township leader to accompany us dismounted and spoke a few words to them. Nobody cared who we were or where we were going; they only wanted to check what we carried. A seated commander soon recognized the UN insignia, letting us pass without further search. On the way down a timber yard—signs of the illicit trade—then three trucks laden with timber crawled up the slope, eastbound for China. I recalled how a Wa official chortled, when Chairman Bao issued an edict banning logging in 2014 in Wa Region: "Sure he did. But now there is nothing left already." Also en route were two trucks full of cows from the Myanmar side—compared with Pang Yang, these bovine kin had it easy, riding aboard trucks, bound for slaughter in Cangyuan in China. It took thirty minutes to reach the bottom of the spur, the edge of the majestic river we had tracked throughout our descent. Commodities continued to trickle under the watchful gaze of two small, earth-packed bunkers, etched into adjacent small hills overlooking the river crossing.

Mobility and Human Capital

It became apparent that many employed Wa young men were either in the lower rungs of the UWSA administrative or military apparatus or in the households of Wa leaders as drivers or attendants. Those on the football field were the lucky ones, with freedom to leave their posts in the evenings. Other young men relied on personal contacts or kin to establish small businesses trading in food items, construction materials, and houseware imports. Burmese were skilled mechanics or furniture makers, or casual laborers attached to a boss like Ah Chit or Saw. The more itinerant figures like Ah Yong or Shwe seemed to be ethnic minorities whose kin and hometowns bridged the margins of Wa Region and Shan State.

While the value of education was widely touted, and the corollary self-effacing sense of being "uneducated" was widespread, at least on the surface, formal education itself offered little actual opportunity for social mobility. On my first visit to Wa Region in 2012 I asked a Wa man what job he did for a living. He snorted and replied, "We have no jobs because we have no education. We do a little buying and selling of small items to survive." Many border inhabitants seemed to have internalized Chinese and international modernizing discourses prizing "education" and saw themselves as lacking. Ron Renard writes, "Wa leaders themselves, as shown by their ignorance of the Wa written script, often see Wa as backward, far inferior to groups they perceive as civilized, such as the Chinese."[20] Similarly, Chin's rural village interviews yielded the following: "People like us who do not have education or know how to do business can only do hard labor; if we don't, we would starve."[21] The subsistence economy had been partially pulled into surrounding capital and labor markets, without institutional mechanisms for making this transition.

Formal education was in crisis—enrollment rates were an estimated 44 percent for school-aged children in 2014, but more startlingly the attrition rate between Grade 1 and Grade 6 was 92 percent.[22] For every one hundred children who enrolled in Grade 1, only eight made it to Grade 6.[23] There were 354 primary schools (Grades 1–6, though many village schools only offered Grades 1–2) across Wa Region, but only nine middle schools (Grades 7–10). Schools operated in three different mediums—Chinese, Wa, and Burmese.[24] Middle school was sparingly available as an added expense, and there were no high schools (roughly ages seventeen to eighteen) in North Wa, except for two classes in the Myanmar school in Pangkham. When rural parents spoke of the importance of education, they had in mind basic schooling from Grades 1–2. The lack of governmental support for education could also be seen through the measly wages teachers were paid—for village schools, wages were between 150 and 400 CNY (between 25 and 66 USD) a month and paid either by the township or the villagers themselves, with a standard monthly ration of twenty kilograms of rice.[25]

These disastrous educational statistics seemed an obvious target intervention for development specialists seeking to assist the region's economy and wean it off reliance on the drug trade. But to what extent was lack of education an impediment to development? The truth was that even with formal education, there simply were not many jobs. Employment in Pangkham and other towns was mainly in the service industry—for girls, working in the casino (3,000 CNY per month or 500 USD), health centers for foot reflexology (4,000 to 5,000 CNY per month or 660 to 830 USD), or as shop assistants (1,500 to 2,000 CNY or 250 to 360 USD). These were higher wages than elsewhere in Myanmar, and girls were often expected to get married not long after. For boys domestic opportunities seemed fewer; the fortunate ones ended up as drivers or aides for Wa leaders and officials. Other positions in the Wa government struggled to earn 1,000 CNY per month on the high end. Most joined the army, voluntarily or through conscription.[26] Almost all of my ordinary Wa friends (those not children of leaders or rich businessmen) were in the army, as drivers, logistics, or soldiers or in the personal entourage of Wa officials. There was, then, no tangible difference between a Grade 3 and a Grade 6 education.

Wa youth traveled to China for employment, but often not in any significant numbers or for sustained periods of time.[27] In contrast, Wa leaders and those with means sent their children for studies in Lashio, Mandalay, Yangon, or China. Some made it to Singapore, Australia, or the UK for tertiary education, but these numbered in the low dozens at best. Many in Pangkham sought to start their own businesses—small shops selling goods imported from China such as CDs, electronics, underwear, apparel, or alcohol or selling items over WeChat. Skilled labor was not often done by ethnic Wa—hairdressers, clerks, and teachers in town were Chinese and the car mechanics and skilled craftsmen were Burmese—much less engineers, doctors, or accountants. Many administrative posts in the government were staffed by local ethnic Chinese.

Ethnic Chinese who came to work in Wa Region peddled an implicit narrative of laziness or "lack of desire" among locals, the Wa in particular. A Chinese hairdresser from Kunming told me that there was no way they could train local Wa in hairdressing: "They are just not hardworking enough; they don't stay long enough to learn." This, in earshot of his Wa assistant in the salon, seemingly a diligent understudy. The hairdresser had come to Wa Region after reading about the Golden Triangle; he returned home twice a year, living in Pangkham on a temporary residence permit that cost 960 CNY (120 USD) a year.[28] Here, he earned 7,000 to 8,000 CNY (1,200 to 1,300 USD) a month, compared to 4,000 to 5,000 CNY (700 to 800 USD) in China. Wa officials cited figures of sixty thousand Chinese migrants in Wa Region, including the tens of thousands working in the mines near Man Xiang. Especially when it came to valuable resource extraction, the Chinese bosses preferred to hire Chinese. Ethnic-based networks of trust and affinity, cultural communication, rather than competence, were the chief criteria.[29]

A local Chinese friend who managed various Wa, Shan, and Lahu workers on his father's mineral processing plant and rubber plantations remarked, "It baffles me that the villagers are one kilometer away from a water source, but have all this while never thought or digging a well in their own village. Think of how much time they have spent carrying water back and forth. I always scold them for this but they never change. They could produce so many varieties of vegetables to sell in the market, where there are currently only four types available. They never have this idea."[30] He noted, however, that Chinese workers in the mines were reluctant to train local Wa for fear of losing their jobs. "For the locals, they never have the pressure of finding a well-paying job. If all fails they simply return to the village. They go hunting with a large group of friends for days, without catching anything at all."

Autonomy was also accentuated (or exacerbated?) by linguistic separation from the rest of the country. Rather than a bridge, language posed a barrier to integration. Deciding the primary language of instruction—between Chinese, Burmese, or Wa—would be a central pillar of integration, tying future generations of Wa Region closer to either China or Myanmar. A former UNODC staffer in Mong Pawk interviewed a villager:

> [In the] last few years, with the agreement from local Wa authorit[ies,] [the] Burmese government sent two teachers to establish a village primary school in our village, but after staying for two years the school collapsed as there [were] no children [wanting] to attend the Burmese school. The language barrier between teachers and children was one of the reason[s], the other reason is [that] most of the people in Wa region don't want to learn Burmese as they think that it is not useful in their daily lives since the official and commercial language used in this region is Chinese. It is easier for us to go to China than Burmese control[led] area. When we go [to] China, we just need to register our name at the border checkpoint, in the case of Burmese control area there are a lot of military checkpoints along the road and [they] ask us to show a lot of document[s] which are impossible for us to obtain. So we feel more close to China [than our] so-called country Burma.[31]

The Myanmar government sent nearly eighty teachers across Wa Region to teach Burmese in schools, but their reach was limited. A district secretary recounted, "The kids learn up to Grade 3 here, but in the end, there is no reason for them to speak Burmese; they cannot use it anywhere in Wa Region, and they are not going out anytime soon. They are not good at it." In 2015, the Wa authorities mandated that every work unit in the government should send its staff for basic Burmese language training. But they struggled to find the right books, appealed to the Myanmar government for help, and received none (perhaps they used the wrong channels). The program fell apart shortly after. National policies failed to seize the right channels for linguistic integration, and even worked actively against them.

A Wa official put the figure of Wa inhabitants able to speak Burmese at 5 percent:

> Actually, many more locals than you think can speak Burmese, they just find it awkward to do so, especially when in Pangkham. Why is it that we go to Myanmar and are not recognized, we go to China and we are not recognized? If we speak Burmese here, others suspect we might be [Myanmar] spies. When I go to Naypyidaw for meetings, they think I am from Lashio [because I speak Burmese], but I tell them I am from the border areas proper. They still think we are ethnic Chinese people here in Wa.[32]

Inhabitants of Wa Region, rural or urban, Wa, Burmese, or Shan, were engaged in modes of dwelling-in-traveling, of traveling-in-dwelling. Because they were caught in a structural bind of a weak and narrow economy, the difficulty of reliable migration to China for employment, the reputation of being lazy and unambitious, and the linguistic and documentary barriers to engagement in the national economy, prospects for physical and social mobility were dire. There was little improvement through skills and education; instead, social capital and the fortitudes building of connections were the only way to advance one's lot. There was ease of movement, but with little accumulation. All this while vast amounts of wealth circulated within limited circles.

But perhaps questions geared toward social mobility, human capital, and inequality were not the ones to be asking; perhaps these questions about livelihoods and employment privileged a model of accumulation rather than subsistence. And yet the project of autonomy necessitated a careful blend of both—self-reliance and subsistence were never independent from the need to navigate wider market forces and manage and extract from cross-border flows of capital. Sustainable subsistence and self-reliance required preempting the hazards and vulnerabilities of the borderland political economy.

Unratified Mobilities

"Why don't you pick up your phone?" Liang grunted in a heavy Yunnanese accent, which he ordinarily tempered when speaking to me. He had ridden his motorbike up the hill to my office, uncharacteristically flustered and impatient. Liang was a Hui, or Chinese Muslim, owner of a small beef noodle shop a short walk from the vegetable market, and one of my first few friends in town.[33] His thick, muscular arms were the result of years of stretching sheets of flour to make the famous pulled noodles in Jinghong, Yunnan, as a teenager. He moved to Pangkham in 2003 from Lancang, a large Chinese town four hours' drive from the border. The opium industry and circulating capital made living costs, prices, and profits higher in Pangkham: a bowl of noodles sold for 10 CNY compared with 6 CNY in Lancang. As a Chinese national, Liang used his border pass to enter Wa Region through the Menglian crossing and applied for the Wa Temporary Residence Permit (Chn: *wailai renyuan zhanzhuzheng*). He sold rice noodles in a thick beef- and tomato-based broth, and his little corner shop made a name for itself over the years. Several times a week, he rode his electric scooter across the bridge back into China to secure more meat (Halal cuts were not available in Pangkham) and ingredients from his supplier.

Noodle sales near the market offer a good indicator of town economic vibrancy. Liang sells about sixty to seventy bowls of noodles, perhaps a hundred on good days, but there are not as many people around now in 2014. "It's just like that, always patchy," Liang says. He is perpetually cryptic about his business. Rental has risen from 1,000 to 5,000 CNY following the landlord's renovation of the premises, but he now lives with his wife in a room at the back of the restaurant. His two daughters live in Maymyo in Shan State with relatives, still in primary school. Liang's wife, Ma, is also Hui, but from Dangyan—they met in Wa Region. Liang's has been a trajectory of settling and moving, of intergenerational migration.

Border mobilities were, however, the cause of his troubles today. Ma had just returned from the Chinese Consulate in Mandalay, where she had spent nearly 10,000 CNY (USD 1,600) applying unsuccessfully for Chinese nationality for their two daughters, aged eight and eleven. This included travel costs, the translation and notarization of birth certificates from Burmese into English and then Chinese (60,000 MMK or about 60 USD): "We have no education. How are we supposed to know how we should have filled in these forms? My wife isn't very literate in Chinese or Burmese, and she could not explain our circumstances clearly to the officials." Liang himself had Chinese and Myanmar identity cards and a temporary residence permit for Wa Region, while Ma, being from Dangyan, had a Myanmar ID (Bse: *hmapountin*) and a Wa ID. Liang's Myanmar ID, issued in Pangkham during a visit from a Myanmar government immigration team just after the 2009 Kokang crisis, also listed him as Lahu (much like Ah Yong above): "It's just easier to get Myanmar citizenship this way." Neither Liang nor Ma had passports.

After work, I went over to his shop to look through the documents. Because his Myanmar ID was now missing, Ma had traveled to Mandalay on her own.

"Why didn't you go along?"

"I can only enter Myanmar through the international border gate at Ruili, and that would require me to go back to Lancang, make a passport, then travel north to Ruili, cross into Myanmar (at Muse), and then travel down to Mandalay. Ma wouldn't be able to follow me. We'd have to meet in Mandalay."

Border mobilities were marked by their documentary limits, risk tradeoffs, hassle, and weighing benefits for inhabitants. Border porosities were not all-or-nothing; they came with transaction costs.

None of the documents their daughters possessed were useful for claiming Chinese nationality. Born in a Pangkham hospital, both had three forms of identification—a Wa identity card, a Wa Hospital birth certificate, and a Myanmar birth certificate that gave the daughters' place of birth as Mandalay. The unratified status of Wa Region meant Wa documents were unrecognized at the Chinese consulate, and their only national document—the Myanmar birth certificate—unfortunately left blank the column for the father's nationality. "This is the problem—there is no link connecting them to China; they are born in Wa Region, without proof of a Chinese father," I proffered, unhelpfully restating the obvious.

"We have this letter from the Wa authorities. It cost us 200 CNY," he said as he unfolded a document with the stamp of a Wa Ministry, dating from seven months ago and addressed to the external affairs branch of the Chinese authorities in Lancang:

> Living at xxx address in Pangkham are Ma (Wa ID: xxxx) and Liang (Chinese ID: xxxx) who were married in China in 2009, and have two children Rou and Xun born on dd/mm/yy and dd/mm/yy, this certifies that they have registered under our household registration records and requests that they be offered assistance in their relevant applications.[34]

The Chinese consulate in Mandalay ignored this letter and referred Ma to the local Chinese authorities in Liang's hometown in Lancang. Liang was 10,000 CNY poorer and no closer to having his daughters recognized as Chinese citizens.

"You know the people at the Wa ministry, talk to them for me."

"There's not much they can do; the letter they wrote was obviously not enough," I replied. Showing up to remind the Wa authorities of the ineffectualness of their certification would cost face all around.

His daughters, it seemed, were now restricted to Myanmar citizenship, having been born in Wa Region—not the most appealing prospect for Liang. Had they made a point to have their daughters in China, birth documentation would have been more careful and the path to citizenship easier. But Ma would have had to travel there under a Myanmar passport to give birth (if even possible). Valorized mobilities and "flexible citizenship"[35] must be complemented by the lifelong consequences of ignorance of or failing to exploit the correct systems, along with the temporal delay with which consequences materialize and realization dawns upon people. "Let's go to the office tomorrow morning. I'll introduce you and at least the minister will consider your case," I offered.

"There's not much we can do," came the reply the next morning, as unhelpful as expected.

This was a tragedy of legal personhood at the peripheries. Lacking the literacy and knowledge of how to navigate the bureaucratic systems, large groups of people fell between the cracks, with grave implications for citizenship and mobility of their offspring. Liang had a Grade 6 education in China, and his wife was not a strong reader. It was intimidating for them to make appeals to authorities, or to understand the options available to them. There was little public awareness of the significance of documentary records, or ensuring that details such as parents' nationalities were clearly recorded. Their daughters would be eligible for Myanmar citizenship, but a future life in China, where Liang was from, could now only take place as migrant workers (if at all). They were stuck on one side of the border—either in Wa Region or in lower Myanmar. Another alternative was for Liang to send his daughters to Northern Thailand to study, in the hopes that they might eventually naturalize there. He would remain in Pangkham with his noodle shop. As modes of belonging became institutionalized, people at the peripheries of country and society would be further marginalized and left out of integration efforts. Meaningful autonomy would have to resist the forces of isolation, fighting to retain access and keep a foot in the door.

I was back at Liang's noodle shop another evening, watching him fry bean curd triangles. The creamy white paste was flattened onto a tray and cut into triangles with a knife, flung remorselessly into a deep wok of boiling oil with chopsticks. A friend was over to play Chinese chess and gossip about the ongoings in town. "They've introduced a new ruling and now residence permits must be renewed every three months. That's 320 CNY a year, and taxes are now 400 CNY a month, to that add another 80 for garbage disposal. The health certificate is 400 CNY a year, and the business registration is more than 1,000 CNY. I buy the beef from Menglian, but it still costs between 10,000 and 20,000 CNY a month." Living costs continue to rise, just as the town itself seemed to be stagnating.

"Why do you stay, then?" Shopkeepers always offered good insight on public safety and the economy.

"Fixed costs are 200 CNY a day. I lose this if I don't open the shop. Here, at least there is less competition than there is in China. I've been here so long, where else can I go? As long as taxes aren't too high and I can still make a living, I'll stay." The bean curd triangles, now golden brown, were laid out on paper towels. Liang chopped cabbage, a side dish to be mixed with chilis and vinegar.

"When I first opened in 2005, a bowl cost 3 CNY, and rental was 400 CNY. Sometimes this shop feels like a prison." These were the people who rented buildings from the relatives of Wa leaders, whose shops catered to traders and businessmen, whose taxes then went into the coffers of the Wa authorities to raise soldiers to protect the region. Attracting visitors and investment was central to the sustainability of the Wa economy.

Freedom felt curtailed at times. "It is the taxes and regulations that are killing our businesses." This was, as elsewhere, a common refrain, complaints that regulation was too strict (Chn: *guande taiyan*), destroying petty livelihoods and driving businesses away to other less stringent towns like Monglar.[36] It reminded me of another friend, also a shopkeeper, also annoyed with the regulations: "The commerce department came round to enforce its new regulations, which now requires the prices of all items to be labeled on the shelf. We explained that this doesn't work for small businesses like ours whose stock changes and that don't have the same items in the same place all the time. But of course they insisted. This is just like the Wa government, doesn't do the big things, only the small things."

In July 2014, inhabitants of Pangkham woke up to find that the string of gaming shops that ringed the casino compound had been shuttered. More than twenty such shops hosting the popular videogame "Fish Hunter" (Chn: *dayu pai*) had been forced to close down.[37] "Fish Hunter" saw players sitting around a video machine "pond" and firing virtual bullets at all kinds of unsuspecting ornamental fish. Owners sold off their machinery and lost their businesses overnight. Rumored reasons were that it was a highly addictive game that drained the incomes of families, including children; it was a form of costly illicit gambling; being open twenty-four hours, it attracted all kinds of unsavory characters (methamphetamine abusers, who found themselves unable to sleep). This was undoubtedly intended as a public service, reflecting the responsiveness of the UWSA to some social ills. For instance, price gouging during crises was another activity harshly punished, offending UWSA sensibilities of fairness. This time, no compensation, no advance notice, just an immediate order to close. The main casino, however, loomed large behind, unscathed by anti-gambling operations.

In these times of regulation, people spoke fondly of the liberties and openness (Chn: *kaifang*) in neighboring Monglar, also on the Chinese border, a town run by the National Democratic Alliance Army (NDAA), close allies of the UWSA and more recently in the international headlines for its wildlife trade.

Casinos, brothels, and hotels were flourishing there under such permissive laws. Monglar was occasionally open to Western journalists, churning out sensational headlines like "The Myanmar Town Where You Can Buy Drugs, Sex, and Endangered Animals," "Dirty Old Town," "Debauched Land of Drugs and Vice," and "Lawless Region Where Anything Goes."[38]

The Chinese government temporarily shut down the border crossing to Monglar from Daluo in 2005 because Chinese officials had reportedly gambled public money away there. In response, the NDAA shifted most casino complexes to a field thirty minutes away from the border. It also operated online gambling from there, forcing the Chinese government to shut down cable service in 2012 to disrupt the flow of money. Several meetings and compromises later, service was restored. Lax governance and fewer crackdowns meant shadow economies would thrive, attracting border denizens of all kinds to these towns. Raids drove traders from one town along the border to the next, and it was in the interests of local authorities to avoid being too harsh, yet keeping up with the pretenses of law in order to avoid antagonizing the Chinese government.[39]

The borderlands for Liang were not about a lack of mobility but the inability to have property and legal personhood affirmed—falling into the cracks and incongruities of national citizenship regimes and Wa governance. Property was always at risk; petty thieving and burglary, scams, counterfeit money and fake products were widespread—most went unreported. Liang was ambivalent about security: "Yes, they are very strict and punishments are harsh, but there still is a lot of theft. My motorbike was stolen a few years ago, but I found it myself. I still had to call the traffic police, send the bike in to them for paperwork [Chn: *ban shouxu*], was charged 500 CNY for it, and at the end of all that it got damaged in storage. I lost another few months ago when a friend borrowed it, I don't think I'll get this one back. The police are only useful if you are powerful."

Yet Wa Region took tough measures to offer reassurances of its stability. Despite its purported lawlessness, enforcement could be draconian—the death penalty was imposed for armed assault, rape, murder, and child abuse. This was despite Myanmar's abolitionist status at the national level. Punishments were reported on the Wa State TV News with scenes of men with bowed heads in handcuffs. In July 2015, four men were paraded through town on the back of pickups, a convoy of eight police cars, sirens blaring. A sign bearing the misdeed hung around the offenders' necks: they had burned down a house, killing someone inside. Three loops of town, then up into the hills outside Pangkham to the firing squad, buried in a hole they were reportedly made to dig the night before. Another two men were executed for murder in March 2016.[40] "That's why there's so little murder in this town, even though many are armed," a Wa official proudly announced.

Forced Mobilities

Wa governance fit poorly into external models of governance and statehood. It comprised a host of contradictory processes: a careful dance of regulation and permission, with adequate consideration for the sensitivities of China and Myanmar. It combined a laissez-faire space for movement, livelihoods, and trade, with a mix of centrally planned campaign-styled interventions, top-down and directive-driven, a legacy of the Communist-era. These included crackdowns on drug abusers (Chn: *saodu*), on prostitution (Chn: *saohuang*), and on gambling (Chn: *kangdu*), adopting militaristic language like that in China. The Wa authorities launched yearly campaigns to crack down on drugs after the 2005 opium ban, with the months of May and June seeing the most intensive clean-up operations in the lead up to June 26, the International Day against Drug Abuse and Illicit Trafficking. Groups of men were shackled outside township offices, drug abusers thrown into pits in the ground for "rehabilitation." Harsh drug enforcement was an iconic part of reputation management—it targeted (selectively) reviled characters, and through draconian spectacles served as reminders of the administration's authority. Authority was partially for security but also an assertion of autonomy.

Nowhere was the heavy-handed authority of the UWSA administration better seen than in the 2005 opium ban, a watershed event in Wa history. Weaning several hundred thousand opium farmers off poppy as a cash crop was no mean feat. Hideyuki Takano, a Japanese writer who traveled into the opium-growing Wa hills of the 1990s, lived in a village and wrote of the dire travails of the peasantry.[41] The overall strategy, in hindsight, involved five prongs: harsh enforcement, opium-substitution programs for farmers, searching for alternative revenue for the polity, consolidating access into the hills through roadbuilding, and a controversial population relocation into disputed territory. What transpired was the forced migration of around one hundred thousand Wa villagers down to South Wa, the territory on the Thai border "promised" to the UWSA by Tatmadaw Military Intelligence Chief Khin Nyunt for helping to defeat the Mong Tai Army's Khun Sa.[42]

Between 1999 and 2006, the UWSA began voluntary and forced resettlements from districts in North to South Wa on the Thai border, with anywhere between fifty thousand and one hundred fifty thousand villagers moved.[43] This was a massive humanitarian and reputational disaster for the UWSA at the time, but it soon passed. Wa officials I spoke to put the figure at around one hundred thousand (a staggering one-quarter of the population of North Wa), noting that relocations were not all to South Wa but also a redistribution of population within North Wa itself. These were to other less populated or flatter-relief townships like Mong Phen, Mong Kar, and Wein Kao. Many were moved from the hilltops to spur lines beside roads, and large villages were carved into several smaller ones.[44]

The mass relocation was drastic and brutal. Fiskesjö describes how the uprooting of such large populations affected the social and traditional fabric of village communities, as it "cut large numbers of people off from their traditional maps of local gods and spirits, their sacred groves, in effect the entirety of familiar ground and local historical memory."[45] Malaria and travel-related deaths wreaked havoc among the population, physical and social suffering compounded by their loss of access to traditional and ritual means of propitiating local spirits.[46] A health official recalled that there were eight hundred deaths from malaria alone, others giving a total figure of four thousand.[47] It also angered local Shan who were displaced. The land in South Wa around Mong Yawn and Mong Hsat was widely rumored to have been "sold" by Khin Nyunt to the UWSA, fueling grievance against the Tatmadaw.[48] Wa settlers arriving reportedly told local Shans, "General Khin Nyunt has given us this country. If you want it back, go and ask him."[49]

Ostensibly, the relocation was to provide livelihoods and farmland for a population heavily affected by the poppy ban, but motives and figures were riddled by rumor and bias. Chairman Bao argued in a rare television interview that movement was needed to centralize small far-flung villages and provide electricity, schools, and protection:

> We used to be like monkeys, there would be 2–3 households far away, another 2–3 households further away, it was hard to even find them to talk. . . . This is why they are so backward. They go an entire day without speaking to anyone else. Look at the people in the towns, they move and interact, every day they are receiving exposure in their mind . . . so backward, I decided to change this.[50]

Some sources suggested that the migration was possibly to make room for Chinese agro-business and rubber plantation interests, or to consolidate UWSA territory in the south.[51] Others claimed that the UWSA intended to bring in more ethnic Wa from China and needed to clear out the central Wa hills for this; yet others suggested the UWSA planned to exploit silver deposits in the areas their villages had vacated, or had been pressured by China to shift opium farming down to the Thai border.[52] The Tatmadaw was also said to have encouraged this, with a view to spreading the UWSA's military forces more thinly out over a greater area.[53] Most of these claims were far-fetched. The obvious explanation held the most weight: a strategic military move to lay claim and secure routes to the Thailand-Laos border areas.

Reducing population pressure in the hills of North Wa allowed for the expansion of rubber as an alternative cash-crop. Yunnan Province started an Opium

Replacement Fund in 2006, offering tax incentives and subsidies to Chinese companies to start plantations in Myanmar's peripheries, investing USD 26.5 million by 2007.[54] From a livelihood perspective, these were reported to be a failure, with Chinese companies often abusing the subsidies through fraudulent projects, or alienating Burmese farmers through poor compensation and a heavy-handed approach. Still, through joint ventures with UWSA officials and military commanders, rubber plantations burgeoned. By 2009, the UWSA boasted more than 400,000 mu (26,667 hectares) of rubber planted, and 1,200,000 mu (80,000 hectares) by 2015.[55] A TNI report declared that the Chinese fund was "financing dispossession," as land grabs removed farmers' access to land, reducing food diversity with monocropping, leaving low wages and forced labor caring for rubber trees.[56]

But rubber quickly became a massive disappointment. International commodity prices climbed to a high of USD 6.26 per kilogram in February 2011, then halved precipitously to USD 3.11 per kilogram by December 2012. It continued falling to a low of 1.24 per kilogram in November 2015, and remained around 2 USD per kilogram for most of 2015–18.[57] This was disastrous for the UWSA's legitimate revenue, but more so for rural inhabitants whose income from rubber tapping was now minimal.[58] Many plantations, given rubber's gestation period of seven years, had not even matured yet when prices plummeted. Rubber trees were cut down in several areas in 2015 to be replaced by other crops.

The village of Yaong Soi is blanketed in a tired canopy of gray, the cool air moist and misty, the grass damp.[59] It is just an hour's walk away from the frontlines facing the Myanmar fortifications, where this chapter began. One can vaguely make out the lighter white tufts of cloud in the valley below, just beyond the perimeter of trees that protect the village from strong winds. Perhaps the clouds have entered the village; perhaps the village has entered the clouds. Yaong Soi is nestled in a gentler east-facing slope on one of the many mountainous ridgelines that run through Wa Region. A patchwork of dark brown thatched roofs is interspersed with the occasional zinc roofing of the better-off households, cheap foot-long Chinese-made solar panels planted carefully on the corners of the roofs. There are twenty-three households here, all ethnic Wa, all relying on subsistence farming and livestock (see figure 11).

Chickens roost in a neat line on the bamboo platform that rings the veranda of a thatched house, supervised by a slumping dog. A man feeds his pigs boiled jackfruit seeds and bamboo shoots, fending away unwelcome imposters from a neighboring household. Jackfruit and banana trees, clumps of bamboo, and a variety of garden plants fan out among the houses. Piles of cow dung, food wrappers from Chinese-made snacks, chopped firewood, and mossed-covered

FIGURE 11. The village of Yaong Soi, July 2015. The neighboring township can be seen on the next ridgeline.

stones flank the well-worn paths that run among the houses. Building material is strewn beneath houses, awaiting the next project. Dusk approaches, and movement returns; villagers, dogs, and cows make their way home.

Yaong Soi is said to be the oldest village in Man Xiang Township, at three hundred years old. From the five-day market in Man Xiang, where the bus services from Pangkham end, it is a treacherous twenty-minute motorcycle ride downhill, the narrow and steep track impassable to four-wheeled vehicles. Overgrown with tall grasses in certain parts, the track then continues into the valley and reaches the Nam Rai River an hour later, where a rickety bamboo footbridge provides a crossing into Ka Laung Pa Township. Before this dirt road, there were footpaths; villagers gesture to these invisible arteries fanning out across the scrub and forest of the hills. The records and accounts of travelers passing through Wa Region centuries ago chronicle the traders, muleteers, soldiers, foragers, migrating villagers, and farmers who have crisscrossed these hills, as Fiskesjö carefully curates in his book *Stories from an Ancient Land*.[60] One imagines the bedraggled and heavy-laden battling gravity, resilient undergrowth, and the scourges of mud and rain. The hills are an unforgiving corporeal experience, an accretion of local knowledge, skills, and histories.

"They would raid us, and we would raid them," a villager recalled of the headhunting period, gesturing at the village sitting atop the opposite ridgeline. The two ridgelines faced each other down; that village is now part of Ka Laung Pa Township, a township reportedly even poorer than Man Xiang. Rainy season, and villagers weed their light green upland paddy fields, a short walk downslope from the village. The paddy runs to the edge of the slope, then falls away into the darker secondary forest of the valley. As mist clears, the adjacent spur is dissected by dirt roads meandering downhill, bright orange trails of exposed soil bearing testament to the ubiquitous feats of everyday engineering in these hills. A man beckons toward the undergrowth and saplings just off the main path. "See that moss-covered stone there? That's where they used to lay the severed heads." The flat stone now sits obscure among the leaf litter.

Harvest, and the villagers knot bundles of cut rice stalks together, piling these in a circular fashion and forming a stack in their fields, much like elven straw houses. Villagers call out to one another as they walk through the fields. The citrusy scent of cut grass fills the air. This year, only half of Yaong Soi's households produced enough rice for twelve months. The others have gaps of between two and four months, which they cover through paid labor, selling livestock, or borrowing. Upland paddy has been the key staple in these hills, a swidden agriculture that sees the rotation of the annual crop between ten different planting areas surrounding the village. The current plot being used this year is close to the village, easily discerned by the makeshift fences of thorny branches and sharpened stakes which dissuade opportunistic cows from entering. The hills have for centuries bestowed their gifts of soil and water inequitably—springs well and dry up; soils and minerals wash away with rain, only to gather abundantly in other areas. Upland paddy is hit-and-miss, at the complete mercy of the gods. Disparities of yield between households, villages, and townships are common—creating disparities in wealth and food security. The villagers of Yaong Soi could dig terraced rice paddies, as in other parts of Wa Region, but the water source is more than a kilometer away, and not abundant enough to water their fields. They could dig terraced farmland to retain fertilizer, as in other parts of Wa Region, but they worry about removing the fertile topsoil, or not having the correct variety of seed, or developing land only to have it claimed by a local leader. In recent years, eight of their ten plots of land for rotation have been lost to rubber plantations, or other villages enforcing their customary claims to the land. The hills give and the hills take away.

In 2004 the Wa authorities ordered the Yaong Soi villagers to move up to the township seat of Man Xiang to consolidate the population. The villagers built new houses in the township center but returned after a year because of a lack of water and firewood. A few families, however, stayed behind after the return, starting small shops in the market area. Man Xiang is a transit point for traders arriving from Dangyan, baskets of peanuts, rice snacks, fruit, and cartons of cigarettes dangling precariously from both sides of their motorbikes. Pajero taxis from Lashio pass through here, and a daily bus service runs down to Pangkham. Permanent stalls in the market area are restocked with goods every five days on market day, when villagers walk up from the surrounding villages to sell produce. Here the full repertoire of languages can be heard—Burmese, Chinese, Shan, and Wa, including the different dialects and accents. Cucumbers, pineapples, groundnuts, home-brewed spirit, and rice sit alongside the cigarettes, fried snacks, *thanaka* (Bse, sandalwood) paste, bottles of petrol, clothes, salt, and cooking oil brought in from either Myanmar or China. Goods are laid out on tables under large red umbrellas. A bus arrives, and a trussed-up pig is unceremoniously dragged out from the trunk underneath and flung squealing onto the side of the road.

Other than the odd patrol of soldiers around the township, little suggests that the Myanmar checkpoints are only a stone's throw away. Despite this proximity, only one person from Yaong Soi, a novice monk, has been to the Myanmar areas—they have no identification documents or any desire to acquire any. Few speak Burmese, though several speak Shan and could communicate with others there. In the last eight years, Man Xiang Township has risen to prominence for extractive capitalism, following the discovery of large tin deposits (see chapter 4). Large hills have been carved apart, and the roads leading down are smothered in a blanket of dust. Apparently, there are around ten thousand to twenty thousand Chinese workers in the Man Xiang mines, brought across from neighboring Chinese provinces to work machinery and extraction. A shantytown of eating places, massage parlors, zinc-sheeted motels, and wooden shops has arisen. The mines are less than an hour's motorbike ride away from Yaong Soi, but few villagers travel there to work.

Yaong Soi's is a story of many appropriations: the maize devoured by birds, the papayas destroyed by insects and fungi, the cow they lost to an attack by a tiger. Seven or eight young men from the village went over to the mines to work, but the boss ran off without paying his staff when the venture failed. In 2002, five households were moved from their village to South Wa; they have not been heard of since. A cow of theirs wandered into a rubber plantation and was shot. Other cows break into rice fields and destroy crops. Four young men have only just returned from their mandatory militia training with the army. The relentless curse of gravity takes its toll—erosion eats away farmland and roads, while water runoff draws fertile topsoil down and away.

The plots available for swidden agriculture have receded, most of them claimed by a local commander who then enlisted the villagers to tap the rubber plantation he set up on their land. There were no land titles, only the dictates of customary use.[61] Now there is a meager wage for collecting latex from "his" trees, about 25 CNY (4 USD) a month for tending to 150 trees about an hour's walk from the village.[62] The township agricultural officer did little for them, only gathering villagers together annually to suggest crops they can grow, without actual input of seedlings or agricultural products. Road repair duty occurs about three times a year, every household sending an able-bodied member for two days' work each time. Taxes paid to the township authorities are a basket of rice (twenty kilograms) per person aged between ten and sixty per year, even though directives from the central authorities have banned grain taxes across Wa Region. I share with the Yaong Soi villagers the English saying on death and taxes, and they improvise one of their own: "here there is tax even without income."

"If You Want to Prosper, First Build Roads"

In Afghanistan and Colombia, the problem of illicit drugs growing in remote areas has been often put down to a lack of connectivity; roadbuilding is often touted as one solution, the promise of development and progress. Roads and access to markets might integrate far flung villages, drawing them into agricultural markets for alternative crops, thereby weaning them off opium. The Wa authorities brought remote farmers to settle in larger villages. Chairman Bao reasoned, "I gave the order. Ideally it would be two hundred households and above [per village], but in cases where we had no choice, it was a minimum of fifty households in a single village, at least with one child per household. We can have a single class [for school].... It is easier to bring electricity as well as have meetings."[63]

Under the Chinese mantra of "If you want to prosper, first build roads" (Chn: *yaoxiangfu, xianxiulu*), the grand project to link all townships with all-weather asphalt roads began in 2012. A series of main arterial roads that ran through the entire Wa Region were to be completed by 2019, the thirtieth anniversary of the UWSA. By late 2014, asphalt roads already ran through the northern townships of Wa Region with remarkable engineering (see figure 12). Tellingly, perhaps, they linked the Chinese towns of Cangyuan and Ximeng to the Wa townships of Kunma, Nam Tit, and Mengmao, the home areas of top-ranking Wa leaders. Now, three main thoroughfares targeted: (1) a north–south road from Pangkham to Mengmao and Nam Tit; (2) a northwesterly road toward the mining areas and then Lashio in the Burmese-controlled areas; (3) a southeasterly road through the lower lands and onward to Monglar Special Region 4 and Kengtung in the Burmese-controlled areas. In mid-2015, the travel time from Pangkham to Meng Mao, the second largest town in Wa Region, a road distance of about 150 km, was reduced from five to six hours to three to four hours.

FIGURE 12. The road from Mengmao descends into the valley, past a hydroelectric dam in the distance, January 2015. This road was vulnerable to landslides in the rainy season.

In the CPB period, the road from Mengmao to Ban Wai (Sao Pha) and then downward to Pangkham was mainly a dirt track for horses and mules. The road was painstakingly widened by hand, carved into the hillsides and paved with cobblestones, completed in 1988 and passable by motor traffic.[64] It made its way to Cangyuan in China. The cobblestone remnants can still be seen today in higher sections of the hills, or at the sides of the asphalt road. Other segments in the hills, including a more direct route between Mengmao and Pangkham, were built in 1995 by the UWSA. The Myanmar government during Khin Nyunt's rule as intelligence chief had played its part, providing materials to connect Dangyan in the West up to the Salween edge of Wa Region with a narrow asphalt road.

The new roads devoured the old cobblestones and the edges narrow spurs and ridgelines. Scars of progress were etched into the terrain—rows of houses partially demolished to widen roads, exposed bright orange slopes, and fragments of gates and porches left in its wake. The roads descended sharply into valleys, complete with drainage and even safety ramps in certain areas.[65] By order of the Wa government, there was no compensation for owners whose properties had succumbed to the imperative of the greater good: people bore the loss without (risking) complaint.[66]

Bumpy surfaces pooled with muddy water were now replaced with a smooth glide across asphalt. This was the feel of progress, a stark contrast with the relentless bouncing about or meandering of a vehicle in second gear. Overzealous drivers rounded bends at breakneck speed, and skid marks on the asphalt, or large flattened portions in the vegetation besides roads, testified to misjudgments, injuries, and even fatalities. Along the road to the north sits the rusted carcass of a goods lorry, pushed onto the roadside to warn others of the dangers of road travel.[67] And the battle with the elements continued. Large sections of the tarred road had collapsed in several areas. Friends blamed this on the cheaper material and substandard contracting work carried out by one of the construction companies, pointing out that another main road built by another company had fared better. Landslides caused during rainy season (May to September) rendered roads in frequent need of clearing, rupturing travel without warning.

It was tempting to buy into the narratives of UWSA leaders and see in road-building some grand developmental design—an attempt to buttress governance, opening thoroughfares for the mastery and legibility of its own territory, or to "enchant" inhabitants and subjects with the promises of connectivity and modernity or, perhaps, a spectacular showcase of progress in contrast with the neglect of the Myanmar state.[68] Roads were touted to connect and grant access to markets, education, and wage labor. They would also facilitate quicker transport of troop reinforcements between north and south.

Yet despite their physical construction (and constant repair), roads in Wa Region always seemed to remain aspirational, always in anticipation of something else. The remoteness and sparse population density made few ventures feasible. With the lack of access of many ordinary people to cars and larger vehicles, they did not stand to gain much from smoother roads. Roads also would allow commodities, especially rubber and minerals, to be shipped off to Chinese markets— but profiting a select few. They would attract the investment of Chinese companies by connecting markets and townships in the hills—but only if there were sizable markets worth tending to. For ordinary people there was nothing valuable in the hills besides opium; as the British noted in the 1930s, "it is their only industrial crop; it is the only agricultural product which is sufficiently valuable to stand the high cost of transport."[69]

Road construction within Wa Region, however, played another, more important role. It was an efficient means of laundering capital: roads, I was told, were being built at an exorbitant cost of two million CNY (330,000 USD) per kilometer, with companies parceling out road contracts in sections to other bidders from China who brought in their own construction equipment and workers. There was a high premium for building in unstable territory but also much opportunity for rent extraction along the way. Wa-affiliated companies had great expertise in construction projects in the 1990s and 2000s, with much of the capital garnered from the narco-trade reinvested into legitimate business conglomerates involved in construction and resource extraction. These large conglomerates had ties to Burmese and Kokang networks, legacy connections from the Khin Nyunt era that continued long after his removal.[70]

Roads were infrastructural icons of the Wa Region frontier economy. But while they offered promises of connectivity and access to remoter regions, real integration seemed always deferred by the structural limitations of Wa Region's marginality. What good were roads without IDs, without employment at their ends? Checkpoints and other legal barriers to movement also tempered the ostensible porosity of the borderlands. And while they promised to facilitate the movement of capital and labor, roads were in their material selves part of capital circulations for elites—used to convert illicit wealth into legitimate income through the act of construction. Between and across the Salween and the Chinese border, travel for Wa Region inhabitants was always a latent possibility, aspirations complemented by a rhetoric of freedom and opportunity, yet ever in waiting. Dwelling and traveling, rupture and connection, and regulation and permission were part of the endless dissonances of highland autonomy.

2
TOPOGRAPHIES OF POWER

> The war machine does not last. It is always captured. Deterritorialized, active forces are always eventually reterritorialized, made reactive, either because they are captured by the state or because they ossify into state-like hierarchies and become the state itself.
>
> —Danny Hoffman, *The War Machines*

Early 2015, dust got everywhere in Pangkham Town—smothering car doors and windscreens, ledges and balconies, collecting on the zinc roofs of warehouses, suffocating the green facades of roadside trees and plants. Dust was a constant scourge these last years. Even the rainy season provided little respite for a town so unfavorably located in a basin surrounded by ridges. Up in the hills, cars could be spotted from afar by the little plumes of dust they kicked up as they traveled the winding roads. Shopkeepers splashed water at entrances to keep the dust down. "The air here is unhealthy, so much better to be up in the hills," a friend complained. "It's so hot and puts everyone in poor spirits."

The dust was a product of construction, both of buildings-in-waiting and of the project to pave the entire town by 2019, the thirtieth anniversary of Wa Region. Some roads were still concrete, webbed cracks and depressions haphazardly filled in with gravel. Concrete embankment walls or orange exposed soil ringed the slopes of the ridges encircling the town. Pangkham had the aesthetics of a fourth-tier Chinese city, only the gleaming Buddhist pagoda and the stained zinc roofs of older houses rendering some semblance of Myanmar. Ceramic tiled roofs on dour gray houses of the early 2000s were interspersed with the blue corrugated iron of warehouses, or the orderly metric curtained windows of hotel frontages. Signboards overhanging shophouses were garish pinks or blues, with Chinese script pronouncing the variety of enterprises—eatery, clinic, barbequed foods, supplies, wellness center, provision shop, or computer shop. Telephone lines were coiled or knotted on concrete poles, with banners in Chinese advertising some new opening or discount strung across them. Grand buildings now were being built more than twenty stories high, with cranes dotting the skyline, changing the landscape of town. Their height was testament to a steady supply of electricity for elevators—a luxury not found across most of Myanmar.

Pangkham was an aspirational and transitory town. There was not much of a tourism industry, yet every other building seemed to be a hotel of some sort, with lit signs, red or gold lettering, and large faux-leather armchairs in the lobby. "They just use it to hold land—that's what has the most value," a friend remarked. The centerpiece of town was the casino, drawing Chinese gamblers from across the border. Built in 1998, the three-story complex, a pastel structure lit up by warm orange glows at night, was billed as an entertainment center by its glittering signage. Unlike in other border towns like Mongla to the south, the gambling scene in Pangkham was more centralized, a single enterprise that provided employment for hundreds of young men and women. They dealt cards, transported chips, or served drinks at the baccarat tables. The casino was constantly refurbished, additional wings renovated, structures on its peripheries torn down to make way for newer facilities.

People of all means could participate in the casino—there was a large "wheel of fortune"–styled game where gamblers threw grubby small-denomination notes onto pictures of animals, hoping the dial struck the requisite creature. Another involved pulling large dice (again with animals) down onto a board, where losings were swept unceremoniously off the board with a broomstick. The casino was divided into areas based on stakes. Luxurious private rooms were on the higher floors, along with an entire karaoke complex and a large wing for sports betting. TV screens broadcast football matches from all over Europe. Opposite, heavy bass, strobe lights, and techno beats emanated from the dark halls of the main club area, where rich businessmen sat around tables and launched competing bids hanging garlands of flowers around female Chinese dancers. But beneath the gaudy appearance, casinos were one of many nodes in the money-laundering circuits, the movers of "black money" through the hidden undercurrents of capital in the borderlands.

A strong smell of rubber took hold in the mornings when the processing plants across the border in China were in full swing. The sickly stench filled the basin, fueling residents' complaints about insalubrious conditions. Well-lit electronic shops sell the latest mobile phones operating on three of China's main mobile networks. Electronic tones of an annoyingly popular Chinese dance number blare every morning from the indefatigable garbage truck, manned by convicts shackled disconcertingly around the ankles. The roads were not particularly bustling, just the average person heading to the market to buy produce. The clutter of parked cars and motorcycles along the narrow roads near the market made for a tricky drive.

This street was where older Wa women would have gathered in the early 2000s, squatting along the road in wrapped black headdresses, smoking their silver pipes, and peddling large, compressed cakes of dried opium paste. The old market was now being renovated into a three-story complex, its outer structure now festooned with scaffolds and netting. During this interim period, sellers laid out their produce on tarpaulin sheets by the main road—mainly Chinese petty traders on whom Pangkham depended for nonstaple foods and household wares. Exotic wildlife—pangolins, black bears, civets, porcupines, bamboo rats, and even leopards—could still be found here, though numbers fell noticeably over the years. The previous Sichuanese vendor was no longer present in 2014, his supply lines had dried up. Dozens of men waited outside the main casino entrance, eating steaming hot buns, a wary eye watching for the pickups and trucks arriving to recruit labor for the day. As the morning wore on, the casino staff changed their shift; a huge assembly of two hundred uniformed men and women in their early twenties descended upon shops and the market or retired to their dormitories.

In the evenings of the hotter season, women danced choreographed at the peace pagoda to popular Chinese electronic tunes blaring from portable speakers. These rhythmic aerobics continued until the sun went down, providing a spectacle for others strolling around the People's Park. Dusk fell, and youth tore down the roads in their Toyota pickups, heading home for dinner with friends piled into the back. Others gathered outside barbeque shops to drink beer. Nightfall was a scattering of glows—young people shouting drunkenly under the dancing neon lights of the nightclubs, others absorbed in the LED screens of their mobile phones. The tired, warm pink light of massage parlors and brothels bathed gaggles of young women smoking cigarettes on armchairs, veiled by long dyed hair and thick makeup. The headlights of pickups illuminated gaudy hotel signboards and entrances; the casino was lit by bright orange spotlights of fortune. Despite the sizable number of men in worn-out military fatigues, there was little visible law enforcement, a freedom of the frontier.

Visions of Autonomy

Autonomy was partially produced through imaginaries. Wa Region was envisioned differently by its neighbors, each imposing their own framings and interests on it. China saw an unruly buffer zone on its peripheries, a place known to be the source of trafficked narcotics or weapons, a potential crucible for the spread of disease. It was a hideout for unsavory characters fleeing the Chinese mainland; they remembered the KMT adversaries who fled across the border to stage counterattacks. They recalled the massacre of thirteen Chinese sailors on the Mekong in 2011, along the Laotian border, allegedly by militias and drug traffickers.[1] Yet Wa Region was also a frontier for economic opportunity, easing pressures on the national economy by having Chinese entrepreneurs seek wealth abroad through plantation and resource extraction. Most importantly, it was a bargaining chip, an ally to be used in wider geopolitical negotiations with the Myanmar government. Autonomy's potential lay in its ambivalence.

To the Myanmar state, Wa Region was a thorn in its side, a bastion of insurgent resistance too difficult to presently disarm but one that needed to be kept in check. There was a paternalistic sense toward the "backward" minority inhabitants of the hills, whose territory was coveted yet whose populations were troublesome. With no meaningful Myanmar government presence in Wa Region, a part of the nation's borders was beyond its control, an insult to national sovereignty. It was widely rumored that the Tatmadaw leadership regretted the concessions Khin Nyunt had granted the UWSA, which had now led down an irrevocable path to aggrandizement. For the large part of the 2000s, the Tatmadaw was content to let the UWSA be, if it stayed out of overt national ethnic politics. The UWSA had to be contained and enclosed, to prevent its form of autonomy from becoming a model for others.

This influence was already taking shape. The modest levels of development in Pangkham were the subject of envy of other armed groups. Visiting in 2015 for the first Ethnic Armed Organizations' (EAOs) summit organized by the UWSA, ethnic minority leaders touted conditions here as an exemplar: "This is an indication of what we could achieve if we were able to run our region," a Mon representative told the Burmese media.[2] Years later, the Arakan Army leader, present at this summit, would remark that mimicking UWSA autonomy was the only way to develop its own economy and standards of living: "We prefer [a confederation of states] like Wa State, which has a larger share of power in line with the Constitution."[3] Wa autonomy pushed the boundaries of other EAOs' aspirations, refusing to allow the Tatmadaw to dictate the terms of federalism. With more than twenty EAOs across the nation, modeling political organizations and governance off what neighbors had was commonplace, in what Cynthia Weber calls a "citational practice."[4]

Down in the embassies and head offices of Yangon, the UWSA was to the international community just one of the many distant threats that destabilized the strong yet fragile Myanmar state, its pet project and fledgling democracy. Impressions were of a lawless fiefdom in the hills run by intransigent rebels. Little was known of it beyond its involvement in the narcotics trade. In 2005, the US Eastern District Court of New York indicted eight top UWSA leaders for narcotics-related charges, just months prior to the UWSA's announcement of its opium ban. That same year, the US Treasury Department announced sanctions on eleven UWSA leaders and associates along with sixteen companies based in Thailand.[5] As was common in China and Myanmar, businesses simply shifted registrations to the names of relatives and affiliates, creating an inscrutable network of shadow capital ties.[6]

But the UWSA had its own imaginings of autonomy. An early clue to how this translated outward came in 1993 when Saw Lu, then UWSA spokesman for international affairs, made a demand for autonomy and a plea for international assistance in eradicating opium. This statement came at the beginning of Myanmar's National Convention, a nationwide attempt to draft a new Burmese constitution. The Wa proposal noted how the Wa had been "pawns in the violent, destructive games of others," and it made an explicit political demand:

> Our political goal is to restore real democracy for all of Burma, a democracy in which the majority rules, but equally important, where minority rights are protected even if the minority is a minority of one person. . . . We want the restoration of Wa State within Burma. We are not separatists, but we want some autonomy for our people. Under the British and until 1962 there was a Wa State in the northeastern corner of Burma. After Ne Win's 1962 coup, his government redrew the map. Wa State just disappeared. It was swallowed up in Shan State. We have historic roots in and an historic claim to the area east of the Salween River from Ko Kang south to the Thai border. We want to administer the area as part of a federal union in Burma.[7]

But autonomy was not simply a set of political demands, of which all sides often had incongruent understandings. It was its own lived reality in Wa Region. It was not restricted by codified terms and conditions of ceasefires or political arrangements envisioned in Yangon through peace commissions. It was a de facto autonomy seemingly borne of raw military might and the strategic defensive affordances of the highlands. A proud leadership saw itself as self-reliant, entrepreneurial, nondominated, responsible only for itself and its people. Autonomy was about traveling where you wanted, negotiating with whomever you wanted, buying whatever you wanted. Autonomy was also a value in Wa Region, expressed through social meanings and material manifestations of power and authority, of self-determination and self-respect grounded in strength and wealth.

But for all the proud assertions of might, autonomy treaded carefully. It seemed that there were strong parallels between the way the UWSA navigated relations with the outside, the way in which individual leaders projected authority within Wa Region, and the way in which local inhabitants made sense of the capillaries of power. Autonomy was based on the same logics of how power should operate, on evaluations of authority, on the embodied sensibilities and mental maps of who was important and why. In the absence of state institutions and mandates, norms and relations filled the void. Wa elites applied these values when dealing with outsiders. They scaled up to regional politics: Which representatives from the Myanmar and Chinese governments, or EAOs, were worth negotiating with, whose words could be counted on, and who had the capacity to implement promises? Who was powerful, whom could they influence, and how long would they stay influential? The topographies of power were not simply networks and connections but fluctuating temporally.

In this chapter I chart a course through this terrain of power and authority, showing how it is based on both *autonomy as a social value* expressed through wealth, self-reliance, and ability, and the *management of relations* through generosity and patronage. Autonomy as a social value[8] can be observed ethnographically in embodied sensibilities, contests and competitions, practices of visitation and hospitality, and deferential reciprocities. This social realm is also the very fabric through which political relations play out. As Marielle Debos, in her work on "men in arms" in Northern Chad, argues, "the art of governing consists in managing power relations."[9] Any understanding of autonomy in Wa Region relies on examining the logics of power and authority in Wa Region, as well as mapping out its topographies and relations. The autonomy of the polity, subsequently, is inherently relational, a scaling of these values, practices, and relations up to the geopolitical level.

The War Machine, Past and Present

Autonomy as social value has a long history in Wa highland imaginaries, interacting with the claim-making and impositions of external forces. The desire to have autonomy respected and be left alone appears deeply entrenched in the histories of the Wa hills, based on accounts of travelers who entered at the turn of the 1900s. These travelers depicted a social landscape in a "near-permanent state of war," dotted with "village stockades" and "farmer fortresses," defensive fortifications "selected with an eye to the tactical position and inaccessibility," built in the absence of a sovereign overlord.[10] The Wa hills were described as isolated: "mountainous, insalubrious, and largely inaccessible," with tales of their notorious headhunting playing well into stories of British expeditionary daring:[11] "The escort [of sixty rifles] was in a state of nerves, the men sleeping in their boots, for terror of the Panghung Wa (& these are not wild Wa, but comparatively tame)."[12]

The British deputy commissioner of the Shan States, James G. Scott, noted that prior to his initial visit in the 1890s, rumors of Wa cannibalism were rife, but he reassured readers: "The Wa are not cannibals, at least not habitual cannibals."[13] He continued in his *Gazetteer of Upper Burma and the Shan States*, "A Wa must go out with the same reflection as a self-respecting dog, who never takes a stroll without the conviction that he is more likely than not to have a fight before he comes home again. Nevertheless there are rules of the game [headhunting]. . . . To behead a man from a community even on the same range of hills is looked upon as un-neighbourly and slothful."[14]

Headhunting constructed a discourse of barbarians beyond the pale: it was given simple "explanations" such as being a primitive ritual meant to boost crop fertility.[15] The Wa also had fearsome reputations for wildness and violence. Another missionary wrote admiringly in the 1930s of a "warrior culture" among the Wa: "The Wa are superb fighters when on the war path. They become so brave in battle that their actions often reach the degree of recklessness. . . . There is mysteriousness and strangeness about the Wa nature that few can understand."[16]

There were values of self-reliance and egalitarianism. The headhunting reputation came together with an aversion to hierarchy and the refusal to allow single kings or chiefs to rule over Wa country.[17] Magnus Fiskesjö, the leading anthropologist of the Wa who conducted fieldwork on the Chinese side of the border in the 1990s, summarizes this:

> Until the end of Wa autonomy in the 1950s, in the central Wa country every man, and generally also every woman, was regarded as independent and autonomous in themselves, according to an ethos that strongly emphasized equality and that was bolstered by codes of honor and moral norms. . . . People would also unite to defend villages and, in larger conflicts, the genealogically connected networks known as *jaig' qee* ('realms'), or even, when necessary, Wa country in general. But personal and local autonomy was retained and exercised as far as possible.[18]

Resonating with James Scott's thesis, Wa autonomy was about preventing the emergence of hierarchical political structures. If a chief or king were to arise, he might pledge the allegiance or subordinate his realm to a foreign power, without the consent of his people.[19] For this reason, the Wa reportedly undermined hierarchizing tendencies: "The Wa placed curbs on internal competitive trends, calibrating the rotation of duties in ritual community feasting, thus restricting the aggrandizement of individuals, who might otherwise, if permitted to rise in political stature, become vulnerable targets of co-option by threatening external powers."[20]

Fiskesjö points toward a period of autonomy and egalitarianism that appears to have been disrupted in the 1950s once KMT raiding began, and militarily superior outsiders entered the hills, seeking the allegiance of Wa chieftains. The loss of autonomy arguably began once Chairman Bao and other militia leaders "joined" with the CPB (see chapter 3), now co-opted by external powers.

At first instance, these accounts and impressions of Chinese and British colonial explorers seem to fit neatly with Deleuze and Guattari's notion of the war machine: bands and nomads exterior to the state, "nonmetric, acentered, rhizomatic multiplicities that occupy space without 'counting' it."[21] Inhabiting what Deleuze and Guattari call "smooth" space that remained unenumerated and classified, the war machine resisted the "striated," organized, and metric space of state logics. The headhunting Wa and their later guerrilla bands were not nomadic peoples in the sense of perpetual migration, but rather an intermezzo, a distributed deterritorialization that refused fixity.[22] Fighting was not the primary concern of the war machine; rather, it was to stay outside the forces of state capture. It resisted co-optation by the state and resisted interiorizing the very logics of the state, the propensities to classify and make legible. The Wa quest to remain autonomous outside the state makes them seem the quintessential war machine, a nomadic force finally co-opted by the state when they formed alliances with the CPB.[23]

Northern Chad offers an instructive parallel, demonstrating how local values shape society despite the apparent absence of political order. Julian Brachet and Judith Scheele's study of Tubu "anarchy" examines how the narrative construction of Tubu areas as a disorderly and wild periphery are not merely external but "have been accepted and partially created locally, imbued with value, and endorsed as a description of what it means to be 'Tubu.'"[24] Stereotypes of negativity—"archetypical raiders, thieves, and predators," are appreciated by local people themselves, describing dangerousness and disorder not as problems but as values that are valorized—personal autonomy, disobedience, and a capacity for violence.[25] Such values, situationally enacted, affirm and make up the Tubu social world, giving meaning to the supposed absences within anarchy. In fact, "The key virtues in Faya are autonomy, originality, self-affirmation. They translate into a vision not only of what it means to be an excellent person but also of social interaction."[26]

But the war machine analytic risks creating the impression of a pristine, pre-1950s egalitarian Wa community that fended off encroachment, engulfment, and hierarchy until it was finally overwhelmed. Or until militia leaders rose and were co-opted. While accounts of Wa militias rising in the 1950s to fend off KMT raids fits snugly with Scott's prognostications for the demise of Zomian freedom around that time, the shift from egalitarian society to authoritarian militarization took decades to unfold. The arrival of the CPB in the late 1960s and its introduction of militarization and bureaucratic organization saw the gradual embodying of state logics in Wa society. For the common man, the autonomous egalitarianism of the pre-1950s would be replaced with a subservience to military leaders and elites. The highland world of Wa Region must be thought of not as a stark rupture between past egalitarian autonomy of Wa realms and the present militarism of the UWSA but as a process of continuity and change.

Instead, ethnography uncovers continuities of social values and logics expressed in contemporary political practices and relations. Self-reliance is valued only to the point where reliance becomes prudent. Engagement is not just warding off external impositions but also accepting and subverting select political values. These logics and values are not discernibly "Wa" or "Chinese" but an agglomeration of a changing borderland sociality. Autonomy was as much enacted through political relations and practices as through social values of self-reliance, ability, patronage, hospitality, and wealth, all of which shaped one another in everyday events. Tactical dissonance is about selectively adapting values and practice, in the service of a project of autonomy.

Parceling Up the Wa World

The Wa called their own land Wa Country (Wa: *Meung Paraog, Haktiex Paraog*) or the Wa hills (Wa: *Gawng Paraog*), without a clear, bounded sense of spatial demarcation. The British colonial project was the first to embark on territorial delimitation in the Wa hills. Following the annexation of Upper Burma in 1885, the Wa hills became part of the minority-dominated "Frontier Areas" from 1891, separated by the British from the Bamar-majority "Ministerial Burma" of the central lowlands. This colonial division sowed the seeds of divergent futures, as Mary Callahan notes: "No other Asian colony suffered such a radical bifurcation in its population's fate."[27]

But the British remained ambivalent to governing the Wa hills, seeking only the occasional flag march or prospecting trip for minerals. The Wa hills were troublesome to govern militarily and would produce little revenue from taxation. Making territorial claims there would anger the Chinese.[28] The Wa hills were not included in the British census of 1901.[29] And while the British accepted that rumors of gold were exaggerated, the presence of other minerals like silver and lead created hesitation about simply abandoning their claims.[30] The subsequent creation of the Federation of Shan States in 1922 for the indirect rule of Shan areas left most of the Wa hills out of its administrative arrangements, as did the Government of Burma Act 1937, which created governance structures integrating the states of the Frontier Areas into Ministerial Burma, allowing them to elect members into a new national parliament in Rangoon.[31] The Wa States were excluded throughout, left almost unadministered with only a small British garrison present from 1934 onward—"a sleeping dog that is best left to lie."[32]

The carving up of highland realms took decades. Wa inhabitants would have seen boundary posts erected decades prior, in the 1890s and 1930s. Disputes over the two-hundred-mile stretch between the Nam Tit and Nam Hka Rivers, which ran through the Wa hills, began in 1897–1900. James G. Scott and the Qing general Liu attempted to demarcate boundaries based on an 1897 agreement that created the Burma-China Boundary Demarcation Joint Commission, an endeavor befuddled by the absence of accurate maps and consistent place names.[33] Rumors of gold tracts within the disputed areas made both sides postpone reaching a definitive agreement, preferring to hold out for more geological information. The boundary posts along the border started in 1898 but were abandoned for the stretch through Wa country (from present-day Nam Tit to Kunma) when a British-Chinese joint expedition was attacked by local Wa.[34] The British only reentered in 1929 to resume demarcation efforts, by which time the posts had been destroyed by local Wa.[35]

Nonetheless, disputes between the great powers flared up on occasion. In 1933, the British protested Chinese incursions across the Scott line and sent their own survey party in 1934, which was attacked.[36] The Banhong Incident, touted by Chinese propagandists as loyal Wa protecting the Chinese frontier from British incursions, led to the British burning villages around Ban Lao.[37] A Boundary Commission chaired and arbitrated by Swiss colonel Frederic Iselin produced a boundary in 1937, a ruling that was accepted but not ratified, as World War II began in China.[38] The Iselin line ran past today's Nam Tit, Ban Wai, Kunma, and Longtan Townships and past Banlao on the Chinese side, and it became precisely the eastern boundary of Wa Region today. The demarcated geo-body, the hallmark of the nation-state, was replacing unmarked zones of influence and tribute.[39]

The nature of Wa autonomy did not fit into states' conception of territorial boundaries. Fiskesjö notes that Wa communities were part of the "heavily armed, yet only loosely associated and fiercely egalitarian polities—called 'the Wa states' only because [the British] had no word for such stateless sovereignty."[40] British reports betrayed an inability to comprehend autonomy in the Wa hills, a naïve belief that territoriality would guarantee allegiance:

> "The Wild Was should be retained, together with convenient routes into their country. Experience on the North-West Frontier indicates that it

is best to have unpleasant people of this sort under one's own sovereignty, rather than that they should be in a position to raid into our territory from a base in China. It is understood that there should not be much difficulty in bringing them under control and stopping their headhunting practices."[41]

The British began planning for Burma's independence after World War II.[42] Leaders of highland ethnic groups were concerned about their political autonomy in the future nation, and in 1947 the British Frontier Areas Committee of Enquiry (FACE) consulted them about their futures in the new Burmese state.[43] Four Wa representatives (mainly from areas more proximate to the Salween, and none from Chairman Bao's area) were interviewed, yielding the most-cited example of supposed Wa isolationism: "We do not want to join with anybody because in the past we have been very independent. . . . We are very wild people and we do not appreciate these things [education, clothing, and hospitals]. . . . We live entirely by ourselves."[44]

This exchange, circulated and reproduced in most accounts of Wa Region, lent itself to an exaggerated narrative of the Wa as politically naïve, disengaged, and disinterested.[45] Other statements included the following: "Was are Was and Shans are Shans. We would not like to go into the Federated Shan States" and "We have not thought about that [political future] because we are wild people.[46] We never thought of the administrative future. We only think about ourselves."[47]

Nonetheless, Burmese independence went ahead in 1948. The terms of federal autonomy were based on the 1947 Panglong Agreement signed between Aung San, leader of the Burmans, and leaders of the Kachins, Chins, and Shans, guaranteeing them "full autonomy in internal administration."[48] But there were different arrangements and terms for each group, each negotiated bilaterally.[49] Excluded from the Panglong Agreement were smaller ethnic groups such as the Naga, Ta-ang, and Wa.

The Wa were now subjects of a newly created Burmese state with which they had little conception of or contact with, and even less political allegiance. The long-autonomous mountain realms were now divided in two with the final demarcation of the China-Burma border in 1960, even as its effects on the ground would take decades to materialize.

Logics of Authority

It is in Pangkham where one starts to get a feel for the logics of authority and political relations refracted across town. People refer to places less by street names, more by landmarks—the casino, government offices, the old and new markets, and prominent hotels but also houses of the elite. It was the register used to give directions: "It's down the street near the river just past Minister so-and-so's house," "Same street as the Hong Pang company's hotel," or "It's behind district leader's shophouse." Stories, too, dot the built landscape, locations for narrations of past events, senses of place that impinge upon the passerby. As Keith Basso prompts us, "places served humankind as durable symbols of distant events and as indispensable aids for remembering and imagining them."[50] Oral histories were engraved into landscapes: "This is so-and-so's hotel, which he built after getting out of prison. . . . This street used to be just a muddy road that caused jams. . . . This was where Chinese opium traders gathered in the market."

The headquarters of the Wa administration and the main meeting hall sit in the center of town, within the compound of the military school, adjacent to the People's Park. The seven "Ministry" offices of the Wa administration—Agriculture, Political Works, External Relations, Military Headquarters, Finance, Development, and Justice—were dispersed across town, but offices were not always staffed. Wa State TV News was broadcast most days in Chinese, Wa, and Shan languages and mainly reported on the meetings in these ministries. These ranged from biannual workplan meetings, the hosting of other EAO representatives, or staff exchange training run by Chinese government delegations. Across town, signboards pronounced the branches of companies and enterprises, some private joint ventures with Chinese capital, others widely known to be owned by figures from powerful families. Embedded in the town landscape were these intimations of the vast networks of political and economic relations, radiating out across Wa Region and beyond.

The authority of individual leaders in contemporary Wa Region relied on values of autonomy, expressed in wealth, self-reliance, ability, and strength, and manifest in both spectacular and spectral performances in Wa Region. Little of the egalitarian ethos seemed to remain. Nowhere was this seen better than in the regal persona of Chairman Bao Youxiang himself. Bao was the commander-in-chief of the UWSA, the chairman of its political wing, and the head of the Wa administration, and his name took on an almost mythical life of its own. He was the warrior king of the Kunma guerrillas in the 1960s, deputy commander of a CPB brigade, and later leader of mutiny against the CPB. Mansion complexes belonging to him and his kin were undoubtedly the central seat of power in Pangkham, down a small street guarded by uniformed armed sentries. People, places, and projects associated with him were invested with authority and respect. Members of his wider family were heads of administrative and military units and businesses ventures, all seemingly "untouchable." On special occasions, the skyline of Pangkham was lit up by a grand display of fireworks, and anybody who was anybody gathered at his mansion for lavish celebrations.

Bao Youxiang was born in Kunma, the heart of the Wa hills, in 1949, just after the formation of the independent Burmese nation-state. Up in the hills, however, de jure incorporation into a lowland polity meant next to nothing. An endless period of warfare and turmoil continued. Bao married at fifteen and founded the Kunma guerrillas two years later in 1966 to protect his area from other Wa guerrilla groups, some of whom were allies of the Burmese state. Bao described how headhunting raids became retributive warfare: "I wrote an edict—from now on whoever cuts a head from my troops, I will cut a hundred, a thousand from his."[51] A bold statement perhaps, but prescient, with the hindsight of success.

Bao's figure circulates through the hills. Photographs of him in full uniform donning a military cap are on display at many ministry and township offices. In one iconic poster, he is pictured saluting, rays of sunlight emanating from clouds behind him in messianic fashion. Armed soldiers march beneath his frame, a text borrowed from Chinese military imagery. The red Chinese text superimposed over the image reads, "If no one offends me, I offend none; if someone offends me, I must offend him" (Chn: *ren bufan wo, wo bufan ren, ren ruofan wo, wo bifan ren*). In another image, he wears an oversized Communist-era olive green military jacket and cap, paired with gray sneakers for comfort. Videos of him inspecting troops from 2012 circulate online; he is perched out of the sunroof of a specially modified Porsche Cayenne, roaring greetings and supervisory words to parades of soldiers commemorating the UWSA's twentieth anniversary. In other scenes, rows of singing villagers welcome him into township celebrations.[52]

There is a palpable reverence as people speak of him; rarely a bad word is heard; aspersions are only found in silences. A friend recounted with some reverence, "I never started smoking, because when I was young, my aunt brought me to see Chairman. . . . He offered me a cigarette, but I declined. He then told me I should never smoke unless in his presence. So I don't."

Others described him as having the well-being of his people at heart, even if the inability to travel out of the region (many Wa leaders are on blacklists) had resulted in a "lack of exposure" to the outside world among key Politburo leaders. Even Chinese businessmen understood the aura and adulation: "His car was traveling on a narrow road in the hills, with a whole line of cars gathering behind, simply because no one dared to overtake his vehicle. He finally stopped to allow others to pass, realizing that he was holding up traffic." Implausible as it might seem (the chairman's cars are not known for sloth), circulating tales demonstrated the reverence with which he was held.

Arguably, it was Bao who precipitated the demise of the uncaptured Wa war machine, despite his status as the indefatigable leader of the UWSA. By joining the

CPB in 1969, along with three other key Wa guerrilla groups, he brought the untethered peoples of the highlands into a wider state-form and network. This compromise (see chapter 3) was made to push Burmese government–affiliated Wa groups out of the hills, with Bao successfully building up a reputation as a capable warrior, becoming a CPB battalion commander and later brigade deputy.[53] The state-form was here to stay. As Danny Hoffman writes, "The war machine does not last. It is always captured. Deterritorialized, active forces are always eventually reterritorialized, made reactive, either because they are captured by the state or because they ossify into state-like hierarchies and become the state itself."[54]

The alliance not only incorporated the Wa hills under CPB governance from the 1970s onward but more importantly began a process that interiorized state logics and classificatory practices within Wa political society—the impetuses to make legible and striate space (however ineffective), an association with territory and fixity, a mimicry of the state-form, in particular through CPB taxation and enumeration.[55] Even when the external domination of the CPB was toppled, political structures had irrevocably changed—an adoption of the hierarchizing state-form (however partial), no longer an exteriority, no longer able to resist the emergence of chiefs. Gone was the supposed egalitarianism of the autonomous highland realms. Authority was now embodied in the persona of the chairman and other leaders, their titles, ranks, armies, and administration. Yet continuities would be found in the different forms autonomy took.

Wealth, Self-Reliance, and Autonomy

The turn toward hierarchized and centralized forms of authority had much to do with militarization and the expanding political economy of opium in the Wa hills. These broader changes were often reduced into an overdetermined link between wealth and power, encapsulated in the figure of the ruthless drug lord. A sensationalist *Time* magazine interview by two Westerners brought this caricature to international attention. In a self-laudatory 2002 piece, they depict Chairman Bao as the "tribesman," "a squat man in his early 50s with a bulldog face": "His reputation, fueled by rumor, is gaudy, befitting the lord of a narco-fiefdom. Bao is reputedly so rich that he would need two trucks to carry around all his money. . . . To meet Bao, we plunged into the lawless hills of northeast Burma to the heart of an empire built on guns, drugs and blood."[56]

Such caricatures emphasized the belligerence of the UWSA, tying them to the wealth generated by shadow economies, buttressed by authoritarian rule. Accumulation, it implied, was the point of highland autonomy, cloaked in a tenuous political agenda. Greed rather than legitimate grievance. While interviews conducted by Chinese news agencies in the early 2000s yielded great insight into the attitudes and demeanors of UWSA leaders (many now retired or deceased), these complex answers to questions about child soldiers, narcotics, and their wealth never reached Western audiences.[57] Instead, representations fixated on the hypocrisy of Bao's denials: "'These drugs!' he cries, karate-chopping the air for emphasis, revealing the diamond-encrusted gold Rolex he wears on his wrist. 'I detest them! You think drugs have been harmful to others? Let me tell you: they have been a much greater disaster for the Wa! Our people are stuck in such poverty they haven't even got clothes to put on their own backs.'"[58]

The reputation of illicit wealth and power was worsened by the other notorious family in Wa Region, the Weis. Wei Xuegang was the shadowy ethnic Chinese financial controller of the UWSA, said by observers to be steadily filling the coffers with drug money and business investments, a "remote control" giving the UWSA "the opportunity to deny that they are actively involved in the drugs business."[59] Having left Wa Region in the 1970s when the CPB arrived, Wei worked with the Shan drug lord Khun Sa before striking out on his own, returning to the UWSA just after 1989. Several large business conglomerates linked with him and other UWSA leaders invested profits from the opium trade in precious stones, timber, construction, rubber, and agriculture in the 1990s.[60] These did business locally and across Myanmar, Thailand, and China but retained offices in Pangkham. In 2000, Wei was one of the first UWSA leaders added to the blacklist under the US Foreign Narcotics Kingpin Designation Act,[61] and other associates of his Hong Pang investment company followed in 2008.

Personal wealth became a key social idiom of autonomy and hence authority in Pangkham, as elites profited off extractions from the narcotics industry, either directly or through informal taxation. Rent-seeking and reciprocity quickly translated into cultures of patronage, providing for one's kin and affiliates in sometimes spectacular fashion. Being a leader with businesses and companies meant the ability to fund and run a work unit or ministry, to pay for the hosting or festivals or gifts, and to raise armies and followers. UWSA rulings placed limits on the number of people each household could "raise" (Chn: *yang*), increasing with political rank. The larger one's entourage of soldiers and helpers, the more important they appeared. Chin Ko-lin, a criminologist who carried out research on the opium trade in Pangkham in 2001, recorded an interviewee speaking of Chairman Bao: "Bao is perfectly clear who is doing what, but he needs money to develop the Wa State and to maintain his power. Here, money talks and it is everything; if you don't have money you cannot be the top leader. Bao is the most powerful leader mainly because he knows how to make money."[62]

Such statements were commonplace, but they also effaced the competing regimes of value introduced by charisma, historical accomplishments, and kinship ties of leaders. Wealth was an easy but reductive explanatory factor for power, as Hoffman finds among the *kamajor* in Sierra Leone: a "host of value regimes seem to operate simultaneously and in competition."[63] Outside the Baos and the Weis, other officials' authority was contested and shifting, interpreted differently by actors—a combination of wealth, influence, and "ability," personal histories of valor or origin, kinship ties, and institutional standing within the Wa administration. It was not easily apparent which of these variables would hold more weight, and these deliberations constantly emerged in conversation—people gossiped over poor political decisions or leadership, debated who would be able or unable to solve a problem, or disputed who had jurisdiction in any particular area.

One Leads Ten, Independent, Speaks, and Listens

Midranked Wa government officials taught me the most about local webs of relations that buttressed authority. Wang was in his seventies, living in a sizable but unassuming house in the middle of town. A Sino-Burmese from Shan State, he had been studying in Yangon in the early sixties when Ne Win's military coup of 1962 took over the Burmese government, beginning the fifty-year military dictatorship. He joined the Communist Party in 1964 and moved up into the hills of Shan State to take up arms, surviving the campaigns of the 1970s and 1980s. He finally opted to stay with the UWSA when it was formed. He was an informal liaison to international guests in town, a role he took on with feigned reluctance: the windows of his bookshelves were peppered with photographs and mementos of their visits, and he rattled off the names of previous aid workers and embassy representatives. He saw the NGOs who arrived in the immediate years following the opium ban, he took them to meet senior leaders, and he arranged dinners and tours of rubber plantations and the former CPB headquarters. Yet despite holding his present post for nearly three decades, as an ethnic Chinese he was always a partial outsider. Moreover, it seemed that his long-suffering and more amenable personality was not always suited to the steely brashness often required for progression to the Wa Central Committee. Younger officials interrupted him at meetings, he was not an automatic pick for a seat at the first few tables at dinners, and his diminutive frame did not exude the sturdy masculinities required of a big man.

Wang sat alone in his living room after dinners, watching Burmese and Chinese news on television, the perfect time for our weekly conversations. He washed out a pot of Kongmingshan tea, a special produce of Wa Region, and laid out some cut fruit and a knife, gesturing toward a bunch of bananas hanging from ceiling. Unlike other leaders, he did not put on shows of patronage—no one attended to him, no driver, or cook, or young men in his household to pour tea or run errands. Wang was never short of admiration for Maoist policies and the Chinese Communist Party. "Mao used to say that Chiang [Kai-Shek] was his logistics officer; he knew how to raid the KMT for supplies." Or espousing the qualities of political leadership by describing the pictorial origins of the Chinese word for cadre (Chn: *ganbu*): "Look, it is beautiful—one leads ten, one stands strong and independent, speaks, and listens."

A favorite theme of Wang's was a social critique of authority. He relentlessly expounded the notion of ability (Chn: *nengli*), or business and leadership acumen. While the Wa Central Committee set up policies and guidelines—for example, the goal for each township to spend 5 percent of its budget on education and 5 percent on healthcare by 2019—no central budget was regularly allocated to townships to meet these targets. And because government officials were paid low salaries (between 150 and 1,200 CNY [between 25 and 200 USD] and around twenty kilograms of rice a month), all were expected to use their positions of power to access business opportunities. This meant that individual leaders had to rely on their titles and influence to invest personal and public funds in businesses and projects—ranging from rubber or tea plantations and petrol stations, to tin mines—generating revenue for public services. They also received gifts and favors from visiting businessmen, or tax concessions from the Wa government for these businesses. The distinction between individual and public wealth was never clear, and many businesses were owned partly by a work unit (Chn: *danwei*) and partly by the leader himself.

Wang was himself a midtier exemplar of such enterprise. Like others, he constructed a hotel on the land in front of his residence and had leased it out to a Chinese entrepreneur from Hunan Province for a reasonable rent of 300,000 CNY (50,000 USD) a year. On a survey in mid-2015, I counted at least eighty-five hotels and guesthouses in town: "There can't be *that* many visitors in town, such that everyone is building hotels. Are there no other enterprises for this land?" "The hotels are always full," came the somewhat incredible reply; "there are so many tourists and businessmen, tens of thousands of visitors a year." Perhaps he knew better. The hotel had, after all, been running for the last twelve years despite changes of management. Wang had invested in a series of businesses over the last two decades, and his son was managing some of the family wealth. In recent years, he had switched to real estate and properties, tracking increasing land prices in both Wa Region and Myanmar. On the upper reaches of the hill overlooking Pangkham, he was building a huge mansion. I teased him: "Perhaps the Myanmar army will attack Pangkham just to take over your house."

"There are three things you need here for business—confidence, capital, and connections," Wang explained.

What Wang continually gestured toward was the intertwining of leadership ability and business acumen that made a strong leader. Successful revenue generation and smooth administration would bear testament to an official's "ability" and "leadership qualities." Conversely, poor management would lead to being replaced or reassigned. He told me of a certain leader who had been newly appointed to head a ministry but supposedly lacked the personal wealth to do so successfully: "This will be very frustrating and strenuous [*chili*] for him; he does not have enough capital. In the end, the ministry will suffer. They should not have put him in charge." The new minister would not be able to afford to fund ministry projects or cover shortfalls with personal wealth. The central authority budgets were not adequately distributed to the ministries and townships. Understandably, it was often difficult to find township leaders at their offices, since they were busy running personal or public businesses, leaving a contact number on the office board instead. A friend dryly dubbed this phenomenon "Only his name shows up for work" (Chn: *mingzhi shangban*).

A strong leader conducted himself with ruthlessness and pragmatism where necessary, responsible for keeping his own house in order, and demonstrating the capacity to enforce discipline and protect followers. Phone calls were made to military units or to the police to have them "reconsider" arrests; others exerted their influence to shape outcomes. Everywhere I heard hushed sympathetic stories about leaders of whose children or subordinates were said to be disobedient (Chn: *butinghua*), as if it were a cause for shame. Moral discipline and the upkeep of appropriate appearances were essential to the leader's corporate unit, part of his "ability."

Indeterminate Ranks—Complex Relations

Logics of authority were anchored firmly on autonomy as a social value—self-reliance, wealth, and "ability" of leaders. But there were also relational ties that were equally important amid the politics of town. Connections and other personal attributes complicated the logics of authority—it was not simply about wealth or ability but the relations one was able to navigate or cultivate. Personal autonomy, indeed, was relational, not solely borne by individuals but ratified by others. Each took their spot in the webs of patronage relations and lived up to the expectations of their place.

One tries to piece together these "ranked" relations of patronage but is never certain.[64] There were the Chinese veterans sent by China in the 1970s to assist the CPB, who stayed on even after its collapse, widely respected for their sacrifice and counsel (though many remained puzzled by their ideological commitment to

Communism). There were the ethnic Wa leaders in the Politburo, who originated, however, from the Chinese side of the border, and not from the traditional Wa heartlands of Kunma and Ban Wai. Their positions in government, though high, were more functional than powerful. There were the older Wa commanders who had begun in the 1960s as leaders of guerrilla groups, whose military prowess was legendary yet had little temperament for administration or business. Some lower officials had symbolic roles in the 1989 mutiny and were rewarded for this with lifelong government positions. Then there were the ethnic Chinese or Kokang, seen as meticulous (or less charitably, scheming): "When you talk to him, you can always see his mind is swirling with thoughts" was one description I heard. Still others were relatives—sons, brothers, cousins, nephews—of the Baos, often given some position of sorts. And while positions in government conferred status and invoked deference, they were not necessarily commensurate with the authority held.

Locals themselves did not always agree on the hierarchies and relations between leaders. Largely self-evident among the top tier of leaders ("Whatever he says goes" or "As long as he says it is fine" [Chn: *shuo jiusuanle*]), authority was contentious for everyone else, and arguments between ordinary people were full of discrepancy and disparagement. They made dismissive assessments of other officials' authority, particularly those in a different faction or of competing patrons: "He doesn't have any power at all" (Chn: *meisha quanli*), "This guy is a nobody," or "No one listens when he talks." They mocked the hapless positions given to certain "retired" officials, with the superfluous titles like "Political Commissar" and "Assistant," which were in effect polite demotions. They dismissed others' assertions and readings of politics with aplomb ("You've got it wrong; that's not possible") or warily refused to engage ("This one is not good to speak of/guess at"). Some simply did not know but chose to provide answers nonetheless. Others were inclined to boast about the connections they had or to exaggerate someone's influence to curry favor. Many bragged about drinking or visiting with a leader or being good friends or familiar (Chn: *shou*) with the leader's relatives and children, raising these in conversation in some subtle way.

Relations and position shifted constantly. Leaders rose in influence, and fell out of favor over time, plagued by mismanagement, debt, or bad luck. One favored arena of speculation surrounded intrgiue in the Politburo, who was being pushed out, who was not talking to whom, and who were the candidates for promotion into the Central Committee as "second-generation" leaders. Seeking patrons for any deal yielded competing interpretations of power relations, some of which might be terminal for the enterprise. Being able to accurately judge the relative power of leaders was a form of social capital.

Generosity and Protection

While many of the attributes of leadership were up for debate, one thing was agreed upon: a good leader was generous and big-hearted (Chn: *dafang*) and protected and provided for his followers. The late Li Ziru, then the UWSP vice-chairman and Bao's commander under the CPB, had said of him, "He is the only one who can unite and lead Wa Region. . . . He has one great attribute: his heart is big; he can tolerate many kinds of people."[65] I often asked people what they imagined made a good leader, and I received a collection of answers: "One who takes care of the people below him," "One who is generous and not petty," "One who has the wealth to do things," or "One who has the capability to handle tasks." These utterances might have been vague but were over time accompanied with plenty of specific examples and social critiques of particular leaders and the expectations they left unfulfilled.

Stinginess (Chn: *xiaoqi*) was perhaps one of the worst attributes a leader could be accused of. I often heard gossip about which leaders were constantly making purchases and embarking on construction projects without paying the right tips and "introduction fees" (Chn: *jieshaofei*) to middlemen who had brokered the deals, or forgetting to "take care of" (Chn: *zhaogu*) those who had helped them along the way. Others conveniently overlooked debts incurred, most reprehensible for the powerful. Leaders were expected to foot the bill at events; they often hosted entertainment sessions or dinners where guests and friends arrived and left at will. Guests were well fed and spoiled with expensive cigarettes and premium beers, commensurate with the host's rank. Within months I had learned to situate the alcohol and cigarettes (Myanmar beer was more expensive and premium, as was authentic red wine; only "ninety-nine" or premium blends of cigarettes were ranked). At hosted gatherings, no money changed hands, nor were bills paid—discreetness was part of the sense that these costs were trivial and irrelevant to a magnanimous leader, already "dealt with" behind the scenes. The powerful needed no acknowledgment of their provision; gratitude and obligation were implicit.

Generosity was also seen in individual sensibilities, a material but primarily a moral disposition. I was told cautionary tales about leaders who were too stingy to provide for their own people. "Who would want to go with [follow] that guy?" friends asked, having described a leader who only offered his driver a pig upon his proposed marriage out of the household, failing to contribute money to the driver's new household. Given that the driver had grown up in his family and had no chance to work outside, it was expected that the leader then provided for his marriage at the appointed time. The driver, unable to raise a family, remained unmarried into his thirties. Such oversights were often whispered and gossiped about, tarnishing reputations. Not all transgressors faced the same retribution; evaluating generosity was never consistent.

Leaders' obligations also included extending their reputation to protect and provide for others. A leader granted an audience to people he accepted, and in so doing demonstrated to wider audiences how they were protected by mere association with him. A good leader followed up to "look after" his associates, with name dropping commonplace, and one-upmanship a competition among subordinates. Authority took the form of pronouncements. Permission granted by a big leader was license to operate, a vouching-for anointed by his power. "Tell him I sent you" or "tell him you are a friend, and he will help you." On the flip side, not receiving the endorsement of a leader could be a cause of consternation for an individual, an insecurity that one now had to be on their toes.

Strong leadership required tough and decisive action while demonstrating loyalty and keeping subordinates and allies happy. Chairman Bao was asked in a video interview in 2004 about the whereabouts of the elusive Wei Xuegang, charged with drug trafficking in 2002. It was unclear if he was still part of the Central Committee. Bao replied uneasily, shifting in his seat, not wishing to speak badly of his associate but unable to deny the bare truth.

> INTERVIEWER: "Is this about a code of brotherhood?"
> BAO: "That is one aspect of it. . . . I am the leader of this place; my first thing is to protect my people; this is my responsibility. . . . These are businessmen who at times have helped the economic and agricultural development of Wa Region and I at times am also grateful to them, not only him. Some people may have committed crimes elsewhere, but it is not about political things and we can still forgive him, to put it this way."[66]

Protection involved a counterthreat of violent reprisal and sanction, an economy of power around Wa leaders with a potential for brutality and spectacle. Gossip and rumor added to the auras, sculpting the reputation of particular leaders and their capacity for violence, with few retributive acts actually made public. Among the stories that spread were a leader reportedly killing a subordinate who slept with one of his wives, and then divorcing the unfaithful wife. Another shot the ear off a soldier who cut him off driving on a road. Alleged affairs were rumored to be dealt with through beatings or even murder. Tales were told of certain leaders' blasé (and hyperbolic) spoken reactions to troublesome business acquaintances—"Why not just kill them?" (Chn: *shadiu jiusuanle*). Many were just rumor, and veracity was hard to determine.

Violence was also a competitive arena of authority—I heard stories of people literally running to the house of a leader to seek protection from reprisal harm. Yet with the possibility of the display of harsh spectacular sovereignty, inhabitants of Wa Region generally felt safe from physical harm; homicide and assault rates were low, with petty thievery and scams being the main criminal scourge. Armed robbers were publicly executed. Tales of spectacular violence were said to be a thing of the 1990s, a period, it was said, dominated by influence from (apparently Chinese) "secret societies."[67]

Tournaments of Value

Despite a movement toward incorporation into the striated space of the state, disciplinary institutions that enumerated populations and demarcated territory, Wa Region seemed to retain the exteriority of the war machine through webs of contested relationships. Wa Region was neither autonomous nor incorporated, nomadic nor rooted. It always contained elements of both. Lacking rationalized institutions to enforce legal personhood and personal property (there was a constitution and a justice ministry, but judicial processes were summary), patronage relations and generosities filled the political milieu of Wa Region. Values were contradictory. Rules that governed social interactions were full of caveats, subject to differing interpretations.

Anthropologists have offered the notion of "tournaments of value" to think through competitions for influence, the political and moral contestations among people and audiences for honor and respect.[68] In Wa Region, competitions emerged not just between officials but among their followers by association. These had varying stakes, involving strategies and tactics, building on the establishment and maintenance of relationships. There was no clear consensus; assessments depended on shifting and subjective evaluations of success or "performance." These tournaments of value were frequently about fissure and competition. In everyday conversations, if one were to boast of being close to a particular minister or deputy, another interlocutor might undermine it: "He actually has very little power; there is no use asking him for permission" or "It doesn't matter what he says; there is no meaning to it (or it holds no weight)." But they could also be thought of as attempts at transformation (establishing familiarity) and symbolic incorporation (breaking down of boundaries between people), using shared patrons as a reference point.[69] Sometimes I would ask friends if they were acquainted or knew (Chn: *renshi*, with a sense of being familiar with) a particular leader. Embarrassed that they did not, or finding it ridiculous that they might possibly be familiar with someone so highly ranked, they would jokingly reply, "[Of course] I know him, but he doesn't know me!"

Festivals and ritualized settings, social gatherings, and government meetings formed arenas where officials and ordinary people interacted, producing relationships (Chn: *guanxi*).[70] These events created windows of insight into the state of political relationships—who was doing well and close to the chairman? Whose name was read out last or sat the farthest from the center? Who spoke to whom, and who avoided others? Who had an axe to grind with another? Competition between Wa leaders for personal influence and prestige was mediated and tempered by the institutional setup of the military administration and the official party hierarchy, a structure of authority that ran parallel to individual leaders' personal influence.[71] These structures imposed restrictions on how leaders might behave in public and determined the theatrics of power such as seating arrangements and protocol.

An invitation to the wedding of the daughter of a key Politburo member arrived at my office one afternoon. Names were embossed in gold lettering on a stiff red card, inviting representatives from our work unit of the World Food Programme to attend. The weddings of children of top leaders were huge affairs characterized by a large banquet spanning days, with police called in to block off entire sections of road for hundreds of visitors to park. The events were also laid out over several sessions to optimize the number of guests. Patronage in Wa Region often resembled what Francois Bayart calls the "politics of the belly,"[72] closely linked to the provision of sustenance through material benefits and consumption. Invitations were sent out to companies and work units across the entire region; neglecting to send at least a handful of representatives would be impolite.

I drove to the wedding with a colleague, who would help me recall the who's who of Pangkham political society and preempt embarrassment. Rows of cars lined one side of the town's main thoroughfares, with tents and tables stretching for more than a hundred meters on the other. The wedding couple's entourage was parked right down the center of the road, a queue of black Range Rovers, Porsches, Land Cruisers, and a single Humvee, festooned with red ribbons. Confetti and rose petals littered the entire street, and the sharp smell of firecracker smoke lingered in the air, rising up between the pennant banners and gaps in the tentage. There must have been two hundred tables outside and another forty inside the venue. Guests signed in at the registration table, conspicuously listing the amounts of their cash gifts in the guestbook. The table was covered with samplings of sweets, sunflower seeds, and cigarettes; here guests collected their door gift—two face towels and two bars of an overpowering Chinese laundry soap. Important guests were received by the Politburo member and his family themselves, ushered to tables in the center of the courtyard of his large house, where an emcee cheered on performers, accosted by loudspeakers blaring contemporary Chinese electronic tunes.

Leaders and officials occupied the five central tables under the main tent, with key government ministers and deputies spread between two tables, a comfortable distance from the strobe glows and thumping sound system of the main stage. The office manager of an administrative department, an elderly Chinese man from Northern Wa whose additional responsibility it seemed was to emcee every wedding and official event, announced the arrival of the bride and groom. I was ten minutes late, and while the tent was full of guests, high-ranking officials were yet to fully assemble. Another minister had brought his own Johnnie Walker Black Label, not content with the host's home-brewed liquor stored in a mineral water bottle. Twelve dishes were laid on each table, but no one was eating; it was, after all, four in the afternoon. The color theme, unsurprisingly, was red—from the red ironed tablecloths and white chairs with red sashes around them, to the red lanterns hanging from the tentage roof, to the jarring metal candleholders placed at the center of each table bearing bouquets of red and pink roses. The groom pottered about nervously on stage in his light blue suit, as bridesmaids giggled to one another.

"This wedding looks more like a contemporary Chinese wedding?" I asked my companion.

"I don't know. I'm not sure what Wa weddings should look like anymore. Surely there wouldn't be a grand stage and emcee like this."

There were a couple of Chinese-run wedding-planning studios in town, boasting white Greco columns, pink bouquets, and themed photo shoots, one of which was surely responsible for the episode underway today. As we struggled to decipher the rules of the drinking game unfolding on stage, a ranking Politburo member walked into the tent alone. He was ushered toward the center tables, but there was no longer any room at the table where the host and another minister were sitting. Nor had the host come to greet him. Instead, he had been ushered to the table where some military commanders, a minor department head, and I were seated. We were of lower rank by some distance. He fumbled about, claimed that it was too hot and that he had already eaten, got up, and walked straight out.

Guests looked furtively about at each other, shrugging shoulders below the din of the electronic music. They turned back toward the stage as the host, notified of the incident, debated whether to rush out after the offended guest. He laughed uneasily and sat back down. There was another iteration of celebrations that evening, so perhaps he would set it right there.

"Did he just leave angrily?" I asked.

"Maybe sometimes things here are done without care [Chn: *taishuibian*]," came my companion's reply, hiding his concern and remaining polite about the mishappening.

There had been a failure to properly respect the rank of that leader. Perhaps the seemingly "informal" and celebratory nature of the wedding meant that the Politburo member should not have shown his displeasure, coming across as petty himself. It was undiplomatic of him to leave. It was rumored that he had recently been falling out of favor, with the rest of the committee unhappy with his "performance" for several reasons, including his handling of relations with the Myanmar military. Nor did he have booming businesses of his own, lacking the finances to fund programs, spend lavishly, or support subordinates. Authority did not necessarily map onto political rank, and people present reacted accordingly—"They see who it is" (Chn: *tamen shi kanrende*)—an understandable yet unacceptable differential treatment. Perhaps the host would have scrambled to greet and seat another Politburo member who had more power and influence.

Knowing One's Place

Certain transgressions were forgivable. Tradeoffs, compromises, and unspoken rules guided appropriate conduct for people in positions of power. I learned gradually that one should not live in a house too large for one's status, or drive a car too flashy for one's age, or strut around in the presence of superiors. A friend whose mobile phone and wine import business was flourishing dared not upgrade his Land Cruiser: "The minister will have a word with me if I drive a newer model than his." One should demonstrate forbearance but know when to draw the line. There were outliers, of course, often younger men who did what they wanted, but these were regarded as immature, whimsical, or unreliable, seen as small boys who failed to transition to men.[73] True aspirants had to learn to embody the generosity and dignified manners of the powerful, not overstepping the relevant boundaries.

Authority was often expressed through mannerisms and aesthetics, how others reacted to it; one quickly developed a sensibility and even a visceral response to inappropriate acts or gestures. How one might sit or speak in front of a more senior or powerful person. Or how walking instead of driving to a meeting was below one's status and "ugly" (Chn: *buhaoqiao*, lit. not good to see), embarrassing (Chn: *diulian*) all those around who had allowed this to happen—"Surely you should have picked him up and sent him there?" Other topics were sensitive and beyond the limits of proper conversation (Chn: *buhaotan*, lit. not good to speak about or Chn: *buyongtan*, lit. no need to speak about); they damaged the reputations of all present if discussed. Or another's comments or criticisms were taken to be unpleasant (Chn: *hennanting*, lit. difficult to hear), disrespectful when aired in certain contexts. A sense of propriety was embodied as shame or embarrassment (Chn: *buhaoyisi*); conversely, others might criticize a person for having the audacity or lacking shame (Chn: *haoyisi*) in acting in a certain way.

But while humility was valued, a frugality unbecoming of rank was derided. Knowing one's place also required acting appropriately toward those lower in rank. One senior member of the Wa administration had a small house on a main street of town. Meals with him were modest affairs, vegetables with a single meat dish. "I don't understand why he doesn't want to engage in business"; "He's not wily, he doesn't use his position to run businesses, he had a petrol station that failed"; "He's more of a bookworm or scholar, doesn't know how to make the right connections and network"—most commentaries I heard about him congealed around the unseemly disparity between his political position and his family assets. While he was respected for his long years of service to the cause, his roles were largely ceremonial, presiding over events and government meetings about education, veterans' welfare, and cultural policies. These were "Old Guard," respected volunteers whose education and exposure to Communist ideology and governance had helped the UWSA cause in its early days. Now, without wealth or military command, their positions were less integral to the confident, well-equipped UWSA.

Part of the reciprocal obligations and responsibilities were "knowing one's place," involving a respect and reverence for authority in return for protection and provision. The great disparity between people and their leaders was enabled and amplified through honorifics used in languages of address, embodied deference shown when speaking to and about leaders, a bodily comportment when in their presence, and a willingness to comply or provide.[74] This is what Achille Mbembe describes as the "intimacies of tyranny," "reproduced . . . in all the minor circumstances of daily life."[75] These intimacies are central to situating external concerns over "good governance" practices—why stark inequalities are tolerated, why respect for leaders is maintained despite hardship and inadequate social services, and why simplifications of UWSA leadership as authoritarian do not render a full portrait of Wa political culture.[76] In the place of the metrics of "good governance" was a local logic of authority reproduced across society, embedded in the expectations people had of their leaders. This backdrop is crucial to the encounters I describe in chapter 5.

The topographies of power were shot through with moral idioms. There was the story of the district leader who had fallen from grace. The tale was frequently recounted in travels on the concrete paved roads and metric layout of his district seat. The local school and clinics were part of his attempts to provide for the people of his area by running businesses owned by the district. But after several years in office, he was removed from power and put in charge of an obscure department back in Pangkham. People told a variety of reasons for his downfall:

"He built a new market and invited the villagers to sell their goods there, circumventing the authority of a ruling family, who had built the original market that was now emptying out. Nonetheless after he was displaced, his new market was accepted. He was too arrogant—one should know their place and not compete with the main family. People [referring to the district leader] should be reasonable and not overstep their authority."

Another man suggested, "He had built roads, gas stations, and set up a whole series of companies to generate revenue, but it was the organization of the celebration of the UWSA 20th anniversary [in 2009] which landed him into trouble. It was too grand and caused a loss of face for the other leaders. He was replaced a few years later [in 2013]."

"Well, he is not a Bao. What did he expect? He doesn't have the support of the military," came an even more cynical reply. Or similarly, "He is not from Kunma."

Social values of propriety were central to order amid a seemingly disorderly borderland.

With the replacement of this district leader, grand plans for the conversion of his township into a special township fell through. This area was closer to the Monglar area and though small, was close to a border crossing with China. It had a casino, a sports gambling center, a series of hotels, a large pond for recreation, a golf driving range, and a large department store selling a wide variety of household products from China and Thailand. Laid out along a single road, the town was by 2014 lined with new but empty shophouses and apartments, testament to fallen hopes and ambitions and fallen leaders. A reminder of political precarity, the nagging insecurity of the borderlands where a host of factors might always conspire to bring failure—global market prices, the regional security situation, closure of checkpoints or bans on trade,[77] and of course rifts between leaders.

Attending Court

"We're here," Huang grunted as he shut off the engine. Huang had brought me to visit a minister and key Politburo member, a leader I had met several times before and whose authority was founded on safeguarding the UWSA coffers and taxation. It was winter and the sun had already set as we drove toward the outskirts of town, where a large mansion complex on a small hill overlooked the western road to Pangkham. Carefully manicured palm trees and fluorescent street lighting led up to a lower reception area where some garages and storehouses stood. Another slope wound up and around to the main residence, which comprised five large buildings, the central two with an outdoor seating area and large mahogany armchairs around varnished ornamental tables, highlighting the centrality of hosting visitors. Reception rooms were located on either wing of the building, but I never had occasion to visit. The main driveway that ran around the front and eastern sides of the complex were lined with cars. "Hah, look at all the visitors here to curry favor [Chn: *paimapi*] tonight," Huang said, and chuckled, his eyes narrowing.

We walked under the night sky toward the sounds of laughter. The men were drinking in a nondescript building at the edge of the mansion compound. Perhaps it was cooler here, perhaps the minister did not want too many unfamiliar faces under his roof, or perhaps he preferred the symbolic informality of the annex for men to speak freely. Occasionally he would take more private meetings in the sitting room in the main mansion. We entered the room, and the dozen or so men barely looked up. They were seated in two rows facing one another, with a large television ahead, on which a Chinese variety program was broadcast. "Minister, I've brought the rep from the UN." The minister sat at a low table at the back of the room with four other companions, behind him a low wooden bed with a thin mattress and linen. He recognized me and beckoned me over to his table with a (friendly?) grunt. I was not the most regular visitor and was usually given a place at his side on the occasions I showed up, where I presented him a program report on our activities. He looked it over with polite interest and handed it to a nearby soldier, taking great care to place it back in the plastic folder, but no follow up inquiries were ever made.

Naturally, a shot glass materialized from an attending soldier, and the toasts were underway, one to the minister (glass proffered with both hands, nodding, tilting one's head forward) and one each to those seated at my table, addressing each by (Chinese) title: "*fubuzhang*" (deputy minister) or "*lingdao*" (leader, if I was uncertain of his actual post), "*laoguai*" (Yunnanese term of respect for elders), "*tax*" (Wa honorific for older men), or even "*dakor*" ("big brother," more familiar).[78] By this time, I was comfortable enough performing the niceties without a chaperone and deciphering the who's who in the room, so Huang sat on the couches with the other visitors. They were Wa and Chinese businessmen from both China and Myanmar, former Chinese military or police, and officials from the lower ranks of the Wa government. Today's drink of choice was whiskey, not the minister's specialty brewed liquor normally served at dinner, or perhaps only when the crowd was smaller and more intimate. Cigarettes were offered and toasts made, as the television raved about the capabilities of the latest Chinese fighter jet. It was late 2015, and the Chinese news had taken a decidedly more jingoistic tone. Peanut and sunflower shells piled up below the table, as side-dishes of roasted pork or fried bees arrived at appointed times in the evening.

The minister always spoke softly and was reserved in his actions ("It's not just you; none of us can hear him either," another senior leader once reassured me), in contrast to the men around him who mocked one another and guffawed boisterously, competing for the best or funniest story. His movements were slow, raising his hand up to eye-level and leaning forward to build dramatic tension, before muttering a barely audible slur at some political figure. Rigid and regal, this was the bodily comportment of a powerful man but also the effect of health and age. An austere disposition concealed sentiments, leaving the subordinate or petitioner always guessing. Sometimes he half-nodded and waved his hand solemnly to acknowledge someone's departure—the precious jadestone protruding menacingly from the gold ring on his finger—"You may leave, goodnight," or "That's okay, let him sit." Occasionally the grave demeanor was punctuated with laughter at mistakes or incompetence by others, Wa, Chinese, and Burmese stories alike. Telling stories of Burmese soldiers, hand in a dismissive wave: "They were very scared" (Chn: *paaaaaa de heng*), in typical Wa fashion dragging the vowel with a rising pitch for emphasis.

The minister retreated onto an adjacent mattress, the cue for soldiers and guests to jump to their feet and help him remove his black leather shoes. Part of being in the entourage was an attentiveness and care for the minister's health, a most royal yet intimate affair, and at one stage four grown men were massaging his arms and legs as he reclined on the mattress. More distant friends and visitors around him jostled for room to crack jokes or run commentary, and rowdy competitions of masculinity and familiarity often ensued. Different personalities turned up each evening—the plump, baby-faced Chinese man who managed Pangkham infrastructure and utilities, the grizzled Wa businessman from China with a sympathetic demeanor, the jovial Chinese aide with a mischievous grin who handled day-to-day operations, the gems businessman from Kengtung. Doing "business" covered a multitude of legitimate and less legitimate trades. There were also less-familiar visitors, who were not close enough that they still performed sycophantic flattery: "In Wa Region only our minister here has the clout and relationships to take on this [difficult] role." Then there were the regular Wa officials from separate departments—Finance, Taxation, External Relations, Justice Ministry, and so on, many related to the minister's kin by blood or marriage.

Seating arrangements were an indicator of who was the main guest of the day. It was a contest of knowing one's position, ushering others to the main table and not oneself, until beckoned or instructed by others. There was always some nervousness when I visited, even though expectations for my being able to perform the required etiquette were somewhat lowered: first, knowing that I would only be able to leave after having become sufficiently inebriated (staggering, slurring, or heavy eyelids were almost required attributes for guests to depart) and second, a fear that I might not be acknowledged. It was strange to be sucked into "tournaments of value" I was meant to stand outside of. Yet at the same time good ties with this minister yielded social capital and reputation—"So-and-so spends time with the minister"—with spillover effects on other relationships, and the potential to insulate people and projects against gossip and petty badmouthing.

A similar anxiety was present for businessmen and visitors, worried about what mood the leader was in at that moment. There was a feeling of coming before the emperor, who lay latent and reserved, reclined on his rest bed ready to pronounce judgment. A Chinese man once showed up to pitch his business: "This is my card, I am Yang Wei, and I sell steel framings and other construction materials," he said earnestly as he distributed his name-card with both hands and a slight bow to those of us seated around the table. Greeted with hesitation, he overelaborated: "Not the word for impotence; see, it's written differently, like this." A calamitous attempt at clarifying the Chinese homonym only called further attention to this misfortune, cueing stifled grins all around (some less stifled than others). The minister himself succumbed to a short outburst of laughter, relieving all present from the burden of politeness. Yang Wei's business prospects went limp. Meeting the minister in the intimate setting of his house and in front of his entourage of regular visitors was no simple task.

Conversely, having a few allies among the entourage boosted one's chances of success. Endorsements were important, the necessity of being introduced or framed by someone already familiar and trusted by the leader. One of the minister's relatives by marriage was also the deputy minister of another department, a kindly older man with whom I was familiar. "Come join us. It is great that you are here. Sit." His strategic questions opened up the chance for subtle self-promotion: "I heard you just returned from the trip to Man Tun? How was the situation up there?" And turning to the table, "He is very serious about his work and travels all across the region to visit villages."

Wa officials and acquaintances, and often Chinese visitors, took it upon themselves to be the advocates and juries on petitions and propositions, inserting (un/)solicited opinions into the fray often to demonstrate their knowledge or to denigrate another. Strategic one-upmanship was commonly the order of every day. In other cases, they were simply thoughtless remarks partially meant as jokes. Of course, power and standing could afford thoughtlessness.

"Oh, I've heard that the prices of rubber are falling again. How can it be profitable to start a new plantation?"

"Surely this guy doesn't know what he is talking about. Where would the money for a new ore processing plant come from? If he really had money, he wouldn't be coming here."

"This guy is talking nonsense; he is one of those who likes to go out and brag."

"China has become so tough; the West doesn't dare to mess with them anymore. All it takes is for them to pull out debt and the American economy is in ruins."

On the Xinjiang Uighurs: "If anyone can do this, it would only be the Chinese government, to so determinedly move villages in an entire area."

"It's now very hard to get a loan in China. The government is much stricter nowadays in ensuring collateral and running background checks. Investments into the borders is drying up."

Then there was the collectively reassuring and virtue-signaling narrative of Burmese duplicity: "Ah, I've spent so long in Burmese areas but I have never been able to figure out what they're thinking." "How do they expect to lead the country when they can't even speak nicely to the minorities?"

And sometimes to rattle me, "Does the UN still give out that rice with the funny smell? I hear the villagers complain and try to sell it off." This was rarely done in full earshot of the minister, who might interpret it as rudeness to his guest. Accuracy was rarely an objective, rather a rehashing of hearsay that formed the verbal jousting under the influence of alcohol.

The nebulous and oft-cited "Chinese influence" took shape through these drinking routines. They lubricated the everyday circuits within which opinions and worldviews were shaped. Reduced in think tank reports to "pressure," economic incentives, or strategic dependence, "influence" also consisted of the daily attendance of Chinese visitors and "wise men" pontificating on regional and borderland politics, making pronouncements of the shortcomings of the West, and embellished with tales from their life experiences and stories.[79] And all this unfolded with Chinese Central Television news playing in the background on the big screen, featuring out report after report of Chinese economic progress, Communist government campaigns, and the successes of diplomacy through the Belt and Road Initiative.

Hospitality and visitation were a fundamental mode of relations in Wa Region. It was part of a regular exchange, the intimacy of what James Scott calls the "face-to-face quality" of patron-client relations, contrasted to the impersonal connections of a state bureaucracy.[80] They were a form of what Julia Elyachar calls "phatic labor," the social work done to maintain channels and keep connections open.[81] Anthropological studies of hospitality have traced the reciprocity and exchange of gifts and obligations, material practices of feasting, spectacles of excess and consumption, and the fluid networks of patronage and power relations.[82] All took one form or other in Wa Region. Leaders showed care for those seated alongside, a loyalty to friends but also a callousness to some followers, a miserable sight of asymmetry. Petitioners and followers perpetually reevaluated where they stood, as a friend described: "I can't say that he [a minister] will listen to me, but, put it this way, he will definitely take care of me." Hospitality became a "tool for managing strangers"[83] and nonstrangers.

Visiting and accompanying a big leader was the mastery of a bodily comportment of deference, a blend of seriousness and casual intimacy. People bowed and bent their bodies when approaching leaders, with nods of the head, ushering others to sit, receiving gifts and glasses with both hands, seated with closed bodies. Some moved calmly and with grace, others exaggeratedly polite, in overt willingness to please. Others were deliberately boisterous and animated—the possibility of being rowdy demonstrated familiarity and ease in the presence of the leader. Transgressions of the rules indicated leeway and favor. Much like one never made appointments to visit "big men" once they were acquainted, intimacy hinged on the possibility of showing up unannounced in the late afternoon or evenings to sit with them, never calling ahead or making appointments. Spontaneity was in contrast with the planned and curated events such as festivals and weddings, and a demonstration (to others) of "closeness."

I, too, embodied these sensibilities and responses after countless visits, especially in the arts of toasting. Not accepting a drink is ugly. Not finishing it in one gulp if you meet a person for the first time is ugly. Not clearing your glass with a fresh full toast of alcohol for a superior with whom one is not familiar is ugly. Not accepting a gift, or staying for dinner—all have a variety of meanings, sending signals to another. Qualities of stinginess or calculativeness and lack of excess were registered as aesthetically unpleasant, often connoting a lack of respect, intended or otherwise. I once watched a group of Burmese police and intelligence officials visit with a Wa leader. They sipped on their whiskey instead of downing it, and they smoked but failed to distribute cigarettes to all present. These were the nitty-gritties of stalemate, the everyday details that accentuated difference and made it difficult to build bridges.[84]

While guests were socialized into appropriate behavior, the hosts performed generosity—the "communal enactment of the values of hospitality and the gracious receipt of it."[85] The ability to "accompany" (Chn: *pei*) or "receive" (Chn: *jiedai*) was integral—words that conveyed the importance of physical presence, someone of appropriate rank sitting with guests personally, entertaining, and "giving face."[86] Mastery of the rules also involved knowing whether and when to ask for something or give in return, as Bourdieu famously elaborated.[87] Asking for something another cannot give might cause one to lose face. It might not be appropriate where one's capital is insufficient. It might be an abuse and misuse of one's position to ask for something trivial, or a card played only when desperate. It could also force the other to refuse the request, and in so doing appear ungenerous. Alternatively, it was also a sign of intimacy to be willing to approach another for help. The rules always retained room for situational behavior and improvisation. These norms, and their tactical transgressions, filled the spaces vacated by formal institutions. In this manner, Wa political society shares many similarities with other societies across the globe.

Ghosts and Ruptures

The constant construction in Pangkham, including Wang's house, which was taking more than four years, was an index of capital flows and ruptures behinds the scenes—joint ventures, debts, investments—in a cash economy with no formal banking system. Construction was also a means of laundering money and commoditizing value from shadow trades, swapping materials and labor for illicit goods. A small hotel took about six months to construct; constructing a large mansion was slightly quicker. "With the opium ban and crackdowns on drugs, the economy is slowing," an official surmised. Xi Jinping's anti-corruption campaigns and stricter rules on loans and financing across the border in China had knock-on effects for the availability of capital for investment in Wa Region.

At the same time, infrastructure was being upgraded. Road repairs saw entire channels dug up through town and large drainage systems installed. Houses and buildings adjacent to roads saw walls demolished and gardens repossessed by the Wa government. This ordering endeavor was reminiscent of state-driven infrastructural projects in neighboring China. No compensation was paid, and no appeals heard—it was for the "good" of the people. It cost 300 CNY (50 USD) per square meter to build the roads in town, and in addition to the road tax on vehicles, landowners whose properties faced roads were expected to fork out some money for construction. Although construction was sometimes touted as a means of technological transfer and employment for local Wa, it seemed that the steamrollers and heavy machinery were always operated by Chinese workers, donning straw hats and bright orange visibility vests with the names of Chinese construction companies as they spread asphalt and water on roads.

Details about property ownership and trade trafficked in the domain of rumor and gossip, revolving around commercial endeavors and life histories of public figures. In downtown Pangkham, where the basin limited flat land, I was told that one *mu* of land (one-sixth acre or 666 square meters) cost a minimum of 1,000,000 CNY (160,000 USD). There were few public documents in Wa Region. The only source of official pronouncements were Party documents and the nightly Wa State TV broadcast. There was the Dragon Traders Hotel, more than ten stories high and painted a bright blue, and conveniently situated at the rear entrance of the casino. There were a couple of other tall buildings nearing completion, said to be built by a Politburo member and another by the daughter of a key leader. Finances and shareholders were never clear, narrated accounts often discrepant. The casino, too, was being renovated. Walls were built to mark out private land, to keep out fly-tippers and trespassers. Turnover of building material under the blue zinc roofs of warehouses was constant, the flow of material for construction, demolition, and construction again. The town expanded outward and upward.

But etched into the architecture of the town were unfinished buildings and abrupt endings, icons of the unpredictability of the borderland economy. Some roads were half paved, leading down an alley into an abandoned private jurisdiction. Other buildings remained incomplete for years. The dark grays of concrete stood out among the gaudy blues, pinks, greens, and yellows of surrounding blocks. "The Chinese businessman who built that must have been arrested; he just never came back," a friend said, gesturing toward an unfinished five-story building overlooking the football field. "What was he arrested for?" "Not sure, but what else could it be? Drug offenses, or perhaps his businesses failed elsewhere, and he ran out of money." Elsewhere on the edges of town an entire residential complex of houses stood empty, built in a joint venture between Wa businessmen and Chinese developers, either assets that served as vessels of capital exchange or laundering, or in anticipation of a property boom that had yet to arrive.

These concrete carcasses and dead-end paths, the crumbling and abandoned scaffolds were relations ruptured, of relations-in-waiting, of bearers of potentiality. Perhaps they were networks that had come to an end or reached their limit. Perhaps they were testimonies of poor "ability" and miscalculation. Or betrayals of a relationship or reneging on reciprocity. Autonomy through wealth and self-reliance could never alone guarantee survival; it was relations, patronage, and norms that enacted it. The capriciousness of the borderland economy had to be constantly hedged against through relational engagements with the outside.

3
OSCILLATIONS AND INCONGRUITIES

> **He was a businessman. He was like water, flowing wherever it flows. We are like a rock; we cannot be moved.**
>
> —UWSA chairman Bao, speaking of Khun Sa

> **But if we bought it, where do we use it and for what? It is very surprising to hear the report from foreign media, but I have nothing to say. We have heard about aircraft, which fly in the sky, but we have not considered how to use them and get them to fly.**
>
> —UWSA spokesperson Aung Myint, on alleged Wa helicopters

In May 2015, Pangkham was a flurry of political excitement. Roads were blocked off by UWSA checkpoints, and Wa police in their black uniforms and shiny helmets patrolled the streets wielding automatic rifles.[1] At the invitation of the UWSA, twelve other Ethnic Armed Organizations (EAOs) traveled by "small roads" (the nebulous term for bypassing sanctioned checkpoints) across government-controlled areas to reach Wa Region. The UWSA, asked by other EAOs to host, began preparations months in advance, securing accommodation for its guests at the best hotels in town, facilitating travel arrangements, and readying the military for conference security. Eight media groups from lower Myanmar were allowed, the first official press invitations to Wa Region for nearly a decade. More than a hundred guests converged on the town for the first-ever EAO summit hosted by the UWSA, a place to discuss a joint opposition strategy. No Myanmar government representatives were invited.

The sense of intrigue from outside Wa Region was palpable. What form of conspiratorial insubordination was transpiring? Why was the previously detached UWSA now taking the lead in a coalition of armed opposition to the government? Traveling through armed Wa checkpoints, journalists painted Wa Region as a reclusive stronghold. They passed the skeletons of a derelict passenger airplane, helicopter, and ferry in a "Secret Garden" on their way from Kengtung, reigniting absurd rumors of the UWSA acquiring attack helicopters two years earlier.[2] In town, they wandered around the casino and People's Park, snapping photographs of everyday life in Pangkham, paying particular attention in the evenings to the vices on offer. EAO delegates visiting for the first time observed the relative prosperity of Wa Region and compared it enviously with their own areas: "They [the Myanmar government] are not working to develop our region, they are destroying our region. If we look at the Wa, this is an indication of what we could achieve if we were able to run our region."[3]

The UWSA took this moment to showcase its achievements, its spokesperson effusive: "In the past, you only heard the bells around the necks of oxen pulling carts, and the only homes you saw were small bamboo huts.... But nowadays we all have cars for traveling. The things you can buy in Rangoon, you also can buy here. There is no difference. Today, our region is developed."[4]

Grand photographs emerged of thirteen EAO leaders—some in military uniforms, others in traditional garb—seated on red-and-gold ceremonial chairs surrounding a central circular table, the various acronyms of their organizations proudly displayed on large cards in front of them. A large mound of pink flowers stood in the center for good measure. Microphones at each seat, with two additional rings of representatives surrounding the core group, lent an air of congressional officialdom and unity. Chairman Bao proudly declared the summit as the beginning of a common platform for political dialogue with the government. He asked the attending groups to support the UWSA's application to the Myanmar government for an autonomous ethnic state. Pressured or otherwise, most declared their support by the fourth day of negotiations, though noticeably not the two Shan EAOs, reluctant to see Shan State further fractured and UWSA claims to South Wa legitimated.[5]

On the third day of the summit, I visited a Wa ministry for a vehicle permit for ease of travel through the restricted parts of town. One of the clerks for the event, a friend, unfurled long lists of administrative passes for representatives, cars, and media groups, issuing me one of the spare numbers listed at the bottom. Differently colored passes gave access to specific areas of the conference venue, and media permits allowed journalists into the central hall at select times to take portraits of the attendees.

"How are things going so far?" I asked, his flustered appearance already betraying his response.

"It's so tiring organizing this thing—the media, armed groups and all the security needed, not to mention the hotel and meal arrangements we provide as hosts," he said as he furrowed his brows and shook his head. "We're too polite to tell groups to limit their delegations to six or eight, but they should know better. This task is a big headache—many groups demand a VIP pass for all their representatives, but we can only give them two VIP and the rest observer passes; there's simply not enough space in the conference room. Obviously not everyone can sit at the center table," he said as he exhaled with exasperation. The very act of recounting the delegates' attitudes seemed an ordeal.

This week in Pangkham, gestures of respect and reciprocity were watched carefully by all: who met with whom, who was invited to the houses of which hosts, which room they sat in and in what order, which hotels they were accommodated in—each act laden with meaning. The politics of summit behavior— "They should know better"—was intriguing. One should not demand too much hospitality (risking angering the hosts) or too little (admitting one's own insignificance). A twelve-point statement was released at the end, calling for the cessation of recent fighting in Kokang areas and amendment of the 2008 Constitution, requesting support from China and the UN, endorsing the UWSA's calls for its own ethnic state, and committing to future EAO summits and political dialogue with the Myanmar government.[6] With the May 2015 summit, the UWSA had temporarily taken up the mantle of forging EAO solidarity.

Despite Wa and other media descriptions of the watershed meeting as "a tremendous boost for non-Burman ethnic unity," the actual dynamics of gathering were rife with disagreement and petty posturing.[7] Another friend chimed in: "The names of the [other EAO] leaders are so tricky, they get upset when their names are misspelled, as if we speak any Burmese ourselves." The UWSA wanted its arrangements to match those of prior peace conferences elsewhere in the country, or better, improve on previous protocols and standards. Yet there were clearly mismatches in expectations for both guests and hosts—pettiness was frowned upon, and generosity and forbearance were expected. "Their hearts are so small, how can there be any lasting solidarity among us?" He handed me the car pass and scribbled in a row at the bottom of the sheet.

The tenuous solidarities between the EAOs were part of a longer history of intermittent and capricious relations in Myanmar—skirmishes and ceasefires, alliances and betrayals. The now-defunct National Democratic Front (NDF) of the 1990s, the waning United Nationalities Federation Council (UNFC), and the present-day warring Northern Alliance were among the cross-ethnic coalitions, countering the Tatmadaw's legacy of divide-and-rule politics. Members were sometimes simultaneously part of different alliances; lines between strategy and convenience were blurry.

This chapter examines tactical dissonance first through these *oscillations* of political relations—the making and breaking of ties between actors, the failed negotiations and reneged promises, the empty gestures or grudges borne. Oscillations are fluctuating, ambivalent, and intermittent, the frequent changing of multidirectional relations that work to constitute autonomy. I do not use this term with a sense of regular frequencies and wavelengths. Here, I examine contemporary political relations between the UWSA and the Tatmadaw, juxtaposing them against their political histories. I trace how relational autonomy has been imagined from the 1950s and enacted over seven decades, the outcome of intermittent political ties. Suspicion and mistrust are borne out of history, repeated patterns of integration and disintegration.

The second element of tactical dissonance surrounds the *incongruities* between how the UWSA envisions autonomy, through control over its economy and foreign relations, and the Tatmadaw's notion of how Wa Region should fit into the sovereign Myanmar nation-state. These incongruities are evident in their different emphases at the negotiating table. While political observers focused on whether the UWSA (and other EAOs) would sign the Nationwide Ceasefire Agreement (NCA)—what talks the UWSA would attend, what terms would be acceptable— the incongruous imaginaries remained a fundamental problem. Though norms of hierarchy and appropriateness ensured that a degree of decorum would be observed in talks between them, the UWSA would make outlandish demands to scupper talks, where it remained unconvinced of the other side's sincerity. The relationship between the Tatmadaw and UWSA was a tango, concomitant postures of accusation and reconciliation.

In 2015, Bao's speeches at the EAO summits were diplomatic and measured, calling for unity and peace, with an insistence that autonomy was for development and livelihoods, not independence: "If there is no village to live, there will be no place for Wa people to work and survive."[8] Yet in the same breath he scoffed at suggestions that Thein Sein's civilian government was any improvement from the previous military regime, and later condemned the Tatmadaw, describing it as a wild tiger that tries to kill others.[9]

Stalemate in the peace process was, then, not a static intransigence but the dynamic intermittence of relations, recalibration and repositioning, underpinned by a fundamental incongruity in understandings of sovereignty and autonomy. The Tatmadaw, the NLD government, and the EAOs talked past each other, with different handles on what self-governance, power-sharing, confederation, and federalism meant (exacerbated by the language translations of key terms). They disagreed over nonnegotiable prerequisites to talks such as a nonsecession clause and over different technical arrangements for ceasefire monitoring yet kept channels open for engagement. These misfits and failed talks, olive branches and compromises, were and are the relations that enact Wa autonomy.

Merchant of All, Subject of None: Chen and Navigating Histories

"How could they possibly come to any sort of agreement between this many groups? It's the same old endless talking," Chen, a cynical fifty-five-year-old Chinese businessman who was also an official in a Wa government ministry, said, snorting, as we sat sipping tea in the courtyard of his house. Chen had been assigned to hospitality duty during the EAO summit. For guests, the rank of their assigned chaperone would be interpreted as an indicator of the regard with which they were held. Officials like Chen were responsible for personally bringing their assigned guests around town, checking their requests for meals and entertainment, and setting meetings up for them with their hosts.

"Some Wa officials aren't themselves very good at the work of hospitality; they always need the Chinese among us to do this," another friend explained. He was referring to an ethos of attentiveness and decorum that made a good host. Indeed, there were several ethnic Chinese across the entire UWSA administration, all long-term inhabitants of the borderlands, some of whom, like Chen, spoke both Chinese and Burmese.[10] Most were overwhelmingly not, despite insinuations from the outside, "Chinese nationals" or "Chinese agents" sent by China to co-opt and control the UWSA.[11] They were enterprising, often leveraging kinship or ancestral ties and language skills to take on brokerage roles or commercial opportunities. This was exactly the case with Chen, as another friend noted pithily: "He does everything and has traded in everything; the only thing he doesn't sell is women."

Chen's entire life history was a tale of maneuver, seeking refuge and chasing opportunity, traversing the political turmoil and shifting terrains of the Burma-China borderlands across his lifetime. It was through his life history that I began to situate contemporary UWSA political engagements—foot-dragging and detachment—as part of longer turbulent chapters of history.

Chen's close-cropped hair gray at the sides, his teeth protrude, and crow's feet spread from the sides of his eyes. He looks comical at times—shorts, a gaudy polo T-shirt, and a baseball cap to shield him from the sun—his sartorial demeanor not befitting a serious businessman in the hills; an indicator of someone with little to prove. His laughter is cynical, a disarming mix of humor, disappointment, smugness, and a dash of anger, as he speaks candidly about the state of affairs in Wa Region. Many Wa officials, I found, possessed a sense of humor and self-deprecation about their world.

Chen's various businesses profit from the gaps in legal enforcement or authority, the surpluses and disparities across boundaries, ever seeking out investment prospects and joint ventures. "I would be a fool if I cannot succeed in this place," he laughs, seeing vast permissiveness and freedom in Wa Region. He owns a large rubber plantation, a copper mine and an ore processing plant, various farmlands, a furniture and wood products factory, and residential properties in Pangkham (Wa Region), Kunming (China), and Hopang and Mandalay (Myanmar)—the invisible tentacles of capital that enmesh Wa Region in the wider world. While this puts him among the wealthier of Wa Region, he is nowhere close to the top. His family, too, has a global spread—one of his daughters has studied in Australia, and his son in the UK. His eldest daughter is now married and lives in Mandalay; the son has returned to help him with business in Pangkham. His position as a midlevel official in the Wa administration gives him access to cross-border contacts for copper and tin extraction and support from top-ranking leaders in dealings with outsiders.

Chen was born in 1959, the third of four children, to a Chinese family settled in Hopang, a Burmese-controlled but ethnically mixed town just on the northern edge of present-day Wa Region. To the north and east lies the hilly Kokang region, and beyond that, China. To the south, the Wa hills, and to the west, the Kunlone Bridge and the Shan State towns of Hsweni and Lashio. Hopang was a town at the crossroads of control, along one of the key trade routes eastward to China along the river Nam Tit that skirted the Wa hills.

The 1950s were a period of increased transgressions of the Burma-China frontier, and the beginning of challenges to Wa autonomy. This came after decades of near complete neglect by British colonial administrators and the preoccupations of World War II. With the Burma-China border finally demarcated in 1960, ethnic Chinese and other minorities moved freely and settled outside the gaze of the Burmese state in large swathes of the northeastern Shan states.[12] In the early 1950s, chaotic scenes surrounded the newly independent People's Republic of China. Soldiers of the defeated Chinese Nationalists (Kuomintang, KMT) crossed into Burma and around the Wa hills, with the Chinese Communists in pursuit.[13] The KMT troops reorganized with US support and launched several unsuccessful counterattacks into Yunnan between 1950 and 1952, later forced to move down toward Kengtung.[14] At the end of 1951, there were fourteen thousand KMT troops in Burma, and the fledgling Burmese government brought this violation of its sovereignty before the UN in 1953.[15] These border transgressions were used partly as the justification for rapid modernization and expansion of the Tatmadaw and entrenched a sense in the Tatmadaw that the borderland peripheries were vulnerabilities for the center.[16]

Chen's father was one of tens of thousands of Chinese migrants to move westward when he left his hometown of Baoshan in neighboring Yunnan Province of China for Burma in the early 1950s. They were not all KMT stragglers—until December 1958, an estimated one hundred and fourteen thousand Yunnanese had fled China and the Great Leap Forward, with 80 percent heading to Burma.[17] These included Chinese refugees displaced along with the KMT, blurring civilian and military distinctions.[18] This was the 1950s milieu of Hopang, where Chen's father settled, a thoroughfare for the movement of migrant Chinese across the border, following the Nam Tit River westward down toward Lashio and Mandalay.

The Wa hills were not spared the chaos and raiding of the KMT period, even though KMT routes ran closer to the Salween and Nam Hka Rivers on either side. A KMT base of around four thousand troops was established in Pangyang, with other bases in Yin Phan (Vingngun).[19] Though the bulk of KMT forces withdrew to the Thai-Burma border by 1953, smaller bands stayed on the Chinese border, some in Wa Region, gathering intelligence and trafficking jade and opium for income.[20] Wa villages were ransacked for grain and livestock, locals enlisted as porters or soldiers, and livelihoods were disrupted.[21] In 1957, Chinese Communist forces entered the Wa hills on the Burmese side of the border, ostensibly in pursuit of KMT forces, creating tensions with the Burmese government. Observers speculated that the invasion of the Wa states by Chinese forces was part of a ploy to gain bargaining capital to exchange for territory in Kachin areas.[22] On the Chinese side of the border in 1958, the journalist Alan Winnington described Chinese Communist work teams cracking down on Wa social life—weapons confiscated, arrests made, drum-houses and skull avenues destroyed, ritual sacrifices of cattle and water buffalo banned.[23] By 1960, most KMT troops had largely retreated from Wa Region, though supply routes and networks of contacts would endure for decades.[24]

Amid the chaotic military movements in the 1950s, Chen's father began work for the legendary Olive Yang, a tough, tomboyish, and ruthless woman from the ruling Yang family and the de facto leader of the Kokang region in the 1950s to early 1960s.[25] Olive Yang's prominent Kokang Defense Force was enlisted by the Burmese government to drive the KMT out from Kokang. Yet after having done so in 1953, her group continued to collaborate with the KMT to run opium routes down to Thailand throughout the 1950s.[26] KMT roots set up networks for narcotics smuggling for decades to come. Soon after, Chen's father left the service of Olive Yang, married his third wife (Chen's mother), and settled down in Hopang opening a provision store.[27] Unhappy about his leaving, Olive Yang sent assassins to kill his father in Hopang. He was not home at the time, and only his opium stocks were looted. Decades later, Chen's father met Olive Yang at a temple in Hopang during the New Year, and they chatted briefly. "My father told her that luck had been with him; otherwise he would long be dead. She smiled, telling him that they were old, and not to quibble [or bear grudges] about the distant past."

Amid the oscillating worlds of the borderlands, stories of loyalty and disloyalty, magnanimity and betrayal were commonplace. The Burmese junta entered into a series of treaties and pacts with the Chinese Communists in the 1960s to address the KMT problem.[28] It also searched the peripheries for loyal local strongmen, incorporating them as pro-government militias under the *Ka Kwe Ye* system (KKY, lit. "defense"), or "home guard," in 1963.[29] In return for their allegiance, these militia groups received "travel permits" or opium smuggling rights and became self-supporting. A journalist traveling with Shan militias noted the similarities between the "chameleon-like" and "anarchic guerrilla situation" of the 1960s and 1970s and the "remarkably fluid mosaic of petty princedoms" once encountered by the British in the early 1900s.[30] The KKY system started in Shan State in 1967, leading to a whole mosaic of groups of with floating allegiances and political goals, vying for control of people, trade, and territory in the hills.[31]

Up in the Wa hills, feuds and headhunting continued between villages on opposing hilltops and realms up till the 1970s, absent any unified political consciousness of a larger Wa polity.[32] Wa chieftains were separated into various villages and realms, with guerrilla bands created between 1966 and 1969 to defend their lands.[33] The leaders of these groups would ultimately form the later UWSA leadership.[34] They were repeatedly threatened by KMT raids, embattled by Lahu groups, and pressured by the Tatmadaw to disarm.[35] Chairman Bao recalled in an interview in 2004 (note the Communist terminology, all in Chinese):

> As I saw it, everywhere there was oppression [*yapo*], resistance [*fankang*], exploitation [*boxue*], and struggle [*douzheng*]. I was displaced. This and that village at times would take grain or money [from us]. It was tough. These people would come to take our grain, when I didn't even have enough for myself. Why should I give it to them? So I grit my teeth and dealt with them.[36]

A type of proxy war took hold in the Wa hills as the Communist Party of Burma (CPB) moved in to search for a stronghold. By the late 1960s, the CPB, which had been fighting the Burmese government mainly from bases in the Pegu Yoma of central Burma, moved its focus up toward the Chinese border.[37] Angered by the anti-Chinese riots of 1967 in Burma, China increased support for the CPB, and the CPB leadership sought bases near the Chinese border from which to base the revolutionary struggle.[38] Despite a mainly Bamar leadership, the CPB recruited heavily from the ethnic minorities to fight the government. In 1969 the CPB entered the Wa hills to enlist Wa guerrillas. Under the CPB, Wa groups attacked small Burmese government garrisons and Wa KKYs in Mengmao and Ban Wai (Sao Pha) from December 1969.[39] Other Wa guerrillas simultaneously battled KMT and KMT-affiliated groups, capturing Yin Phan (Vingngun) by April 1971. The Burmese military was driven out of Mengmao on May Day 1971, and present-day Wein Kao and Mong Pawk districts were captured later between 1971 and 1973, establishing more or less the territorial boundaries maintained by the UWSA today.[40] On one side were now the Burmese government and its Wa KKY groups; on the other, the CPB and its aligned Wa guerrilla groups.

The CPB arrival consolidated some Wa guerrilla groups, driving others out. KKYs who fought on the Burmese government side fled into Burmese-government-controlled areas, along with their families and villages.[41] Mahasang, a respected leader of the KKY in Yin Phan, fled to the Thai border, where he started the Wa National Army (WNA). His brother-in-law Ai Xiaoxue began the Wa National Council (WNC), representing the splintering of Wa militia groups westward and southward into Burmese areas, moves that would become significant in the latter stages of UWSA history.[42] Other Wa moved West to Shan State, settling in the thousands in Dangyan, Hsweni, Kunlone, Hopang, and Panglong. Passing through these towns on my way from Lashio to Pangkham, my drivers would often point out Wa villages along the way, inhabitants now all fluent in Burmese, interspersed among other Shan, Lahu, or Ta-ang villages. They returned occasionally to Wa Region to see relatives, noting the painfully obvious disparities between Burmese and Wa living standards during the 1970s through 1990s, when infrastructure and markets in the Wa hills remained poorly developed.[43] This would later be reversed.

Communist Rule and Mutiny

Life under CPB rule in the Wa hills was poor. The CPB had not always been willingly received; rather, in many areas of the hills it had pummeled the "Wild Wa" into submission with bazookas and automatic weapons.[44] Yet under the CPB (with Chinese support) the Wa hills were relatively rid of internecine warfare and Burmese attacks. The CPB's modern weapons were attractive to Wa guerrillas in this alliance, even if Communist ideology did not find a hold. "We used the pages of the little red book to roll cigarettes," a Wa official recalled. The CPB period, however, seeded a consciousness of political unity among disparate warring Wa realms.

Pangkham, which later became the CPB headquarters, was mainly a town of rice fields and dirt tracks, nestled into a basin and set apart from China by the Nam Hka River, with several wooden thatched houses and a market for the contraband trade. Located on trading maps between Thailand and China from the 1970s, it was previously a travel stop between Kokang region and Kengtung in Eastern Shan State.[45] Food insecurity was rife, child mortality extremely high.[46] The journalist Bertil Lintner, one of the few Westerners to visit during the CPB period, walked across Wa Region in 1986, finding some restaurants, a video hall, a field hospital with operating theater, and a small hydroelectric station nearby supplied by the Chinese.[47] Chang Wen-chin's informants describe Pangkham as a market stop on the trading route from Dangyan (west of the Salween) to Menglian in China.[48] Most of today's UWSA leaders only began to settle their houses in Pangkham in the early 1990s, and development would only begin in earnest around 1996.[49]

The CPB widened dirt roads and mule tracks through the region from Pangkham to Mengmao, but there was little commercial trade beyond mule convoys. Villagers found it hard to avoid opium cultivation, since it appeared the only possible cash crop in the hills. The CPB collected a 20 percent tax-in-kind on opium grown locally, which it then sold on to opium traders. It also imposed 10 percent taxes on locally traded opium in the market.[50] It earned some revenue by taxing trade to and from China at the Panghsai crossing in Northern Shan State, but in 1980, the opening of other crossing points by China saw this revenue decrease. Older informants recounted tales of suffering and hunger during the 1970s and 1980s, including plagues of large rats that destroyed crops and attacked people—"strangely, they only bit the ones sleeping in the middle."[51] This historical memory of hardship, death, and oppression during the CPB era set a low bar—from which the UWSA could easily demonstrate progress and increased standards of living for its people.

Adding to Wa hardship were the constant military campaigns. In 1979 the Tatmadaw launched Operation Min Yan Aung I to attack Pangkham, capturing the mountainous area of Maw Hpa in Matman Township, and creating today's southwestern boundary of Wa Region. The 1980s saw the CPB and its predominantly Wa foot soldiers making annual dry season raids into the western areas of Shan State and up to Taunggyi, returning by April before the rains began. Human-wave tactics caused devastating casualties but never amounted to serious territorial gains, and by the mid-1980s morale among soldiers was low. Future UWSA leaders would build personal reputations and histories in this period, some remembered for their valor in battle, commanding great respect over the military; conversely, the lack of military experience was an impediment to the political careers of leaders. Many farmers and civilians of the present day had spent years in the military, fighting across Shan State, a widespread militarization of the Wa population prior to the formation of the UWSA.

Just as the CPB was battling for the highlands around Hopang at the turn of the 1970s, Chen completed his high school studies in Lashio, a relatively stable Burmese government-controlled town in Northern Shan State, in 1976 at the age of seventeen. When he returned to Hopang, the CPB was in full control of the Wa hills. Chen traveled soon after to the famous jade mines in Hpakant, Kachin State, where he spent two years working in shafts, portering canned food and supplies, learning the tricks of trade. He was once buried during a cave-in with four others, an accident that killed a coworker.[52] One of these mining bosses he worked for was the cousin of the famous Shan drug lord Khun Sa, and a relative of Chen's later mother-in-law. Chen was gradually exposed to the business dealings and networks of Shan militia and entrepreneurs. The mines were relatively small at the time but numbered in the thousands, employing largely Han Chinese workers and some locals. Conditions were tough, packing journeys of two days from the nearest road. Workers stayed in the mining areas for months at a time, and accidents were common, with the constant danger of broken bones and cave-ins.

Chen returned to Hopang in 1979, started a shop of his own, and began bringing cow hides, beans, chilies, and other household products from Burma across the border to nearby market towns in Yunnan, China. Starting off with two mules and traveling on foot, he later hired helpers and bullock carts for the journey to these Chinese markets, where the end of the Cultural Revolution had seen some stability return. For many years, there was little competition, since few others dared to travel through the CPB-held areas into China. This was Chen's comparative advantage as a border inhabitant. He brought all kinds of items, from radios and spices to mosquito nets and watches, seeking out new markets in the neighboring Chinese towns of Mengding, Cangyuan, and Yunxian. Among the goods moving into China was opium, fully banned there by the 1950s. Opium had been banned by British decree in Shan State from 1923, but the areas east of the Salween (including Kokang and Wa areas) remained exempt due to the impossibility of enforcement.[53] By 1986, when Chen finally married and gave up trading to China, he had fifteen mules and three bullock carts. He retained the shop in Hopang but no longer embarked on the month-long journeys. "My father warned me not to be involved in two things at the time: ideology and drugs. I only followed his advice to avoid one of them," he said as he chuckled.

On the evening of April 16, 1989, mutineers from the Wa ranks, led by Zhao Nyi Lai and Bao Youxiang, took over the CPB headquarters in Pangkham, expelling the Burman leaders across the border into China. The Twelfth Brigade of mainly Wa troops seized the armory, radio station, and headquarters, destroying portraits of Marx, Stalin, Lenin, and Mao (and the CPB archives) as they went. Burman CPB leaders swam across the river into China, where they were given asylum. The mutineers declared on April 28 in a radio broadcast,

> We, the people of Wa region, never kowtow before an aggressor army, be it local or foreign. Although we are very poor and backward in terms of culture and literature, we are very strong in our determination.... It was a hard life for the people. The burden on the people became heavier with more taxes being levied. We faced great hardships. Can the people avoid staging an uprising under such a condition?[54]

Disaster had long been in the cards—an earlier radio broadcast by the mutineers denounced the "narrow racial policies of the Communist Party of Burma."[55] Wa troops, making up two-thirds of the CPB fighting force, bore a disproportionate burden of fighting and dying. They were increasingly alienated from the Burman leadership, who were engrossed with ideological persuasions and class struggle but had little respect for ethnic minorities.[56] The CPB was full of different ideological groups and political persuasions to begin with—Burmese Communists, ethnic Chinese dissidents fleeing lowland Burma, various local Wa and Kokang strongmen, Kachin nationalists, and advisers and supporters from China.[57] Its leadership had failed to militarily capitalize on the 1988 uprisings across Burma and the troubles of the Tatmadaw, and no longer had full support from China.[58] The CPB army halved from twenty-three thousand to ten thousand between 1976 and 1986,[59] with a crumbling civil administration, opium control and high taxes. The Wa male population had been ravaged by war casualties: CPB records from 1986, showed a population of 263,029, with 18,231 more women than men, a male-female ratio of 1:1.15.[60]

"After 20 years of struggle there was little economic development or outcome to show for the people of Wa Region, so we asked [the Bamar CPB leaders] to take a rest," came Chairman Bao's ominous understatement.[61]

Following the April 17 mutiny, Wa leaders Bao Youxiang and Zhao Nyi Lai created the "Burma Nationalities Democratic Solidarity Party" and the "Burma

Nationalities Democratic United Army" (Chn: *miandian minzu minzhu lianhe jun*) in May 1989,[62] inspired, an interlocutor reported, by the Solidarity movements in Poland. Zhao Nyi Lai became the general secretary and Bao Youxiang the commander-in-chief of the army. The military junta's State Law and Order Restoration Council (SLORC) was keen on a ceasefire, weakened by popular uprisings across the country.[63] This verbal ceasefire, agreed on May 18, 1989, was brokered by the Burmese general Khin Nyunt, then chief of Military Intelligence, with the further promise of development programs in the border areas—roads, hospitals, schools.[64] In return the Wa would keep their area and weapons and would abstain from fighting the government, discussing secession, or supplying weapons to urbanite Burmese or other EAOs. It was only the second EAO to sign a ceasefire with the military junta at the time, soon followed by several others. The breaking with other insurgent groups arguably harmed the overall momentum of anti-government forces.

With the relative stability brought about by the ceasefires between the Tatmadaw and former CPB groups, Chen decided to try his luck down in lowland Burma. In 1989, he bought a pickup and started bringing goods from Mandalay to Hopang, where his wife ran the provision shop. He made purchases as a shareholder of a frozen shrimp company in Yangon, supplying a Hong Kong wholesaler. Between 1994 and 1995, he started moving cars from Yangon to Simao in China, driving them up in groups of three or four. When the Chinese government shut down this cross-border trade, he turned to the car repair business, bringing skilled mechanics from Burmese areas into China to run workshops. Chen was relentless in sussing out new demand and opportunities.

A hiccup along the way shifted his fortunes. In 1992 Chen was arrested in Lashio by the Myanmar police, jailed for two weeks for having illegally brought two visitors from China to purchase cars there. The visitors lacked the appropriate permits for travel and the Myanmar police were fishing for a bribe. Chen was later released because a friend of his was close to one of the top leaders of the then newly formed UWSA. Through the UWSA liaison office in Lashio, this leader made requests to the Myanmar police to release Chen, and a goodwill agreement was reached. The liaison officer for the UWSA in Lashio who negotiated Chen's release was later promoted to head a Wa government ministry. When Chen moved into Wa Region to Pangkham in 1998, he was recruited by this minister to join the department, in a broker "operations" role.

Chen's long stint in the administration furnished him with an abundance of stories, from politics to history, from gossip about personalities to conspiracy theories, with observations about all governing parties: The illiterate district leader pretending to examine a report. The drug trafficker beaten during interrogation until he figured out that the "right" answer was to absolve an infamous official who authorities were trying to protect. The Burmese military commanders who underestimated the rapacious logging capacity of a Chinese businessmen (an entire knoll felled in a week). The Tatmadaw patrol mauled by a tiger. The themes were consistent—always an irreverent jibe at power.

"This is ridiculous (Chn: *taihaoxiao*). How can we succeed when the district leader can't even read?" Chen always used the collective pronoun.

His accounts are laced with the bizarre: a cynicism that described events and places as "fun" (Chn: *haowan*), or literally "fun to play," calling out the ludicrousness of an event, one beyond belief, even entertaining. His dark humor made irreverent light of grave situations—stories of shadowy trade, of betrayals and crimes, of unexpected helping hands. Chen was accustomed to absurdity in the shadow economy: "The one who shouts the loudest always is the guiltiest," he noted with glee.

Like others traversing the borders, Chen possessed the attitude of entrepreneurial daring encapsulated in the Yunnanese saying "You may die but you cannot be poor" (Chn: *side qiong bude*)—expounded by anthropologist Chang Wen-Chin as a ridicule of those perceived as too timid to embark on these trade journeys.[65] Chen's creativity, movement, and navigation occur within the oscillating histories and overlapping forms of authority and jurisdiction in the borderlands. Political instability becomes accepted as a way of life, with livelihoods and aspirations responding to the continual opening and closing of commercial opportunities. Respite comes from managing connections and networks, using the patronage of strongmen in vouching for him—all essential to movement, commerce, and security in the hills.

Chen is a borderland inhabitant, dwelling-in-traveling—of Wa Region, a veritable *wabangren*. His story tells of chaos and opportunity, ingenious agency among the bleakness of protracted conflict. His tales remind us how movement shapes narratives of history—he offers a particular perspective, an itinerant, multisided yet partial view, a situated knowledge colored by place, time, and intent. This long and convoluted journey ushered Chen to exactly where he was now—an ethnic Chinese hosting EAO leaders in Pangkham in 2015, on behalf of the UWSA administration. Region-making of the Wa polity was an amalgamation of the myriad political trajectories and travels of individual and groupings.

Reluctant Rebels: Autonomy and Its (Ethnonational) Expressions

Wa autonomy would be recognized only in dribs and drabs, and never as a distinct politico-legal entity. After the 1989 ceasefire, the Wa area was dubbed "Shan

State Special Region No. 2 (Wa Region)" by the Myanmar government, symbolically subordinate to the Shan State government in administrative terms. The UWSA continued to call it *Meung Vax* in Wa, and *wabang* in Chinese, mapping the nomenclature of the Wa hills onto this new polity. Yet the word *Meung*, also from Shan, refers to country, or town, and does not necessarily have a territorially bounded connotation. At the national level, the inconclusive early 1990s National Convention discussions on a new constitution left Wa Region an indeterminate entity with little legal basis, given the absence of a written ceasefire or constitutional amendments.[66]

Wa autonomy, the very same statelessness that the British had difficulties fathoming, was slowly cajoled into conventional political terms used to understand insurgency—warlordism, separatism, rebellion, or ethnonationalism. It had to be called something that resembled something else. This pigeonholing resonates with what Louisa Lombard calls the "conventionalization of rebellion" in the Central African Republic—a mutual adaptation through which rebels adhere to forms of armed resistance that can be recognized and engaged by international humanitarian organizations and regional leaders.[67] Rebel groups made explicit a particular type of relationship with the state, in order to seek entitlements from it. Lombard argues that it is precisely the state ideal that lets all "perpetuate the idea that they are fundamentally different social groups, with different interests, rather than people involved in a joint endeavor." They first emphasized their separateness, before coming together to re-create political order through peace talks and dialogue.[68] What appear to be postures of EAO antagonism and civil war can also be read as a form of political order created together with the Tatmadaw.

Nonetheless, ethnic conflict and notions of warring drug lords remain the dominant language for speaking about the civil war in Myanmar, forcing projects of autonomy into a conflict lens. The new Wa polity was not initially Wa ethnonationalist in nature—it was haphazard, and inclusive of former CPB comrades. As noted above, it was called the "Burma Nationalities Democratic United Army" (Chn: *miandian minzu minzhu lianhe jun*). The Military Directorate in Pangkham, where the original signage of the Wa army still stands, reads, "Headquarters of the Military Directorate of the United Army" (Bse: *thwe-si nyi-nyunt-yay tat-ma-daw sit-u-si-tha-na-kyout*)—Note: "United" or "One Blood" (*thwe-si nyi-nyunt-yay*), and not the "Wa" army.

It was Khin Nyunt, a friend insisted, who during negotiations with the new group dubbed them the "Wa State" Army, and the name quickly stuck.[69] Whether a deliberate effort by Khin Nyunt to divide groups along ethnic lines or simply a convenient shorthand, by November 3, 1989, the "United Wa State Army" name had crystallized. With the incorporation of elements of the Wa National Council based on the Thai border, the new organization was now embedded in the ubiquitous ethnic-based politics of Myanmar.[70] It was also, as a Politburo member acknowledged, a means of laying claim to a place within the Myanmar Union, a ratified territory or an ethnic State (e.g., Kachin State, Shan State), which could only be identified with an ethnic group.[71] The adoption of the Wa identity, in the Wa hills, was a means of fitting autonomy into the acceptable registers. This was the "conventionalization" of rebellion, adopting forms ratifiable and recognizable to outsiders. Autonomy of people and place in Myanmar, it seemed, was always tied to ethnicity in the accepted political imagination.

The fledgling UWSA attempted some initial involvement in national federal conversations. In 1993, just as a new federal union and constitution were being discussed under the Myanmar National Convention (1992–1995), the UWSA leadership penned an open letter to the international community, calling for the "restoration of Wa State within Burma." The Wa portrayed themselves as "Pawns in the violent, destructive games of others. We have been used as fighters for both the Ne Win government and in the Burma Communist party's military arm. Neither army was under Wa officers. The Wa fought other people's wars in return for food and clothes. Finally, we have come to realize that we were being used to kill each other off."[72]

This was not merely strategic posturing, but a genuine sentiment that paralleled Wa self-narratives of being tricked and taken advantage of. Wa officials often reminded me that the Communist battles with the Burmese government "were a Burman affair," between the Burmese themselves, and little to do with them. Another prompted, "We are a peace-loving people; we have never gone out to colonize and dominate others." The language of colonialism (Chn: *zhimin*) and its demonization had been adopted from Chinese political registers.

The constricting of the UWSA into an identity-based organization fit with ethnic identity as the central political register for the expression of political projects across the country. It found a seat among the "alphabet soup" of ethnic-based EAOs (now the received nomenclature) that burgeoned across the country throughout Myanmar's civil war. But the UWSA had not begun seeking the path of ethnonationalism. The 2004 *Wa Region Gazetteer* published by the UWSP continued to reflect a more inclusive spirit, at least in word: "[to] reject majority [Burmese] ethnic chauvinism, reject narrow local ethnic nationalisms."[73] Another slogan reflected the idealized imperatives of unity across ethnic lines: "The Wa cannot be separated from the other ethnic minorities; the other ethnic minorities cannot be separated from the Wa."[74] And yet, whether these endorsements reflected good-faith intent or mere lip-service, the political frameworks and models across the country would push Wa Region toward a more narrow form of ethnonationalism, playing precisely into the "divide and rule" strategies of the Myanmar military. The militarization of the UWSA also heightened ethnonationalism, setting it off on a trajectory of its own.

Autonomy, in practice, was a series of maneuvers. The UWSA made unilateral assertions of zones and territory even as it continued to negotiate economic concessions. The area called the Wa Self-Administered Division (Wa SAD, divided into six townships) recognized under the 2008 Myanmar Constitution did not map neatly onto the areas controlled by the UWSA.[75] While the UWSA holds de facto control over most of Wa SAD's delimited areas, and parts of another two townships outside it (Minepauk and Mineyan), Hopang and Matman were controlled by the Myanmar government.[76] Territory demarcated today follows the defensive frontlines of the 1980s—to the north, a road along the Nam Tit River; to the east, the Salween save a sliver of ridgeline near Tar Gaw Et Bridge controlled by the Myanmar government.[77]

In 2009, frustrated by the lack of progress on political recognition, the UWSA officially declared the "autonomy" of Wa Special Region 2 based on its de facto territory, with twenty-four Wa townships (Chn: *qu*) forming three districts (Chn: *xian*) (Meng Mao, Meng Neng, and Mong Pawk) and two special townships (the "capital" Pangkham and Nam Tit).[78] These Chinese-language administrative units do not map onto the Myanmar government-mapped districts and townships.

The autonomy of the Wa hills—the colonial bifurcation of their realms, military invasions and cooptation by ideologues, mutiny against the masters—was not reducible to evasion or rebellion. Instead, it was a constant search for acceptable modes for its expression, adapting or making do within the incongruous political affordances of the time.

Compromise and Fracture: Making and Breaking Relations with the Tatmadaw

"It wasn't always like this—we used to have good ties with the Burmese, particularly through the Military Intelligence [MI]," Li, another close friend who held a middle rank in a Wa ministry explained, as we sat discussing the history of Wa ties with the Myanmar military. This was not a forthcoming conversation. Most Wa officials dismissed this with a glib "They can never be trusted" wave of the hand. But it would be found in Li's stories: there was a logic to the relationship in the past, centering around General Khin Nyunt and the boon he presented for Burmese-minority relations. Himself of Chinese descent, Khin Nyunt built a rapport with many EAO leaderships, especially the UWSA, negotiating ceasefires with four splinter groups of the CPB. Beginning with a visit to

Wa Region in 1998, plans for economic development and commercial pursuits were made.[79] This was bolstered by the opening of the 1988 "postsocialist" business sector and the gradual formalization of Myanmar's underground economy. Wa autonomy in the 1990s was based on the permissiveness of wealth and business, including alleged links to criminal triads and Chinese secret societies across Southeast Asia and Hong Kong.[80] Believing him to be a strongman in control, the UWSA remained loyal to their patron Khin Nyunt, despite overtures from other groups to switch allegiances.[81]

"Khin Nyunt was a friend; he knew how to treat us with respect," Li said as he told stories of interactions with Khin Nyunt's feared and powerful MI agents, how they would be taken around Burmese regions when they visited and hosted at restaurants and karaoke joints. A Burmese friend in Yangon in 1998 recounted how cars tore down streets at fearsome speed, granted immunity by bearing license plates that distinguished them as part of a "peace group" from the border areas.[82] These special privileges elevated borderland businessmen and representatives above the law, and they were resented by lowland urbanites. "At that time, there was even a Burmese military garrison that was allowed in Pangkham," Li claimed, "and the MI agents were so powerful in Myanmar, they could organize whatever small permits we needed. There was a sizable Burmese population in Pangkham as well, laborers and other civil servants. Now they have all but left."[83]

In fact, just after their formation in 1989, UWSA and the Tatmadaw were in an alliance of convenience—battling the prominent drug lord Khun Sa's fifteen-thousand-strong Mong Tai Army (MTA) from Southern Shan State. Khun Sa had become greedy, it was said, and fought other militias and EAOs to seize territory.[84] The Myanmar government requested assistance to suppress this Shan nationalist who had declared independence, and UWSA was happy to oblige, perhaps with an eye on control of the drug trade. Khun Sa surrendered to the Tatmadaw in 1996, and as recompense for the two thousand troops they lost, the UWSA took over a large swathe of his territory bordering Thailand. This resulted in the diversification and atomization of the drug trade, and the splintering of Shan militias into smaller groups, contests that drew international and US Drug Enforcement Agency (DEA) attention to Eastern Shan State to stem the flow of narcotics from the Golden Triangle.[85] Later skirmishes against Shan militias and Thai military forces also took place in 2001–2002.[86] General Thein Sein, who was to become Myanmar's president in 2011, was the Golden Triangle military commander at the time, making him an old acquaintance of the UWSA leadership. It was these campaigns against Khun Sa that the UWSA have cited as evidence of their "coming to the aid of the nation" and helping to protect its sovereignty, as Chairman Bao did in his speech at the thirtieth anniversary celebration.

Collaborative relations with the Myanmar government did not last long. Khin Nyunt was arrested and removed in October 2004, just a year after having been made prime minister.[87] Many of his associates were jailed. The MI networks, which had become a "supra-entity within the military over the years [causing] structural tensions with the army," were dissolved, and assets seized.[88] Khin Nyunt and his MI officers had lost the struggle for power and economic competition with other Tatmadaw figures; the MI was said to have controlled even foreign relations and national security.[89] Others felt threatened by his influence and alliances with the EAOs. Businessmen from Wa Region told me how plans to do business in lower Burma, including the exporting of mineral ore down through Yangon, were abruptly shelved. Future Tatmadaw leaders would blame Khin Nyunt for enabling the fledgling armed group to accrue wealth and consolidate its military, creating a problem now too big to solve. China would remain the sole route for export, and other routes for contraband material through Thailand or Laos would have to be maintained carefully.

From here, Wa relations with the Myanmar state struggled to recover. In 2009, the first Kokang crisis, known locally as the "88 incident," sent waves of insecurity along all the EAO-controlled areas on the border.[90] The Tatmadaw entered Laukkai, the capital of the Kokang group (Myanmar National Democratic Alliance Army, or MNDAA) just to the north of Wa Region, on August 8, 2009, on the pretext of raiding a weapons factory. It drove out Peng Jiasheng's MNDAA, allies of the UWSA and former CPB comrades, ending their twenty-year rule of the Kokang region. The Tatmadaw installed Bai Souqian, a rival commander friendly to their interests. Weakened by factionalism, the MNDAA leadership and army fled, and thirty thousand Kokang refugees crossed the border into China, angering the Chinese government. Throughout the hostilities, the Tatmadaw had sent reassurances to the Wa that they would not be attacked—they would not risk the entry of the UWSA into the conflict. To the EAOs, this was yet another instance of the Tatmadaw picking off enemies one at a time—"They sign [a ceasefire] with one and attack another; there is no meaning [in negotiations]" was a common refrain.

But locals' fears of spillover along the border were not assuaged, including in Pangkham. Li retold the anxieties of that period:

> There were long queues at the Menga crossing to China; it took half a day to get across the checkpoint. Many people sold their cars and properties for whatever cash they could and took it with them—cars dropped to 10,000 CNY in value, and motorbikes to as little as 500 CNY. Even petrol became very cheap. The prices of crossing the river into China illegally rose from 100 CNY to 800 CNY. But then nothing happened, and people returned to town after a week.

Foot-dragging was favored where the UWSA saw no benefit from engaging yet did not want to be the first to sever ties. In the year that followed, negotiations continued over the Tatmadaw's demands that they transform into a subordinate Border Guard Force (BGF).[91] Lieutenant General Ye Myint traveled to Pangkham to meet Chairman Bao in September 2009, who reportedly avoided him for days.[92] The sides met again in Dangyan in February 2010, with little headway made, only more verbal threats and posturing.[93] An interlocutor from the UWSA recounted the events (with perhaps some degree of exaggeration):

> Initially, the UWSA agreed to many of his terms for the BGF. But the final sticking point came when Ye Myint, feeling that the UWSA was weak because they kept agreeing to his terms, pushed for the training of UWSA troops to be held in government-controlled areas. This was too much and unacceptable, and he was told to leave. The UWSA took back all of the concessions they had been willing to agree to, because it appeared he was being greedy and untrustworthy. On his way out his troops were so afraid of being attacked, that they did not reclaim their weapons at the checkpoint where they had deposited them, making for government-controlled areas in haste. But the UWSA was willing to agree to most terms; we value peace.

The region prepared for conflict. Burmese workers, schoolteachers, medical staff, and a military garrison present in Pangkham grew anxious, and NGOs were ordered to withdraw in March 2010.[94] The Wa vice-chairman attempted to reassure frightened Burmese personnel, who, fearful of reprisals, fled Wa Region by private means. In September 2010, two hundred Burmese government staffers left Wa Region, returning to their posts only in December 2011.[95] In September 2011, three more meetings between the Tatmadaw negotiators and the UWSA took place, with a bilateral ceasefire agreement reaffirmed.[96] Yet top Myanmar officials largely stopped visiting Pangkham by late 2013, and the only remaining meetings between both sides were discussions on the implementation of the Nationwide Census for 2014.

The 2009 Kokang incident appeared to signal the decline of Burmese living in Pangkham. There were reportedly only about ten thousand when I arrived in 2014.[97] By 2014 there were few Myanmar government personnel remaining beyond eighty or so Burmese schoolteachers spread across the townships, a handful of medical staff, and a single Myanmar Border Affairs officer in Pangkham. Relations had entered the nadir of yet another cycle. The vice-chairman would reassure Burmese people and international groups during tensions: "Don't worry. If fighting ever breaks out we will escort you personally down to Lashio."

Mistrust and Failed Generosities

Mistrust is the decades-old breaking of promises—the broken ceasefires, the military encroachments, the agreements withdrawn from or left to expire. Unreasonable demands and bad faith were a familiar part of political machinations. Mistrust is also cultivated in the detail. Gifts are given, some poisonous, some half-heartedly, partially, or miserly. Appearances are stern, upright, taut, unyielding. Tones are harsh, cold, proud. Speech is monotonous, forceful, or restrained. Representatives sit apart, or closer, lean toward, or away from, creating either openness or hostility. These qualities and sensations are interpreted by peoples and groups who possess their own sensibilities of what actions constitute kindness, or warmth, or sincerity. As Alaina Lemon writes in her analysis of Cold War relations, "people formulate judgment about social values" through the qualities and material affordances that they perceive—"words, gestures, images, demarcations of space."[98] These are unspoken sensibilities for many, the jarring feeling or uneasiness when rules of propriety have been flouted, the "common sense" of decorum. Such sensibilities are not reflected in risk analysis reports or other political commentary pronouncing political divisions, deadlocks, and strategic dilemmas. Nor are they reflected in media summaries of events—walkouts, breakdowns in talks, firm statements or denials. But these sensibilities are the quotidian forms of peace.

Shortly after the EAO summit in Pangkham, and prior to the NCA signing in October 2015, I visited a Wa ministry early in the morning to sit with officials and discuss regional politics. These chats about goings-on in town were part of my weekly routine. This morning, the minister entered the sitting room in great annoyance, having just finished a meeting next door with Myanmar immigration officials, over the provision of Myanmar identification (ID) cards (Bse: *hmatpountin*) to the people of Wa Region. "Ah, these people are longwinded and never to the point," the Wa minister snorted as he sat down in the mahogany seats of the department's sitting room, imitating the Myanmar officials' upright pose and stern faces during the meetings. "They keep talking and discussing, as if a longer meeting is a better meeting, but they are only here to give out 150 IDs." Of Wa Region's four hundred fifty thousand or so inhabitants, over 90 percent are technically "stateless" or unregistered by the state[99]—although they have identity cards from the Wa authorities (see figure 13), they lack Myanmar ID cards. From the UWSA perspective this was a simple task—to finalize the numbers of Myanmar IDs the immigration department had come to issue and grant them permission to travel to the districts to issue them—one they did not feel warranted two hours of politeness.

FIGURE 13. ID card issued by the Wa authorities. It reads, "Myanmar Special Region 2," with no mention of Shan State.

Outside, the immigration officials stood imperiously in the courtyard, doing their best to embody the gravitas of the Myanmar state. Rigid postures were adorned with the symbols of authority—pressed dark-brown uniforms and shined shoes, briefcases filled with documents, black hat with curved corners and insignia badge, polished belt buckle. They talked loudly and officiously on their mobile phones, reminding those present of their higher mandate.

"They are nobodies" (lit. they are not anything), a Wa official next to me scoffed as we looked out into the courtyard, "yet they come here and hold court with our ministers and impose on their time without shame." The negotiation was a theater, with requisite performances of hierarchy. While the UWSA sent the vice-chairman and the external relations minister to the meeting, the Myanmar representatives who traveled to Pangkham were low-ranking district-level immigration officers. The Myanmar officials "should know their place," the Wa official suggested, pointing to the mismatch in rank and implying that the Myanmar officials should speak less and behave less haughtily.

"One hundred and fifty cards? And yet we still provide lodging in hotels, buy them SIM cards, bring them for meals." The Wa minister was not angry; he was more bewildered and disdainful, finding his impression of the Myanmar as full of gestures and empty promises vindicated yet again. "How are they not ashamed to receive hospitality, and give so little in return? It is always the same."

"It is not right that you call people your citizens but do not issue them even with IDs," another official chimed in. "This should be a small issue [and easily provided]."

The Wa authorities often raised the provision of ID cards during negotiations with the Myanmar government. Weeks later, I followed up on the registration process in a district to the north and was told by a secretary that "the government issued 173 in total, reluctantly increasing it from the planned 150." Providing IDs was performance of a gift, yet the manner of interaction and inadequacy of numbers only served to exacerbate mistrust.

The motives and sincerity of the Myanmar government were always doubted. The minister laughed it off: "This is just like in 2010 [during the BGF negotiations], when they offered to make token registrations so they can claim the inhabitants of Wa Region are registered. Then they take the votes for themselves in the upcoming election. This is what they do." This fraud likely never happened, as Wa SAD townships were never eligible for elections, but the minister's distaste, founded on experience from across the country, was palpable.

Other Wa officials disparaged these IDs: they came without an accompanying household registration document, meaning they were worthless for purchasing land or passport applications. The Myanmar ID cards were also said to have restrictions on the range of movement they permitted.[100] In the face of what they perceived to be caprice, stinginess, a lack of sincerity, or hidden ulterior motives, the Wa response was one of disdain. An inadequate gift was more damaging than no gift at all.

On another occasion, a group of Wa officials were discussing the allocation of Myanmar car plates among the leaders. The Myanmar government provided around fifty vehicle license plates to Wa leaders, a "confidence-building measure" allowing their cars to enter Myanmar areas legally. Wa vehicles ordinarily have their own license plates beginning WA, WB, and so on, but these cannot legally travel to Myanmar-controlled areas. But with only fifty offered, there were hardly enough to go around the Central Committee, ministers, commanders, and deputies. And it was said that the plates had to be paid for, costing the same as the car itself. A Toyota Land Cruiser, or Lexus SUV, costing several hundred thousand CNY after being driven up to Wa from factories in Thailand, would now cost double with official plates. Of course, while the cost was hardly prohibitive to Wa leaders, it seemed unnecessary and miserly. The sense was that those who make the rules control them, and the licenses could have easily been given freely, if only Myanmar knew how to "do things right" and were sincere about building relationships, providing for the regions they considered part of their country.

In 2014, the first Myanmar Nationwide Census since 1983 was carried out with help from the international community, and covered Wa Region. Some officials saw this census-taking as a means of espionage, and the Wa authorities did not allow census-takers to go door-to-door in more "sensitive" or remote villages. Why should these data, including information about access to electricity and water supply, be provided to the Myanmar government if there was no corresponding tangible output or developmental support? Why should the Myanmar government ask about demographics if only 150 IDs would materialize after? Or literacy rates if educational assistance would not be proffered? Would knowing the number of households without proper toilets or water supply lead to sanitation projects? A state that sought to surveil and know without providing reciprocal assistance was one that did not know how to behave as a respectable patron.

While occasions of governance (census registrations, inspections of resources) held potential to build ties and trust, they often fell short because of inept performance and dissonances with local understandings of trust and generosity. At other times, they were outright obstructed by the Wa authorities seeking to preserve their own interests. What were the strategic trade-offs for either side—the promise of limited citizenship and vehicular access in exchange for gradual inscription into the state's legibility or legitimacy project? The balance between autonomy and incorporation was delicate. Who would make the first move to propose forms of integration, and how would it be received?

Allies and Rivals

The relational autonomy of Wa Region was also dependent on the strategies and positions of other EAOs, each with its own historical baggage and hierarchies, riddled with tensions. In 2015, the Kokang group launched another round of attacks to take back its region from the Tatmadaw. Other groups rallied around it, and this sustained conflict precipitated the first 2015 EAO summit in Pangkham with which this chapter opened. UWSA Chairman Bao described camaraderie with the Kokang as a "jaw and teeth" relationship: "We . . . cannot be divided."[101] Another CPB breakaway, the Monglar group (NDAA), was the closest contemporary ally of the UWSA: both were situated along the Chinese border and conversed together in Chinese.[102] The NDAA guarded the UWSA's eastern flank and supply routes from Laos and Thailand. Yet in 2016, the UWSA sent one thousand troops to occupy several Monglar military positions. Rumor had it that the Monglar leadership, perhaps due to some personal relations, was leaning too close for comfort to the Tatmadaw. Afraid that the Monglar might sign an agreement with the Tatmadaw and allow Myanmar troops into its area, cutting off the UWSA's indispensable supply routes, UWSA troops occupied key positions on Monglar front lines.[103] They ignored orders by the Tatmadaw Triangle Regional Command to withdraw, only resolving the issue months later.[104] Taking matters into their own hands was never off the table. A Chinese friend described this strand of the Wa leadership's "bad habits": "If the government rejects their request to trade a good, they will not argue, but simply find a way to do it themselves [also meaning smuggle]." This willingness to go ahead regardless and alone was a hallmark of autonomy and self-reliance.

And unlike the Kachins, Shans, and Karens who have better English-language skills, colonial-era connections to the Western world, and dispersal of an international diaspora, Wa populations have been comparatively far more cloistered. Wa political culture is heavily influenced by China. Chinese mobile networks, Internet, and television were the largely restricted sources of information available on world politics. And while some top-level leaders understood Burmese, it was only in the last five years that the Burmese media had become more mainstream. In Pangkham, Al-Jazeera was the only English news station broadcast (through Chinese cable television), and none but a handful of youngsters spoke English. "Civil society," "elections," "democracy," "grassroots participation"—these were not a part of any local political vocabulary, only the "people," hallmarks of a now-defunct Communist proletarian ideal.

With Khin Nyunt gone, ties with the Tatmadaw weakened from 2009. Tensions were expressed mainly through disputes over the territory of South Wa, consolidated under the UWSA's 171 Military Command led by Wei Xuegang. The area remains central in ensuring a route to the Thai and Laos borders. Tatmadaw demands that the land be returned give rise to mutual blockades—the UWSA refuses to return this territory without compensation for the investments in infrastructure they have made. A friend in the administration dismissed this: "How can we return a land we have lost so many lives for, without any compensation?"

"No. [We cannot give it back.] We did not get this land for nothing; it was fought for, and we gained the government's permission," Bao Youyi, the vice-chairman of the party and elder brother of Chairman Bao, snorted in disbelief at an interviewer in 2015.[105] Indeed, the UWSA suffered more than two thousand casualties fighting the various Shan groups over the 1990s, a figure frequently repeated by Wa officials.[106] Both sides maintained a cordial front, though tensions simmered. In June 2015 there were a series of standoffs, triggered by the arrest of more than twenty workers of a Wa company charged with illegal logging near South Wa.

A UWSA minister described the event with nonchalance: "They block us, and we block them, each trying to prevent the other from resupplying. But sometimes we also allow each other to resupply, allowing food through out of compassion, since we are all soldiers." Another Wa soldier and Burmese counterpart were shot in a business dispute in September 2015, but stability stemmed from norms in place between old adversaries to prevent escalation. The minister explained, recalling his history spent at the frontlines: "Tatmadaw commanders take their soldiers' guns and put them together, to make sure nobody fires at us either out of anger or by mistake, or nobody revolts and demands food. They don't want to trigger fighting because of poor discipline."

This minister was also aware of their reputation among other EAOs as less politically sophisticated and intransigent. "They can think what they want, but we already have a ceasefire; to sign another one means that all this agreement in the past was meaningless." The UWSA was negotiating from a position of strength and had not engaged in conflict with the Tatmadaw since 1989. "Look at many other groups—many of them negotiate peace while fighting the military. This is a joke!"

"What about the Karens who have just left the UNFC?"

"Which Karens? There are so many of them. We wouldn't even know whom to speak to." The UWSA took pride in its unity and avoidance of factions. Another friend remarked, "We know that the Myanmar government will be delighted to see factionalism among us. We must stay united. There may be disagreements, but everyone tolerates one another, as long as none is over the top" (Chn: *dajia renshou yidian, bu yao guofen jiu keyi le*). The narrative of unity among the different Politburo leaders has been central to the UWSA's self-described ethos, despite the varied backgrounds, interests, and ethnicities within the Central Committee.[107] As a popular (Chinese) military song bellowed by Wa soldiers went, "Unity is strength, unity is strength, this unity is like iron, this unity is like steel, harder than iron, stronger than steel!"

Yet unity beyond the polity was never assured; one's own interests came first. The UWSA did not join the UNFC coalition formed in 2011, and in the years leading up to the first Pangkham EAO summit in 2015, it largely refused to join peace talks, concerned that the Tatmadaw would use the UWSA name to pressure other groups to attend: "They will tell others: Even the Wa are coming, how dare you stay away?" a friend explained. During the buildup to peace talks, a Wa minister I sat with took calls from EAO counterparts, reiterating that they would not attend: "I keep telling this guy that we are not going to the meetings, but they keep calling back to check. We do not change our minds so easily."

Certain other EAOs were described as "snakes" for changing their positions all the time, an interlocutor from the Politburo winding his hand in a mock slithering motion. Other EAO leaders were accused of agreeing on personal terms and concessions with Tatmadaw officers, in exchange for pushing their group toward agreement. There was always the threat of sellouts from within; stability required vigilance. There was a sense among the UWSA that "we will keep our promises, but we are not sure the others will." Trust between the EAOs was low, based also on experiences of past failures.[108] A UWSA official recalled, "But everyone later signed agreements with the government, leaving behind the Karens to fight on [alone]; they suffered greatly."

Failing to hold firm to stances, or going back on one's word, was an affront to Wa political sensibilities of power, even as maneuvering took place in practice. Self-narratives of trustworthiness were distinct attempts to contrast themselves with the perceived treachery of the Tatmadaw, or fickle leaders of other EAOs: "We already have a ceasefire; we will never fire the first shot [to break it]"; "We said we will not sign a new ceasefire, and we won't," went the oft-repeated refrains. Despite fluctuating tensions and provocative stances on both sides,[109] the ceasefire between the UWSA and the Tatmadaw held, a record Wa leaders raise proudly during peace negotiations.

"The NCA was drafted between the Myanmar government and the UNFC coalition; it did not involve us. How can they now ask us to sign onto something that we were not involved in discussing?" a Politburo member remarked on another occasion to me. It was quite the conundrum—the UWSA had refused to participate previously, and now refused to sign what it had not participated in.[110]

Months after the May 2015 summit in Pangkham, the historic NCA was signed in Naypyidaw on October 15, 2015, between President Thein Sein's government and eight EAOs.[111] Though hailed by some as a "historic" deal, or at least some form of visible progress, what was meant to be the cornerstone of President Thein Sein's peacebuilding legacy lacked the crucial participation of the larger EAOs. Only eight EAOs signed, comprising less than a third of insurgent strength in the country. Many remained skeptical, especially since the NCA itself made few clear provisions for the actual implementation and monitoring of the ceasefire. Of the eight EAOs that signed with the government, four had been at the May 2015 summit in Pangkham. It appeared that desire for EAO solidarity was giving way to self-preservation and judiciously calculated interests. Most of the groups that signed were closer to the south areas (perhaps coming under pressure from the Thais) and had fewer proximate allies for holding out against the Tatmadaw.

"This is exactly how it starts: one by one they agree to sign," Hein, a friend in the Wa military, remarked. "They say we are uneducated and only think of fighting, but they are fast to fragment and sell out. Meeting with the Tatmadaw always creates temptations to agree to terms, with few reliable promises made on their side—this is why we often stay away. When we make promises, we do not go back on them." It was apparent, though, that geographical location, terrain, military might, and proximity to China meant that the UWSA held a stronger bargaining position. "The other trick," Hein elaborated, "is that they break up the ethnic minority armies by offering smaller subunits a status of *pyithusit*, militia status, granting them local autonomy and control over smaller areas and preventing them from becoming a larger group."[112]

Ultimately, the narrative of honor and reliability, of keeping one's promises and sticking rigidly to positions, was more idealized norm than practical guide. Chairman Bao, with rhetorical flourish, compared the rigid trustworthy promises of the UWSA to the unscrupulous businessman–drug lord Khun Sa: "He was a businessman; he was like water, flowing wherever it flows. We are like a rock; we cannot be moved."[113] But the UWSA position was hardly rock-like, far more flexible than it appeared. A willingness to compromise was part of its history—with Khin Nyunt, with the BGF negotiations, with attending peace talks; there was no guarantee it would stay the course. Though it was common to hear people say of respected leaders, "If they say they will do it, they do it," there were expectations and compromise built into these yardsticks, particularly in a region of narco-trafficking and military governance. Political culture was rife with concurrent internal contradictions.

Intermittence and Incongruity

Shortly after the signing of the NCA, Aung San Suu Kyi's National League for Democracy (NLD) won the 2015 national elections in a landmark victory. There was great cynicism among Wa leaders that the elections would not be free and fair ("Don't worry. They have already arranged who will be in charge"). Yet she took power in March 2016, consequently making the peace process her explicit priority.[114] Friends in the higher ranks of the UWSA expressed a willingness to engage with her, encouraged by the potential for a new negotiating partner.

"We used to think she was an instrument of the West, but now it appears that she is the only one who can lead the country," Hein remarked on a separate occasion. Others were somewhat skeptical—they had no prior relationship and thought of her as having spent a lot of time overseas and rarely with ethnic minorities in the country. Wa Politburo members met with her in late July 2016 but downplayed the significance of the event: "We are just going for a chat, to establish relations; there is nothing specific to talk about," a minister told me in the weeks prior. It was unclear then if Aung San Suu Kyi would continue the commitment to peace. Or would the military, no longer in government, continue to undermine the peace process, refusing to heed a president's calls for peace, and continue skirmishes and territory grabs? Would it signal an opportunity for constitutional amendment?

Aung San Suu Kyi announced the formation of the Twenty-First-Century Panglong Conference in 2016, named after the 1947 pre-independence agreement with ethnic minorities. On August 31, 2016, seventeen EAOs gathered in the Myanmar Convention Centre in the capital Naypyidaw, dressed in the mandated "ethnic" garb, their military uniforms and ranks not permitted or recognized.[115] Dozens of Tatmadaw officers, politicians, international dignitaries, and ambassadors were invited, entering on red carpet under banners of Myanmar colors and logos of peace doves. Opening speeches were delivered by Aung San Suu Kyi, Tatmadaw commander-in-chief senior general Min Aung Hlaing, and UN secretary-general Ban Ki-Moon, under the bustle of reporters and cameramen. "Ethnic harmony" was on full display as attendees were entertained with "traditional" costumed dances from the diversity of the Union.

At the apparent urging of China, the UWSA sent a group of four representatives to Naypyidaw, clad in the traditional red Wa vest lined with white trimming, faux silver buttons, and a water buffalo totem embroidered on the breast. They posed grimly for photos at the entrance to the large hall. But these were low-ranking officials—a clear sign of disinterest since their top leaders had met with Aung San Suu Kyi in Naypyidaw just two months before. Perhaps they had not been convinced.

The UWSA representatives walked out on the second day. They alleged disrespect: "We left because we didn't like the accommodation, the environment and the way they treated us. I want to see peace prevail in the entire country. We came to the conference for peace."[116] One of the disputes was over the provision of "observer" passes to the representatives, an indication of their diminished status rather than that of full-fledged participants who came prepared to read a speech from the UWSA Politburo. The UWSA claimed that it had been asked to participate on the pretext that it would be given a chance to speak, but the opportunity was removed when they arrived.[117] On hindsight, perhaps they should never have expected a platform. The Tatmadaw, and not the conference organizers, decided who was allowed to speak, an indication of the rifts to come in further negotiations.

This seemingly petty excuse was a blow to the prospects of the peace conference. The Wa representatives had clearly been ordered by higher-ups to leave, who had themselves been urged by China to attend. With the departure of the largest armed group, others would feel emboldened to break ranks.

It was, however, in the details of negotiations that incongruities in the imaginaries and registers of autonomy between both sides became evident. Peace talks revealed different emphases and concerns of the UWSA and the Tatmadaw. In April 2017, the UWSA announced the formation of the Federal Political Negotiation and Consultative Committee (FPNCC), or what commentators dubbed the "Wa Alliance." A twenty-seven-page document of "General Principles" was issued, but upon closer scrutiny, seemed to have been drafted unilaterally by the UWSA, retaining even phrases such as "Wa will positively support" and "Wa recommends."[118] The other allies were simply asked to adopt it, leading to many misgivings.

The FPNCC terms were clearly unacceptable. Demands were broad and called for "a high degree of autonomy" for ethnic states in a federal system—control over their own legislation, economy, natural resources, border access and customs management, foreign currency exchange, and even foreign relations. It called for the stripping away of the Tatmadaw's seats in Parliament and allocating them to "disadvantaged groups" and minorities. It even proposed granting autonomous regions, prefectures, and states based on minority population figures.[119] Were these sweeping demands a sign of bad faith? Or was the FPNCC asking for the sky as a negotiating tactic?

It turned out that in early April 2017, the UWSA submitted an amended NCA to the Tatmadaw and the National Reconciliation and Peace Center which it would be willing to sign.[120] Intriguingly, the key modifications in this amended NCA were *military specifics*—including the establishment of a ceasefire boundary with landmarks that would be mapped out in a separate subagreement.[121] No fortifications were to be allowed within two kilometers and no artillery above 105mm deployed within ten kilometers of the boundary.[122] It rejected restricted travel and arbitrary taxation at unilateral and "random" checkpoints and made provisions for the travel of military commanders through the other party's area with prior notification and armed escort.[123] And in a UWSA-specific demand, it asked that the Myanmar government push for other countries' removal of sanctions against EAO leaders.[124]

Political dialogue was a secondary concern in the FPNCC's amended NCA, glossed over more broadly in wide-ranging autonomy, development self-governance provisions. Some clauses were clearly unacceptable to the Tatmadaw—in particular the call for Tatmadaw, rather than EAO, troop withdrawals.[125] The amended NCA also attempted to establish terms for the termination of the ceasefire, such as breaking the territorial boundaries currently controlled by the UWSA, or failing to hold political dialogue within ninety days of signing.[126] Interestingly, it called specifically for the UN and China to be participants in the ceasefire monitoring process. All these seemed deal-breakers for the Tatmadaw.

A follow-up document released by the UWSA read, "Wa State has made its own efforts and its sincerity of peace has been exhausted. This situation has been beyond the control of Wa State, *Wa State can do nothing about it!*"[127] There was no significant progress after.

The debacle over negotiations revealed the differences between the way both sides understood and expressed autonomy. Three things emerged from the involvement of the UWSA in the national political arena. First, the UWSA was more interested in how de facto territorial and military lines were to be enforced, rather than how the constitution might be altered to devolve powers and incorporate them into the legal fold. It was clear that the UWSA was more comfortable in speaking specifically in military terms and less the language of political reform.

Second, the FPNCC formation signaled the beginning of formal and concerted Chinese intervention, a potential broker to bridge the incongruous imaginaries of the two. Chinese Special Envoy Sun Guoxiang was shuttling back and forth between the Myanmar military and the EAOs. The Tatmadaw was also forced to include as "special guests" the three EAOs that they had listed as terrorist organizations and with whom fighting continued.[128] Rumor had it that the Chinese had asked UWSA and FPNCC leaders to explicitly request their facilitation. Rather than genuine engagement, the need to "give face" to Chinese efforts was propping up the moribund peace process.[129] An *Irrawaddy* interview with a UWSA minister illustrates this:

> China also promised it would make sure we were able to give an opening address and that we needn't sign the DoC [Deed of Commitment] to attend. China negotiated with us on May 21, but the conference was scheduled to start on May 24, and we needed time to make preparations. They [Burma government] usually play that trick—they only made arrangements when the conference was too close. This made it difficult for us to attend. Our assessment is that they wanted to create a situation in which they invited us, but we did not attend.[130]

Third, autonomy meant retaining flexibility and dealing with contradictions among its own allies. By mid-2017, the UWSA were no longer the remote warriors of the hills; they had emerged as a leader of the EAOs, replacing the UNFC coalition with the FPNCC. They were envied for their cunning and ability to drive a hard bargain with the Tatmadaw. At the same time, rumors of rifts continued, the Kachin Independence Organization (KIO) supposedly unhappy at the UWSA domination of the coalition. An observer commented, "They say they only negotiate as a bloc, but they all still meet with the government in smaller groups." This was the world of ethnic unity in Myanmar—historical suspicions, alliances and rifts, the everyday practices of trust and mistrust.

A Third Panglong Conference in July 2018 was disappointing. The UWSA sent two top Politburo leaders down to Naypyidaw, but they fell ill from exhaustion on the second day. Little substantial progress was made—the UWSA sent no representatives to the working groups to discuss specific political and ceasefire arrangements. This was "bare bones" diplomacy—acquiescing to another's demands by turning up, but in no meaningful way, only semifulfillment and foot-dragging.

"This is why we do not want to meet General Min Aung Hlaing too often. It is embarrassing for all sides when he makes requests that we know we cannot give, such as signing the NCA," a Politburo official remarked.

In 2019, no Panglong Conference was organized, and the FPNCC avoided the 2020 iteration, citing COVID-19 concerns. Refusing discussions was an ambiguous means of rejecting anticipated terms, rather than outrightly confronting the Tatmadaw.[131]

Watching the stalling peace process and the dormant FPNCC years after I left the field, I recalled Chen's disparagement of the political posturing and constantly shifting allegiances, the incompetence and tragedy. Chen's laughter recalls what Bakhtin terms the people's laughter: "It is ambivalent: it is gay, triumphant, and at the same time mocking, deriding.... The people do not exclude themselves from the wholeness of the world.... He who is laughing also belongs to it."[132]

Exasperated with the hospitality work, deference, and niceties required to engage the powerful all around and cultivate connections, Chen once remarked, "When I retire I will go back to China. I'm tired of bowing my head all the time."

4

FRONTIER ACCUMULATIONS

> **Surplus capital can be lent abroad to create fresh productive powers in new regions. The higher rates of profit promised provide a "natural" incentive to such a flow and, if achieved, raise the average rate of profit in the system as a whole. Crises are temporarily resolved. "Temporarily" because higher profits mean an increase in the mass of capital looking for profitable employment and the tendency towards overaccumulation is exacerbated, but now on an expanding geographical scale.**
>
> —David Harvey, *The Spatial Fix—Hegel, Von Thunen, and Marx*

In July 2015, a new bank opened its doors in Pangkham. Smart white signboards touting the "Southeast Asia Union Bank" were foisted on its façade—a fresh coat of anemic yellow paint with brown windowsills—yet air conditioning units at every window gave away its previous status as a run-of-the-mill hotel. Two ATMs were installed across town, but no one was ever seen making withdrawals. Outside the bank lurked two disinterested security guards, their disheveled uniforms and dirty lanyards suggesting a lack of supervision. The bank's glass doors were only ever partially open; it was unclear if this was to keep out the unrelenting roadside dust or curious passersby. There were no lights, and it was hard to get a glimpse of any tellers or staff inside. The grandiose "Southeast Asia Union Bank" had arrived in the Wa hills, yet a quick Google or Baidu search did not reveal any other branches across the region.

Wa Region remained a largely cash-based economy. Prior to this, there was only the Wa State Bank run by the Wa Finance Department, which offered fixed deposits and safe boxes, but no electronic banking system. Customers would wire money to the Wa State Bank's Chinese bank account across the river and receive cash in Pangkham. Inspecting physical currency was part and parcel of any large transaction, given the numbers of counterfeit banknotes in circulation. Even cars and property were paid for in cash, with buyers wielding black plastic bags filled with thick stacks of 100-CNY notes, portable money counting machines at the ready. Though the Myanmar kyat was not used in Wa Region, it could be exchanged for Chinese yuan at money remitters (Bse: *hondi*) across town, shifting money between Myanmar bank accounts in Yangon or Mandalay. Another increasingly popular method for smaller amounts was WeChat Pay through the social networking app, which required a Chinese or overseas bank account.

The opening (or otherwise) of this "Southeast Asia Union Bank" was part of a larger set of sudden changes across Wa Region. A few months earlier, a quixotic complex of country houses and facilities had sprung up in the hills of Ai Cheng Township, a two-hour drive north of Pangkham (see figure 14). A large plot of earth on a ridgeline had been leveled, possibly for an entertainment complex or hotels. Armed uniformed guards in desert fatigues patrolled the construction sites, shielded from the road by advertisement hoarding. These large boards proclaimed the investments in Wa Region by the "Yucheng Group" from China, adorned with photographs of luxurious hotel rooms, artists' impressions of hospital complexes, complete with illustrations of gentle, fair-skinned nurses. A temporary arch was erected over the entrance declaring the opening of the "Ai Cheng Free Trade Zone"; other posters declared the net worth of the "Yucheng International Holdings Group" to be 80 billion CNY, or 13 billion USD. Yucheng claimed to offer financial services and "peer-to-peer" lending called "e-*zubao*," a financial concept I would only make sense of after having left the field. Construction was still ongoing, and while the carefully manicured country houses were structurally complete, there was no sign yet of larger buildings or the free trade zone. Nor had the lucky hillside homeowners arrived yet. The new neighborhood was an

FIGURE 14. Luxury homes being built in the Wa hills, by a Chinese developer under the Yucheng Group, August 2015.

absurd sight, opulent advertisements and publicity hoardings lining the highway running through one of Wa Region's poorest townships.

Wealth never traveled unaccompanied; rumors started spreading throughout Pangkham about the group and what their motives really were. Yucheng were said to have purchased a fleet of nearly eighty vehicles, employed hundreds of workers, brought over managerial and skilled employees from China, and taken over entire hotels to house their staff. Well-dressed Chinese working professionals showed up at the nightclubs. Alongside the bank, they purchased land and property developments that had lain empty for years. People gossiped about the huge sums of money they were investing—hundreds of millions, even billions of Chinese yuan. I was told by friends that property belonging to Wa leaders had been purchased at prices two to three times the market rate in a thinly veiled attempt to curry favor. They were said to have the tacit approval of the highest level of Wa leadership.

A friend joked, "They have good knowledge; they have been well initiated—they knew who to curry favor, and where power really lies. Did they come to look for me? No! Did they go to look for so-and-so [another less-influential member of the Politburo]? No! Instead, they went to the chairman and other key Politburo members and military commanders."

It was a bizarre moment to enter Wa Region. Why were they here, and what commercial potential could they possibly see in this area laden with political and security risks? Where did the money come from? What sort of industry had they in mind ultimately? Who would buy the strange, modern, European-styled cabin homes perched on a ridge in the middle of nowhere? What sort of ties did they have to the Chinese government? Rumors spread of their affiliation with this and that Chinese leader, all the way to the highest rungs of the Chinese Communist Party (CCP), but nothing could be confirmed. In the borderlands, everyone naturally suspected some form of money laundering; yet surely it must be impossible to bring so much capital across the border without the knowledge or consent of the Chinese authorities. Or perhaps it was some kind of mining that they were making inroads into, initially prospecting in secret to ultimately dominate the extractive industry? Some officials even posited that this was a nascent manifestation of the Belt and Road Initiative (BRI), private companies advancing the interests of the Chinese State.

And yet despite misgivings and suspicion, the group was welcomed into Wa Region and allowed to purchase the land and assets they needed (for a hefty price), move freely, and inquire about various investments. It was almost too good to be true, but none of the Wa officials dealing with them let their guard down: "They have their own motives" (Chn: *you ziji de mudi*), came a deputy minister's cryptic reply.

But accepting the visitors was not simply opportunism. The moral economy of frontier commerce was pithily summarized by an acquaintance: "If you do not take the money offered, others will say—stop pretending [Chn: *buyao zhuang*, to be morally upright and incorruptible]."

"How dare you not take when something is given?" (Chn: *renjia geide ni haibushou*) was a common rhetorical expression of complicity. This heavily laden phrase connoted not just that it was rude to reject a gift but also that it was unbecoming to behave as though one was above the fray, too righteous to engage in the norms of the border world. In the absence of formal state institutions, transactions were regulated by a series of norms and expectations. And these transactions writ large were the cross-boundary relations that co-constituted the autonomy of the region.

The frontier arrives; it shifts and is unstable. Anna Tsing, writing on Kalimantan's forests and their relations to global circuits of capital, argues that the frontier is "not a natural or indigenous category.... [It is] a traveling theory, a foreign form requiring translation.... The frontier, indeed, had come to Kalimantan. It hadn't always been there."[1] Contrary to the American frontier depicted by Frederick Jackson Turner as a *terra nullis* ripe for the expansion of "manifest destiny," Tsing argues that the frontier is produced through "resourcefulness"— the turning of nature into resources for extraction, land into plantations for cultivation, and people into subjects.[2] The frontier arrives, drawing new spaces into circuits of capital and political imaginaries. Myanmar, as Masao Imamura argues, is itself described as a frontier, imagined by regional and international media as a place facing an "expansive force" and due a transformation.[3] In a similar vein, the Wa hills were both imagined as a frontier gradually incorporated into circuits of migration and flows and produced through disorderly forms of capital accumulation.

In this chapter I explore relational autonomy through five different and overlapping modes of accumulation as they unfold in the region, deploying them as windows into the structural constraints of the borderland economy. Resourcefulness is about improvisation, a sensibility adapted to the precarity of commerce in the absence of formal state institutions. Resourcefulness operates within a local moral world, drawing upon oscillating connections, obligations, or the power and authority of patrons, to turn opportunity into capital. Modes of accumulation draw together a variety of individuals, capital, and commodities, alongside forms of governance that tread a fine balance between permissiveness and regulation. In turn, the autonomy of Wa Region, sandwiched by the Chinese and Myanmar economic and legal regimes, is enacted by actors (elites and ordinary people) seizing onto these disparities and dissonances through arbitrage and regulation. Accumulation shapes and is shaped by the limits of the borderlands.

Spatial Imaginaries

Yet while the frontier, with its connotations of lawlessness and opportunity, seemed the most apt spatial imaginary for Wa Region, other external interests imagined it in different ways—as a buffer zone, a proxy, a node in a wider ecosystem, or a rebellious stronghold to be crushed or co-opted. The UWSA's formation in 1989 created a new set of balancing acts along the Myanmar-China border—a strong autonomous polity whose allegiance was up for grabs by its neighbors. Naturally, historical support for the CPB meant China began with a closer affinity. Observers argue that the UWSA is "unquestionably the biggest stick Beijing wields" in its negotiations with the Myanmar government; supporting the UWSA is China's political means of keeping the Myanmar government in line. More sympathetic political commentary propagates a sense that Wa Region is "caught in between," a pawn in a larger "chess match," sandwiched between powerful countries who manipulate it for their strategic interests.[4] When President Thein Sein suspended the Chinese Myitsone hydroelectric dam project in Kachin State in September 2011, which would have sent 90 percent of its power to China, the Chinese were outraged. Months later, US secretary of state Hillary Clinton's visit to Myanmar signaled the beginning of closer relations with the West under a "democratic transition" and opening. Chinese arms reaching the UWSA were reported soon after, in 2012.

China's strategic interests were both military and economic—a need to secure an alternate energy supply route to the Straits of Malacca, seen as a pro-US chokepoint.[5] China completed oil and gas pipelines from Yunnan to the Bay of Bengal by 2014 and planned a China-Myanmar Economic Corridor with road and rail networks. A series of hydroelectric dams (of which Myitsone was the largest), economic zones, and a deep-sea port at Kyaukphyu were further parts of the attempt to harness the resource potential of Southeast Asia's "last frontier."[6] This would form but one part of China's ambitious BRI. In addition, Myanmar was reportedly key to a "String of Pearls" geopolitical strategy, a series of Chinese-controlled ports and naval bases across the Indian Ocean to protect its westward geostrategic interests.[7] In this geopolitical climate of the mid-2010s, the UWSA, as a key EAO in Myanmar's internal politics, grew in regional importance.

A powerful Wa Region would be useful as a bargaining chip for China, but while it allows arms (mostly indirectly) to the UWSA to keep the Myanmar government in line,[8] it is wary of fueling actual fighting that might disrupt BRI investment plans in the country. Border stability would see Wa Region form a buffer zone from drugs, disease, and disorder (of refugees, ethnonationalist sentiment, economic instability, and crime) for the Chinese but only if it contained rather than conducted or channeled these elements. Concerned with stemming the flow of heroin and methamphetamines, joint border drug enforcement operations were launched periodically, involving a host of Chinese agencies—the Chinese Border Police, People's Armed Police, Public Security, and the People's Liberation Army (PLA)—supported by an extensive surveillance and intelligence apparatus.[9] China also provided training and equipment to the Wa Health Department for disease control and epidemic containment, and it trained doctors and nurses in China.[10] Wa students were brought to Yunnan on study exchanges, easing immigration requirements to allow short trainings and middle-schooling. Officials of neighboring Yunnan counties and prefectures were often invited to Wa Region for celebrations and festivals, and Wa officials traveled to China for visits, short courses, and governance exposure. These exchanges however, paled in comparison to the actual needs of the region.

For others, Wa Region was one of many nodes in the cross-boundary networks of highland Southeast Asia (SEA). This nodal form was epitomized in the casinos of Pangkham and smaller Wa towns, gathering points for a variety of illicit enterprises. Casinos had a centripetal ability to draw together customers from neighboring areas, described by the NGO International Crisis Group ICG as "crucial enterprises not just for gambling and money laundering, but also for racketeering, drug distribution, human trafficking, prostitution and wildlife smuggling—part of an interlinked illicit political economy in the area."[11] In this form of "casino capitalism," Wa Region was a stepping-stone, a linkage in wider networks to be bridged, a route to elsewhere, with profit to be made along the way.

Growing anti-Chinese sentiment in Myanmar meant that associations with China were latched upon easily as proof of Wa disloyalty to the Union. Online blogs and Facebook posts drummed up misrepresentations of the Wa as ethnic Chinese, as proxies of China, armed by China, seeking to be part of China, treacherous subjects.[12] Such narratives had surprising traction, harnessing the criminal reputations of the UWSA. It is still commonly believed that most of the Wa leaders were ethnic Chinese. A Yangon interlocutor recounted a sentiment: "There is no point fighting the Wa. They are Chinese, and more Chinese would simply come over the border to join, a never-ending stream of soldiers."[13] This, of course, had close parallels and precedent with China's support for the CPB in the 1970s.

In May 2015, the *Global New Light of Myanmar*, a propaganda newspaper of the Tatmadaw, lobbed a series of denunciations just as EAOs were gathering in Pangkham for the first summit: "Civil administrative positions are being taken by ethnic Chinese and local culture is being swallowed.... Now is the time to monitor if they all are real ethnic Wa tribesmen or if they are [Chinese] people pretending to be [Was] and trying to use Wa image for their own selfish interests."[14]

It continued, accusing the UWSA of taking the "path toward secession," hijacked by Chinese interests with "antagonist characteristics," and the biggest manufacturer of opium and methamphetamines with forcibly conscripted child soldiers.

Outsiders fomented these misconceptions, building on popular narratives. A Reuters visit to Wa Region in 2016 exaggerated the "monitoring" by Beijing and repeatedly highlighted the few Chinese citizens present among the Wa administration as if this were evidence of grand infiltration and not simply migration for livelihoods.[15] The rush to allegations of a diluted and "inauthentic" Wa identity, manipulated by China, seems a convenient Western reproduction of China's essentializing and overdetermined views of its own ethnic minorities.

Others highlight the role of UWSA as a military proxy for China: "Any military action against the UWSA would pit the Myanmar army against China. The Wa leaders are always accompanied by Chinese intelligence officers, and it is no exaggeration to say the UWSA is an extension of China's People's Liberation Army."[16]

Notably, Wa leaders reject totalizing depictions of such reliance and control. "Nobody else offered any assistance," a township leader suggested. He emphasized that it was the CPB leaders with Chinese Communist support that brought Chinese as a working language to the Wa in the 1970s, and not something they had deliberately chosen. Chairman Bao himself reminds visitors that he is grateful to the Chinese for providing his basic education in the 1960s—the only source of assistance. Other officials often made comments or statements distancing themselves from China, for instance, when declaring their desire to have the UN and China as external observers to the peace process in 2015, the UWSA vice-chairman was quick to justify this by pointing to China's role as neighbor. Yet while he explicitly rejected "foreign powers meddling in our affairs," he also urged Myanmar's NLD government in a 2016 statement to remain nonaligned and take advantage of the economic benefits of China's BRI.[17] Wa officials clearly value ties with China, occasionally bemoaning how historical affinities and sentimental ties with China are gradually wearing away as leaders and officials on either side step down: "Nowadays among the younger officials, there are no longer any old sentiments" (Chn: *yidian ganqing doubuyou*). This relationship is filled with ambivalences—demonstrating gratitude for past assistance through amenability, relying on continued Chinese support because there is no other, yet having to prove to outsiders that their loyalty remains to the Union of Myanmar.

But China is also clearly a patron to Myanmar, resulting in an idiosyncratic strategy. While China's official stance has been to encourage dialogue (Chn: *qua-*

nhecuitan) and respect the principle of nonintervention and the sovereignty of Myanmar, China demonstrates its indispensability to the Myanmar government in managing to bring all sides to the table through heavy-handed pressure. At times China calls for negotiations; at others it allegedly encourages the EAOs to scupper talks.[18] When the Kokang (MNDAA) launched concerted attacks in 2015, fighting with the Tatmadaw yielded hundreds of casualties and fifty thousand displaced, with no clear gains. Several Myanmar bombs landed by mistake in Namsan, China, killing five civilians, and the Tatmadaw was accused of disregard for China's security, damaging relations. The Tatmadaw also capitalized on widespread anti-Chinese sentiment to gain national support in the battle against the ethnic Chinese Kokang, a move that consequently softened China's approach to the border EAOs.[19] Weapons were allegedly sold to the UWSA that year, just as they were reported to have been in 2012.

The following year, Aung San Suu Kyi's NLD government came to power and showed a willingness to accommodate and renegotiate China's Myitsone hydroelectric plans. In return, the Chinese special envoy Sun Guoxiang was sent to persuade the Wa and Monglar groups to attend the government's Twenty-First-Century Panglong Conferences. The groups did so reluctantly. Despite its political support, China's heavy-handed pressure on the EAOs to sign the NCA was a reminder that its own interests came first.[20] The Panglong Conferences of 2016 and 2017 cost China much political capital on all sides. The relation—not proxy, not pawn, but constrained by the complex political economy of the borderlands—might be as a UWSA official put it to me: "Like any other relationship, if you ask something and we do not give, the relationship weakens, it is not to say we are forced [to comply]."[21] The EAOs (mostly on the border with China) still refused the NCA, straining their relations with China at that time.

But border geopolitics entailed constantly shifting interests and demands, betting on the political fortunes of different factions. Such vicissitudes were complicated by China's "multi-layered policies," with Sun's Guoxiang's diplomatic channel, the International Liaison Department of the CCP, and the Chinese PLA all lending different faces to its intervention, as Lintner points out: "Through its traditional policy of separating 'government-to-government' and 'party-to-party' relations, China is able to send diplomats to take part in the peace process at the same time as its security agents are arming the UWSA."[22]

Wa Region was a dissonant space, framed differently by different actors and their political imaginaries. A buffer zone for the Chinese security apparatus, a rebellious periphery embarrassingly illegible to the Burmese state, a stronghold base and ally to other EAOs, and a frontier for the aspirational accumulation of

Chinese entrepreneurs. Or a satellite whose loyalty was up for grabs, a proxy for external interests. Or perhaps one of many nodes in the complex shadow networks and associations of the Golden Triangle. These contradictory political imaginaries occurred within the structural constraints of the borderlands—international political sanctions, topographical limitations, logistical difficulties, a lack of legal personhood, and susceptibility to market prices of raw materials, to name but a few—structures that fashioned the limits of autonomy and its contours.

Parasitic Accumulation

Yet the autonomy of Wa Region was not only a political imaginary. It was constituted partially through the oscillating economic practices of various borderland actors. One of this was a form of *parasitic accumulation* drawn to Wa Region to capitalize on lower levels of state legibility, regulation, and surveillance, leeching off present commercial transactions. Here, counterfeit and fraudulent outsiders were juxtaposed with images of the honest (Chn: *cunpu*) and unassuming local inhabitant (Wa or Shan or Burmese), the "frogs in the well" too trusting and too truthful to really "do business." Stories and warnings of being cheated, scammed, and duped with fakes permeated Wa Region as did the material itself. Fake medicines, money, herbs, alcohol, tea, electronics and mobile phones, luxury products, and a range of other consumer goods were sent from China to the areas where inhabitants were supposedly unable to distinguish authenticity.[23]

Most strikingly, parasitic accumulation drew on parallels with older narratives of "backward" minorities at the fringes. The missionary Harold Young recounted stories of the "gullible" Wa from his stay in the 1920s and how "the Chinese had started wild rumors among the Wa" that if white men were to walk in their fields, the fields would become barren.[24] In 2003, a failed joint venture between Wa investors and a Chinese company to start a paper mill near Pangkham caused much consternation. Renard describes how the paper produced was ultimately of substandard quality and could not be sold in China; "after several efforts to turn the project around, the Wa gave up, and assumed they had been cheated."[25] The tangled and ambiguous cross-jurisdictions of the border required a constant vigilance—to check authenticity of any product or venture being purchased.

In patronizing fashion, Wa Region and the UWSA were sometimes dubbed a "copycat" version of China (Chn: *shanzhai zhongguo*) in Chinese media.[26]

Everyday resentment of exploitative and opportunistic Chinese economic influence, and the condescending attitudes of Chinese entrepreneurs and businessmen, surfaced occasionally among locals: "They are very arrogant, but their mouth is sweet. They know how to flatter."

"No, thanks [in English]. I wouldn't buy any of these [fake] Chinese goods."

"Perhaps it's harder to make a living there [in China] because people are more calculating and give fewer tips."

These contrasted with an assertion of the toughness of Wa society versus the empty bluster of Chinese visitors: "The average Chinese pickups can't cope on our muddy roads here; their engines are too weak."

Several borderland figures emerge. The first, the savvy trickster (mainly Chinese). One story was recounted by a Wa official, disgruntled with the exponentially rising prices of land in Pangkham. "In the mid-1990s, Pangkham was still rice fields and muddy roads; land was still available and cheap. Chinese businessmen saw the potential value and came to purchase land in the center of town in the early 2000s. Plots of undeveloped land were simply bought up at undervalued prices, offering cigarettes and beers to local Wa officials to smooth the deal. Now they regret. The Wa officials were too trusting and unsophisticated, too easily charmed by the Chinese gifts."

Laments about fakes and warnings to remain on one's guard were ubiquitous. In one supposed scam, tricksters were said to blow smoke into a person's face, inducing a type of hypnosis that would make a compliant victim hand over assets or cash to them. A friend also told me about how Chinese companies would come to Wa Region and invite Wa businessmen or leaders to participate in a joint venture, hosting tours to their offices in China to display their facilities and capabilities. As it turned out, these companies were complete fakes, with receptionists, workers, and office space hired temporarily for the brief period of the "tour." A successful scam would see the fake company disappear with the initial capital investment (always in cash). Yet another story told of a con man who invited investors to visit a mine he claimed was his own. He brought the unwitting businessmen into the mining areas of Man Xiang where hundreds of mining shafts were being worked and showed them a site, machinery, and workers and ultimately absconded with their capital once the investments were made. Such scams were conducted over a long process of courting, dining, and entertaining the investors to convince them of his wealth and success.

These caricaturizing tales illustrated a disgruntlement at the structural constraints of economic and political reliance on China, yet they were interspersed with polite statements of gratitude acknowledging how integral they were to Wa Region's economy—"They are our neighbors and we have close ties." At the same time, there were occasionally attempts to paint even longtime ethnic Chinese inhabitants of Wa Region as outsiders—*zhongguoren* (Chn, Chinese nationals)—from China. This ambivalent Wa-China relationship was deeply embedded in tropes from Chinese narratives disparaging non-Han ethnic minorities within its borders; Wa Region inhabitants were well aware of these prejudices.[27]

Tricksters, however, operate within a local moral economy; it was not a free-for-all lawless zone of deceit and fraud.[28] A form of pragmatism guides interactions—*guanxi*, connections, and trust operated alongside a habitus of vigilance and the principle of *caveat emptor* or "buyer beware." Individuals took caution in their own transactions and dealings, seeking advice or help from others, performing their due diligence by undertaking their own investigations into the legitimacy of investments and partners. Fraud and deception might result in resentment but also a sense that one deserved the outcome for having been so foolish—"doing business is like this." As Chang Wen-Chin writes of the jade trade across the China-Myanmar borders, "One would assume that trust was a necessary foundation cooperation among partners and between traders in transaction. In fact, trust was a value rarely observed in practice, receiving only lip-service. Informants frequently talked of distrust between traders and told me in confidence stories of betrayal."[29]

Another friend, also an official in the Wa administration, recounted a story over tea:

> There was this time in the past [around the mid-2000s], when some of Tax's [a military commander] men were arrested in Myanmar areas by their police for carrying drugs. In broken Burmese, they claimed to be Wa from China. This meant that the Myanmar police would send them back to China rather than putting them in jail. At that time, they were sent back to China through the border crossing at Pangkham [escorted though Wa Region by Myanmar police], with the Chinese border police waiting to receive them. Of course, we had to find a way to intercept this.
>
> So our guy [an ethnic Chinese] dressed up in shirt and trousers. He even put two pens in his pocket [to look official]. He drove a car with Chinese plates from over the border and pretended to be the Chinese representative arriving in Pangkham to take over custody. "Why is there only you to receive so many prisoners?" He explained it was a public holiday in China, so they only sent him over. The Myanmar police even took photographs of the "handing over" of the prisoners to the "Chinese detective."
>
> But of course we didn't drive them back across the border. They took a small path down the side of the bridge and came back on our side. The Myanmar police saw it from afar and realized they had been tricked. I told them this was because it was easier to travel [to where they were going in China] using the roads inside Wa Region, but they did not believe it. In the end, I went to Tax, and told him "Now you have to give some blood [Chn: *chu yidianxue*, meaning incur costs]," so he gave money to host the Myanmar police—eating, drinking, and dancing

with women. The next morning the police left for Myanmar areas; they couldn't find the prisoners anyway.

Being deceived was clearly not a one-way street. Quick thinking and improvisation were valued as "ability," manipulating the other side to gain an advantage. They operated within a broader calculus of retribution, cost, proportionality, and obligation. Sometimes trickery was understandable, or even acceptable, used as a means of ensuring outcomes alternative to the law of the state, that were not detrimental to the immediate parties involved.

What this friend implied in recounting the story (however true) was an outcome that was not entirely a wrongdoing—the Myanmar policemen had little to gain from handing over the prisoners. They were simply carrying out protocol. It was "appropriate" that the Myanmar police be hosted (and thanked for doing their jobs) after realizing they had been fooled; it was "appropriate" that they close an eye to the transgressions; it was only right that it would cost the commander to free his men. The men had not been carrying large amounts of drugs either, so in borderland terms the outcome was a just one.

A second figure of the businessman (Chn: *shengyiren*) is a wonderfully flexible entity that accommodates the complex array of registers and tones that defined their subjectivity and the wide range of illegal and illicit enterprises on the border. It provided the image of freedom in being a self-made man, one who was not employed by another in a salaried job (Chn: *dagong*). It provided an explanation for one's wealth and willingness to spend to build connections. It provided cover for all types of motives and occupations. Many in Wa Region were coy about their sources of income, and the capaciousness of terms like "trade" (Chn: *maimai*) or "work travel" (Chn: *chuchai*) provided the perfect umbrella for any activities ranging from mineral water importation to heroin trafficking. The devil was often in the subtext—the line of business one was in. Any key snippet of information, spoken in conspiratorial tones, revealed probable histories. "This hotel is owned by a Hui businessman" might hint at the Huis' complex histories of migration and movement that took them across the mountains of northwestern Yunnan down toward the northern Thai border, drawing allusions to the smuggling industry.

There was another sense to the term "businessman," a moral descriptor used for an individual whose objectives were mainly personal accumulation without considering the wider welfare of Wa Region. Chairman Bao once used this term in TV interviews to describe the infamous drug lord of the Golden Triangle, Khun Sa, contrasting Khun Sa's private ambitions with his own concern and political responsibility for the people. On Khun Sa (as in chapter 3), Bao said: "He was a businessman. He was like water, flowing wherever it flows. We are like a rock; we cannot be moved."[30] They were, in the eyes of other Wa officials, *just* businessmen,

142   CHAPTER 4

concerned with profit and not the politics and governance of the region. They had no higher goal, as it were, beyond the making of money. Yet as it often turned out, almost every significant person was a businessman of some sort.

Parasitic accumulation followed money and capital from China to the borderlands, either through private or state-led enterprises. It tracked these flows and sought ways to extract capital in parallel at every turn and transaction.

In one of the most remote and poorest Wa townships on the boundary with Myanmar, an amateurish "artist's impression" poster hung outside the township office (see figure 15). It was aspirational—a proposed dam project on the Salween River, complete with power station and pylons, roundabout gardens, a riverside walkway, SUVs, and luxurious homes. Small groups of people took evening saunters along the manicured riverside. There was even a yacht on the river, and red-roofed pagodas perched on the sides of the idyllic gorge. The scene depicted a hydroelectric power station to be built by a large Wa company owned by a top Wa leader. When I inquired about its progress, the township secretary cackled. He recounted how the Wa company had been cheated of one million CNY

FIGURE 15.   Graphic designer's impression of a hydroelectric dam project on the Salween River, October 2015. It never materialized.

(166,000 USD) by a Chinese architect, who after "surveys" and "consultation visits" had returned nothing more than this monstrosity of a graphic.

The Wa company had now begun preparations with another Chinese contractor, but discussions stalled, with the Myanmar government facing stiff opposition to hydroelectric projects on the Salween River from local environmental groups.[31] It was a testament to the audacity (or perhaps naiveté) of certain Wa leaders, that they would contemplate building a dam across a river control of which was jointly shared with the state. The painting was an extrapolation of this absurdity—images of Chinese luxury and prosperity juxtaposed into the security landscape of a river boundary that separated Myanmar fortifications from their Wa counterparts across the river. Appealing to an infrastructural enchantment, a trickster artist had woven the visual appearances of prestige necessary to secure contracts.[32] There was, of course, the possibility that the project had simply failed, instead of being an elaborate ruse. Now, the sorry picture hung next to a dated township office calendar, covered with a layer of dust and traces of fingermarks that once gestured excitedly at its promise.

Spatial Fix: The Yucheng Group

Two women arrived at my office one August morning, the sharp sounds of northern-accented Mandarin filling the reception, a stark contrast with the melodious tones of Yunnanese I had by now become accustomed to. As it turned out, one claimed to be the head of the mysterious SEA Union Bank and working for the Yucheng Group. She did not have a name card ("It hasn't yet been made") and explained that they had just arrived in Pangkham and were trying to get a sense of the region. When driving around, they stumbled upon the signboard of a UN office. She spoke of the possibilities of "working together" and bragged unabashedly of the hundreds of millions of CNY invested, vehicles purchased, and hundreds of employees that the company had hired. She referenced the development zone starting up in the hills, and reaffirmed its plans to build a four-thousand-bed hospital and luxury complex, as well as a zoo. Ironically, of all the boasts she proffered, it was the claim that Yucheng had already acquired three tigers that seemed the most plausible.

The woman wanted to borrow some maps of the area and claimed that the Wa authorities had been unable to provide her with one. Broadly suspicious, I rehearsed a default set of polite bureaucrat excuses about the complexity of UN procedures and information sharing ("I'm very sorry our rules from above are so tedious") and deferred the matter to a later date. Her presumptuous and unsettling arrogance invoked little goodwill; it beggared belief that a company with serious plans for large-scale investment did not even possess a reliable map of the region. Colleagues and I searched the Internet for background information about the company but found little beyond basic information on their headquarters and the peer-to-peer lending system.

Back at a government department days later, one of the deputy ministers was baffled about what the bank actually did. "It doesn't allow people to create savings accounts, nor does it give out loans. this is a strange bank," he mused. "I'm not sure what they do, but they have their own intentions," he caveated without elaboration. A minister, when I asked whether Yucheng was affiliated with the Chinese government, seemed unsure: "Probably not," he replied, "but it doesn't seem they are here to earn much." He had himself met with their representatives, who hinted that they had some approval from people within the Chinese government and were part of the development of China's western frontier, but the minister did not go into further detail. Formal and informal Chinese government policies like "going out" (Chn: *zouchuqv*), "development of the West" (Chn: *xibudakaifa*), and the BRI were useful catch-all enterprises that private interests could leverage to grant themselves a veneer of legitimacy without the possibility of verification by borderland inhabitants.

The manager of my apartment building (owned by a Wa deputy minister), during our evening gossip sessions, told me of the tens of millions of CNY Yucheng had offered certain brokers and leaders' sidekicks and the exorbitant fees paid to purchase property from leaders. Other government officials whom I was close to gave different but also astronomical figures. Others said they were financing the road construction in town and across the region. A township leader was said to have been relieved of his duties after it was discovered that he had received tens of millions of CNY in "loans" from the Yucheng company. The shady dealings were all around, Yucheng supposedly contributing to the public good with hospitals and road construction yet also brandishing huge amounts of money to win favor with Wa leaders for unclear private motives.

Months later, the Yucheng Group bought over the News Agency of the Wa administration, which had been a bureau under the Political Works Ministry. The News Agency was responsible for the monthly magazine *Wa State Today* and the televised "Wa State TV" news. Yucheng brought in producers and editors from China and rebranded the news with fonts, formats, and logos. They retained local staff to continue newscasting, since none of their Chinese media hires could speak Wa or Shan, but took over journalistic production. Two teams of journalists hired from China to produce content for the *Wa State Today* magazine were constantly roaming the town, desperate for stories to publish—shadowing street cleaners in Pangkham or interviewing people taking evening walks around the main stadium. They purchased a new plot of land upon which they were to build an eight-story tower which would headquarter the News Agency. This, too, was bizarre. Were they trying to manipulate the local media, with whatever limited reach and significance it had? Currently it reported broadly on the meetings Wa officials had on any given day—a drug bust, a road collapse, or a thief punished. It seemed there was little to no profit or influence to be garnered.

People continued to gossip—apparently the head of the Yucheng Group was based in Anhui Province and had ties that led straight to the top of the Chinese Communist Party. Not long now, some thought, the bubble would burst, and the truth would be revealed. The Chinese police from counties across the border in China were now making inquiries, suspicious of the large flows of capital and people across the border but unable to cross the border and properly investigate. Nor did they want to wade into dealings above their jurisdiction. The lines between legal and illegal were often blurred, since it was almost taken for granted that no one would be able to accrue or move such great sums of money without having protectors or patrons in the Chinese government—in other words, tacit approval from the "top," whichever echelon that was. It was unclear if anyone (on both immediate sides of the border) really knew what these ties were; all that reached the borderlands were impressions and assumptions.

Capital, in what David Harvey famously called a "spatial fix," searches for new global territories and spaces to solve the problem of local overaccumulation.[33] It seeks out from overseas cheaper labor and inputs, new consumer markets for its goods, pouncing on favorable (often underregulated) political, legal, and economic situations in other countries and zones to maximize profit and accumulate. Here in the Yucheng case, capital was exported from eastern China to its western borderlands looking for productivity in this spatial fix: "Surplus capital can be lent abroad to create fresh productive powers in new regions. The higher rates of profit promised provide a 'natural' incentive to such a flow and, if achieved, raise the average rate of profit in the system as a whole."[34]

The "fix" here, however, differs slightly. It is less material and more imagined. "Resourcefulness" takes on new meanings, as capital assumes powers not through production but by turning land into a canvas for a speculative project. The hodge-podge spectacle of potentiality—the news agency, the jobs created, properties purchased, the hospitals and mansions to be built—these were all imaginaries that might increase investor confidence and attract more capital to the peer-to-peer lending scheme back in China. Recall the minister's comment: "but it doesn't seem they are here to earn much." While Yucheng was not directly extracting from Wa Region, they were harnessing its potential as a canvas to create visions, what Anna Tsing describes as the "economy of appearances":

> The self-conscious making of a spectacle is a necessary aid to gathering investment funds.... In speculative enterprises, profit must be imagined before it can be extracted; the possibility of economic performance must be conjured like a spirit to draw an audience of potential investors. The more spectacular the conjuring, the more possible an investment frenzy.... Dramatic performance is the prerequisite of their economic performance.[35]

What made Wa Region particularly attractive to capital was the ambivalence of its visibility. It brought together *both* the spectacular performances of frontier accumulation and the concealment of the shadows, a complex play between visibility and invisibility.[36] It was a murky canvas upon which projects could be imagined: where it relied on the spectacle to create value, it also relied on its imperviousness to scrutiny, just beyond the reach of the law or verification. Investors could not ascertain authenticity and legitimacy; they could only see images, the advertisements placed on the Beijing subway, pictures of economic trade zones and luxury mansions in an idyllic faraway land. These images beckoned them to imagine a worthy investment, to imagine potential profit. Intriguingly, such imaginings were as foreign to them as they were to the local inhabitants of Wa Region, living on the same ridgeline as a massive boarded-up construction site.

This was the dual nature of relational autonomy—it drew in capital and flows by being beyond the reach of states, while remaining anchored in economic networks and institutional appearances to attract potential investors. Its reputation relied on both legibility and illegibility—much like the bright and gaudy flashing lights and thumping music, reverberating from the dark caverns of the casino complexes.

Spectacular Accumulations

Mao, a mining investor from Zhejiang province on China's east coast, is a quintessential representation of a third figure—the entrepreneur. Mao had been back and forth across the river countless times. Differing legal and economic regimes run up against one another in Wa Region's frontier market, offering surpluses and premiums for exploitation across the legal geographies of the border. Mao, in his early forties, left his wife and two kids in Zhejiang and arrived in Pangkham in 2011 just as the mass exploitation of tin was beginning in the Wa hills.

Pooling money with four other Han Chinese acquaintances, he operated a tin mine in Man Maw, a four-hour drive from Pangkham. But within a year, operations were delayed while permits from the Wa authorities were being renewed, leaving him to spend his days waiting aimlessly in Pangkham, only traveling to his mine once a fortnight. "Mining is a risky and bitter job; you have to be tough and daring to do it. It's always possible you find nothing at all."

Tsing's "economy of appearances" demonstrates a linking of scale-making projects, where finance capital, cronyism, and the frontier as a fluid region of extraction come together.[37] "Spectacular accumulation," according to Tsing, occurs where "investors speculate on a product that may or may not exist... looking for the appearance of success. They cannot afford to find out if the product is solid; by then their chances for profit will be gone."[38] And to conjure such appearances, businessmen, tricksters, and entrepreneurs engage in a medley of bodily performances, of masculinity, of daring, and of success.

I met Mao early on in my travels to Wa Region, when he lived in a small room in the low-tier motel (this motel later turned out to be owned by Wang, the Wa official of chapter 2). That evening, he perched on the edge of the bed in his underwear fiddling around on a laptop, an overflowing ashtray in close proximity. The television broadcasted a low-grade Japanese pornography channel, a staple of Pangkham's seedy motels.

"Nothing much has changed," he said as he looked up. "We're still waiting for the permits. Roads are bad; I won't be heading out to the mines this week."

Mao had spent his entire afternoon at the casino; gambling seemed to him a predictor for the direction his luck would turn. We walked out to the apartment complex at the river's edge, across from China, to use the kitchen of his business partner who had returned to China for the time being (this apartment complex was owned by a Politburo member whose daughter's wedding I described in chapter 2). The apartment showed few signs of habitation, though a crusty drill bit lay on the floor, beside a small bed with mattress still wrapped in plastic sheet. The stove worked, however, and Mao browsed the stored condiments available for his use. "The food they make here [in restaurants] is so oily, I can't stomach it." He had been to the market in the morning and now brandished a bagful of ginger, spring onions, and pork. He drew a chopper and sliced the pork thinly.

"A group of friends told me about Wa Region. China is big; there are many people; you need to keep moving if you want to find money. There's no point working for other people." Mao had no mining expertise whatsoever but left his adhesives factory in Hangzhou to someone else to manage and departed for the border where tin was underexploited. "There's a large pool of miners and engineers with expertise from Yunnan, where the Gejiu mines have run dry; they are always looking for investors." Mao and partners would strike deals with local Wa authorities for concessions, rent mining machinery and laborers, and use local and Chinese processing plants before selling the ore back into China.

"There was a mining boss from Guangzhou, who bought a mine and dug it for four months but did not find anything and gave up. He sold it on to another, who extended the shaft for only another twenty feet and struck it rich. Mining is tough but you must keep going no matter what, even though it is difficult."[39]

Masculinity and entitlement were part of this frontier subjectivity, an imperious sense that audacity and cultural and economic capital should allow mobility across borders and business deals. Mao's hair was spiked up with glistening gel, cropped at the sides; his yellowing teeth and large frame were accompanied by a confident swagger. He clung to an imagined Chinese privilege in Pangkham, adopting a "big brother" persona, greeting Chinese shopkeepers and restauranteurs as we went on our post-dinner strolls. "These guys here respect me. We have a community and I treat them well," or "Don't worry. As long as I am here, the police won't dare to touch us." Cultural capital (as he imagined it) would mix with audacity and convert resources into wealth for him. Perhaps this bravado was ultimately a hint of anxiety. When Mao had gambled away his cash, he crossed back into China to withdraw money at the border ATMs: "This is no issue. Nine out of ten people here have come across the river; the authorities are only searching for drugs. On the Wa side, it doesn't matter what ID you produce; the most important thing is that you pay the 30 CNY [5 USD]."

But Mao always stood out to me as a Chinese outsider, especially when I became more familiar with Pangkham. Perhaps it was the long-sleeved polo shirt and jeans, the fake Adidas sneakers, and the leather fanny pack, apparel locals rarely wore. Finishing the sliced pork dishes, we ventured up the peace pagoda to the small funfair. Shooting games, darts and balloon games, beanbags, and balls into barrels surrounded a defunct bumper car arena. An inflatable pool was set up with miniature remote-controlled boats to for children to pilot. The boats were labeled "Chinese Navy," manned by tiny plastic soldiers perched on them. In the middle of the pool, a sign read, "Protect China. Diaoyu Islands, China's territory." Vendors had clearly reused secondhand games from across the border, with little regard for their messages. Mao chose a fishing game, small balls of dough used as bait for small fish trapped in a grubby Styrofoam box. We sat and waited for a good half hour, Mao's fishing rod dangling over the box. Perhaps the fish were not hungry enough. There were nibbles, more nibbles, but no bites.

Competition was fierce by 2014; the Man Maw area was mined by dozens of companies, each digging their own shafts toward, under, and around the main lode.

There were no systematic geological prospecting surveys, only quick registrations and permits given for the right payments. Costs ran high—permits, fees for importing equipment, ore processing and transport costs, wages for drivers, workers, engineers, and surveyors, and taxes, which amounted to 25 percent of the value. But taxes could be minimized with the right patrons, giving Wa-affiliated companies an edge, as a friend described the predicament of the tax bureaus: "Everyone knows one another. How can I ask you for taxes [Chn: *dajia doushi shouren, wo zenme haiyao nideqian*]?" Enforcing taxation and careful accounting were pettiness, and pettiness toward friends was unbecoming. Beyond the reach of the Myanmar state and of international oversight standards, mining was unfettered by environmental protection, labor laws, extractive quotas, and mining safety requirements. A confidant of Myanmar state counselor Aung San Suu Kyi was quoted in the media as saying of the Wa mines, "Even for us, it's still a mystery. They are quiet and very wise—and they keep their movements low-key."[40]

Performing power and success, daring, and confidence were central to the entrepreneur. It was having guts (Chn: *danzi*), and as Chang Wen-Chin describes in the borders, a "wild temper and adventurous disposition . . . a fearless spirit of risk-taking."[41] It was a masculine environment, rules of propriety and politeness underwritten by ruthlessness, not dissimilar to the entrepreneurial and business culture described in China, with strong tones of sexual consumption.[42] Because of the ubiquity of scams and swindles of varying scales, there was a perpetual fear that business dealings and commerce were constantly perched on feet of clay, the hidden, the counterfeit, and the ghostly. A tough demeanor was then essential to avoid being taken advantage of—a brusque manner of speaking, of beckoning, of chiding others and compelling them to do one's will. It was ordering of subordinates and service staff around, the dismissive wave of the hand, the frowns, the scowls, the raised voices of irritation and impatience. It was the constant explaining and the know-it-all condescension, an affected wisdom and passing of commentary. Hearty laughter, flattery, and "sweet-talking" at the right moments. A capable, no-nonsense, streetwise person who could not be bullied or manipulated at others, willing to confront others when needed. A person who was polite and mild mannered, who did not have the requisite connections, was at risk of being an easy target. Moments of confrontation were tempered by shows of generosity through gifts, tipping, and the writing off of small monies.

Six months later, Mao had left Pangkham. While the lack of formal regulations rendered potential for profit, it also meant unrationalized, unpredictable authority. The permits never materialized, and his mining operation was taken over by a local military commander. Across the board, concessions in the Man

Maw area were requisitioned by the true sovereigns after 2013—local Wa leaders, military units, and their associated companies. The initial heyday for Chinese medium-holder extraction was over, and by 2015, few remained, with most concessions operated by around ten large UWSA-affiliated companies. Where permits and legal provisions could be revised or ignored, might was right. Retroactive or forged contracts displaced Chinese shareholders and speculators, as a friend in the Wa government recounted:

> [They told them]: sure, contest ownership of the mines through the legal means, but everyone knows that the UWSA's Justice Department will rule on the side of its officials and units. Good enough that some compensation is offered; in front of a commander during a meeting, I advised a friend carefully [and performatively in front of the commander], "Commander is so good to you, to even offer you this [minimal] compensation. Just take it and leave."

Knowing Chinese mobile phone sellers and three-wheeler drivers in the markets was one thing; it was another to be ingratiated with the right patrons. It became apparent that Mao was a dilettante. He did not have the right Wa patrons, nor did he cultivate them through introductions, gifting, and visiting. He was caught in treacherous local power relations that he had underestimated. Central was the "politics of knowledge"—"the knowledge of languages, of trading routes, of evaluation, and of markets"—that Chang describes in her case of the jade trade. Brokers and middlemen were central to the navigation of the commercial terrain, the topographies of power.[43] Too confident in his cultural capital, Mao was caught off-guard by the changing landscape.

"You must not get ahead of yourself; in the end, this is Wa country [Chn: *wazu difang*; implying you must know your place]," I recalled of a friend's cautionary tone; "they don't take too kindly to braggards."

Where Mao's spectacles failed, others' discreet accumulations worked. Another Chinese investor I had heard of ingratiated himself with one of the daughters of a key Wa leader, his profits untouchable, which he shared with her. Other Chinese investors ran ore processing plants or transportation services, sold construction material, or leased out mining equipment, tapping surplus along the production line but not competing with Wa interests for extraction itself. In 2016, tin ore from Man Maw made up 95 percent of Myanmar's tin output, its prolific production hitting even headlines in international media—"Mystery Myanmar Mines Shake Up World Tin Market."[44] By this time, Mao had been long gone.

Accumulation by Proxy

Narratives of fraud and deception by outsiders omit the ways in which local leaders and inhabitants, too, are happy to welcome capital and people that arrive. Recall: "How dare you not take when something is given?"

In 2015, there were an estimated thirty thousand to sixty thousand migrant Chinese nationals in Wa Region, according to a friend in the UWSA administration, a number with great seasonal variance. Without Myanmar government presence, the border crossing at Pangkham cannot be an international one. No passports are accepted. Only Chinese citizens registered in the prefectures adjacent to the border and others with special permissions can apply for a border pass to cross legally. Everyone else from other parts of China and beyond crosses illicitly by raft or dinghy. They come as investors, truck-drivers, miners, shopkeepers, laborers, and market traders. Many were supposedly wily wheeler-dealers who had found themselves in good stead with key UWSA leaders, a source of simmering unhappiness for local lower-ranked officials. "These Chinese who come over to find positions of power are bad people; they stick to Wa leaders and say whatever to win their favor. Some of our officials are easy targets," Wang once surmised.

While Chinese entrepreneurs flocked to Wa Region from the 2000s in search of opportunity, relations were not completely unequal. It was not a one-sided rapacious exploitation of a frontier zone. Unlike the peripheral groups in Kalimantan described by Tsing, who had to find creative ways to redefine their marginality in relation to the center, elites in Wa Region were in a far stronger position, still the "predatory periphery" able to forestall the peace process in the country, traffic narcotics, and arm its allies with powerful weapons.[45] Exploitation was no one-way street in the Wa hills. Actors preyed on each other, visitors and hosts alike.

Various Wa leaders were known to have big business interests and properties in China and Myanmar, ranging from hotels to domestic airlines, plantations, land, and other properties. Many of the jade mines in Kachin State were rumored to be at least partly owned by certain Wa companies, a fact never easy to confirm.[46] Statistics and numbers were even harder to verify. Even from trusted friends, I received wildly varying figures—of the cost of a particular property, for instance, constructing a kilometer of road, or the annual turnover of a particular silver mine. Reticence and secrecy were ubiquitous—a friend of mine who ran a hotel was unwilling to speak of his costs and profits. Another, having left the service of a top leader after marriage, recalled that many of his contemporaries who stayed with the leader had by now, twenty years on, become remarkably rich. They were always guarded about where their wealth came from. Even to him, they described their work as "business" or "buying and selling" and their products vaguely as "goods" (Chn: *huo*). Public secrets and "common knowledge" were inevitably subject to a blend of exaggeration, guesswork, or falsehoods.

A portly Chinese businesswoman came by the ministry one summer day in July 2014. A local guide brought her on motorbike and made brief introductions, and they sat themselves down in the sitting room where we gathered to gossip in the mornings. Sporting frizzy permed hair and two necklaces of precious stones, Zhao was in her mid-fifties, and sat nervously at the opposite end of the room reserved for visitors and petitioners. Officials from the department ringed the room. Zhao was from Changsha, Hunan Province in China, and had traveled the borderlands investing in various mining prospects across Shan State. "I have been cheated of 530,000 CNY [90,000 USD] from a mining venture that went bust. I am now trying to get to Monghsu to look for this company. Can you give me a pass to access the Burmese areas?"

"Who is the person [your contact] you know?" asked the minister, sussing out the level of her backing. It was, after all, his job to deal with such requests.

She named a high-ranking Wa military commander.

The deputy minister next to me nodded his head knowingly. "Who did she say that was again?" I whispered to him, not yet then familiar with the titles of commanders.

"A northern commander. He has a tough reputation. She should not have trusted him," came the quiet reply. "It seems he has taken some money but is not recognizing her claims or responding to her now. But who knows? This is her side of the story."

Zhao described the places she had been to across the borderlands, traveling for months on end. Yet each region had an entirely new political landscape, and knowing officials in one area did not necessarily help in another. She was edgy about her presence and not willing to reveal whom she knew and who her other contacts were, perhaps because they might betray her lack of standing, or perhaps they were divisive figures. Being in the entourage of one leader might mean estrangement from another. Or perhaps she knew no one.

Her illegal crossing from China was not an issue for the Wa officials, but beyond that they would not help. "We cannot help you to get to Monghsu. You have to go back to China, come to Myanmar through the proper crossing point at Muse, or fly from Kunming to Mandalay, and from there travel to Monghsu."

"But I don't know what the route is."

"Then you have to find someone who does. It is dangerous if you don't know anyone; we don't travel there ourselves."

Throughout the conversation her broker, who had brought her to the office, remained seated and silent. Zhao looked disappointed and brandished her Chinese passport, but he remained unmoved, telling her to go through Kunming.

"May I have your name?" she asked. "Just call me Old Man Liu," the minister replied, again, to hearty cackles all around. It was hard to believe that she had showed up not fully knowing whom she was meeting, not able to place such a high-ranking leader in the hierarchy. These were cues that she was a nobody, not worth the trouble to help, someone who might namedrop the minister in her next meeting, an annoyance he wanted to avoid.

Zhao sipped from her almost empty glass of tea, not offered the respect of a prompt refill. Her nerves showing through, dismissiveness in the room turned to a mild pity for her. The minister commended her spirit: "You are a strong woman. Where is your husband? How does he let you travel to these areas alone?" She claimed to have "fellow villagers" (Chn: *laoxiang*) now living in Kengtung, and other parts of Wa region and Shan State, who had made introductions.

"Well, take this 530,000 CNY as the price of a lesson [Chn: *maige jiaoxun*]. I'm not trying to pour cold water, but you should cut your losses and not invest in places you do not understand. You are an older woman [Chn: *laomama*] already. Even Qing here, who is Chinese from Myanmar, has been unable to close a deal for timber after payment."

"This place is very undeveloped," she ventured. "I saw villagers here wearing grass shoes out in the hills. There must be room for more development." Perhaps she was trying to convince the officials of their need for her capital, as buyers disparage a product they intend to purchase, to lower its price.

"No, they normally wear suits and leather shoes. The ones you saw had already taken them off for the evening," came the minister's curt reply, provoking guffaws all around.

Like Mao, she, too, exhibited a patronizing attitude in the border regions, believing that all she needed was to buy the right patrons to gain unfettered access. Her mode of arrival—by motorbike—and her broker gave away her social standing in town. Any businessperson with the appropriate connections and capital would be driven around in the car by a host who was familiar with local officials. Instead, she had hired a rider for the day, and probably badgered him to bring her to the minister, embarrassing the rider for his lack of standing. Zhao did not just require a boatman to row her across the river; she required a broker with understanding of the social infrastructure. She could be cheated, dispensed with, ignored.

"You see, these Chinese always do it this way. They travel however they want, and then turn to us for help when they run into trouble. If we don't help them, they badmouth the place and say that we are thugs," the minister grumbled to me. I spotted Zhao several months later in the hills outside Pangkham, traveling in a rented pickup around the Man Maw mining areas in Wa Region, perhaps having found another patron.

Like Mao, Zhao was a convenient scout for Wa leaders to suss out resources on their behalf, whereupon the real powerholders could swoop in to develop the opportunities. Perhaps the Wa, too, had their own proxies.

Becoming Logistical: Prospecting within Limits

It is several months into my stay in Wa Region, and Chen, my businessman friend from the Wa administration, is driving me and another official out to visit his copper mine and processing plant. The Toyota Hilux glides smoothly up into the hills along the winding new roads, and past the newly designated garbage dump, where all manner of waste is tipped into the valley below and set on fire. Children play amid the garbage; some teens and elderly rummage through debris for salvageable material. The wind scatters plastic and other fragments back up across the road. We round the corner where the barrels of tar are gathered, hundreds of abandoned dark brown cylinders rusting beneath the jet blue sky, remnants of a successful roadbuilding project. The other companion traveling with us, an official in the military headquarters, remarks on the excellent precision job done by the Hong Pang company carving the roads into hillsides. A much better job than the road from Pangkham to Mengmao, which has seen precarious rock fall and disintegration at many points. The hills will stabilize in five years, he says.

We reach the fork in the road where a smaller dirt track runs down to the processing plant. A makeshift signboard shows that the mine is named after another government department; Chen has ensured that he adopts the unit name (and gravitas) of his minister patron. It is a steep, dusty trail down into the valley, a veritable nightmare for the truck drivers who cart large rocks down to the processing plant. Here, the rocks are dumped into large metal drums along with iron balls the size of large baseballs. The noise is disconcerting. Finer ball mills follow after the coarse crusher; they rotate like a cement mixer, after which the smaller rocks are funneled into spiral separators. They wind up in a trough and are mixed with liquid chemicals, the resultant mush then dried out to leave fine powder. In this particular plant, the ore is refined to a 6 to 8 percent purity from the roughly 0.5 percent purity of the original rocks brought in from the mines. The laboratory retains a daily log where purity of processed ore samples is tested with chemical reagents to determine whether the batch is worth refining further. For a batch to be profitable, the purity level of incoming rocks must be at least 0.3 percent; the numbers in the logbook have been hovering suspiciously just above this figure all month. Piles of rock lying around the sides suggest a sizable amount of discard.

Late 2014, and Chen's copper mine is not doing well. The copper ore found in the rocks there is simply not valuable enough, with purities around a mere 0.2 to 0.5 percent. With eighty employees, both locals and specialists from China, operational costs are high. Finding the right skilled labor is costly and difficult: wages for a digger operator are around 7,000 to 8,000 CNY a month, machine operators at 3,000 to 4,000 CNY, and lab technicians at 5,000 to 6,000 CNY. These have all been adding up.

We step out of the pickup and are welcomed by Chen's plant manager, a uniformed middle-aged man in crisp military dress, pocket-sized revolver holstered at his hip. The manager shows off the ambitious facilities—mill, laboratory, dining area, and living quarters equipped with electricity and television. The conditions at his mine are far better than in Man Maw, our other companion points out encouragingly. We are just in time for lunch. The workers arrive from the mine shafts piled on the backs of pickups. Bedraggled from the drizzle, they eat quickly in the plant's canteen, feeding scraps to the resident dog. There are digger operators, blasting specialists, mill operators, chemical specialists, and other odd laborers who dig or spray water on the sorting machines. There might be as much as two million tons of usable rock here, the engineer says; they must just locate and excavate it. The operation could run for ten years, he says.

Chen unveils his new prize, a handheld X-ray Fluorescence (XRF) spectrometer gun manufactured in Massachusetts, able to determine the mineral composition of a particular rock just by pointing at it. A group of well-dressed Chinese merchants had showed up at his office one morning to demonstrate its capabilities, handling it with great reverence as they removed it from its casing. Capital, it seemed, beckoned through frontier crevices, drawing cutting-edge technology to the far-flung reaches of the borderlands. These are the technologies of resourcefulness; they turn unremarkable spare rock into resources. Chen now presses the gun against some samples from today and asks me to confirm the mineral elements shown in English. The figures for copper are disappointing, and so too with the following samples. The conversation shifts to the weather and its effects on transportation.

Shortly, Chen's engineer emerges from another pickup truck—we are about to embark on an inspection tour of the mines. Chen has two mineshafts in operation here, both copper, but the yields have not been good thus far. The mineshaft entrance is a further two kilometers downhill from the plant, where a large valley fifty meters wide has been blasted into the hillside. Quaint wooden logs

FIGURE 16. Inspecting minerals outside a copper mine, August 2014.

frame the entrance of the shaft, 100 meters deep and 560 meters long; one almost expects dwarfs to emerge at any moment (see figure 16). Two workers in rudimentary safety gear are drilling a new vent for explosives with a pneumatic hammer. A digger ambles noisily across the upper echelon of the slopes. The engineer, sporting a yellow helmet and brandishing a trusty small hammer which establishes his geological authority, points to small rocks on the ground. He and Chen are bent over in hopeful conversation, discussing the potential locations of further deposits. All around us in the valley are strata of exposed rock—orange, red, stone, metallic, and even the sharp blue-green of oxidized copper. If only the treasonous laboratory numbers were as brilliant. Chen hides his disappointment. We drive in silence back up the hill for lunch.

Mid-2015, and Chen tells me he now has a new engineer—the previous one came highly rated but soon left, unsuccessful in his search for ore. "They are liars, all full of talk. Who can tell what is really in the ground? The engineers from China are from all over; it is hard to know whom to believe, and whom to hire. Their rates are so expensive," he laments. A far cry from a year before, when that very same engineer was praised as a graduate from an affiliate school of Beijing University, paid a handsome 200,000 CNY (33,000 USD) per year. It seems Chen has given up on paying for such expertise with low returns, preferring to spend only 84,000 CNY (14,000 USD) for the new engineer. A Karen laborer of Chen's, whom I know from the football field, disparaged the quality of the ore at Chen's mine: "It's a well-run group. The problem is that the ore isn't valuable enough." He had left the sinking ship after a couple of months. Almost none of the laborers and machine operators are ethnic Wa.

Perhaps it is the stress of the venture—Chen has lost weight and has shaved his head to hide the balding patches. His skinny arms emerge abruptly from the baggy sleeves of his polo T-shirt. He smiles less, and his eyes no longer sparkle amid the wrinkles, but the cynicism remains. He rarely sits around for tea after lunch, instead heading home to his apartment, where he is mostly on the phone, checking for updates on mineral prices and speaking to buyers and contractors. He gambles more at cards in the office, despite clearly being one of the weaker players at the table.[47] He now owes more than one million USD for his mining enterprise. He thinks about selling some of the several houses he has in China and Myanmar. He could liquidate his machinery and other assets, but those would come at a loss.

Our conversations have turned philosophical—on inequality and unfairness—though the political gossip continues. Chen is cynical about governance, perpetually comparing the situation in Wa with that of China. He is an ardent admirer of the Chinese government, whom he says has a billion people to work for it, which will never change. We talk about nepotism, about the vicissitudes of life, about a friend who has recently contracted stomach cancer while his healthy eighty-year-old mother continues to weed the fields. Chen is nostalgic, proud that he has sent his children for education abroad and given them a chance at a bright future.

"*Qihunanxia*," he says drily, citing a Chinese idiom that literally means "When you ride the tiger, it is difficult to dismount." We laugh at the imagery. This tiger of the mining venture is capricious. He has invested so much and must keep going.

Prices for tin and copper have fallen even further.[48] Blasting and digging at his copper mine have now ceased, the ore no longer present in viable purities. Chen now leases out the operations of his processing plant to tin-mining companies at the Man Maw areas (see figure 17). His work now primarily consists of convincing other mining bosses to use his processing plant for processing, since it is halfway between there and Pangkham. He has also bought out a mine shaft there, but it seems a desperate venture, a far cry from his previous optimism. Chen's son is

FIGURE 17. The Man Maw tin mines near Man Xiang Township in Wa Region, October 2015.

now managing parts of the operation and rattles off the prices of tin per ton: 2014, 160,000 CNY; May 2015, 116,000 CNY; September 2015, 100,000+ CNY; October 2015, 98,000 CNY. He makes a pitch for their new operation, carefully describing the various costs per ton of transport, processing, and profit. "It makes much sense for the companies to send their rocks to our plant, rather than processing it onsite for higher charges, or bringing the rocks even further toward Pangkham," he says. "They save 100 CNY per ton to process it to 20 percent purity." He sounds confident, but there still is the issue of the debts they owe.

Tin stocks in the Wa hills were said to be limited and winding down, and by the time I left in December 2015, I was hearing complaints from mining bosses about how quality ore had become significantly harder to find. It was unclear how much more wealth was present, and intensive tunneling was required to find lower-grade ore deposits. Cognizant of the capriciousness of the industry and the lack of reliability of data, Reuters concluded in a video report, "In the meantime, and without proper geo-exploration of the secretive and restricted region, metal analysts and the world market face uncertainty."[49]

Chen has become logistical. He has sought to capture value by shifting from an extractive (mining ore directly) to a logistical operation, as the geographers Mezzadra and Neilson would have it: "Logistics moved from being an exercise in cost minimization to becoming an integrated part of global production systems and a means of maximizing profit."[50] The transport of loose worthless rock is costly, so it makes sense to process it into lighter concentrated ore for movement toward China. The processing plants closer to the mines themselves charge a premium, so Chen's plant offers a midway solution, halfway to Pangkham. Becoming logistical also suits many of Wa Region's other economies. A level of deniability ensues: "We are not the producers; we only make the conditions conducive and facilitate." Becoming logistical extracts surplus value from along the production chain.

The mining hills remain littered with rock and some debris, some with mineral content too low (less than 2 percent) to be yet worth the costs of processing. The miners are waiting for the prices to rise again, which might turn all this waste rock into value. At other times, they have no choice but to process the rock at a loss, simply to recover sunk operating costs. Chen tells me that there is more than one million metric tons of such rock lying around in the Man Maw area. There is much latent potential in these rocks, in these hills, yet all of it is dependent on forces beyond the control of the region. Perhaps Chen's words, "I am a fool if I cannot succeed in this place," were once too bold. Not for want of connections, or knowledge, or acumen, but a victim of wider economic forces at play beyond the hills.

Fallout

Right around the same period as I was preparing to leave Wa Region, the Yucheng project was gradually unraveling. The Hong Kong–based *South China Morning Post* reported in December that Yucheng was under investigation and funds had been frozen;[51] arrests were being made in Anhui Province. Chinese secretaries, journalists, and other staff working for Yucheng and the Wa News Agency were stealing back across the border into China by January 2016. Many were picked up and questioned but released—they had thought themselves working a salaried job for a legitimate company.

It was not until early February that reports of the largest Ponzi scheme in China hit Xinhua News and Western newspapers. The sums were extraordinary. Xinhua News reported the astounding figures of nine hundred thousand people cheated of more than 50 billion CNY (7.6 billion USD) across China, with about 95 percent of the investments being fake.[52] Several Chinese companies had been promoted on the E-*zubao* platform without their knowledge, the scheme falling apart when the company finally fell short of cash to pay out principals. The E-*zubao* company in Anhui was reported to have buried documents in a pit twenty feet underground, later retrieved by excavators.

Soon, further details emerged explaining how so many had been duped in China, despite a public already vigilant against scams and fraud. The *Washington Post* and *Los Angeles Times* reported how the Yucheng Group had advertised the E-*zubao* peer-to-peer lending services on the seven o'clock China Central Television (CCTV) news and on bullet trains, lending it a veneer of government legitimacy.[53] Staff had had a meeting at the Great Hall of the People in Tiananmen Square. The company had also participated in the twelfth China-ASEAN (Association of Southeast Asian Nations) Expo, where it appeared to have been affiliated with Xi Jinping's BRI strategy. Little wonder that these rumors of government backing and official connections filtered into Wa Region. The *LA Times* also reported that "public wrath has rapidly shifted toward the government" and that the backlash in China was censored online, with protesters detained.[54]

Back in Wa Region, the Wa authorities were busy dividing up the properties and assets of the now-defunct Yucheng Group. Developments were unfinished, properties without legal owners. Some money was returned to the Chinese authorities, but the bulk of it was not easily liquidated. Who would buy these assets back from Yucheng's holdings at nearly the same prices they were sold for? The cars and building remained in place even a year after, having been requisitioned by the Wa authorities. Nor could these assets be given to Chinese creditors. The promise of capital in the frontier, now faced with a need to reenter the formal market, failed miserably. This capital was stuck in the shadows and revealed for what it really was, a complex of half-finished buildings on a ridgeline in insurgent territory overseas.

There were losses all around, and some of the profits made by Wa leaders were returned into a central fund. A committee was put together to return monies to local contractors for work and labor that had been partially completed or materials that had already been delivered. The Wa authorities did not seem shocked, or at least concealed it well: "Doing business is like this."

Wa Region had been used as a frontier staging ground for the economy of appearances, where illicit gains were made material and spectacularly manifest in the quest to attract more capital investment. Wealth was converted into property, buildings, vehicles, and tigers, which then served to generate further potentiality. There was no real plan for Yucheng to make profit; Wa Region was certainly not a viable financial investment, even in the odd chance that wealthy buyers were drawn to hillside property in the remote, conflict-wrought peripheries of Myanmar. Top Wa leaders seized an opportunity to retain profit themselves, and there were suggestions that in return, Yucheng had arranged the supply of arms sales to the UWSA.[55] While media reports revealed how wealthy Yucheng executives in Anhui Province splurged their salaries and bonuses on property and designer goods, their employees in Wa Region had gained far less.

The Yucheng director in Wa Region was said to have been arrested, but many below him were released.

By 2017, reports circulated that much of the capital had likely been laundered overseas via Thailand and Singapore.[56] Twenty million USD was recovered in Singapore, where the former Yucheng president purchased a 17.5-million USD house on the luxurious island Sentosa Cove of Singapore.[57] Laundering was a key reason why they had chosen to invest in Wa Region, where Wa autonomy stood beyond the regulatory reach of the Myanmar and Chinese states. While Wa Region was clearly not a place to stash wealth in the long term, because Chinese law made it difficult to move capital overseas, the borderlands were attractive for their well-established and illicit routes for moving money out into the global circuits of capital.

The extravagant hoardings surrounding "Ai Cheng Free Trade Zone," with its luxury hillside homes and planned hospital, were torn down by mid-2016. The specters of capital were gone, leaving behind small plateaus of rock and dirt engraved into the hillside, a monument to that which was given and then taken away.

5

GESTURES OF GOVERNANCE

> **Beyond the basic demand of a Wa State, the UWSP has not developed a clear vision for the future of such a state, or how it should interact with the rest of the country. Nor has the organization developed a comprehensive strategy to achieve such a state. Furthermore, the UWSP is a very hierarchical organization, with a top-down leadership style and little room for participation in decision making for local communities.**
>
> —Tom Kramer, *The United Wa State Party: Narco-Army or Ethnic Nationalist Party?*

> **We sometimes saw only the backwardness and misled ourselves into ignoring the progressive ingredients of the situation, and we sometimes made the mistake of thoughtlessly transplanting ideas here which were based on experiences in other places where conditions were different.**
>
> —Ping Fu-chang, secretary of the Communist Party Working Committee in Ximeng in the Wa Hills in the 1950s

Chattering schoolchildren and other townspeople lined the tarred road leading up to the Longtan township office; coordinated black and red outfits snaked nearly half a kilometer down the hill to the main market.[1] Under the gray skies, guests had assembled in the hours prior, inundating the township courtyard with neatly parked rows of cars. The schoolchildren, each donning a dark red traditional Wa vest for the event, practiced waving and chanting welcomes but were now distracted and jostling among themselves. Teachers struggled to keep discipline, while a row of somewhat less enthusiastic villagers in black traditional dress and knotted turbans wandered into place on the lines. Women in bright red ornamental dresses with fine trimmings squatted at the roadside, their silver-beaded headdresses and necklaces forming a jarring contrast with their gaudy Chinese-made platform sneakers. Other men strolled past, partially clad in dark green military slacks, the durable apparel of choice for the working man.

The small town comprised a main road of no more than two hundred meters, with the main market and bus station at its center, flanked by shops selling produce, hardware, and Chinese household goods. Longtan was the Wa township at the highest elevation, of around twenty-five hundred meters, and rainy days often saw the town shrouded in mist, a cold grayness that went on for months in winter. Today was a cautious September morning, bright, not sunny. Chilly temperatures still meant people huddling around fires during the day. A short drive away in a restricted area was the mystical "fairy lake" of Nawngkhio, which the British searched for and charted in the 1930s, the dwelling place of the "wildest and fiercest of all the Wa," and where ancient tea trees grew.[2] A hotel had opened just in time for today's event; important guests would be put up there. Uniformed police with startling white gloves cordoned off the road with cones and flags, waving commonfolk to the roadside. It was market day, too, once every five days when villagers would hoist baskets of produce over their shoulders, secured to their heads with a forehead strap, and begin the long trundle uphill with children in tow. Downhill from the waiting guards were a row of women in bright headscarves seated over vegetables laid out on mats, and the occasional man selling captive poultry or fertilizer. Small Chinese goods trucks parked in rows behind, arriving today to sell goods from across the border. Women clad in blouses and loose-fitting pants hurried to the bus station, traditional Wa bags slung diagonally across their shoulders, indifferent to the unfolding scenes.

This was the third day of the New Harvest Festival, the biggest celebration in Wa Region, occurring every August or September after most rice harvests were complete. Festivals were hosted at region or district level, but wealthier townships occasionally organized their own event. Longtan Township had organized four days of celebrations, with basketball tournaments between competing military units, games for children (100-CNY notes attached to the top of a two-story-high pole for any child who could scale it), and Wa dance troupes performing reenactments of the harvest. Pennant banners festooned the main township building, the sort used at grand openings in China, with temporary fun-fair shelters and umbrella stalls set up. Damp of yesterday's drizzles was still drying off thatched huts. Having spent the previous night in the spare rooms of the township office, curled up in a floral blanket while water seeped under the zinc doors, I now slurped down a bowl of "convenience noodles" at the market with a companion, waiting for the event to begin.

Soldiers scurried about, and people murmured to their friends, a cue that the convoy was on its way. Twelve SUVs soon rolled up, halting at the foot of the slope. The district and township leaders were ready and waiting to receive their guest. The doors of the lead gleaming white Land Cruiser opened, and a stout regal man, the minister, was helped out of the vehicle by guards. In a flash, all doors of the other vehicles opened. Two dozen soldiers leaped out, dashing to the front clutching assault rifles and grenade launchers despite the lack of any apparent threat. People clapped rhythmically and schoolchildren began their synchronized welcome chants, shrill rhythms reverberating up the hill. The minister was not in the prime of his health, making slow progress on this symbolic trudge up the hill. Everywhere, villagers and leaders bowed politely, welcoming him with a nod. Others snapped pictures on their mobile phones. He waved imperially to the crowds, escorted by officials from the township and district, the convoy of cars following slowly behind (see figure 18).

The entourage eventually arrived at the township government office where two rows of mahogany chairs, facing one another, had been laid out under the porch. The minister sat down with his hosts, and drinking and greeting began in earnest. Flanked by other senior officials, his ever-attendant soldiers poured out his own home-brewed *lingzhi* liquor from a canteen into small shot glasses for those around him. My companion and I observed at a distance, as all those lurking at the ready lined up to toast and greet him—local officials from Mengmao district, ethnic Wa businessmen and guests from across the border in China, representatives from China's Ximeng County, and other Chinese businessmen. They came to "give face" to the Wa celebrations and to the officials of Longtan. They came as visual reminders of their presence, their plans, and requests. These were the visits, the being with, the slight bows and two-handed toasts, the drinking, smoking, laughter, and dining that drew people into wider circles of association, just as

FIGURE 18. Procession of vehicles follows a Wa official uphill to the township office during the New Harvest Celebrations, September 2014.

the minister's reputation and presence had honored the authorities of Longtan Township.

Lunch followed an hour of toasts, with meals prepared in the outdoor temporary kitchens behind the township offices. Hundreds of festival participants ate in shifts in the downstairs hall, while dining tables were laid out carefully in the upper rooms of the township office for officials. I pottered around all morning. Most of the local officials I knew were busy with duties; others I knew from other places. Many were unfamiliar. There was the nagging social anxiety of waiting. I had been in Wa Region for a few months, now only beginning to find my way among the various social circles. My companion had left; it was "not his place" to mingle with leaders. A tea hut where an enterprising Chinese businessman was giving out free samples offered a temporary haven. I savored the flavors together with the one-armed secretary from another township, who grunted niceties: "Have you eaten? Join us later. Have you yet visited the lake?" Everyone was waiting for lunch, after which the obligations of presence would be complete.

I joined the minister only as lunch was winding down, partly out of hesitation and partly to avoid being plied with liquor from the get-go. His standard refrain of "This liquor doesn't give you headaches" (a means of differentiating it from mass-produced or fake Chinese liquor in circulation) I knew to be false. One of the minister's personal bodyguards who recognized me earlier brought me into the dining room and whispered in the minister's ear. At this stage of the drinking (around 11 a.m. in the morning), the minister was largely inebriated, and raised his gaze, squinting foggily at me.

"I know we have met, but I do not recognize you now. You are a completely different person from before. You have become black," he mustered.

"The sun in the Wa hills is very strong"—I struggled a polite reply to this evaluation of my complexion. "You've met him before, Minister. That's why I didn't bring him in earlier," said Aik, a Wa businessman friend from the Chinese side who was seated next to the minister and was surely greasing the wheels for some cross-border venture. Aik proceeded to introduce me with kind words, the type of vouching-for so integral to the building of ties but also to preempt any accusation that he had been negligent in failing to invite a guest to the table.

"Sit with us." The minister went straight to the shot glass, as other soldiers rushed to add a chair next to him. We fumbled through the rest of the meal, spicy marinated MSG-infused chicken, stir-fried roots of dubious forms, braised pork, and clear vegetable soup. By this stage the frequency and volume of toasts had fallen markedly, and a Chinese businessman seated at our table, visibly drunk, had begun to rant on and on about how close he was to the leader. He put his arm around the minister's shoulder and continued to blabber away to the table: "This job of running the ministry, is one that only our minister can take on"—a standard-form flattery device adopted by countless Chinese businessmen. He soon crossed the line from intimacy to annoyance, just one slobber short of harassment. Since the soldiers were not of sufficient status to physically restrain the minister's guests, it was the unspoken task of other aides to intervene, gradually prising him away. Aik had not stepped in; a business rival was welcome to make a fool of himself. "Rest; we have all been up early" and other polite excuses were offered. The minister insisted it was fine, but others at the table repeatedly exhorted the businessman to "retire and rest." Pleasantries upheld propriety all around, and the minister had not needed to disrespect the drunk man himself.

While the New Harvest celebrations were proudly broadcast by Wa State TV on the evening news, outsiders might view such events as a cruel juxtaposition between "long-suffering" Wa villagers, or "serfs of the army" living in poverty, and the grossly unequal enrichment of elites in Wa Region through the extractive, narcotics, and plantation economies.[3] It was hard to discern levels of poverty, of course, in a subsistence economy. Social indicators, insofar as they can be reliably gathered, are dismal. Illiteracy is an estimated 77.5 percent, with 64.7 percent of people aged five to twenty-nine having never had schooling of any form. Only 8.1 percent of those aged twenty-five and above have had some primary school education.[4] Healthcare indicators are disheartening, even with the potentially overoptimistic statistics of the Wa Health Department.[5] Food security indicators are poor. The World Food Programme's Vulnerability Analysis and Mapping (VAM) branch classified 43 percent of surveyed households at "Borderline" and 25 percent as "Poor" in food consumption patterns, with 60 percent of households with less than two acres of land, and only 48 percent of households with access to irrigation.[6]

The provision of meals during a festival and the hosting of visitors from within and without the region were costly. Longtan township authorities were said to have lavished 3 million CNY (500,000 USD) on this New Harvest Festival, with dance performances on an outdoor stage with lighting and sound system, prize money for basketball and tug-of-war competitions, the fun-fair, and cooked meals over four days for thousands of people—officials, villagers, and soldiers alike. An observer attuned to other norms of governance might be forgiven for wondering if such money could be better spent on schools, healthcare, or other social services for a vulnerable rural population. One might also be deeply discomfited by the shows of adulation of a leader, welcomed by deferential subjects. Nor was there any accountability of public expenditure and income, no consultative input to policy priorities, no public or systematic vetting of investors in mining and the plantation industry, many of whom contributed large sums to these events.

I struggled to confront the nagging question posed by colleagues visiting from Yangon: "Why are we [WFP] still working here when the leaders are so rich? What are *they* doing for their people?" In this was implied, as was the general sense in Yangon when the UWSA was (rarely) discussed, why do Wa people not revolt against their rich leaders when conditions are dire and inequalities stark? Had the UWSA not just replaced the exploitative CPB with its own form of elite rule? Was the relation between leaders and people in Wa Region one of fear and coercion, an authoritarian regime? And if so, were outsiders condoning or perpetuating this repression?

These were questions asked from the very beginning, when the UN entered Wa Region in the late 1990s to work on opium substitution programs. Working with UWSA authorities, the community of development practitioners and observers quickly (and reasonably) concluded that the UWSA had "weak capacity" and was "hierarchical," "with a top-down leadership style and little room for participation in decision-making for local communities."[7] The late Ronald Renard, head of the United Nations Office on Drugs and Crime (UNODC) in Wa Region, concluded that Wa leaders "[often] did not have their people's best interests in mind," adding, "The next issue [after the opium ban] with the Wa is good governance."[8] Another UN official was quoted as saying, "The Wa are very much influenced by China, they want to make big projects. It is very difficult to make them understand community development."[9]

Nor did UWSA leaders help their own cause, often issuing callous soundbites that resembled a nonexistent form of trickle-down economics: "The Wa State wants overseas investment. Bosses get rich first, and then the Wa State can develop."[10] Elites' lavish expenditure on houses, cars, and construction projects were reportedly justified by Chairman Bao's assertion that "it was natural for the top man to have so much."[11]

How, then, should the UWSA be supported or reformed or have its "capacity" built? What might the terms of engagement be, for internationals to assist in "sustainable" or "equitable" development? What types of governance and public goods should they provide, and what were the ultimate goals for development here, or even an "exit strategy"? There were none of the conventional signs of civic participation—elections, civil society groups, or representation; popular support was accrued differently. In more charitable moments, outsiders wondered: What was it that inhabitants of Wa Region expected from their leaders?

But perhaps forms of governance in Wa Region are doing something else that does not adhere easily to the registers of state-led developmentalism and technobureaucratic rule. Here, celebrations and festivals are a spectacular mode of governing and establishing authority, with leaders providing for ordinary people through festivities and commensality.[12] Partaking in these collective rituals, individuals are located as recipients within the social hierarchy and members of the wider polity. The generosity and authority of the patrons are established and acknowledged through attendance and acceptance. Sometimes "providing for" backfires—another district organizing a similar festival was said to have borrowed large sums for an unremarkable celebration, becoming a target of mockery: "*qie*, they have no money but still want face," a friend snorted. Longtan Township, however, was one of the wealthiest of the twenty-four townships in Wa Region, bordering China with easier access to commerce and technology, and some silver and tin deposits that turned a handsome profit.

In this chapter, I explore the incongruities between logics of governance in Wa Region and the logics of governance espoused by the model of the developmentalist state. The logics of governance in Wa Region are, predictably, deeply intertwined with the logics of authority introduced in chapter 2: how powerful leaders should behave, the types of generosities, providing for, and obligations of protection placed upon them—all emphasizing the social value of autonomy. As such, governing was aimed more at demonstrating a "providing for" and protecting of subordinates and subjects than attaining bureaucratic competence, state legibility, and technocratic ability to administer the population. These logics of governance and authority were self-understandings that defined the political project of autonomy in Wa Region and turned governance into a field within which political relations with the outside were carefully navigated.

Governance in Wa Region was an arena where *governance by gesture* unfolded, most vividly seen in the New Harvest celebrations. The celebrations were not simply conspicuous consumption but a display of provision for the people. The extravagance of these celebrations has parallels with Judith Scheele's work among the "anarchic" Tubu of Northern Chad. Scheele argues that seeking wealth is driven "not by competition for scarce resources, nor indeed by an ideology of communal sharing, but rather by notions of competition for personal glory and cleverness: the only reason for accumulating wealth, in things and in people, is to be able to give it away publicly, in grandiose fashion."[13]

While wealth in Wa Region has other material imperatives such as raising an army to keep out enemies, extreme displays of generosity, even unto waste, were also expressions of personal autonomy and self-reliance. Extravagance demonstrated authority.

Further, festivals were theaters for instituting patronage relations, within and beyond the region. They were events through which businessmen within Wa Region and from across the border fostered relationships with local officials. Guests inscribe their names and their companies or departments upon arrival, leaving a cash gift recorded in the very public official ledger, a demonstration of generosity and means. Guests drop by to be seen, to craft a persona—flattering and earning favor, bringing informal proposals to big leaders in evening visits. The grandeur of hospitality reflects the state of township finances and their "ability" in management. Rather than a form of bureaucratized governance, regulations unfolded through patronage, seeking permission for ventures not by fulfilling an environmental protection or safety standards criteria but by earning favor and trust. Due diligence procedures were affected through shot glasses and skewered meat.

Governance and Its Ends

A recent field of political science dubbed "rebel governance" seeks to make sense of nonstate governance by insurgents, secessionists, de facto states, and separatists.[14] Scholars examine the internal dynamics, organizational structures, and "set of actions insurgents engage in to regulate the social, political, and economic life of non-combatants during war."[15] By shifting attention away from the violent actions and criminal conduct of insurgents during wartime and toward the interim management of resources and administration, rebel governance research has sought to provide a more accurate picture of civilian life under the governing mechanisms and authority of armed groups. The bulk of these studies examine contextual factors and attributes of different armed groups to account for variations in their forms of governance.[16]

Mampilly, for instance, reasonably imagines rebel governance as an interactional process. He combines analyses that focus on elite motivations and ideologies with materialist political economy explanations that examine how rebel governance is shaped by the nature of its funding (relying on either external or internal support). For him, rebel governance is a process of adaptations between the initial preferences of armed group elites and the changing political and social environment of the movements' histories: "Interactions can have important effects on governance performance.... The agency of rebel leaders is restricted by other actors with whom they are forced into interaction."[17] His processual approach avoids a crude reductive analysis—that rebels are either criminals seeking to maximize profit or bandits settling into the process of state formation.[18] Instead, he points to rebel governance as "counterstate sovereignty"—in competition with the state, yet mimicking it symbolically to build legitimacy—with a series of hypotheses about different attributes such as secessionism, centralization, Maoism, and factionalism and how these affect the nature of rebel governance.[19]

Many such rebel governance approaches appear to make two assumptions about the ends of governance. First, they assume that "rebels" are oriented toward *optimizing* their organization and administrative institutions—creating as effective as possible bureaucracies, public services, or legibility projects—ultimately for military or material benefits.[20] This purportedly helps rebels to recruit people as participants or supporters, ensure their compliance, or gather economic resources and funding. The link between "better" rebel governance and increasing military capacity, however, has been called into question.[21] Second, rebel governance studies often assume that effective governance aims to build *legitimacy*—to win over hearts and minds internally through providing organization and social services for people or through whitewashing international reputations externally vis-à-vis outside audiences and to gain desired recognition.[22]

But governance unfolds alongside other logics of authority in local political culture. It goes beyond an instrumentality of outcomes, not merely oriented toward efficient management of resources (recruitment and revenue) or the accrual of legitimacy (internal or external). Here, Hoffman and Vermeijen's study of the Mai-Mai is instructive. For them, rebel governance is not solely about institutions and leaders but a form of governmentality where "clusters of techniques of Mai-Mai rule, relating to ethnicity and custom, spirituality, stateness, and patronage and protection" shape political relations between leaders and followers.[23] This less common approach broadens notions of governance to include the role of sociocultural values and practices.

Governance in Wa Region must first be seen as informed by local logics of authority, and itself as a realm navigated by the UWSA's elites and leaders to manage political relations with Burmese, Chinese, and international nongovernmental organizations (INGOs) across boundaries. Governance was both a mode of *performing authority* and *building political relations*, part of the processes through which relational autonomy is constituted. First, it involved a gestural performance of authority by powerholders themselves, rather than simply a form of communication (or propaganda) for audiences—whether "the people" or the "international community." Reputation management was more complex than a whitewashing of the armed group's sins. The UWSA leadership was not trying to convince outsiders that all drugs had been eradicated (security services knew better), that its administration was being reformed, or that it cared for the well-being of everyday people. It did not aim for "good governance" and efficient management of its resources. Rather, leaders were acknowledging the norms and expectations that came with authority. A "proper" authority should show that it was listening to and aware of the needs of the people; that it was aware of its obligations to neighboring state governments in drug enforcement; that it was aware of the expectations to provide for subordinates with generosity and magnanimity. Governance was *gesturing* toward an acknowledgment of the social expectations of authority.

Second, governance was an arena through which relations with the outside were managed. Relations operated across boundaries at different scales—

building and balancing ties with Myanmar, China, and the international community. Assistance programs were conduits for building cross-border ties, by granting access to outsiders and accepting aid in return—the provision of healthcare services across the townships, the distribution of grain and food supplies, and the expansion of an education system. It was a realm through which obligations were created or reciprocities refused. Rather than regarding material assistance as central to the development of Wa Region, Wa elites (despite their public rhetoric of gratitude) were more concerned with navigating political ties with the outside through development assistance, to ensure autonomy. While accepting gifts afforded the giver recognition and respect, these same gifts also created debts. UWSA leaders did not want obligations they could not fulfill.

Consequently, measuring the UWSA administration by "good governance" or standards of efficiency misses the point—this is not mainly what the UWSA aspires to. If governance is first seen as a means of performing authority and building relations, then it becomes a domain for understanding UWSA officials' interactions with the international community. These are the local terms and sensibilities upon which to orient any external assistance efforts. Governance is a domain for making sense of the UWSA's engagement in development initiatives and their moments of candid, self-critical reflections on the inadequacies of their administration. Their actions were not about legitimacy as social or political capital to be accrued but rather situated in a local moral economy, where gestures acknowledged expectations—what people expected of their leaders, what the international community and neighboring countries expected of the UWSA. This is not an excuse for failures of healthcare provision or for dire education services but a means of understanding governance in local terms.

Skeptical Audiences

The influx of development professionals and INGOs after 2005 for opium substitution programs in Wa Region opened new interactions across different political fields.[24] A high of nine INGOs were present in Wa Region in 2008, working mainly in the livelihoods and health sectors, constructing water and sanitation systems, agricultural inputs and fish farming, and immunization programs. Very quickly, INGOs found the truly ramshackle social services, skeletal public infrastructure, and rudimentary record-keeping to be a dereliction of the duties of any administration. Resource management was poor, with rapacious extractive industries in mining and logging. Land grabs by powerful leaders went unchallenged. Timber was long gone before a 2014 edict outlawed logging. The seemingly unsustainable hunting and trade of endangered wildlife offended external sensibilities. The UWSA administration perpetuated glaring inequalities in livelihoods, healthcare, water and sanitation, and quality of housing between elites and everyday people. Political appointments in the UWSA were seemingly based on nepotism, social capital, and connections.[25] Nor was there any separation between lawmakers, enforcement, and policy implementers, despite the organizational lines between party, military, and administration. Young men were conscripted into the army per household, with no appeals or exemptions. Observers were troubled by their inability to convince the UWSA leadership of the need to alter these "bad governance" practices.

Of course, by "good governance," observers were referencing Western norms of strong institutions, a professionalized bureaucracy undergoing "capacity-building," participatory procedures, anti-corruption, empowerment, and transparency initiatives.[26] INGO or UN visitors to Wa Region often had reasonable doubts about the UWSA leadership, finding Wa leaders unable to articulate a feasible plan for developing their area.[27] There was no "consultation" or civic participation, no representation of the people's needs, no civil society groups. UNODC staffer Jeremy Milsom was more sympathetic, suggesting that the UWSA lacked support (assumed to be vital) from outside: "Pursuing its development goals in relative isolation, the [Wa administration] has embarked on a number of sometimes poorly informed and poorly planned initiatives to support its people after 2005."[28] Yet it was precisely because these development workers were allowed access to the top rungs of the UWSA leadership that they were able to gather insights into "leadership styles." Similar access to the higher echelons of the Tatmadaw or Myanmar government would have been, and remains, unimaginable.

One also notices the striking parallels between contemporary "good governance" criticisms and patronizing colonial attitudes of the past. "They buy fancy cars, gadgets, and weapons to cover their insecurities," a fellow aid worker argued, depicting the UWSA as amateur rulers, blinded by their wealth, ignorant and lacking in technical capacity. Early British and Chinese travelers and administrators visiting the Wa hills downplayed the ability of local Wa to work the mines within their areas: "The barbarians here do not know the methods, and *all the extraction and management is done by Han people*. When the Kawa come, they are treated with liquor and food, for fear of otherwise provoking their anger and stirring up trouble."[29] All this was despite Wa smiths being reputed in Shan sources for mining and processing iron. Elsewhere, the American missionary Harold Young infantilized the Wa temperament when discussing political feuds and headhunting raids: "The Wa are extremely sensitive and take offense at very trivial things."[30] He recorded accounts from the 1920s of how feuds were triggered at the smallest insult, the whimsical and unreasonable demands Wa raiders made on their neighbors, concluding with critiques of "Wa nature and its apathy and indifference to emotion or excitement."[31]

Other moralizing undertones were embedded in embellished colonial accounts of Wa insalubrious and basic living conditions: "The state of dirt of both men and women is absolutely beyond belief and is only limited by the point beyond which extraneous matter refuses to adhere to human flesh."[32] The lack of interest in engaging the outside—"not an enterprising, or an ambitious race"—conflicted with acknowledgments of their grit: "extraordinarily diligent cultivators [of opium] . . . independent, energetic, ingenious, and industrious."[33] These accounts contributed to notions of Wa supposed disinterest in innovation, yet malleable under the forces of education and civilization. Implicit was the potential for such a civilizing mission to relieve them from the throes of ignorance and backwardness, a theme highly resonant with the treatment of minority groups in China.[34]

British journalist Alan Winnington, visiting Chinese Communist Party work teams in the Wa hills in the 1950s, noted that "tradition and superstition have to be surmounted before any appreciable results can be got in farming," for "farming was, and remains, of the most primitive kind.[35] An area of jungle is burned off and the land scratched a little before the seed of dry upland rice is scattered by hand. No fertilizer is used . . . animals are not used."[36] He described the painstaking efforts to introduce the Wa to wet-field rice farming, which would double the yields from the same seeds.[37] Under the supposed threat of having their heads removed should crops fail, the Chinese cadres introduced the Wa to the co-operative system, with shared use of buffalo for ploughing, diversified crops, fertilizers, new planting methods, and equipment distributed by the Chinese government. The Wa were gradually taught "not to quarrel and fight," with feuds mediated by the party's cadres, and headhunting itself "shown" to be unnecessary for a good yield.[38] The Wa hills had no shortage of skeptical outsiders who questioned the effectiveness of local techniques.

626: Spectacles of Reform

Some aspects of UWSA governance appeared to be explicitly engineered for external audiences, with a view toward reshaping its image, in particular its role in narcotics production. The UWSA's primary reputation as the drug lords of the Golden Triangle was hard to shake, not least because production and trafficking were still going on. Drugs were the primary issue that placed Wa Region on the maps of UN and Western governments from the mid-1990s—the few books available on the UWSA had covers adorned with poppy fields or soldiers.[39] As early as 1990, the UWSA began planning for a ban on opium-growing and trafficking in their territory, eventually gaining support from the UNODC in 1998.[40] They had learned of the reputational costs following the US "war on drugs" and from the experiences of other groups in the Golden Triangle, attracting sanctions and the threat of military action.[41] The draconian ban took effect on June 26, 2005 ("626"), penalizing offenders with jail and heavy fines for the growing and sale of opium.

Sympathetic UN observers argued that the region was not prepared for this transition, that the "misguided image" of the UWSA as a dangerous drug cartel had forced the new leadership to enact the opium ban at a drastic pace, imperiling the livelihoods of its own people.[42] Poor planning, harsh measures, and the lack of appropriate development assistance sent hundreds of thousands of farmers deeper into poverty. Heavily food-insecure Wa farmers had become dependent on opium as a cash crop, de-skilled by capitalism—in expanding their poppy fields, "they grew fewer food crops and produced less tools and handicrafts so that they now lack the initiative and skills to survive without opium."[43] Consequently, the UNODC's opium substitution projects began in 1998, bringing support for livelihoods, agriculture, healthcare, and infrastructure to the UWSA.

Other observers were dubious about the ban's success. The UNODC was accused of naively giving legitimacy to the propagandist attempts of a narco-trafficking organization; while UNODC believed Wa Region to be responsible for 40 percent of Myanmar opium production in 2004 (16,750 hectares), the US government alleged the figure to be 55 to 65 percent.[44] Even if satellite pictures could disprove the mass production of opium, observers I spoke to were unrelenting: "They must be growing it somewhere you cannot see." Strangely, while opium cultivation in Myanmar declined from 1997 to 2006, it then doubled from 2006 to 2012 after the Wa opium ban, shifting from Wa, Kokang, and Monglar Regions to other parts of Southern Shan State, driven by a price stimulus.[45] Heroin-refining and trafficking were even harder to monitor, and it was impossible to convince outsiders of their cessation. Observers also noticed the marked shift to methamphetamines, seizures of crystal meth across Myanmar jumping from about five thousand kilograms in 2008 to more than twenty-five thousand kilograms in 2017, and meth tablets from 25 million to 450 million in the same period.[46] Statistics, however, often remained at aggregate levels for the whole Golden Triangle, with distribution between regions unclear or not meaningful. The United States, refusing to concede that its sanctions and strategies had failed, gradually withdrew support for the UNODC. The UNODC project in Wa Region closed in 2008, and its presence in Myanmar was significantly reduced, with

FIGURE 19. The Tenth Anniversary Commemoration of the eradication of drugs in Pangkham, June 2015.

most projects petering out by 2010.[47] Drug eradication was a thankless affair for everyone involved; it was hard to track trafficking flows, harder to boost livelihoods, and even harder to disprove accusations.

The People's Park field, a football pitch during the week, was today a flurry of activity. Several rusty steel cauldrons stood on the concrete track right in front of the grandstand, filled to the brim with colorful pills and powders half-wrapped in plastic packaging (see figure 19). Contingents of hundreds of schoolchildren, "representatives of the people" (Chn: *qunzhong daibiao*), and soldiers from the Pangkham military units lined up on the grass behind, settling in for the speeches. A large banner was strung up over the People's Park grandstand, "Celebrating the 10th Anniversary of Wa Region's Eradication of Opium." At one corner of the field was the ambulance donated by a Chinese healthcare NGO, with police cars deployed at the park entrance, dark navy uniforms and caps surveilling the crowds. Under the grandstand, VIPs and invited guests arrived at the rows of tables set up facing the field, with small cards in front of each seat indicating the name and title of the official. Several top Politburo leaders were in attendance, but not the chairman himself, who had not been seen in public for more than a year, reportedly in an extended period of poor health. Today's leading dignitary was the UWSA vice-chairman, the customary political speechmaker.

It was not a particularly formal affair. Despite the neat lines of students on the field raising placards exhorting others to "value life, avoid drugs," few seemed interested in the speeches delivered by the vice-chairman, the head of police, and two others. Senior UWSA officials were in attendance, however, sitting introspectively in eight long rows under the grandstand. There was little gravity or intrigue with this annual affair. The officials and dignitaries were barely listening; they were smoking cigarettes and taking frequent bathroom breaks. Some chatted among themselves or fiddled with phones in the rows behind, mingling with old friends. Far off on the opposite side of the park, a hundred or so onlookers gathered, perched on the low gallery steps that ringed the field.

I had been given a front-row seat on the VIP platform, just next to the minister of agriculture and the UWSA political spokesman. "What drugs are these they're burning?" I inquired. "Oh, I couldn't even tell you. I don't recognize these drugs myself," came the reply. I looked at the spokesman quizzically (a hardened member from the CPB era and now on the Central Committee) but chose not to pursue this line of questioning. "The BBC and other foreign journalists wanted to come and witness this event, but they weren't able to because of the security situation; the Myanmar government would not allow," he explained. I was not particularly close to the spokesman but was still surprised and vaguely offended that he was feeding me the party line.

Shortly after the speeches ended, soldiers came to the front and doused the cauldrons in kerosene. The students and soldiers were ordered to move backward using military commands, and VIPs were invited below to incinerate the scourges of society. Photographers from the Wa News Agency were on hand to catalogue this year's symbolic repudiation of the white powders and pink and red pills. Wielding wooden torches, Central Committee members and their guests from the front row proceeded toward the cauldrons. A military commander lit my torch, and we winced and ducked away from the flames, shoving the torches into the crystalline forms and retreating from the fumes. The ignited meth was the signal for the dignitaries and grateful schoolchildren to disperse. The fires were left to burn. Someone else would return to clean up the mess after.

After the event, I had lunch with a friend from one of the ministries, recounting my exchange with the spokesman. He snorted and slapped his thigh. "Hah! What nonsense! No journalists wanted to come; they don't want to look like fools! In previous years they invited the media for these ceremonies, mainly the Chinese media, but the flow of drugs continued, and they knew they were being taken for a ride. They stopped turning up. So even though it is the tenth anniversary, this year we have decided not to make such a big deal of it."

"The Chinese put a lot of pressure on the leadership to make sure that drugs do not enter China. It makes them very angry, and occasionally someone here has to take the rap for it." We referenced a handful of commanders and deputies who had "retired" early—"Yes, of course the Chinese know who is doing the drugs; they have very good intelligence over here. If it goes elsewhere, they are not so bothered."

Action and enforcement did occur, and they were not mere shows. In the two months prior to the celebration, nearly one thousand drug users were arrested and sent to prison, detained at spontaneous checkpoints set up along the main thoroughfares in Wa Region. The 2009 Wa Yearbook had pages filled with photos of seized drugs and sorry offenders standing in front of the contraband spread, their heads bowed.[48] Security cooperation with China was a demonstration of willingness to collaborate and fulfill the obligations of "toughness on crime." The Wa news (TV and Magazine) was replete with prisoner exchanges. Shaved heads in handcuffs were herded across the bridge into China, marched away by stern Chinese police.[49] Wa leaders frequently blamed crime on Chinese nationals: "Those here are running away from the law in China. Many are thieves and dealers to fuel their addiction." The central debate about the UWSA involvement in drugs was whether leaders were running the operations themselves, providing cover for affiliated businessmen or syndicates doing it, or unable to control fully smaller traders and producers within their territory.[50]

All were entirely possible. Statistics were constantly contested, reports opaque about sources, and outsiders often had no means of cross-checking or evaluating the feasibility in local geographies.[51] "Criminals will always be criminals," an international enforcement officer based in an embassy in Yangon once retorted, after I delivered a briefing about engaging the UWSA. Despite thirty years of abject failure in drug enforcement, few seemed receptive to alternative views on the logics and values of the "criminals." Autonomy was a double-edged sword. Operating in the gray areas of the state also meant the inability to prove and convince others of the sincerity of any eradication efforts.[52]

The easiest explanation for the opium ban was to shed the drug lord reputation and build a more legitimate organization that could engage others on the regional and national stage. By transiting to drugs with more discrete production processes, such as methamphetamines, Wa businessmen could preserve income while avoiding bad press. But the opium ban and spectacles of drug enforcement could not have been primarily a quest for legitimacy, or a shoddily orchestrated ruse to pull the wool over the eyes of inspectors or foreigners. Wa leaders knew that even a visitor, much less security agents, staying a couple of weeks would easily see through appearances. A visitor might even get a straightforward admission from certain members of the Wa leadership themselves. Everything was an open secret if one knew whom to ask.

Instead, drug enforcement and drug-burning spectacles were about UWSA performances of authority, demonstrating an understanding of the basic obligations of governing a polity, acknowledging responsibility for the burden, as it were. The UWSA was not seriously expecting to fool anyone (other than the truly gullible)—but rather to perform gestures that showed it knew how a governing body should operate, how it should take narcotics issues seriously. Elites were aware of expectations that they not transgress certain limits: "Don't be too much" (Chn: *buyao guofen*)—drugs should not be openly trafficked without consequence. Brazen and identifiable breaches of international conventions would cause diplomatic problems for the Myanmar and Chinese states (made to look bad or forced to act), necessitating sanctions or isolation of Wa Region. Performing authority was about taking action to live up to the perceived expectations of the outside, at least symbolically. Drugs could never be eradicated (even if there was real intent to do so), but out of respect to neighbors, gestures must be made.

In this way, drug enforcement was also a mode through which relations with the outside were managed. The UWSA demonstrated its awareness of the rules of a civilized political society, that it knew where the boundaries were. As the Chinese phrase went, "*yisi yidian*" (lit. little bit of meaning), referring to doing something for the meanings it entailed. The phrase also implied complicity between the doer and audience of the performance, neither calling out realities. While not entirely efficacious, the act itself was symbolic and communicative of an appropriate sentiment and intent. The UWSA partook in drug enforcement training from China and hosted visits from international visitors to showcase its contribution to Myanmar's collective action against narcotics. Governance here was an arena for navigating neighbors, managing one's reciprocities with, and autonomy from, them.

Incongruous Registers of Governance

Caught up in a traffic jam caused by an errantly parked car, I entered the meeting late. I was an observer, called along as the UN official resident in town. An INGO had arrived in Pangkham to engage the UWSA on the issue of child soldiers one dusty morning in May 2015. Wa External Relations officials were not enthused: "Ah, it's these same issues they want to talk about again; nobody wants to listen anymore." The Wa authorities were not confident of being understood, the criticisms were long-standing, and the answers were always the same. The Wa vice-chairman and spokesperson were set up on one side of the meeting room, with the two Western representatives on the other. Posters for immunization programs and HIV interventions decorated the walls. Because they had not brought a Chinese translator with them, English was first translated into Burmese by the INGO's staffer, and then from Burmese into Chinese by the Wa spokesman. Jane, the INGOs officer, presented the vice-chairman with the UN secretary-general's *Report on Children and Armed Conflict*—the "list of shame," she called it—that first listed the UWSA as an organization that recruited or used children from 2006.[53] The Wa spokesperson bowed and received the document with both hands, a ritual gesture of politeness. Jane went through the UN's "Six Grave Violations" of children's rights in armed conflict and proposed that if the Wa were to show commitment to an "Action Plan," which ultimately entailed access, verification, and demobilization, the international community would then provide assistance to support the children.[54]

"Yes, it is true, we do have children in the army, but we are in the business of protecting them too. Many are orphans or from poor families. We agree with the six violations you have pointed out, but Wa is a different place."

"Yes, this is what armed groups all over the world have told us," Jane said as she smiled diplomatically; the structural similarities from her vast global experience were clear.[55]

The vice-chairman was obviously prepared for the meeting, copy of the Wa Basic Law[56] in hand, pages flagged at the relevant sections:

1. Protection of children within orphanages is a Wa government duty.
2. Under-eighteens cannot be deployed on the front lines.
3. Under-fourteens cannot be charged as adults for offences.
4. The death penalty for those who abuse children.

He had a whole series of explanations for the presence of children in their ranks:

- "We lost ten thousand troops in the wars; there are many children to take care of."
- "There is a warrior code among us: it is prestigious to be in the army; one cannot be respected if they are not in the army. The children will cry if not allowed to join."
- "There are fifty thousand households across Wa Region, and many have family members in the army. Some are with both parents in the army."
- "One thousand orphans are newly produced every year."
- "There is much poverty in households; we have to send to the army to take care of them and feed them."
- "There is honor in service—much like the Burmese who send their children to the monastery."

He did not mention the conscription policies of the UWSA requiring at least one male per household to enlist in the army or administration, with two for larger families.[57]

"There is almost perfect overlap in our objectives.... We sit on common ground together," came the visitors' acknowledgment.

The Wa representatives grew more confident as the conversation wore on, leaning back in their chairs and grinning periodically. The spokesperson stopped taking notes, even answering without translating for the vice-chairman. Polite smiles soon faded as it became clear that the conversation was making little progress. The Wa explanations had received no clear rebuttals from the visitors, yet the visitors were not conceding their position.

"Well, having heard our explanation, should you still insist on keeping us on the list, there is nothing we can do," the vice-chairman pronounced, mock bewilderment spreading across his face. The room filled with stifled, embarrassed laughter. It seemed to them that the INGO had created the problem by placing them on the list, and it was within the INGO's power to take them off it. If it did not, then surely the INGO was causing the problem. This was how power should work: a decision maker listened and then decided.

One of the visitors told me afterward how she was surprised at the frankness of the leadership, making little attempt to conceal the role of children or their training conditions. They did not see how this placed children and teenagers in vulnerable positions to begin with, susceptible to psychological and behavioral illness, given their accepted roles in farming and hard labor. They did not see "ideological" indoctrination as worrying. Another Wa official remarked, "They must understand that these are not the same child soldiers as in Africa, where they are all on drugs shooting civilians." Unlike other EAO authorities, UWSA logics of governance contained no elements of anything approaching a "human rights discourse," making it hard to find common principles to appeal to.[58]

On the second day of discussions, the vice-chairman changed his tack: "To be clear, what we have are child student soldiers. They are there to learn and school. We too are involved in protecting these children." Discussions were complicated by the fact that the nuances and sequencing of the "Action Plan" were inaccurately translated. It was unclear if assistance would arrive only after the child soldiers had been demobilized or during the process.

The distinction between a commitment to planning for future action and a promise to demobilize was lost not just in translation but through an asymmetry in registers of how development processes and commitments worked. For the Wa leaders, it went like this: "We agree with the six points. We are trying to reduce the children in our army. But what we cannot do now, we do not want to promise."

The Wa communication strategy was poor, with moments of brutal honesty demonstrating how uncontroversial the topic was to the Wa leadership. "In fact, we prosecuted a commander who beat to death a sixteen-year-old soldier for running away."

When told that one of the visitors had urgent business down in Yangon and would leave the following day, the vice-chairman sniggered, "Tell him the work has not even begun and he is leaving. [This is what we mean], you will help a little, then you will leave, but we have to take care of these children long-term." The jibe was strategically mistranslated back to the guest by his Burmese staffer: "The vice-chairman wishes you will stay for longer."

Governance for the Wa leaders was about first acknowledging and addressing the needs of people—not necessarily fulfilling or solving them. The Wa administration often lacked the commitment and organization to respond adequately to social needs, poverty, and orphans. It also seemed to lack concerted political will to spend capital on these fronts; most of it was retained for the military or for individual accumulation. In fact, providing for children in military institutions brought both goals in alignment (though caring for orphans was not the sole objective under a militarized region).

Yet governance entailed demonstrating *some* provision, within reason, for subjects' material needs. As a responsible moral authority, Wa authorities were expected (and expected themselves) to respond to both child poverty and the charges of child soldiering from the outside. Much like the drug enforcement campaigns and spectacles, performing authority meant displaying an awareness of the problems and acknowledging the responsibility to take them seriously. This is somewhat like what Louisa Lombard calls "promissory politics" of capital-based elites in the Central African Republic. Nonetheless, Lombard's assessment of the state there betrays a somewhat more cynical manipulation: "the use of promises about state-generated future welfare to demonstrate authority yet without assuming direct personal responsibility for people's plights or otherwise giving them any direct means to claim entitlements."[59] In Wa Region, follow-up action was often not efficacious due to the lack of organization and the inability or unwillingness to make such organization happen.

Herein also lay the incongruity between the INGO and outsiders' understandings of governance and the Wa leadership's. Wa authorities would entertain the discussions as was their obligation, but policies and substance could not be discussed without first building relations of trust through reciprocity. The INGO was only in town for five days. It did not trust the outsiders ("Why should we listen to your way of doing things?"), nor did the outsiders demonstrate pledge assistance by making material commitments ("You ask us to promise, but what can you provide besides surveys and inspections?"). An "Action Plan" was worth nothing without tangible material provision. This was why collaboration with INGOs was difficult; it was not (mainly) a case of unenlightened leaders but the different systems and procedures through which governance was expected to materially function. Governance was first gestural and relational before it could become effective and instrumental.

At the end of the meeting, the vice-chairman announced that he was delegating the task of liaison to the head of the Health Bureau, who delegated it to his deputy almost immediately, a clear sign of Wa disinterest that seemed lost on the visitors. Over the next few days, the Wa administration assisted by organizing trainings for cadres and military commanders on child protection issues. A second summation meeting was held at the end of five days, the workshops held, the boxes checked, and the delegation returned to Yangon. Wa State media misrepresented the outcome the following day: the organization had heard the explanation and would return to Yangon to try their best to remove the Wa from their list. No follow-ups ever materialized; the INGO turned its efforts elsewhere, to another, "easier" or "more cooperative" armed group.

In 2018, Wa State TV uploaded onto YouTube a series of programs on child "student-soldiers" training (unarmed, without insignias) in military fatigues in school. Videos that to external audiences might be incriminating evidence were to the UWSA a proud showcase of facilities they had built to educate and feed children.[60]

Gestures of Governance

UWSA governance was less about creating a rationalized bureaucracy or biopolitical apparatus to control population and territory, and much less about effectively winning over the support of people through optimal economic development and social services. Instead, Wa leaders sought to live up to the social expectations that came with their authority—at the very least, to listen to petitions and to acknowledge them. Anything else was a bonus. Governance was not "solution" oriented, not even process oriented but about addressing obligations by granting an audience (or else have one's moral authority diminished); it did not require solving them through the technicalities of Weberian state-metrics. The powerful were expected to show *some* generosity, adopting the appropriate signals, even if the final material provision was inadequate or minimal. At its minimum, this entailed safeguarding the inhabitants of Wa Region from

Tatmadaw attacks, and allowing land use and customary land ownership. Governance in Wa Region was through gesture.

This was manifestly not how the registers of "good governance" operated for development workers and NGOs, the only outsiders to be involved in Wa governance. Their senses of what governance entailed focused on both process and outcomes. NGO (and UN) procedures were ostensibly about data gathering, fund-raising, programming, and implementing projects. Providing services first required understanding needs, ensuring access and approvals, designing, and then implementing interventions.

The decentralization of governance structures in Wa Region meant that aggregate statistics from the central authorities in Pangkham were unreliable. The ministries had little interest in township-level policies; they only gave broad unenforced guidelines. Authority came with decisions and instructions and less the responsibility to implement.[61] Farmers told of township agriculture officers giving them lessons on planting sugarcane, "but they didn't provide any inputs." This work of directing labor (Chn: *zhidao gongzuo*) was deeply associated with Communist governance. But for development workers, it was difficult to confirm and collate aggregate statistics. The differing degrees of participation rendered these statistics less meaningful. In fact, the previous Multiple Indicators Cluster Survey (MICS) had been conducted by UNICEF back in 2005, with little follow-up since then. Staff and funding shortages, linguistic diversity at the village level, poor accessibility for security reasons, and the lack of donor interest to begin with complicated the task further. Program managers had to deploy survey staff not based on technical skills but the right linguistic skills—Wa, Shan, Lahu, Akha—or kinship ties among the different townships for access. Even units of enumeration were not standardized. Weight was estimated by baskets, for husked and unhusked rice, or land area by the numbers of rubber trees growing on them. "What will you give us? There are all these people coming here to ask questions, but they always leave and never return" was a refrain I commonly heard from officials.

Programming interventions of INGOs required such data, showing comparative need and lobbying headquarters for resources. How might one represent comparative indicators of poverty and underdevelopment when Wa officials were indifferent to outsiders conducting surveys prior to providing something in return? Needs were clear to local staffers, but they needed to be quantified and placed in comparison with other regions of the country; Wa Region was but one of many needy areas. Food security surveys, for instance, would map out the different townships in Wa Region based on a sampling of villages and households, and assign a color—red, orange, yellow, and green. This was based on a "food consumption score" calculated by recall surveys of diet adequacy and diversity: "How many of these types of vegetables have you eaten in the past week?" The fear was that poor execution or picking the "wrong" villages might color a township yellow or even green, instead of the red and orange it was "known" to be. How would needs of such complex socioeconomic profiles be conveyed in questionnaires from a four-day excursion, augmented by the "correct" statistics, and translated adequately into the registers and languages of the development community? UWSA authorities were not the only ones wary of surveys.

Working in Wa Region was more costly than working in other parts of the country. It certainly pushed the limits of cost-effectiveness. Transportation and travel costs were high. The overland journey from Lashio to Pangkham took ten to twelve hours, not including the time taken to stop over at the Tar Gaw Et Bridge, where rice had to be unloaded onto smaller trucks, brought across, then loaded back onto the bigger trucks, to comply with the load-bearing limits of the bridge. Under such metrics, and with a push to increase beneficiary numbers, Wa Region became a poor candidate for operation or expansion. An NGO could reach two to three times the number of beneficiaries for the same amount of funds in Karen or Mon States.

Field staff had to figure out local networks of authority and associate effectively with local officials but had to be rotated every few years to prevent excessive familiarity. Temperaments differed from township to township. Logistics operators mark on maps the villages that are inaccessible to trucks during the rainy season, others even to bikes. They learned the schools and storehouses that township offices might provide, to pre-position rice rations before the roads closed off for rainy season. They built good relations with transportation bosses to persuade them to submit bids for contract tenders to meet requirements. The Wa administration simply did not operate at the same levels of detail.

The critiques I heard about UN procedures were revealing of these different registers. "One by one they must go up and sign on the form for the ten kilograms of rice they receive; what a waste of time! We are not here to steal the rice. It's such a small amount anyway."

"[A minister] was told to take a photo with the bags of rice received, but it had the Japanese flag [of the donors] on it, and he hates the Japanese. I had to persuade him to just get it over and done with."

"You are here, and you can see the situation, but why is it that your people in Yangon do not understand?"

"If you are going to build a school, just build it. Why are you asking the villagers to contribute sand and stone?"

Participation, consultation, sustainability, pilot schemes, gender sensitivity, and even monitoring and evaluation tasks were a series of activities that seemed cumbersome, unnecessarily exacting, and stingy to local authorities. Some NGOs interpreted this as "resistance" to their methods, or a lack of "awareness," and deemed the UWSA "difficult to work with." In many cases, Wa officials appealed for interventions to be altered to fit their conceptions, and although they often relented ultimately out of politeness: "You should do it your way, but do consider our request"—this undoubtedly dampened their enthusiasm.

Development workers in Wa Region quickly learn that their projects are precarious. The political climate was constantly changing, and from nine NGOs in Wa Region in 2008, only three were left by 2013. Donors' funding priorities changed after the eradication of opium, since drugs shifted from a developmental issue to a security one (methamphetamine production carried out covertly by smaller groups rather than poppy by opium farmers). US sanctions on UWSA leaders made for tricky donor relations with NGO projects, and the UNODC project closed down. By 2012, the concerns of the international community gradually shifted toward the peace process and humanitarian aid (particularly in conflict areas of Rakhine and Kachin States), and longer-term development projects were more sustainable in the relative stability of lowland Myanmar. Senior UWSA officials were perplexed after the mass NGO withdrawals: "We have gradually learned to work with you [since 1998], and now you are leaving before the work is complete."

Denial of access was used a bargaining chip. Following the 2009 Kokang crisis, the Tatmadaw imposed bans and restrictions on the movement of supplies and international staff into Wa Region, blocking international assistance as a means of pressuring the UWSA to sign a new ceasefire. Once, when a request for international guests to visit our WFP office was turned down at the last minute by the Myanmar government, I visited a Wa minister to offer apologies and cancel the arrangements we had made. Instead, he lifted his chin with a quiet smile, inhaling deeply from a cigarette: "It is as we had told you earlier: of course it would be denied. This is what they always do, to pressure us." But concerns about aid strengthening the UWSA were surely misplaced—several sacks of rice and a couple of schools would hardly add to their arsenal.

Development assistance was then a modality of inclusion in the state, a test of the state's sincerity and respect, not out of desperate need. Yet rather than expand patronage to create relations of obligation, the Tatmadaw's isolation of Wa Region from foreign contact inadvertently pushed them closer to dependence on China. Development assistance was crucial not for material aid but for the political relationships it entailed. The UWSA did not seek meager material benefits. Money was not a problem for the merchants of the shadow economy, nor were schools, rice, clinics, and roads. Assistance flows were a litmus test of relations between Wa Region and its neighbors—Myanmar, China, and the international community. Refusals reflected deteriorating relations. The laissez-faire 1990s under Khin Nyunt contrasted with the disdain and stinginess of the present government: "They say they are the national government, the leader [Chn: *laoda*], but what have they given? They show little interest in providing for this region." Withdrawals and withholding were seen as forms of stinginess, a lack of commitment to continuing a presence in Wa Region. It mattered little that the assistance was reduced but that presence was continued, that channels were maintained. In this manner, governance provided a space for what Julia Elyachar calls "phatic labor," the work done to keep channels and connections open.[62]

Representing Need

Understanding the UWSA's particular form of gestural governance is not simply a call for cultural relativist accommodation, or pointing out how "indigenous" knowledge should be equally valued. It was also a practical problem of translation. If in fact UWSA governance operated through different political registers and modalities, then how would development assistance function within Wa Region? How to engage with issues of inequality, poverty, and authoritarian forms of governance, if these performances of authority were so central to the Wa political project? How does one represent such dismal economic, educational, and health indicators, without slipping into the easy portrayal of the UWSA and its leadership as simplistically ignorant, negligent, or callous?

Inequality was indeed jarring and materially apparent as powerful Humvees ploughed through the hills past ramshackle villages and struggling crops. Skeptical political observers I spoke to in Yangon suggested that keeping their people poor and uneducated was a means of ensuring UWSA rule and suppressing dissent. But it did not fit in with the distinctive pride that the UWSA took in its autonomy and flourishing. Governance in Wa Region had its internal contradictions: callous inequality was interspersed with genuine appeals for assistance from some of the Wa political leadership and attempts by many local officials to improve the conditions for their people. "Good governance" rhetoric seemed based on Western institutional metrics of rights and representation, resonant with the "new evangelism" of "democracy jihad," as Michael Aung-Thwin describes the West's forcing of democratization on Burma in the 1990s.[63] Development and assistance were clearly desirable to the Wa leadership, but a level of political will and organizational know-how had to be mobilized, enabled by its internal politics, and not compromising its navigation of external relations.

We sped to the airport in haste, half an hour late for the arrival of our chief. I took a deep breath as the Land Cruiser wove around the infuriatingly slow tractors lumbering along narrow roads, spouting clouds of dark smoke into the damp air. Rounding Kengtung's old City Gate, I regretted not having stopped by the ticket office earlier to doublecheck the seasonal schedules. Flights in Eastern Shan State operated in a circuit, a loop from Taunggyi to Kengtung to Mandalay before returning to Yangon. We had arrived in Kengtung the night before to pick up the chief and drive him in to Wa Region. Perched on a stool under the arrival hall verandah in the light drizzle, he suppressed his displeasure: "Perhaps it was not communicated clearly to you." Because our phones were on Chinese mobile networks, we had no reception on the move in Myanmar areas. Our driver, with decades of experience navigating muddy trails, stalled the engine on paved road with trembling hands. The next four days would be a careful curation of what the chief would see, whom he would speak to, and which roads he would take, to get a "fair" picture of Wa Region. A different type of patron had arrived from Yangon.

Hosting visitors was another exercise in representation. This was the tail end of the rainy season of 2015, and we were keen to make strong impressions of the necessity of the work in Wa Region. The chief would likely make only one trip here in his tenure, since Wa Region was among the most difficult to get to, requiring a full week's itinerary that was hard for UN officials to spare. Because travel to Wa Region was heavily restricted for foreigners, seeing for oneself was a luxury. Those who could get permits rarely knew how to navigate UWSA authorities for access to villages and were often presented with the "developed areas"; the seeming prosperity of the towns was misleading. As we traveled down the main road that ran through the township of Mong Phen, silence turned into dismay. "Why are we even working in this township?" This was the first Wa town the chief was traveling through, and it seemed exceedingly prosperous by Myanmar standards—large cars, supermarket, casinos, a golf driving range, and hotels along this concrete road, mansions with roman columns adorning their frontages.

We abandoned plans to reach one village because the track was muddy, and slipping off the narrow trail would plunge the car into the valley below. "I can drive it, but maybe he will be scared," our driver said, considering the sensibilities of our guest. Concern subsided when we reached the other project village just twenty minutes uphill from Mong Phen, where asset creation projects for terraced farmland were underway. Here, the customary visual markers of poverty were in abundance: thatched roofs and pleated bamboo paneling, muddy tracks and barefooted children in tattered clothing. Our work seemed preliminarily vindicated. There were no reliable data and statistics to go by. Wa Region was generally excluded from nationwide development indicators. "This is definitely at least as poor as Chin State," the chief remarked, referring to Myanmar's poorest region on record. We sighed quietly in relief.

We met with deputy ministers informally in Pangkham on the third day since many of the Politburo were away. The chief's visit would reassure Wa officials of WFP's consideration and allow us to make requests using his authority. Handling the translation from Chinese into English gave me control of the conversation. Certain UWSA officials were not well versed in the role of "beneficiary" and could not be relied on to say the "right" things. They might boast of achievements in developing the region, disparage the quality and quantities of programs provided, how certain interventions should be done differently, how they had "provided jobs" for villagers on exploitative rubber plantations, how women were not present in governance, or might appear exaggeratedly hostile to the Myanmar government. But these fears were unfounded. Wa officials were polite, exchanging simple pleasantries and calling ahead to inform other authorities of our impending arrival.

We routed the visit through a string of villages to display the socioeconomic and ecological diversity of the region—a Lahu village in the flatter, lower hills of Mong Pawk, a Shan school outside Pangkham, and a Wa village near Mengmao. Schoolchildren and villagers welcomed us, lined up with chants on the path toward the school, once again marshaled by teachers and the village tract leader. The low morning sun was bright, shining across the basketball patch, a stony ground flanked by two makeshift hoops, metal rings nailed crudely into planks of erected wood. Here a communal dance transpired to the monotonous blasts of pipes, with rhythmic singing, clapping, and stamping in rotating circle. A brief discussion seated around WFP-donated school desks was followed by questions about livelihoods and education patterns, ending off the visit. The chief was dignified, without overly probing or embarrassing questions for villagers, no micro-managing scrutiny of the programs. This, in my mind, was a fair visit, an "average" Wa village that was not too poor, yet not well off in any sense. "Representativeness" was always relative, but we had offered the visuals of rural life—corrugated roofs and crooked wooden posts, villagers in dirty jackets, military trousers, and rubber slippers; schoolchildren in garish T-shirts and track bottoms, amid the upland rice fields of the hills.

The long drive back through the hills was the space for summative discussion. "What is the UWSA strategy for development? What is yours as an office? What impact does our work have if there are so many needs? Isn't it just a drop in the bucket?" These were fitting, yet difficult questions to answer. With such a spread of villages, the ten kilos of rice provided to each student every month for attending school was useful but still a mere fix and not a "sustainable" intervention. Village leaders asked for water sources to be developed, boarding schools, agricultural inputs to be introduced, rice terraces to be built. But there was not always enough suitable land or appropriate water sources. Rubber plantations had reduced the room for slash-and-burn plot rotation, itself overly reliant on the vicissitudes of rainfall. At best, they would make nine months of food security a year and rely on casual labor for the rest. The mines nearby employed Chinese workers, and locals only seasonally. Schooling would get them only so far, as the practical difference between a Grade 3 and Grade 6 education was minimal, if any. "Why should we be providing for their people if they have no clear plans to do so?" Against these questions, a response of "Don't we work in so many other areas with these types of governments?" would be a reasonable yet disappointing rejoinder.

And there were wider political and moral considerations that chiefs had to make. Some agencies had ethical dilemmas working in areas administered by authoritarian rulers. Long-term projects were difficult to plan without reliable medium-term access from the Myanmar government. NGOs with less political clout were wary of ruining their relationship with the Myanmar government and jeopardizing their projects in other less contentious areas of the country. The rhetoric of "sustainable development" and holistic interventions made for high barriers to entry. UN agencies preferred to work through partners rather than implementing the project themselves. No organization wanted to work alone, and a critical mass was required before each individual group's interventions might be said to be truly impactful. What was healthcare without sanitation and clean water or agriculture inputs without access to markets? Too many international organizations moving around in Wa Region might trigger the unhappiness of the Chinese, as it does in Kachin State. "You may say this is not politics, it is education, but will they believe?" a Wa Politburo member astutely replied when I suggested appealing more concertedly to the international community for assistance. They, too, had considered the implications.

One argument to make was that the office was maintaining a channel into Wa Region for future work when (if ever) the political deadlock was lifted. This was phatic labor in anticipation of a changing time. More funding would become available once the centrality of the UWSA to political stability in Myanmar was recognized. More organizations would understand the relative impoverishment in Wa Region compared with the lowlands. But when? And this would become a political function, not necessarily fitting into the actual mandates of any organization. How would one present this strategy to heads with their mandates, let alone donors? Development and politics were inseparable.

Resignation was the order of the day for donors and organizations down in Yangon: "There's already so much need in other more accessible places." For the international community in general, it was often easier to blame disengagement or failure on UWSA "bad governance," "lack of capacity," "lack of interest," and the vagaries of the "political situation." "This doesn't fit our present mandate." The UWSA was far from the only prickly issue the oft-maligned development community in Myanmar had to contend with. It was hard to begin thinking holistically about the country's problems, and even harder when holistic thinking began. Displaced persons crises across the country, especially the hapless Rohingya, became the main stopgap priority; there would never be a moment for longer-term planning.

Internal Critiques

Some in the UWSA administration were indeed self-critical and aware of their limitations. There were internal UWSA attempts to reform governance and political culture. An eight-year work plan (2012–2019) directive consisting of a set of seventeen "instructions" had been issued to all party members in March 2012.[64] The first principle insisted on adherence to party leadership and principles, avoiding the "erroneous behavior" of "one person says it and it is done" (Chn: *shuojiusuanle*, law unto oneself) and "individuals overriding the party," along with an imperative to streamline the government structure. Much of the parlance was borrowed from Chinese Communism, the only register available, and the spirit was aspirational and vague. The workplan called for 5 percent spending of local government income on healthcare and 5 percent on education, targeting monthly incomes of 1,200 CNY (200 USD) per person by 2019. It explicitly welcomed the arrival of UN agencies and NGOs and ordered local authorities to protect their property and personhood.

Conversations with officials were not all celebration and propaganda, or tales of the proud advancement of Wa Region, an impression the Wa Gazetteers or Wa State TV might give. While outwardly proud of their ability to enforce anti-drug campaigns and maintain their autonomy from Myanmar, many Wa leaders were nonetheless circumspect and critical of their actual abilities to provide social services for their people. In some ways, they reproduced narratives of primitivism and charges of being "uncivilized." Wa officials at all levels would often tell me that they were undeveloped, lacking in experience and exposure— "We recognize we were backward; we used to cut heads"—and other related narratives.[65] They quietly leveled criticisms at the leadership, including themselves: "Ah, many leaders are here just to pass the time [and accumulate money]; there is no chance that there will be any real change." I witnessed a feedback session that unfolded among cadres within a district meeting: "Everyone must speak whatever they ought to speak" (Chn: *gaishuojiushuo*), the chairperson exhorted. But, of course, the conditions were never right for freely speaking. Who would jeopardize their position, cognizant of the wider structural constraints, or make a naïve intervention where it was "not their place"? The unspoken context was overbearing.

Wa elites adopted "poor governance" and "weak capacity" (using the terms "backward" and "uneducated") not only to disparage their own governing capacity but the capacities of their people. A district leader who unceremoniously described his people as "lazy, slow, and afraid" had worked with many previous UN officials in Mong Pawk and was familiar with the operations of development agencies. Adopting the Chinese term for human capital, he claimed that many Wa villagers were of "low quality" (Chn: *suzhidi*), lacking in education and initiative or a drive to improve their own conditions. This was neither arrogance nor tongue-in-cheek flippancy; it seemed borne out of his frustration at their lack of interest to labor eagerly on the rubber plantations the district authorities had ordered them to tend, along with other mandatory work such as road repairs. Or perhaps it was his own self-justification for why subordinates continued to languish in poverty where he and other leaders had amassed wealth of their own. And there were historical parallels for this, a self-conscious styling of "primitiveness" and "wildness" regarded as a source of pride and strength:

> The Wa have also, at times, self-consciously played on their own imagined 'wildness,' casting themselves as being much more like the king of the forest than like their lowland weakling cousins. . . . The image of the Wa as dreadful, wild warrior people, an image which is not necessarily one shared by everyone among the Wa today, has been enormously powerful in the region, and, unquestionably, has also served as a deterrent.[66]

Wa leaders understood far more than they sought to let on, partly an unwillingness borne out of skepticism and mistrust ("You will leave before the project is complete"), partly a lack of interest. This often happened when I asked for demographic information or statistics at township or central levels, or participation of local officials in food distribution programs. There were reluctant nods, or dismissive laughter, a shake of the head, a sense that "you are not the first to come here and suggest this." It also occurred when NGOs requested funding assistance or participation from Wa authorities, perhaps disguising other motives for their lack of desire to contribute. In yet other cases, it was part of the request for assistance—"Look at the state of our schools. Please provide new desks."

External observers may have taken too seriously this manner of humble-speak, leaders embarrassed or apologetic for the socioeconomic conditions and administrative inefficiencies. One researcher's interviews, which revealed a similar sentiment from a township leader, "We are among the least developed people in the world,"[67] were interpreted as weakness and disinterest. In meetings with Wa leaders (one of whom even used the English term "good governance"), I was repeatedly given the "We are backward" rhetoric, delivered not so much in a self-deprecatory manner but rather to end a conversation or dampen expectations: "Do not ask too much of us; our abilities are limited." This is what Gayatri Spivak calls a "strategic essentialism," a self-characterization that latches on to existing stereotypes and impressions to manipulate outcomes (but is often manipulated in return).[68] They were as much admissions of failure as attempts to control the narratives about themselves. Relying mainly on interviews with ministers and commanders who reiterated party lines and mantras, observers described this as "bad governance," their models unable to accommodate or comprehend Wa Region's governance by gesture.

Tax Rang was still waiting around the vehicle when we returned, just after the heat of day had passed. We had walked for nearly two hours around the hill and back again to visit the farmland of Yaong Kraox village, inaccessible by car.[69] I had never known a township leader to wait so patiently for his visitors—usually they just sent a boy to lead the way and left to tend to their businesses. Tax Rang was a portly Wa man with close-cropped hair and broad features, and his bad knee had prevented him from taking the walk with us. He donned the standard green military shoes for mud, a white polo T-shirt tucked into his blue trousers. He had been in this post for twenty-two years: "I will never be promoted; those that speak out are always seen as trouble," he said, and he name-checked another District Education official in the same predicament. He reminded me of another deputy minister, who tilted his head to the side and grimaced: "I've stopped visiting villages; they are dirt poor, yet they still slaughter chickens for a feast when I arrive. I don't have the appetite for it."

We were here to survey the possible construction of a canal that would wind around the side of the hill from a natural water source, providing water to irrigate new rice terraces below. An entire valley could be made productive this way (see figure 20). This was part of the Asset Creation programs that WFP undertook to strengthen food security in Wa Region; used with natural fertilizers, terraced paddy was the most dependable form of agriculture. By contrast, upland rice on slopes had high yields but relied on slash-and-burn plot rotation to avoid depleting soil nutrients. Since each plot could only be used for four to five harvests, it required enough plots of land for rotation, a prospect increasingly difficult with population growth and rubber plantations. Upland rice depended on the luck of rainfall and soil quality and was prone to landslides. Another type of nonirrigated terraced farmland required fertilizer, which allowed the plot to be used for up to eight years. All methods used different varieties of seeds, but in many places it was not worth the trouble to dig terraces when the soil quality was too poor to produce sufficient yield.

This canal idea was exciting, finally a local official who was open to requirements of "participation" and local authorities' investment in the task. I was used to listening to requests for schools, dormitories, water systems, textbooks, chairs, orange juice, and agricultural machinery, most of which WFP's mandate did not

FIGURE 20. Yaong Kraox terrace farmlands, with slope in the distance awaiting water supply with the construction of an irrigation canal, October 2015.

cover. Two five-meter dams would shore up the water source—a hillside spring—and extend a concrete canal for another four kilometers, potentially irrigating more than one thousand *mu* of land (164 acres) for the thirty-eight households of Yaong Kraox and for other neighboring areas. At present, the concrete canal traveled two hundred meters before turning into a muddy ditch, water lost to seepage. Materials and skilled expertise would provisionally cost 250 CNY (42 USD) per meter, with food provisions for laborers to be provided by WFP. This came up to 1 million CNY, or 166,000 USD. My colleagues surveyed the water source, confirming its feasibility.

Along the way, we stopped by a Wa couple resting in their makeshift shelter. Given the three-hour round trip from the village, most villagers slept in the fields overnight during the harvest. With a three-month food gap they had taken a loan of ten baskets of paddy this year. Sam and Ye answered our questions cautiously, politely offering us a fat cucumber. There were few visitors in this part of the hills, and rural inhabitants were very suspicious of outsiders' motives. Sam wore rubber slippers and an oversized military jacket, his thick eyebrows shaded by a military cap. Ye smoked tobacco from a pipe during the conversation, her checkered turban knotted up over her head, standing barefooted in a long skirt. The ground was littered with rice husks, and in a corner was a bamboo basket carried on the upper back with a strap securing it firmly to the forehead. My colleague translated from Wa to Chinese. They had a year-old toddler back in the village and a twelve-year-old son, who, surprisingly, given the extraordinary dropout rates in the region, was still in Grade 6 in a Wa school.

These were the villagers the other district head had described as "lazy, slow, and scared." We left them baffled, to continue sorting some sort of root in a basket. Poverty was a nebulous notion in the Wa hills. There were simply too many indicators involved, from land access, to soil fertility, family size, motorbike ownership, the type of roof on one's house, to their position in the village. How would one determine relative need, balance this with feasibility, and ensure sustainability of any given intervention?

We regrouped and drove back up to the village office, where Tax Rang had gathered blue plastic chairs around a small table with sunflower seeds and a canister of tea. We sat on an open patch overlooking the magnificent expanse of the Wa hills, just as the sun was setting. "Thanks for coming," he said, and he smiled. "People from the office never make it out this far." This was one of the poorest townships, sitting on the Salween River, more than twelve hours' drive from Pangkham (in that same time one could reach Lashio in Shan State). At the tail end of my stint in Wa Region, I was decently placed to have a discussion on government policies and socioeconomic concerns of rural inhabitants. We went through some of the possibilities—1 million CNY (166,000 USD) was not a large sum for a leader from Pangkham, but why should he part with it for one village? Perhaps it could be built in stages. The township had no real resources to mine, but there was a barge crossing point across the Salween in the area, where cows, timber, and other goods crossed back and forth from Wa areas into government-controlled Myanmar. Here, the customs post imposed a tax on imports: "Yes, but we only see a small fraction of those profits; the rest goes to central authorities," Tax Rang said as he grinned and looked off into the horizon. "There is not much here but rubber, and the prices have fallen drastically."

"The plan for 2019 [thirtieth anniversary] is to reach an income of twenty-five baskets (450 kilograms) of paddy yield per person, and 1,200 RMB per year," he said as he laughed, his eyes glinting in the evening sun. "Perhaps if the basket is small we can make it." Tax Rang had a self-deprecating sense of humor not uncommon for Wa officials when they were not maintaining an image. "Look at our education standards. We have had our own place for twenty-six years, but thus far have not produced a single university student."

"Except," he added, "for the children of the big leaders who have gone overseas."

"Perhaps we can get some donations from rich leaders?" A quick route to local development was to have a person from the area succeed in Pangkham, becoming a deputy minister or police chief, then funneling some wealth back to his home area through schools and clinics. I was aware of at least two leaders in Pangkham who originated from that township. "Yes, one of the chiefs has spent money building a monastery, but that's about it."

Back down in Pangkham days later, I proposed a philanthropic fund to a friend, an official in a ministry. Money could be collected from wealthy leaders and central government representatives administer the fund itself. WFP staff could help identify and rank "needy" areas for targeted interventions, developmental projects such as this one that did not require much money. This would work much faster than through UN/INGO systems, since they were not bogged down by survey, reporting, and monitoring procedures. None would dare to pilfer such a project.

But governance would remain at the level of gesture.

"This thing that you speak of," the friend replied, feigning weariness and rolling his eyes, "everyone already knows."

EPILOGUE

> War is not waged because there are enemies; there are enemies because war is waged.
>
> —Marielle Debos, *Living by the Gun*

Late on in my stay, the WFP decided to change its programming for school feeding projects across the country, distributing daily high-energy biscuits (HEBs) to schoolchildren instead of the ten kilos of rice ration on a monthly basis. This was based on post-distribution surveys and recommendations from Nepal, where it had been a huge success. The HEBs would be a big change for the region; schoolchildren brought home the rice rations to their families, as a boost to household nutrition. Leaders from the central authorities had expressed reservations, but since it was assistance received, they had left the decisions up to the donors.

Soon after, we received news from one of our field monitors that a district leader had rejected the new HEBs and refused their deliveries to warehouses. This was a vexation, to say the least, since lorry loads of one hundred metric tons of biscuits had already crossed the Salween River into Wa Region. We were supposed to have ensured acceptance before they were transported, but this was a sudden spanner in the works. I jumped into the Land Cruiser for the four-hour drive up north.

The district leader barely looked up but had clearly been expecting the visit. He beckoned us to sit, deflecting the conversation elsewhere. "Look, this Chinese man builds roofs for me, roofs that leak. What sort of person is this?" he goaded another player at the table, presumably a contractor of sorts. I paused. Should we make some small talk first? Would it be rude to get straight down to business? I was not close to this standoffish leader, who was ranked in the Central Committee. When I first arrived more than a year ago, he had been sure to confirm that I was not Burmese: "Oh, at least then we will be able to communicate."

When the card game was complete, he sat upright and turned to me. My audience had begun, "District leader, I heard that you have instructed that the HEBs not be distributed in the whole of the district. This is a key component of WFP's activities here, a program change that has happened countrywide, and our boss in Yangon has decided that the positive nutritional impact seen in other parts of the world is important for the children of Wa."

"You very well know that rice is better for the children, the biscuits are only a snack, and they will still have to eat rice. They are not used to eating biscuits, and teachers have also reported that it makes the children sick." On the contrary, we had found preliminary increased attendance rates in other townships, and further, distributions had not yet begun in his area, so that was clearly a lie. Perhaps, we thought, it was the Chinese businessmen who interacted with the leader who had disparaged our biscuits, seeking to impress the leader with their opinions. Or perhaps they were trying to force us to return to the more tangible rice distributions. It was highly unlikely that he had already received feedback, given that the distributions had not even begun. There were few feedback mechanisms between people and leaders.

I name-dropped another minister, whom I had been to see the night before: "But Minister has seen the biscuits, and agreed that they be distributed." I did not technically need the consent of the district leader, since I could appeal directly to the central authorities, but while I could ensure the biscuits were ultimately accepted, our relationship with him would be ruined, and the field staff who were present in his area would be afraid of him, since they were of lower position and status. He put his hand on my thigh in a gesture of intimacy, turning solemn. "The most important thing is that we are friends. But regarding your biscuits, it is best that you do not bring them. They cause diarrhea for the children."

We drove the four hours back down to Pangkham the next morning.

I visited with yet another minister back in Pangkham to discuss the next course of action. "Ai, this guy has little refinement. Who is he to reject this?" This minister growled and tilted his head back, referencing the breach of the norms of receiving gifts and irritated by the triviality of the matter. "I'll bring it to the Central Committee; we'll accept the biscuits of course." He made no mention of his prior personal misgivings.

I had learned something from my time in Wa Region: how to navigate its topographies of power in particular ways, with particular consequences. How to respond and to comport oneself, how to consider its effect on colleagues, on reputations, and the program. How leaders, too, were constrained by norms and the political situations they were in. Autonomy was about everyday power plays and assertions of authority. It was about changing one's mind whimsically if needed, about beckoning subordinate and petitioners to approach, about stamping one's mark on relationships, regardless of the substance of the request. My task as a visitor, as for many others before, was to manage relations—building them and leveraging them when needed.

"Now you can help us relay this to the headquarters with your English," colleagues in Pangkham would tell me, after months of patiently explaining to me our operational issues: from politics to logistics to program design. Often restricted to frustrated responses of "It just doesn't work like this here" to queries from Yangon, my colleagues and I were ourselves dissatisfied with these answers. Why would Wa leaders, reportedly extremely rich, not contribute funds to the feeding of children throughout their schools? How cost-effective and sustainable was it to continuously bring assistance up into the hills? Why were participatory processes so difficult to implement locally? How should external agencies intervene with an insurgent group that seemed to hold the peace process ransom, refusing to sign a ceasefire or commit to programs? Or more existentially, was this not a national problem that had to be solved by Myanmar itself? Little wonder, then, that many NGOs had left Wa Region after seeing no measurable progress or exit strategies.

One could try to explain the implications of Wa Region's political culture to representatives of the international community, as I often did in briefings in Yangon, providing more context and suggestions of how to engage the UWSA leadership. One could try to explain the needs of the region, the views of the leaders and ordinary people, the role of China, and its relation with Myanmar. One could try to explain how to introduce development programs, providing material contributions and creating reciprocities to build ties. These were all part of the objectives and audiences I had initially imagined for this book. But nothing would likely change, or if it did, it might bring unintended consequences. I thought it more useful to tell stories to give a feel and sense of how autonomy was imagined and enacted.

This book tells stories of how the autonomy of the Wa polity has been produced relationally across three decades. It argues that what appears on the surface as a static deadlock in political negotiations between the UWSA and the Myanmar government is a flurry of maneuvers and countermaneuvers, postures, and intermittent relations. Tactical dissonance is created through oscillating relations—political, commercial, movements of people and capital, and governance—allowing the polity to navigate a ground of nondomination by outsiders. The incongruities between local logics of authority and governance lead to a slippery and adaptive polity, refusing to be classified as this, that, or the other, building personalized relations of reciprocity, responding strategically to external demands through improvisation.

Relational autonomy is an ongoing process, informed by social values, enacted through practices and relations. It shows us how historical parallels repeat themselves; tropes of marginality, backwardness, and belligerence reappear in narratives from the outside. It shows how moral economies and social norms govern political and economic relations in the absence of effective formal state institutions. The seeming stalemate between the UWSA and the Myanmar state is simultaneously dynamic and disorderly—movements of people and illicit commodities, wealth and nepotism, refusal and foot-dragging in peace talks, parasitic accumulation, governance without provision.

Yet this disorder has produced thirty years of overall stability in Wa Region. Thinking about the region as an autonomous polity avoids the imposition of state-centric ideals on it, rather than predetermining what Wa Region and the UWSA should or should not be. A focus on the relations and values that construct the polity makes room for other logics of governance, of authority, of reciprocities—a region-making at work. Thirty years of UWSA history have taught that autonomy is not evasion or escape but a continual engagement.

Implications of the Autonomous Polity

Reframing polities like Wa Region and the UWSA as political projects of autonomy has a set of wider implications. By not predetermining the political agenda of the polity, it recognizes how what Louisa Lombard calls "conventionalization" might take place—"mak[ing] the armed actors' relationship to the state ideal explicit.[1] Political projects of autonomy can sometimes be either misrecognized by analysts or deliberately performed by insurgents as ethnonationalism, rebellion, or separatism, to fit into the registers already understandable by observers. Where the autonomy of the egalitarian highland Wa realms could not be understood outside the registers of chiefs and rulers, the British called them the Wa States. Where the autonomy envisaged by the UWSA polity could not be cogently expressed in codified political forms, it became simpler for the polity to accept ethnonationalist framing and call for a "Wa State," enmeshing itself in the ethnically based politics of Myanmar's peripheries.[2] And where political observers could not comprehend the autonomy of armed groups at the margins of the nation-state, they quickly dubbed them rebels and separatists. All three examples create a misleading, essentialized, adversarial model of Wa Region.

Relational autonomy suggests, first, that analysts, with the luxury of being on the outside, should not be too quick to impose their interpretations on armed polities. Deciphering insurgent motivations and ideologies, we settle too quickly on apparent political "grievances" or demands—declaring this group ethnonationalist, that group territorial seceders, another narco-profiteering warlords—reducing the complexities of their project-making into simpler characterizations. Eschewing ascriptive forms of analysis and adopting an emic approach to how insurgent groups see the world and understand authority allow a fuller picture of their political relationships. In Wa Region, it is autonomy and relations, even personal ones, that shape political action, rather than commitment to any specific ideology or stance. Attention to logics of authority and local political culture are central in comprehending how polities see the world around them and navigate reciprocal relationships. Analysis becomes less about understanding how their demands can be defined and accommodated and more about how relations of mutual obligation can be established.

In "take me to your leader"–styled approaches to political "grievances," groups are reified based on purported intent, relying on their enunciated statements and manifestos or on assessments of their military maneuvers. Peacebuilders and mediators then seek reconciliation by negotiation and compromise on these listed demands between both sides. Naturally, they either hit an impasse over specific terms that neither side will concede or run into a larger problem of accommodating varied demands under a single Nationwide Ceasefire Agreement or National Constitution. Negotiated settlements have failed miserably in Myanmar so far, not for the lack of funding but because of the sheer difficulty of accommodating varied histories and negotiating positions into a single constitutional or political framework. Similar challenges will be faced in building a country following the military coup of 2021.

Relational autonomy also suggests that approaches seeking "capacity-building" for Ethnic Armed Organizations (EAOs) in Myanmar should also be buttressed by attempts to build relations. If governance is also an arena for performing authority and managing relations with the outside and not solely about managing resources efficiently for recruitment and revenue, or accruing legitimacy, then it makes less sense to model EAO institutions after Western "good governance" metrics or "empowerment," "participatory" and accountability standards. This, of course, is not to suggest that developing healthcare, access to justice, gender sensitivity, civil society, and education services in EAO areas is unimportant; such interventions have been reported to have some impact.[3] Instead, these interventions are not solely for developing EAO institutions in themselves but also used as an avenue to develop meaningful ties with other groups and actors across boundaries.[4] How might such interventions create the conditions for reciprocities and obligations between adversaries, to increase their stakes in one another?

Finally, at the heart of insurgent autonomy, then, lies a higher-order conversation between stability and disorder. The conflict economy in Myanmar—mining of ore and precious stones, narco-trades, business concessions, money laundering, and capital flows—strengthens armed groups and militaries, driving resource-grabbing behavior.[5] But while analyses argue that insurgent politics in Myanmar is currently characterized by "business deals in lieu of politics," it also holds true that these business and extractive collaboration deals are in fact vital modes of politics in themselves.[6] They are part of the cross-boundary relations and alternative routes for forms of diplomacy. As such, blanket suggestions that "cutting off" resource revenues to armed actors will decrease conflict are debatable, if they were even possible.[7] This is not to suggest, again, that recognizing land rights, better environmental and resource governance, and revenue sharing under "resource federalism" will not mitigate some of the negative externalities of extraction fueling conflict.[8] Rather, consider that several of these disorderly movements are economic ties central to relational autonomy at the peripheries, holding the adversaries together. Unqualified "resolutions" of these ties might lead to other forms of instability.

While insurgents challenge state authority in military and economic arenas, on the other, disorder (kept below a certain threshold) has been central to a relative stalemate and stability between the Tatmadaw and many EAOs. Battle lines have held for decades in many peripheral areas of the country, apart from occasional, though damaging, skirmishes. Shadow economies contribute to reciprocal concessions and maintain relations between insurgents and the state. This is more than "ceasefire capitalism"; active relationships and webs of obligations are created between both sides in an iterative process. As Worrall notes, "rebel orders are built both upon and alongside existing social and cultural orders which (re-)emerge both during and in the aftermath of conflict, demonstrating how rebel order endures only if it remains responsive to other forms of order."[9] The autonomous polity is made and remade in this dynamic stalemate.

Where one begins to look to spaces and communities at the edges of nation-states and examines them outside of state-centric registers or models of sovereignty, autonomous polities become not threats or resistors but simply expressions of the limits of the projection of state power or will. They are alternative political projects that have survived particular historical trajectories. The persistence of Wa Region along with many other autonomous regions—Nagorno-Karabakh, Transnistria, Abkhazia, South Ossetia, the Luhansk People's Republic, Zapatista areas in Chiapas, the Turkish Republic of Northern Cyprus, Somaliland, and Puntland, to name a few—suggests that this is not an anomalous state of affairs.

As Diane Davis put it in a 2009 essay describing the changing patterns of state and nonstate sovereignties, the core problem for the nation-state is in "learning how to operate in new sub- and trans-national territorial domains, and determining whether existent institutions, political authority, and social legitimacy available to them now are ready for the twenty-first-century task that lies ahead."[10]

By recentering analysis on how relational autonomy is produced, migration, political negotiations, cross-border accumulations, shadow economies, and governance become but some of the moving pieces that produce the polity. Such analysis implies searching for creative ways to buttress ties and rework them along with our definitions of order and disorder. We might then reimagine peacebuilding beyond the signing of ceasefire or disarmament agreements or the crafting of federal arrangements through working committees. We might come to understand peacebuilding as a renegotiation of the wide range of relationships between polities and political projects.

We need to search for newer, more flexible conceptual vehicles of political authority to understand and accommodate desires for autonomy outside nation-states.

Years later, the football players have been displaced from the field; it was upgraded into a spanking new stadium for the thirtieth-anniversary celebrations. Many move between Pangkham and Dangyan. Ah Yong is still taking care of his nephews and nieces. Liang's shop is still open; his daughters are in Maymyo, possibly heading to Thailand with other relatives. The houses Yucheng built still line the road around Ai Cheng; it is not clear what has happened to its other assets.

The WFP office has halved in size, and there are further reassignments of staff to other parts of the country to come. But the canal in the township from chapter 5 is still being built, bit by bit, extending every year. The township head is still there in the same position. A large mining explosives store in a town in the north exploded, killing nine and injuring dozens.

In 2018 there was a slight reshuffle of officials and their appointments, and it seems gradually clearer what the lines of succession might be. The second generation of sons and nephews are introduced into higher ranks in the military and Central Committee. As usual, there is talk of groups and allegiances among some of them. Many other friends in the ministries have continued their positions; they still visit and drink in the evenings.

Chen sits under his patio on one of my return visits. He proudly shows me a large chunk of gold refined but not completely polished. It looks like a large fragment of shrapnel: "Each time I need some money I just break off a chunk of it to sell. The traders in the market are always calling me trying to buy some." He has relieved much of the financial pressures on himself; he looks much healthier and relaxed. He had truly struck gold in one of his mines.

Postscript

In post-coup Myanmar of 2021, the question remains of how a future country, in whatever form it takes, will integrate Wa Region and the UWSA into the nation-state. Observers have listed the UWSA as an EAO that adopts a "wait-and-see" attitude, non-committal to either the State Administration Council or the National Unity Government. The UWSA remains committed first to its own autonomy, carefully balancing the relations between these two sides, as well as its ties with China. Understanding how the UWSA envisions its autonomy, and enacts it, is the first step to figuring out how to accommodate the Wa polity in a new Myanmar.

Notes

INTRODUCTION

1. Of armed groups worldwide, the UWSA is outstripped only by ISIS and Hezbollah in terms of size, and on par with the Liberation Tigers of Tamil Eelam (LTTE) at their peak. Or just under 1 percent of Myanmar's roughly 51.4 million population, according to the 2014 Census.

2. Based on a GIS mapping of the North Wa Region calculating it at about fourteen thousand square kilometers. Lintner records the four districts in Wa areas controlled by the CPB in 1986 as totaling 12,224 square kilometers (1990, appendix 2). This appears to include Selu and other areas that are no longer part of UWSA-controlled Wa Region. Estimates for South Wa, where boundaries are unclear and contested, are taken from Wa authorities and a Phoenix News documentary from 2015, which put the figure at thirteen thousand square kilometers. This gives the total figure of twenty-seven thousand square kilometers.

3. Young 2014; Marshall and Davis 2002.

4. Chin 2009; Kramer 2007; Lintner and Black 2009.

5. Collier and Hoeffler 1998, 564; elsewhere, Kasfir defines rebels as those who "hold territory with the political intention of taking over the state, seceding, or reforming it" (2015, 23).

6. Prasse-Freeman 2012.

7. Cline 2009; Kramer 2007. These stem from discourses widely circulating in Burmese media and Yangon-based government, diplomatic, and security circles. Tedious as it is to quibble with shorthand and hasty classifications of the UWSA, each misframing implies a set of counterproductive "solutions"—for example, where branded as ethnonationalists (Kramer 2007), drug lords and kingpins (Marshall and Davis 2002), and "de facto independent" (Kumbun 2019).

8. The letters on one's car plate determined the sort of treatment the person might receive at a police or army checkpoint. WA meant a vehicle affiliated to the Wa administration; WJ or WB to the UWSA military and police; and WD, WE, WF, WG, and WH were car plates for civilians registered in Pangkham, Mengmao, Nam Tit, Wein Kao, and Mong Pawk, respectively.

9. Because of the degree of overlap, I simply use UWSA to denote the entire political entity comprising the Wa administration (Chn: *wabang zhengfu*), Wa military (Chn: *wabang lianhe jun*), and United Wa State Party (Chn: *wabang lianhe dang*).

10. Fiskesjö describes the ethic of hospitality in traditional Wa rice beer–drinking rules and rituals, an arena of social interaction in which mutual recognition, inclusion, and exclusion are signaled (2010b). While the practices Fiskesjö (on the Chinese side of the border) described have been gradually replaced with the drinking manners found in Chinese practice (see Osburg 2013), its ethics of generosity and reciprocity prevail. In formalized gatherings with Wa leaders (especially where Chinese guests are present), liquor and rice wine are consumed instead of rice beer. Fiskesjö notes that in China, "many Chinese-trained Wa cadres in county towns see the *lei* [bamboo cup] offered them as the epitome of native backwardness and the contents as bacteria-infested filth.... Sometimes the new local elites are barely able to control their feelings of disgust as they

turn down offers of *blai* [rice beer]" (2010b, 120). Still, I participated in variants of Fiskesjö's described drinking rituals at more intimate township or village gatherings.

11. Reeves 2014, 10 (my emphasis); much like the Ferghana Valley where Madeleine Reeves examines the production of borders.

12. Herzfeld describes the autonomous polity as "a system of governance more generic than 'state' and informed by an ethic of shared understandings of the universe" (2019, 28).

13. Hoffman 2011, 13. This language is widely found across political science: the "nonstate," "quasi-state" (Jackson 1990), "para-state" actors (cf Hagmann and Péclard 2010), "proto-state" or "shadow state" (Reno 2000). Elsewhere, they are framed exhibiting limited statehood (Risse 2011) or ambiguous statehood (Caspersen 2012).

14. Lombard 2016, 41.

15. Scott 2009.

16. For instance, that he mischaracterizes the state as overly malevolent (Krasner 2011), paradoxically downplays the agency of the highlands by making subjects reactive to state forms (Friedman 2011; Clunan 2011), or too quickly attributes their social forms to lowland "state effects" rather than local conditions, and overemphasizing the role of labor and manpower (Lieberman 2010, 345). Jonsson accuses Scott of crafting too stark a separation between Zomia and the state. Jonsson focuses instead on the relations through which autonomy is produced, where "highlanders' political protest seems generally oriented toward making and managing relations with states than avoiding them" (2012, 166).

17. Manicas 2011.

18. Jonsson 2012, 169.

19. Scott 2009, 330, 332.

20. Young 2005.

21. In the first, sovereignty, thought of as the "capacity to determine conduct within the territory of a polity without external legal constraint" (Humphrey 2004, 418), is inevitably fractured or eroded by nonstate challengers—often translating into a zero-sum game.

22. Ong 2000; Humphrey 2004; Slaughter 2004; Comaroff and Comaroff 2006; Trouillot 2001.

23. Literature on sovereignty trends toward such relationality. Ethnographies of tribal sovereignty from North America put greater emphasis on this interdependence—Jessica Cattelino's exploration of Seminole gaming in the United States demonstrates how the wealth accrued for economic well-being and the exercise of sovereignty paradoxically create pressures that deny this sovereignty (2008); Jean Dennison shows how attempts by the Osage nation to assert sovereignty are fraught with interconnection and compromise with the national government, in "entangled sovereignties" (2017). Among the Mohawk in North America, Audra Simpson calls attention to contradictions within claims to recognition, deploying the concept of refusal to reject the unjust authority of the state to grant this very recognition, further highlighting the incommensurability of Western notions of sovereignty with local political logics (2014; Coulthard 2014; McGranahan 2018). Brown 2010, 53.

24. Recall Mitchell's "state effects" (1991), which, building on Abrams's distinction between the "state-idea" and "state-system" (1988), sees the state not as a monolithic reified actor but as a constitutive effect produced by practices and representations.

25. Conversations on settler sovereignty in the United States have prompted scholars toward reminders of how the concept of sovereignty bears a historical baggage—linked to divine kingship, legal settler colonialism, Westphalian statehood, and postcolonial self-determination (Simpson 2014; Jennings 2011; Bonilla 2017).

26. For a history of Wa movement into the hills and interactions with the constellation of Shan principalities in and around the China-Laos-Burma border areas from the 1400s to the 1700s, see Fiskesjö 2000. Fiskesjö provides a useful list of the various Shan polities: now the present-day Ruili and Gengma in the north, the Menglian and Sipsongbanna areas to the east, Kengtung in the south, and Manglun in the west (2000, 60–66). These Shan areas, half in China and half in Myanmar, currently surround the Wa Region mainly to its south and east (see also Sai Aung Tun 2009 for a history of the Shan States).

27. Fiskesjö describes the "anti-state" Wa as fiercely autonomous and egalitarian: "People in the egalitarian Wa area continued to seize on subterranean riches to enrich themselves and to defend their autonomy, while consciously seeking to solidify existing non-hierarchical social structures and prevent the emergence of new hierarchies or the building of a Wa state" (2010a, 259). This egalitarian ethos no longer holds.

28. Fiskesjö 1999, 2002, 2010a, 2021; Wang 2010.

29. Watkins produced a dictionary of the Wa language (2014), based on the Ai Soi branch around Cangyuan (present-day China).

30. The core areas of the "wild" Wa, now regarded as Wa "cultural heartlands," are present-day Cangyuan and Ximeng on the Chinese side, and Kunma, Ban Wai, and Mengmao on the Myanmar side.

31. Smith 1999.

32. McCoy 1991.

33. Ong 2020. Tactics, building on De Certeau's distinction with strategies, are flexible actions, improvisations, and combinations, minor forms of "making-do" which "play on and with a terrain imposed on it and organized by the law of a foreign power" (1984, 37); strategies are a function of an incumbent's greater power or knowledge: "strategies pin their hopes on the resistance that the *establishment of a place* offers to the erosion of time; tactics on a *clever utilization of time*" (1984, 38–39).

34. Inspired, of course, though only metaphorically, from E. R. Leach's analysis of shifting highland political systems (1954).

35. Lintner 2021, 3. Lintner previously labeled them as Chinese proxies but also acknowledges that "they are no Chinese stooges" (Lintner 2021, 211).

36. Sun 2019a.

37. The China-Myanmar relationship is a key topic of geopolitical speculation; see chapter 3.

38. Lintner 2019.

39. I use the term "insurgents" in its ordinary sense of groups bearing arms within the territory of a nation-state. Contra Brenner (2020), I prefer this term over the use of "rebels" for the UWSA, since it avoids presuming a necessarily antagonistic challenge to the state. While Brenner avoids "insurgents" because he believes it is a translation of the Tatmadaw's use of *"thaung gyan thu"* (Bse), I do not validate this labeling by using the English term. Meehan (2015, 264) takes a similar position to mine.

40. U Thein Swe, the minister for immigration, and U Thein Zaw, the vice-chair of the NLD government's Peace Commission.

41. Htet Naing Zaw 2019.

42. Wansai 2019.

43. For example, Aung Zaw 2019.

44. Woods 2011.

45. MacLean 2008; Nyiri 2012.

46. Marshall and Davis 2002.

47. Up to 50 percent of the world's opium and 75 percent of heroin production were said to be from Myanmar in the 1990s (Chin 2009, 8). Opium production in Myanmar

was an estimated 312 tons in 2005, with 40 percent from Wa Region (UNODC 2005, 3). Jelsma et al. 2005; Sai Lone 2008; Kramer 2007.

48. Global Witness 2014, 2015.

49. Welker 2014, 3. Welker makes a case for the study of seemingly bounded entities through their processes of enactment and constitution, as others have similarly done: for a disease (Mol 2002), the state through its "effects" (Mitchell 1991), and the humanitarian camp (Dunn 2018).

50. Global Witness 2015.

51. Woods 2018, 3.

52. Condominas 1977; Michaud 2006.

53. Tambiah 1977; Tooker 1996; Leach 1960, 50; Winichakul 1994.

54. Patterson Giersch calls this "process geographies" (2010), spaces analytically bounded by phenomena that traverse them. Also Giersch 2006; Reid 1995; Tagliacozzo 2009.

55. Ong and Steinmüller 2020.

56. Low and Merry 2010. Michael Herzfeld, for instance, describes his conducting advocacy on behalf of a Bangkok urban community he studied as "engaged anthropology" (2016).

57. Feelings of anxiety and dislocation in the field and moral dilemmas were not insignificant in my research journey. For an extremely useful overview of how personality, networks, race, gender, age, self-presentation, upbringing, emotional responses, and past experience might affect the kinds of access and data collected in qualitative research, see Thaler 2021. Thaler writes frankly about his emotional responses to the stories of interlocutors, and the difficulty of balancing transparency demands in research and a "reflexive openness" against mental health and emotional burdens.

58. Nader 1972.

59. In twenty months of ethnographic research among UWSA elites, everyday people, and administrative offices, I informally interacted with 123 interlocutors, including top-ranked politburo leaders, ministers and deputies, and other officials in the Wa administration. I also met dozens of others at festivals, weddings, and other official events, along with weekly visits to the homes of officials and friends in the evenings. Living in an apartment close to the main stadium, I spent leisure time with a large group of young men with whom I had made friends on the football field, as well as their wider circles. I made three follow-up visits between 2016 and 2018. I also spent a total of three months from 2017 to 2019 in Yangon speaking to journalists, UN and embassy staff, think-tanks, and peacebuilders to uncover the views of the metropolis and international community.

60. Milsom writes about the reporting on drugs in Shan State in his thesis on Wa Region: "The veracity of such information is often difficult to ascertain as there are many underlying factors motivating those who give information, and it is often the case that each one has only a small piece of a much larger and exceedingly complex puzzle" (2010, 61–62).

61. Selth 2010, 431.

62. See, for instance, Lee and Schectman (2016).

63. Steinmüller 2019.

64. Chin 2009; Chin and Zhang 2015; Chouvy 2009; Jelsma et al. 2005; Lintner and Black 2009.

65. Ieva Jusionyte describes such a research ethic as "knowing what not to know" (2015, 3).

66. Fiskesjö 2021, 40.

67. See Hedström 2017 in Myanmar, and the gendered division of labor among the Kachin Independence Organization, where women support the war effort through emotional and physical labor in the household.
68. Lombard 2016.

1. PERIPHERAL COSMOPOLITANISMS

1. Similar accounts of civilians coerced to participate in road building have been described as forced labor in other parts of Myanmar (Duffield 2008, 31), but in Wa Region this practice appears more a form of conscripted (in the sense of service) labor.

2. Like Asia World belonging to Lo Hsing-Han from Kokang, and Hong Pang belonging to the UWSA, which built the Lashio-Kokang and Kengtung-Tachilek roads respectively (Thein Swe and Chambers 2011, 61).

3. Chang 2015, 250. Chang's rare piece on Dangyan demonstrates the centrality of Yunnanese migrants of the 1950s in bolstering networks of trade in Northern Shan State, linking Pangkham to Dangyan and many other Shan towns. Her chapter also describes the interactions between KMT, KKY, Shan armed militias, and CPB forces in Dangyan.

4. Chang recounts the tales of traders taking this eastward route in the 1970s from Dangyan (Myanmar controlled) to Man Xiang and Pangkham (Wa controlled) and onto Menglian (China) (2015, 263). The journey on foot took seven days from Dangyan to Pangkham, during the period when the CPB controlled the Wa hills.

5. In 2015, a Wa visitor with a Wa ID card (but without a Myanmar passport) was allowed to travel to Puer, a six-hour drive away. Checkpoints along the road prevented further travel north.

6. Borderland studies is a huge field of literature interrogating at least three themes relevant to Wa Region: (1) spatial definition of border zones and regions (Baud and van Schendel 1997; Kearney 1991), (2) attention to flows and mobilities of the local political economy that transgress boundaries and produce spaces (e.g., van Schendel and Abraham 2005; Cunningham and Heyman 2004; Das and Poole 2004; Donnan and Wilson 1999), (3) border subjectivities and cultural hybridities produced at the interstices of states (Rosaldo 1993; Anzaldua 1987). For summaries of these conversations and the relation between discursive boundaries, identities, and scale, see Newman and Passi 1998.

7. See Tagliacozzo 2009; Walker 1999.

8. Nordstrom 2004.

9. Endres describes this as a "corrupt exception," where state officials taking bribes from illicit traders on the China-Vietnam border "make law" to allow ordinary people to make a living (2014). This extractive agency of borderlanders is documented across Southeast Asia, for instance, by Tagliacozzo: describing Bornean headhunters' raids into Dutch territory and subsequent escape into British territory to avoid capture, and Chinese woodcutters crossing over Kalimantan boundaries to increase logging quotas (2009, 175; also, Tsing 1993).

10. Clifford 1997.

11. Clifford 1997, 36. The epigraph to this chapter comes from Clifford 1997, 24, 36.

12. On the mobilities turn, see Cresswell 2006; Urry 2007; Xiang and Lindquist 2014. See also Kaufmann et al. (2004) on the notion of "motility," the link between social and physical mobility.

13. Chu 2010, 13–15.

14. Foucault 2009.

15. Clifford 1997.

16. Wen-Chin Chang details the cross-border contraband trade in Chinese motorcycles from Ruili, Yunnan, which continued until 2014 (2017). Traders rode motorbikes

down from Jiegao to Mandalay in groups, paying informal taxes and bribes to police checkpoints along the way, hoping to preserve enough profit at the end, another example of entrepreneurs managing risk and exploiting premiums across borders.

17. At the Cattle Trade Tax Bureau and Immunization Station, running under the Ministry of Finance.

18. The Aini people are a branch of the Hani ethnic group of Yunnan Province (along with the Akha; see Tooker 1996), and one of the fifty-five recognized minorities in China.

19. See Campbell and Prasse-Freeman 2021 for a discussion on class, ethnicity, and racism among the majority Bamar in relation to other minorities.

20. Renard 2013a, 142.

21. Chin 2009, 38.

22. Milsom states that in 2000, "the number of children with access to primary education has increased from less than one thousand in 1989 to over thirty thousand, or roughly 30 percent of all children" (2005, 71+).

23. Calculated from WFP data on school feeding projects, based on population estimates and distribution numbers. Some private schools in town and schools in military camps or rubber plantations are not included, but the figure is generally indicative.

24. Wa and Chinese medium schools (82 percent of total) ran on a Chinese curriculum, while the Myanmar-medium schools adopted the Myanmar curriculum (18 percent).

25. In one back-to-office memo, I wrote, "Oct 2015: Once again the terrible education system and shocking ratios of teachers to students and classes means that the students are spending much time waiting for the teachers to be done with another class and come over to theirs. Pang Yao has 146 students (3 grades) and 2 teachers, Man Tun school has 300+ students (across 6 grades) and 2 teachers. (Action: to continue following up on INGO plans for Wa in the longer term)."

26. Each household was expected to send one male to military or government service (teachers, clerks, etc.), a point of contention for many families (see Steinmüller 2019). Service was for life, but I was told that depending on area, the units were not too strict on deserters. Chin records the following explanation from a Wa official: "If an elder brother who is sixteen does not want to join and the younger one wants to, then we will recruit the younger one even though he may be only thirteen. The new recruits are trained for three weeks in Bangkang and then dispatched to various army divisions or regiments" (2009, 43).

27. The vice-chairman of the UWSA suggested in a meeting in August 2014 that there were an estimated two thousand inhabitants of Wa Region working in China, mostly in regions close to the Myanmar border. He raised this in response to news reports that several young women found working illegally in China had been returned across the border by Chinese police.

28. Renard reports a onetime settlement fee for Chinese nationals of 3,000 CNY in 1999 (2013a, 154).

29. Hansen's ethnography of Xishuangbanna in neighboring Yunnan describes these tensions between ethnic minorities and Han migrants to the peripheries (2005), the latter arriving with more education and capital than locals, quickly monopolizing businesses.

30. One possible explanation might be the Wa reluctance to affect or dig into waterways, where they believe malignant spirits reside (Fiskesjö 2000, 368). James G. Scott makes a similar point when he notes how villages are never built near streams for fear of fevers. He describes the Wa bamboo aqueducts used to bring water into villages, where "considerable engineering skill is sometimes shown in winding, or zigzagging this aqueduct about" (Scott and Hardiman 1900, 507).

31. Sai Lone (2008, 62, edits made for readability).

32. Some Wa inhabitants were also able to speak Shan, which helped them to travel within Shan State and converse in markets. However, this did not appear to be a significant boost to connectivity with areas outside Wa Region.

33. Or Panthay. Liang's ancestors were Hui Muslims from Dali areas in Northern Yunnan, forced to flee south down to Lancang near the Burmese border with thousands of others during the Panthay Rebellion in the 1860s and 1870s. His mother was a Han Chinese and his wife Hui from Dangyan in Burma; they finally settled in Pangkham, halfway in between both their families. See Hill 1998 for a generational history of the travels and trade of the Yunnanese Muslims, and Forbes's 1988 account of a Panthay village at the northern edge of Wa Region.

34. Interestingly, the Wa Ministry did not cite Ma's Myanmar ID number, preferring instead its own Wa-issued ID card.

35. Ong 1999.

36. See Tharaphi Than 2016 for an account on Monglar politics.

37. See Rath 2016 for a US explanation of the mechanics of this game, popular across Asia, and being raided by California police. There are both gambling and nongambling versions.

38. Vrieze 2015; Strangio 2014; Finch 2014; Fisher 2014.

39. This happened again in mid-2021, when the Chinese government drastically ordered all Chinese nationals in the borderlands of Myanmar to return home to their provinces of origin and re-register themselves, in a bid to draw out those working for online fraud and gambling syndicates in Wa, Kokang, and Monglar. The COVID-19 pandemic also created severe curtailments on the travel of people between China and Wa Region.

40. Lawi Weng 2016a.

41. Takano 2002.

42. Several accounts contest the notion of Khun Sa's surrender and that UWSA was not necessarily instrumental in his "defeat," arguing that Khun Sa's laying down of arms was related to a shift in business interests (see Maung Pho Shoke 1999; Buchanan 2016).

43. Sai Lone's interviews with district leaders in 2008 had total figures of around fifty thousand to eighty thousand (2008, 44), while the Lahu National Development Organization put the figure at one hundred twenty-six thousand (LNDO 2002, 3).

44. Sai Lone cites the third official UWSA Five-Year Workplan of 2000 issuing orders to township authorities to enforce resettlement and consolidate villages to around fifty households (2008, 42). This was a practice of both the CPB and the Chinese Communists in the 1960s, part of the attempts to control and administer populations (Fiskesjö 2000, 369).

45. Fiskesjö 2017, 16.

46. The LNDO report *Unsettling Moves*, published in the middle of the relocations and endorsed by the WNO's Sao Mahasang of Yin Phan, reports one hundred twenty-six thousand moved by 2002. Forty-eight thousand inhabitants of the areas in South Wa were affected, their land taken away, with thousands fleeing to Thailand (2002). Interviews with those relocated describe deaths on the journey and disease upon arrival.

47. LNDO (2002, 3) gives this figure for the year 2000 alone.

48. LNDO 2002, 7.

49. ALTSEAN 2001, 15.

50. My translation from a TV interview from 2004. Shenzhen Wutong Broadcasting Corporation (2004).

51. Fiskesjö 2017, 15.

52. LNDO 2002. ALTSEAN 2001, footnote 71.

53. ALTSEAN 2001.

54. TNI 2012, 22–25.
55. Wa State News Media 2009, 138. Conversation with Wa Agriculture Minister, July 28, 2015.
56. TNI 2012.
57. Based on ten-year figures from indexmundi.com, data from Singapore Stock Exchange, accessed at https://www.indexmundi.com/commodities/?commodity=rubber&months=120.
58. TNI 2012, 73.
59. Fictitious name.
60. Fiskesjö 2021.
61. Rubber plantations were first introduced to Wa Region in 1997 in Mong Pawk areas (Renard 2013a, 163).
62. Transnational Institute (2012, 73) gives this amount as 5 CNY per *mu* per month, but the unit *mu* is used inconsistently, sometimes referring to a fixed number of rubber trees rather than land area.
63. Shenzhen Wutong Broadcasting Corporation 2004.
64. Lintner 1990, 88.
65. Runaway truck ramps, or arrester beds, a safety design made of ramps filled with gravel to stop vehicles whose brakes had failed, a curious investment along roads that had relatively little traffic volume.
66. This also happened in Pangkham Town in 2015 and 2016, where roads were widened and tarred and drainage installed throughout the town, all with the use of Chinese construction technology and workers. No compensation was granted for any buildings that saw their porches or front gates demolished by the road widening.
67. A public messaging scare tactic commonly deployed in China.
68. Scott 1998; Harvey and Knox 2012.
69. Correspondence of Wilkie to Lloyd, September 3, 1932, IOR: M/3/196, cited in Maule (1992, 26).
70. Asiaworld, founded by Lo Hsing Han and run by his son Steven Law, was responsible for the construction of various highways through Shan State, including from Lashio to Hopang, the Yangon Airport, hydroelectric dams, hotels, and ports; see Fuller (2015).

2. TOPOGRAPHIES OF POWER

1. A Shan militia leader, Nawd Kham, was captured by Chinese security forces and executed for the crime, though discordant accounts circulating around Tachilek on the Thai-Myanmar border pointed to other shadowy figures, including rogue Thai commando units and a rich Chinese casino mogul. See Howe 2013.
2. Weng 2015a.
3. Pwint 2019.
4. Weber 1995. See also Benedict Anderson's notion of modular nationalism (1983).
5. United States Department of the Treasury 2005. In 2008, the Treasury Department updated its list to twenty-seven individuals in total, now described as a "Burmese Drug Cartel"; United States Department of the Treasury 2008.
6. Of the eight leaders indicted by the US district court of New York, one who shared the same surname as the chairman but was not related in any way was rumored to be a case of mistaken identity.
7. Saw Lu 1993. See Lintner 1994, 328.
8. Scheele (2014) describes disorder and autonomy as key social values among the Tubu in Northern Chad, leading to the supposed anarchic nature of their social organization.
9. Debos 2016, 176.

10. Fiskesjö 2000, 207. Pitchford 1937, 226.
11. Norins 1939, 67.
12. This was an account of British cartographer Barton attempting to enter Banhong in 1929 with a Chinese expedition. Harvey 1933, cited in Fiskesjö 2010a, 249.
13. Scott and Hardiman 1900, 497.
14. Scott and Hardiman 1900, 500, 509. Scott and Hardiman describe them as a grove of huge trees with hundreds of skulls running between Sung Ramang and Hsanhtung (1900, 499), also noted by Pitchford, who asserts Hsanhtung was one of the most powerful conglomerates of villages in the Wa States (1937, 231). Stories of headhunting were also found in Chinese records—including the Chinese traveler Zhang Chengyu, who visited in 1890 along with a British expedition and noted the existence of "skull avenues" where hundreds of heads of enemies were placed (Fiskesjö 2002, 84).
15. People today remember this headhunting past sometimes with embarrassment, and sometimes with pride. Ko-lin Chin recounts three versions told to him of the origins of headhunting (2009, 19), in which the people recounting stories tend to associate its origins with other groups or make claims that their ancestral areas did not participate. Other authors record different local explanations of headhunting—including crop fertility and protection against evil spirits (Scott and Hardiman 1900, 498–503; Pitchford 1937, 225). Origin myths of the Wa are discussed by Fiskesjö in his dissertation (2000, ch. 2), variously involving emergence from a hole, where the Wa were the firstborn and hence take on the responsibility of sacrifice to the spirits (Scott and Hardiman 1900, 496; Young 2014, 2). Rather than simply recording the narratives told, Fiskesjö deconstructs the contexts for the creation of these narratives. One Chinese version has Zhugeliang tricking the Wa into practicing headhunting (2000, 346–49), which appears to displace blame from the Wa onto the Chinese or, alternatively, celebrates the superior Chinese cunning.
16. Young 2014, 8, 21–22.
17. For an account of Wa history and relationship with the Shan, see Satyawadhna 1991.
18. Fiskesjö 2010a, 244.
19. Norins describes this in the 1930s: "One of the sawbwas permitted British entry into his territory. This was taken by the other tribal chiefs as a betrayal of Wa autonomy, and led to a threat of inter-tribal war" (1939, 75).
20. Fiskesjö 2010a, 262. Fiskesjö describes failed attempts at "kingship" or chieftainship in the Wa areas of Banhong and Manglun on the Salween, as examples of the tendency to resist hierarchizing rule. He builds also on Jonathan Friedman's thesis on highland autonomy and warfare as a result of increasing "circumscription" by lowland states, a type of enclosure that reduced the amount of land available for highland societies to expand into (1998).
21. Deleuze and Guattari 1987, 409.
22. Deleuze and Guattari 1987, 419.
23. Clastres 1989.
24. Brachet and Scheele 2019, 32.
25. Brachet and Scheele 2019, 7. Brachet and Scheele 2019, 259.
26. Brachet and Scheele 2019, 266.
27. Callahan 2009, 34.
28. See Woodman 1962, 457.
29. Scott 1906, 133.
30. Scott and Hardiman recorded this in the Upper Burma Gazetteer (1900, 278) and corroborated later by the Boundary Commission of 1935–37 (Norins 1939, 78).
31. Included under the Federated Shan States here was the Wa State of Manglun, which is in present-day Pangyang in Wa Region. The unfederated Wa States were only brought "under administration" in 1935 (FACE 1947).

32. AF Morley, then the private secretary to parliamentary undersecretary of state (February 1933, cited in Maule 1992, 26). Also Maule (2002, 213) on the limited British presence in the Wa hills.

33. See E.G. 1957; Norins 1939, 71; Sino-British Joint Commission for the Investigation of the Undelimited Southern Section of the Yunnan-Burma Frontier (1937) and other records and correspondences within bundle M/3/175 at the British Library. The dispute was over a two-hundred-mile border through the Wa States, with the Chinese government's proposal of the "Liuchen line," west of the Scott Line, regarded by the British as an inconvenient administrative frontier. Both sides considered the status quo in 1936 to be a poor outcome—one that divided the Wa and denied Chinese access to the Salween, even as the British sought a buffer zone east of the Salween in the event of conflict with China. This area was between Hopang and Pangkham in the Wa States; see Woodman 1962, 455–72. Five different proposed demarcation lines were drawn for negotiations, with the allegiance of Banhong (present-day China) and the location of Kongmingshan (present-day Mengmao) the two key points of contention (Norins 1939,74).

34. Young 2014, 49–51; Woodman 1962, 461–63.

35. Norins 1939, 70.

36. Christian Science Monitor 1937; Tinker 1956, 338.

37. See Woodman 1962, 471.

38. From the remarkable efforts of men led by V. C. Pitchford, who mapped the border over two years from 1935 (McGrath 2003). A series of British correspondences and records over the commission and dissents are retained in the British Library (*Sunday Express* 1937; Sino-British Joint Commission 1937). Both sides issued a further set of notes in 1941. E.G. (1957, 87), Norins (1939, 78), and Tinker (1956, 338) all demonstrate a slight disparity in the sequence and dates of the events.

39. Winichakul 1994.

40. Fiskesjö 2010b, 112.

41. Sino-British Joint Commission for the Investigation of the Undelimited Southern Section of the Yunnan-Burma Frontier (1937, 3), bundle M/3/175, British Library.

42. Wa Region was largely untouched by the Japanese in World War II. The only places where I heard of Japanese activity were in Mengmao, Man Tun, and Na Wi, mostly in the northwest of Wa Region closer to the Salween. A Wa official claimed he had found the diary of a Japanese soldier in Na Wi, complaining of three scourges: the enemy, malaria, and steep hills. This official also claimed to have met the Wa widow of a Japanese soldier in Man Tun in 1971. Another official told of a Shan who brought the Japanese to Yong Noone Village near Mengmao where they killed twenty-one Wa. The Japanese were called *hawx rhawm* (Water Chinese) in Wa and had vastly superior weapons at the time. This official claimed he had been given an old, rusty Japanese pistol and rifle that villagers found in a cave near Na Wi. The Wa Historical Committee publication finds no military records of Japanese entry into Wa Region but notes that small groups of Japanese soldiers crossed the Salween River into Wa Region to search for routes east toward China (2017, 291).

43. Silverstein 1980. A concern shared by the British director of the frontier areas, H. Stevenson. Many Burmese leaders in the AFPFL were suspicious of the British, seeing them as partial toward the ethnic minorities who remained loyal to them in World War II (Walton 2008, 895). See Silverstein 1980, chs. 4 and 5, for details on the quest for unity between Bamars and the ethnic minorities post–World War II and in the lead up to independence.

44. FACE (1947, pt. 2, app. 1, 35). These four were Naw Hkam U, chief minister from Manglun State (present-day Pangyang), who was himself a Shan; Sao Naw Hseng from Hsawnglong State, part of Vingngun (present-day Yin Phan) of the unfederated Wa States; Hkun Sai of Mongkong; and Sao Maha of Mongmon in the north. These four areas are all in today's Wa Region.

45. For instance, Kramer 2007, 9; Lintner and Black 2009, 48; Smith 1999, 84. Fiskesjö notes that it was likely the attendees had little conception of the objectives of the meeting and that the Shan or British translators' inputs could have also added to a mischaracterization of the Wa position (2013, 6). A review of the full FACE document corroborates this. Saw Naw Hseng states, "I do not know much about politics. I cannot even speak good Shan. I was sent by the Chief of Ving Ngun to come here" (FACE 1947, pt. 2, app. 1, 36)—resonating with the reluctance of Wa representation at negotiations with the Burmese authorities today. Hkun Sai, when asked about the objectives of the Committee, replied, "I do not know anything" (FACE 1947, pt. 2, app. 1, 37). Sao Maha replied, "One Assistant Resident sent me. I do not know his name. I come from Mongmon" (FACE 1947, pt. 2, app. 1, 38).

46. Saw Naw Hseng, cited in FACE 1947, pt. 2, app. 1, 36.

47. Sao Maha, cited in FACE 1947, pt. 2, app. 1, 36.

48. See Walton 2008 on the promises of the 1947 Panglong agreement.

49. For instance, the Shan and Chin agreements offered a clause for self-determination, whereas the Kachin agreement did not. The Karens observed, but refused to participate, seeking instead an independent state.

50. Basso 1996, 7.

51. Shenzhen Wutong Broadcasting Corporation 2004.

52. Shenzhen Wutong Broadcasting Corporation 2004.

53. Commander of 502 Battalion and later deputy commander of 683 Brigade (Lintner 1994).

54. Hoffman 2011, 11.

55. See Lintner 1990, 86–88, detailing CPB records on population and roads.

56. Marshall and Davis 2002.

57. Shenzhen Wutong Broadcasting Corporation 2004.

58. Marshall and Davis 2002.

59. Lintner and Black 2009, 72. See also Chin 2009; Milsom 2005.

60. Hong Pang company, owned by Wei Xuegang of the UWSA Politburo, has a whole series of associated companies and subsidiaries. Widely suspected of being involved in money-laundering profits from the drug trade, Hong Pang's businesses included timber, fruit and vegetable farms, cement, road building, metal smelting, pig farming, and retail. Hong Pang is involved in many joint ventures with other leaders of the UWSA and Myanmar military, rendering a complex tapestry of ownership and accumulation (Meehan 2011; Shan Herald 2007; Global Witness 2014; Lintner and Black 2009).

61. US Department of the Treasury 2005.

62. Chin 2009, 222.

63. Hoffman 2011, 130. For Hoffman, "ethnicity, family connections, monetary accumulation, spending, religious or political office, each of these threads helps constitute relations of patronage and clientelism in multiplex ways" (2011, 130).

64. Guyer 2004.

65. Shenzhen Wutong Broadcasting Corporation 2004.

66. Shenzhen Wutong Broadcasting Corporation 2004.

67. The "secret societies" have been blamed for much of the ills of the 1990s, particularly for the production and trafficking of drugs (Kramer 2007; Milsom 2005; but see Chin and Zhang's rebuttals [2015]) but also for having introduced certain macabre tactics of intimidation and violence.

68. Appadurai 1986. Anne Meneley (1996) demonstrates how practices of hospitality by women in Yemen are "manifestly political and deeply moral" (1996, 4), creating "dynamic competition" between households for honor and reputation (1996, 5).

69. See Yang 1989, 40–42.

70. See Kipnis 1997 and Yang 1989 for these well-studied notions of *guanxi* and cultivating relationships in Chinese society.

71. See Fredrik Barth's seminal work on the Swat Pathans for the competition between parallel structures of power, the chiefs and the holy men (1959). Scott also discusses how "indirect, office-based property" entrusted to the patron by virtue of their office can be distributed to clientele in exchange for their loyalty (1972, 98).

72. Bayart 2009.

73. Hoffman 2011.

74. A reverence for authority appears in language all over Wa Region, with *"lugyi"* (Bse, lit. big person), *"tax"* (Wa, honorific for elders), *"laoda"* (Chinese, elder brother, senior or boss), and *"laoguai"* (Yunannese, honorific similar to *laoda* but used mainly for older men; also refers to husband). The term "Wa leaders" (Chn: *wabang lingdao*) is deployed more generally for officials at township, district, and central levels. In practice, leaders are largely addressed in by their official titles (borrowed from Chinese political registers)—*buzhang* (minister), *fusilin* (deputy commander), *xianzhang* (district leader), *shuji* (secretary), or *quzhang* (township leader). Alternatively, the more informal and personal terms *laoguai* and *laoda* are also used to refer to a senior respected person in the community. *Ganbu*, or cadres, also adopted from the Chinese Communist nomenclature, is less commonly used, referring generally to "civil servants," and *dangyuan* to members of the UWSP.

75. Mbembe 1992, 23.

76. Commentators, often with developmental backgrounds, have commonly raised concerns over UWSA governance and its failure to approach "good governance" standards (Renard 2013a; Kramer 2007).

77. As the Chinese government occasionally did with the Monglar area, shutting down its border and internet services, when gambling losses by Chinese nationals (and government officials) spiraled out of hand.

78. See Fiskesjö 2021, 57–62, for a discussion of personal naming and honorifics in Wa society.

79. TNI 2016, 2017; ICG 2016.

80. Scott 1972, 93.

81. Elyachar 2010.

82. See Hayden and Villeneuve 2011 for summary. Within analyses of hospitality are themes of reciprocity, debt, morality, calculation, unpredictability, and ambivalence at play within arenas of hosting (Herzfeld 1987; Marsden 2012; Shryock 2012; Swancutt 2012).

83. Brachet and Scheele 2019, 33.

84. The jury might still be out on whether these are deliberate acts by the Burmese to refuse to play the game by the right etiquette, a purposive disrespect for local norms in order to establish hierarchy. I do not believe this to be the case in micro-interactions, although at the level of political negotiations such refusals of recognition are most certainly intentional.

85. Meneley 1996, 35.

86. Elanah Uretsky studies these practices of hosting (Chn: *yingchou*) among Chinese businessmen and officials in Yunnan, describing their banqueting and entertainment activities as a domain of social and commercial action (2016). She details practices of consumption, toasting, and prostitution as part of hospitality. Osburg writes about hosting and entertainment practices among "new elites" in Chengdu, with vivid ethnographic descriptions of the micro-practices of interaction (2013).

87. See Bourdieu's discussion of the temporal dimensions of the gift (1979).

3. OSCILLATIONS AND INCONGRUITIES

1. Epigraph: Mya Kha and Lawi Weng 2014. Material from this chapter has previously appeared in a journal article published in *American Ethnologist* (Ong 2020).
2. Lawi Weng 2015b.
3. Lawi Weng 2015a.
4. Lawi Weng 2015a.
5. SHAN 2015.
6. SHAN 2015.
7. Sai Wansai 2015.
8. Lawi Weng 2015c.
9. Lawi Weng 2019.
10. See Hill 1998 on a similar cross-border community, the Yunnanese Chinese Haw.
11. For example, Lintner 2014.
12. Several ethnic Chinese friends I met in Pangkham traced their lineage to Chinese who had come over during the KMT times but were deliberately vague (or uneven uncertain themselves) as to whether their parents had been active KMT soldiers, refugees, or simply civilians moving along with the soldiers. They spoke of their parents moving southward from Hopang and gradually nearing the Thai border, some through Wa Region and some west of the Salween. See also Ying 2008 on KMT descendants in Northern Thailand.
13. The Wa Historical Committee records six thousand Chinese Communist soldiers attacking KMT troops in Wa Region around 1950, forcing the KMT troops to retreat to Kengtung (2017, 305). The KMT troops which initially entered did not engage the Burmese military camped around Hopang and Mengmao (2017, 360).
14. On US support, see Clymer 2014 and Kaufman 2001; on the attempts to retake mainland China, see Gibson and Chen 2011.
15. From Taiwan Ministry of Defence records (Chang 2001, 1089); Chang 2002, 2009.
16. Callahan 2003; Maung Aung Myoe 2009; Selth 2002; Egreteau and Jagan 2013.
17. Steinberg and Fan 2012, 53.
18. Chang 2001, 1088; Sai Aung Tun 2009, 312.
19. Sai Aung Tun 2009, 308. Lintner 1994, 191; Chao Tzang Yawnghwe marks KMT presence in Yin Phan (Vingngun) (2010), and Winnington writes of KMT raids on Wa villages beginning in 1948, with the Wa counterattacks on KMT remnants (2008, 129). Many informants spoke of Chinese KMT soldiers and civilians arriving, but passing through the areas of Northern Wa (near Mengmao and Man Tun) on the way to Dangyan and Lashio west of the Salween. The bulk of KMT forces had left by 1953, with scattered bases and strongholds remaining until 1973 when the CPB gained full control of Wa Region.
20. Intriguingly, the Wa Historical Committee claims that the KMT provided advanced signals equipment and bribed "honest" Wa chiefs into operating this equipment, gathering intelligence on Chinese Communist plans from Wa Region from 1950 to 1972 (2017, 361). The book claims that the local Wa gradually rejected this eavesdropping practice, leading to the KMT departure by 1972.
21. The UWSA-produced *Gazetteer* recorded four villages burnt in the Wangleng area, where KMT troops cut off the ears of Wa villagers and wore them around their necks (Wa Gazetteer Editorial Committee 2004, 2).
22. E.G. 1957, 90.
23. Winnington 2008; also Fiskesjö 2000, 371.
24. Lintner 1994. The KMT retreated to Northern Thailand by the 1960s, where they were supported by the United States and tolerated by the Thai government as a screen against the spread of Communism. Known as the "orphan army" (Chn: *gujun*), they

numbered about thirty-two hundred (Chang 2002, 130) split between two groups, the Third Army of General Li Wen-huan settling in Tam Ngob in Chiang Mai Province and the Fifth Army of General Duan Shi-wen in Mae Salong in Chiang Rai Province (Chang 2001; Ying 2008). They were heavily implicated in the drug trade in the 1960s, competing with Khun Sa for control of routes. Two withdrawals to Taiwan took place in 1954 and 1961, and those left behind assisted the Thai government in the fight against Communists in the 1970s and 1980s. They were disbanded in the late 1980s, many rewarded with Thai citizenship after (Gibson and Chen 2011; Chang 2002). Along with other Yunnanese Chinese refugees and followers, they resettled in Northern Thailand in about thirty-five villages, numbering forty thousand to fifty thousand (Chang 2002, 131).

25. Lintner 2011, 313; Chao Tzang Yawnghwe 2010.

26. Yang describes postindependence-era Kokang politics in *House of Yang* (1997), detailing the various flirtations and shifting loyalties of Kokang leaders, including Olive Yang, with the KMT and Burmese militaries. See also Myint Myint Kyu 2018 on the Kokang Special Region.

27. A key figure to leave the service of Olive Yang was Lo Hsing Han, who later led the Kokang KKY and fought for the Tatmadaw against the CPB in the 1970s. The KKYs received permits to smuggle opium and Lo prospered, soon dubbed the "King of the Golden Triangle" (Lintner and Black 2009, 25–27). After the government ordered KKYs to disband in 1972, he went underground with other Shan rebel armies, arrested in 1973 and released in 1980. It was common for lackeys to strike out on their own after having made sufficient or social connections while in the service of a leader.

28. See Smith 1999; Taylor 2009, chs. 5 and 6. The outbreak of insurgencies across the country after independence, the threat to territorial sovereignty from the KMT, and the CPB's fleeting but widespread military victories across lower Burma in the mid-1950s undermined the authority of the democratic government. The first prime minister U Nu, facing also revolt from within his own party, the Anti-Fascist People's Freedom League (AFPFL), asked General Ne Win in September 1958 to take over as a caretaker government. U Nu resumed as prime minister in April 1960 after his faction of the AFPFL won the 1960 elections. Two years later in March 1962, Ne Win's military coup dissolved Parliament and took over the reins of government, placing U Nu under "protective custody." Both U Nu and Ne Win, along with the legendary Aung San (Suu Kyi's father), were members of the Dohbama Asiayone (We Burmans Association), who began the struggles for independence against the British, and part of the Thirty Comrades who formed the Burma Independence Army (forerunner to the Tatmadaw), trained by the Japanese to fight the British during World War II (see Lintner 1990; Taylor 2015).

29. Lintner (1994, 187); see Buchanan 2016 for a breakdown of the messy definitions and distinctions between the KKY, *pyithusit* ("People's Militia"), and TaKaSaPha (anti-insurgent groups) of the 1960s, contrasted with the Border Guard Forces (created by the Tatmadaw in 2009) and other local militia.

30. Cowell 2005, 3.

31. Chao Tzang Yawnghwe 2010, 22.

32. There always seemed to be an unease when speaking of the past of headhunting with outsiders, as if local Wa had internalized the shame outsiders had attached to it. Stories of headhunting I heard in the hills almost always shifted responsibility onto another area—"There was no headhunting here, but on the opposite hilltop, or in such and such a township, they used to chop heads there."

33. One township leader gave the figure of fourteen different chieftains, including Zhao Nyi Lai and Bao Youxiang in the 1970s. Sai Lone's interview with UWSA deputy commander-in-chief Bu Laikang in 2008 suggested ten "clans" (2008, 29). According to an ex-CPB informant I interviewed, when the CPB entered Wa region in the 1960s, there

were thirty-four Wa groups, twenty-seven allied with the CPB, and four (from Dangyan, Hopang, Man Xiang, and Panglong areas) allied with the government. The remaining three sided with the KMT remnants and were gradually forced out of the area (including Mahasang of Yin Phan's group, who had joined the Tatmadaw's KKY program in 1969 after first resisting the Tatmadaw's orders to disarm [Smith 1999, 350]). It is difficult to trace direct lines between these militia groups and descendant villages of the traditional Wa realms.

34. They were Bao Youxiang and Bao Sanban of Kunma, Zhao Nyi Lai of Ban Wai, Ai Keng and Ai Kelong of Aicheng, and Lu Xing Guo of Hushuang, taken from a Wa government report—Ting Xiao's *A Report on the Support and Assistance to Myanmar's Special Region No. 2 (Wa State) for the Development of its Drug Eradication Program* (2001)—often cited by writers such as Chin (2009, 21) and Milsom (2005, 66). See instead the 2012 report.

35. Smith 1999, 350; Wa Historical Committee 2017, ch. 8.

36. Shenzhen Wutong Broadcasting Corporation 2004.

37. Lintner 1994, 216–17. Also note the distinction between the Pegu Yoma–based CPB and the CPB group that entered from the Chinese border.

38. Steinberg and Fan 2012.

39. Lintner 1994, 217.

40. South Wa (occupied from 1990s onward) is not included in this. The CPB's attention initially turned westward to Kunlone and the strategic bridge across the Salween River, but defeat there meant that it focused instead on driving southward through the Wa hills, down to Pangkham and into the flatter lands of Mong Pawk. Military monuments to the battles fought during from 1969 to 1973 during the military campaign for the Wa hills now stand in Pang Kham, Ai Cheng, Mong Pawk, and Mengmao.

41. Comparing Lintner's CPB population statistics taken in 1979 and 1986, one finds that populations decreased by forty thousand in the years after the CPB takeover (Lintner 1990, app. 2). This was especially so from the northern areas of Wa Region, where the front lines at Kunlone, Hopang, and Nam Tit were particularly precarious. Lintner 1994, 330.

42. Kramer 2007, 22.

43. In fact, most of my colleagues at the World Food Programme in Pangkham were the children of these Wa migrants to Burmese areas, born in Hopang and Lashio. Because they were formally educated in Burma, they had the basic English and mathematics skills required to gain employment with the UN, whereas almost no Wa born in Wa Region were suitably qualified for the task due to the dismal education system.

44. Lintner 2011, 345.

45. Chang 2009, 559. Other maps drawn by Chao Tzang Yawnghwe (2010) and Sai Aung Tun (2009, 306) show KMT troop and smuggling routes passing through and around Pangkham. By this time, the border was fully demarcated.

46. Anecdotally, a Wa colleague in his fifties was the only surviving child of nine.

47. Lintner 1990, 91.

48. Chang 2015, 263.

49. Chin 2009, 29.

50. Lintner 1990, 40.

51. Lintner corroborates a large rat invasion in 1976, which wiped out any CPB attempts at opium-substitution (1990, 40).

52. These horrendous conditions in Hpakant continue to this day, with dozens of deaths annually as jade pickers scramble in large mining pits alongside heavy machinery to eke out a living. See Global Witness 2015, Prasse-Freeman 2021.

53. See Maule 1992 on British policy on opium in Burma.

54. Lintner 1990, 46.

55. Lintner 1994, 296.

56. Chin 2009, 21–23; up to twelve thousand Wa troops fought in the CPB army at any one time, and the Wa National Organization (WNO) later estimated that thirty thousand had died (Smith 1999, 351).

57. Lintner too, differentiates six types of CPB cadres—Sichuan veterans," "old comrades," "Guizhou veterans," "intellectuals and newcomers," "Chinese volunteers," and "national minorities" (1990, 32, 35).

58. Kramer 2007; Lintner 1990, 1994.

59. Lintner 1990, 37.

60. Lintner 1990, 35–36.

61. Phoenix New Media 2009.

62. See a UWSA Politburo member explain this in a 2019 interview produced by Wa State TV, available at https://www.youtube.com/watch?v=CNb2gT0mns8&t=3m40s. *minzu* is Chinese for "Nationalities," or "ethnicities." Renard translates it most closely as the "United Myanmar National Democratic Army" (2013a, 150). LNDO calls it the Burma National Solidarity Party, which is inaccurate (2002, 6). Smith gives the name as the "Burma Democratic Solidarity Party," retaining the hallmarks of Communist "anti-racial" thought (1999, 353), and Buchanan the "Burma National United Army" (2016, 9), demonstrating the difficulties of translations between Chinese, Burmese, and English nomenclature.

63. In July and August of 1988, pro-democracy protests erupted in Rangoon, following months of standoffs between student demonstrators and the military and police. Attempts to quell protesters failed, and despite Ne Win's resignation, protesters were discontented with his touted replacements. Gen Saw Maung finally took power in a bloodbath in September, replacing the BSPP with his SLORC. See Charney 2009; Taylor 2009; Smith 1999; Steinberg 2001. Deaths numbered in the thousands, military rule clinging to power by a thread.

64. Lintner 1994, 298. The 1989 ceasefires with the former CPB groups were crucial to SLORC, ensuring they did not merge with the NDF, a grouping of other ethnic armies dominated by the Karens. It also freed up more troops for the control of lower Myanmar, still reeling from the 1988 uprising.

65. Chang 2009, 564.

66. Human Rights Watch n.d.; Keenan 2013.

67. Lombard 2016.

68. Lombard 2016, 114.

69. Kramer claims that the UWSA promotes Wa ethnic nationalism as evidenced by its claims for a Wa State (2007, 30). The reality stands somewhere in between, a mix of convenience, other priorities, and genuine ethnonationalist sentiment. The case of Mongla (NDAA), supposedly representing the Aini ethnic minority but whose leaders are ethnic Chinese, offers a case study for the instrumentalization of ethnic identity.

70. Lintner (1990, 89–90; 1994, 435) seems to suggest that part of the ethnonationalist drive to brand the organization as a Wa organization was introduced by these groups on the Thai border. Lintner also records a merger with the Wa National Council led by Ai Xiaoxue on the Thai border (1994, 298, 435); Smith records this as a faction of the WNC that returned north to join the new UWSA, fomenting a greater Wa nationalist consciousness. Lintner also states that the 1986 arrival of a Wa officer from the Wa National Army (WNA) showed Wa troops in the CPB the possibilities of ethnic-based armed resistance (1990, 43). The WNA was formed in 1976 from the pro-Burmese government Yin Phan KKY (Ka Kwe Ye), led by Mahasang, the son of the Yin Phan *saopha* (royal) (Smith 1999, 350), who fled Wa Region when the CPB took over and was based on the Thai border (Lintner 1994). It had narco-trade ties in the 1970s with the KMT forces there and worked with Wei Xuegang, current member of the UWSA Politburo.

71. A UWSA Politburo member expressed this in a 2019 interview produced by Wa State TV, available at https://www.youtube.com/watch?v=CNb2gT0mns8.
72. Saw Lu 1993.
73. Wa Gazetteer Editorial Committee 2004, 3.
74. For instance, in Chairman Bao's 2019 fiftieth anniversary speech.
75. Wa SAD is one of six Self-Administered Areas (SAAs) aimed at granting more autonomy to certain ethnic groups in Myanmar under the constitution. Wa SAD consists of six townships, most under UWSA control, and is officially represented by the Wa Democratic Party (WDP), a party completely separate from the UWSA and which operates mainly in Hopang, a Myanmar-controlled subtownship at the northern edge of Wa Region. Five other SAAs are listed as Self-Administered Zones (SAZs) because of their small size of two to three townships (compared with the six of Wa SAD).
76. That the de facto UWSA territory differs territorially from the legally delimited area of Wa SAD gives rise to much confusion. For example, the 2014 Census relies on the township boundaries of Wa SAD to gather data. Where government documents or policies describe wealth-sharing development activities in Wa SAD, they are merely referring to activities in the small portions of Hopang and Mankan (subtownship) areas, and not to the bulk of Wa Region, where they have neither access nor authority. I use Burmese spellings when describing Wa townships as named by the Myanmar government, and Chinese spellings where Wa townships are named by the Wa authorities.
77. The Appendix to the Frontier Areas Committee of Enquiry 1947 describes this as a motor road in 1941, serving the Northern Wa States, with a dirt road extending seven miles into the States (FACE 1947, pt. 2, app. 3, p. 190), probably toward Panglong. This seems to be the extent of British infrastructural reach into the Wa States, though trade networks of mule tracks undoubtedly existed.
78. Democratic Voice of Burma 2009.
79. Khin Nyunt first visited Kokang Region in 1989, enlisting the help of former Kokang KKY leader and drug lord Lo Hsing-han to convince ex-CPB Kokang leader Peng Jiasheng to sign a ceasefire and participate in development efforts (Lintner 1994, 297). This was the same policy with the UWSA and the forebears of the NDAA (Monglar group). The UWSA controlled many other areas in Shan State up to 1992, areas inherited from the CPB, but withdrew from them after negotiations with Khin Nyunt.
80. Chin (2009, 26). See Steinberg 2001 on the opening of Myanmar's economy following the failure of the 1988 pro-democracy protests.
81. Interview with Bao Youxiang, recorded by Maung Pho Shoke (1999, 195).
82. Buchanan's describes briefly the designation of "peace groups" (*Nyein Chan Yay A'pweh*) as a part of the informal ceasefire agreements and arrangements between the Tatmadaw and the more powerful ethnic armed groups (2016, 2).
83. Milsom (2010, 71) mentions a small military unit of twenty persons in Pangkham around 2005.
84. Khun Sa's infamous journey began as leader of the pro-government Loi Maw KKY near Dangyan in 1966, before being detained by the government in 1969, switching allegiances back and forth after his release in 1973, and forming and re-forming a handful of armed militia organizations, finally the MTA with a headquarters in Homong. He died in Yangon in 2007. See Buchanan 2016, 16; Lintner and Black 2009, 61–64; and Chao Tzang Yawnghwe 2010, 176–77 for a short biography.
85. Some claim that the UWSA did not "defeat" Khun Sa and his MTA; rather, it was a confluence of different pressures from Thailand, Myanmar, and other armed groups that led to his surrender; see Maung Pho Shoke 1999. Disgruntled remnants of Khun Sa's MTA continued to fight on as the Shan State Army-South/Restoration Council of Shan State (SSA-S/RCSS), led by former MTA colonel Yawd Serk, and at least seven other

ex-MTA groups (Lintner and Black 2009, 85–87; Buchanan 2016, 17). The RCSS battled the UWSA and Tatmadaw in 2001–2002, and resisted the migration of Wa villagers down to the South, and has today a hot-cold relationship with the Tatmadaw, continuing involvement in skirmishes with other ethnic armed groups.

86. Ball 2003, 14.

87. Selth catalogues the different theories of Khin Nyunt's fall: disagreement as to foreign policy, a struggle for power, personality clashes, competition for the black market, and his own attempts to hold on to power (2019).

88. Prager Nyein 2009, 640.

89. Jagan 2006; ALTSEAN 2005.

90. The Kokang troubles had begun months earlier, when in April 2009 the Tatmadaw announced a policy for all EAOs to be transformed either into Border Guard Forces (BGF), accepting its officers into their ranks, or People's Militia Forces (PMF) under their command (see Buchanan 2016, 18–19, 26, on BGFs and PMFs). This move proved unsuccessful, with only a handful of smaller and splinter groups agreeing to be incorporated into the new system.

91. The UWSA submitted a nine-point proposal to the Tatmadaw in November 2009 proposing recognition of its territory at Mong Phen and Mong Pawk and maintaining control over its own troops, which was rejected (Keenan 2013, 78).

92. They had met in Pangkham in January 2009, in Dangyan in April 2009 before this (Keenan 2013, 77). See also Wikileaks (2009) containing a US interview with a UWSA liaison officer describing the BGF discussions.

93. Saw Yan Naing 2010.

94. Keenan 2013, 80.

95. Saw Yan Naing 2011.

96. See Keenan 2013, 83, for the terms of a fourteen-point proposal put forward by the UWSA.

97. Friends estimated about thirty thousand inhabitants in Pangkham in 2009. The Burmese population fell from eight thousand to only one thousand in that period, according to their estimates. Chin cites Wa authorities' figures in 2004 of eighteen thousand residents in Pang Kham, with fifty-eight thousand migrant workers and mobile residents (2009, 27). The second figure seems too high, and possibly includes tourists, migrant workers, and traders from China, some of whom might reside in the surrounding townships of Wa Region.

98. Lemon 2013, 67–68.

99. Based on the 2014 Myanmar Population and Housing Census, calculated by aggregating township data and separating out government-controlled townships; the figure is 93.9 percent without Myanmar ID cards. Census data collection in Wa Region was highly problematic, but the rate of 90 percent is generally accurate and corroborated by discussions at village level. This is noteworthy; while the citizenship issue has been prominent in news regarding the plight of the Rohingya, it is rarely mentioned that large portions of the ethnic minorities in the highlands have neither Pink IDs nor White IDs, although they have legal avenues to citizenship under the 1982 Citizenship Law, being part of the 135 "nationalities" of Myanmar.

100. Lawi Weng 2015d.

101. Lawi Weng 2015e.

102. Relations with other EAOs are also precarious. Since the fall of the Kokang in 2009, many northern EAOs have become closer to the UWSA, allegedly relying on it for military support and a supply of weapons. These allegations are made by political observers, for example, Davis 2020. Farther south, the Shan State Army-North (SSA-N) provides a buffer on Wa Region's western flank across the Salween River, even though Shan nationalism has maintained a testy relationship with the UWSA, following the Wa mi-

grations to South Wa. To the north, the Kachins are often seen by China as Christian and Western-leaning and regarded with some suspicion by the UWSA. Other officials recounted an incident when a Kachin group supposedly released a map of a greater Kachin homeland, provoking the Chinese government's fury, since it encroached upon their territory. "That was a big mistake. Of course, China will never trust them. They are Christian, speak English, and have many ties to the West."

103. SHAN 2016. Another rumor circulated that the military action was a hotheaded response to "teach the Monglar troops a lesson" after they had disrespected a Wa military commander who was passing through their checkpoints.

104. Lun Min Mang 2016.

105. Phoenix New Media 2009.

106. Their adversaries, the Mong Tai Army, lost about thirteen hundred (Maung Pho Shoke 1999, 52).

107. This is not to suggest that there is no factionalism among the UWSA; disagreements and rivalries are a source of gossip in town, and the UWSA Politburo is certainly not a singular entity with clearly defined and cohesive aims. Yet thus far there have been no overt adversarial factions or splits such as those seen among the Karen, Kokang, or Shan (see Keenan 2013; TNI 2012; Smith 1999). Chairman Bao and his two brothers, along with one other military commander (retired 2019), are ethnic Wa from the central Wa areas, while the vice-chairman and another military commander are ethnic Wa from the areas now carved into China. These form two-thirds of the Politburo as at 2016. Three others are ethnic Chinese from border areas. Media suggestions that the leadership is Chinese are inaccurate.

108. For example, the failure of the National Democratic Front founded in 1976. See Chart 2 in Smith 1999. The current United Nationalities Federal Council (UNFC) was floundering, too, as six out of eleven members resigned between 2014 and 2017, including the Karen National Union (KNU) and Kachin Independence Organization (KIO) heavyweights.

109. Such as the confrontations and standoffs in South Wa in 2015, around Nam Tit in 2013, and with Monglar in 2016.

110. The UWSA had previously signed the Federal Proposal, submitted to the National Convention by a group of EAOs in 2004, and promptly disregarded by the Tatmadaw (Keenan 2013, 76).

111. For a list of EAOs, and a map of the latest EAO zones of control and territories, see Burma News International 2017, fig. 5.

112. He is also referring to the PMF and BGF policies of the Tatmadaw.

113. Phoenix New Media 2009. Milsom 2005, 81.

114. The national peace infrastructure underwent wholesale changes with the arrival of the NLD government, as part of Aung San Suu Kyi's attempts to control it. The Myanmar Peace Centre (MPC), the Thein Sein–led government's peace center that facilitates peace negotiations with armed groups, was reformed into the National Reconciliation and Peace Center (NRPC), and the Joint Monitoring Committee (JMC), set up to monitor the October 2015 NCA, was revamped (see TNI 2017); the replacement of key personnel with strong ties to EAOs was a further setback.

115. Nyein Nyein 2016.

116. Nang Seng Nom 2016.

117. Lawi Weng 2016b.

118. FPNCC 2017a. The principles appear to have been drafted in Chinese, translated into Burmese, and then translated into English for the international community. The lack of subtlety indexed Wa assertiveness on the diplomatic stage, a disregard for the misgivings of allies. Pp. 11–12.

119. FPNCC 2017a, 11. On April 30, the UWSA released a "Process of Negotiation" document that alleged that the UWSA had been "humiliated" by the government, since the private negotiations of the amended NCA had been rejected publicly without speaking to them first: "The government of Myanmar has always shown no respect to ethnic minorities. This mentality has been vividly and thoroughly presented through this event" (UWSA 2017, 13). The document claimed that it had been willing to sign the NCA, but with modifications.

120. FPNCC 2017b. Lawi Weng 2017.
121. FPNCC 2017b, ch. 2, art. VII.
122. Ibid, ch. 2, art. VIII, clause 2, 3.
123. Ibid, ch. 2, art. VIII, clause 8–11. Ibid, ch. 2, art. X, clause 2.
124. FPNCC 2017b, ch. 4, art. XXII.
125. FPNCC 2017b, ch. 2, art. V.
126. FPNCC 2017b, ch. 2, art. XII, and ch. 8, art. XXXIV.
127. UWSA 2017, 15 (original emphasis).
128. TNI 2017.
129. See Horsey 2017. However, the SSA-N (SSPP) and KIO had their own reasons for attending and were perhaps more willing to engage than other groups.
130. Kyaw Kha 2017.
131. On the potential of the concept of "refusal" as an alternative means of understanding resistance and rebellion, see Prasse-Freeman 2022.
132. Bakhtin 1984, 11–12.

4. FRONTIER ACCUMULATIONS

1. Tsing 2005, 30–32.
2. Turner 1920; Tsing 2005, 31.
3. Imamura 2015, 97.
4. Lee and Slodkowski 2016a; Pye and Saw Yan Naing 2013. The China-Myanmar relationship is a key topic of geopolitical analysis and commentary, with China seen as keen to ensure stability, but not necessarily peace, for its economic and strategic objectives (Han 2017; Maung Aung Myoe 2015; Sun 2019b; Lintner 2017). On the wider geostrategic calculations of China, see the several detailed think-tank reports by TNI (2016, 2019); ICG (2010, 2020); USIP (2018); and Sun (2017). On the longer history of this relationship, see Haacke 2011; Steinberg and Fan 2012; and Maung Aung Myoe 2011.
5. Described as the "Malacca Dilemma" by TNI (2016).
6. Su 2016.
7. The "String of Pearls" theory of Chinese expansionist influence in the Indian Ocean has been disputed as exaggerated by some observers, arguing that ports are not the same as military naval bases. See Klein 2018.
8. Sun 2017.
9. Chinese State TV regularly ran reality documentaries that showcased border enforcement patrols dealing with drug smugglers and criminals on the Myanmar border; see the "Military Affairs" program on CCTV 7, April 17, 2013, for example, at https://www.youtube.com/watch?v=QosJvIbJxRA.
10. For instance, a Wa State TV News Agency Report, broadcast October 15, 2018.
11. Nyiri (2012) describes these casino enterprises (Monglar in Shan State and Boten in Laos) as an aspirational form of Chinese modernity and progress while challenging the nation-state and giving rise to new forms of ambiguous sovereignty. ICG 2019, 15; USIP 2020.
12. A good example is the blog of Hla Oo, a Burmese "exile" who spreads inflammatory allegations of Wa secession or allegiance to the PLA; see Hla Oo 2014.

13. Milsom 2005, 80.
14. Aung Zeya 2015.
15. Lee and Slodkowski 2016a.
16. Lintner 2014. There is some truth to Lintner's assertions of the involvement of Chinese military expertise and hardware. Friends in the Wa administration spoke of retired specialists and the informal arms trade at the peripheries of the Chinese state, without offering details. Lintner's later book (2021) offers a more careful analysis of this relationship with the Chinese.
17. SHAN 2015; Lun Min Mang and Thu Aung 2016.
18. A Burmese political analyst was forced to qualify a statement accusing the Chinese of destabilizing the talks in 2015. See Wee 2015.
19. See Ferrie 2015. The anti-Chinese riots of 1967 (Steinberg and Fan 2012), rumored to be stoked by the military junta, were part of a long history of hostility toward landholding and capital-accumulating foreigners. In today's Mandalay, Northern Shan State, and Karen State the presence of PRC Chinese and their business and property investments are particularly visible, causing Burmese to feel pushed out of their cultural heritage areas (ICG 2009, 25; 2020); Sai Wansai 2015.
20. USIP 2018.
21. A TNI report writes of the relation, "Both the UWSA and NDAA are headed by former CPB supporters who have long maintained close relations with China. Indeed, with Chinese widely spoken in both their territories, the two groups are often regarded as Chinese proxies, although this is not an accurate designation on the ground. Although the UWSA has to take into account what China will think about decisions made by the organization, the UWSA has also made efforts during the past two decades to establish links with the international community, especially with Thailand and the West" (2016, 24).
22. Lintner 2019.
23. See Lin (2011), who studied the counterfeit industry in China, though most of her work focuses on luxury goods that have less purchase in Wa Region. In Wa Region, the counterfeiting of goods pertains mainly to consumable goods like medicines and alcohol or cigarettes.
24. Young 2014, 50.
25. Renard 2013a, 157.
26. For instance, *Lifeweek* magazine from China called Wa Region a "copycat society" (Chn: *shanzhai*) of China in the age of globalization; see Zhongguo 2011.
27. See, for instance, Blum 2001; Fiskesjö 2002; Heberer 2014; Litzinger 2000; Schein 2000.
28. Anthropologists of conflict pay close attention to the norms and rules that continue to govern behavior in conflict areas of supposed social breakdown (Debos 2016; Lubkemann 2008).
29. Chang 2006, 278.
30. Phoenix New Media 2009.
31. This aspirational dam is likely an early iteration, or at least leveraging off, the proposed plans for the Naung Pha dam on the Salween River. See Environmental Justice Atlas 2018. For the Myanmar civil society opposition to dam projects, see Chan 2017; Kiik 2016.
32. Kramer corroborates this enchantment with large infrastructural projects among the UWSA leadership, interviewing an aid worker who recounted, "The Wa are very much influenced by China, they want to make big projects" (2007, 32).
33. Harvey 1981.
34. Harvey 1981, 7.
35. Tsing 2005, 57.
36. Jusionyte and Goldstein 2016; Campbell 2017.

37. Tsing 2005, 59.
38. Tsing 2005, 75.
39. Similar narratives of luck and perseverance are at play in jade *dupo* (Chn, lit. gambling on breaking [of rock]), where buyers try their luck buying unopened or partially opened rocks, betting on the quantity and quality of jade found inside.
40. Peel and Sanderson 2016.
41. Chang 2006, 286–87.
42. See Osburg 2013; Uretsky 2016.
43. Chang 2006, 280.
44. Peel and Sanderson 2016.
45. Tsing 1993; Di Nunzio 2017.
46. In spite of this uncertainty, think tanks and NGOs have produced some information on purported ownerships: Global Witness (2015); ICG (2009); TNI (2012, 2013); and Fuller (2015). Kevin Woods describes the rubber concessions given by the Myanmar state to armed group leaders yet financed by Chinese private actors as contributing to a terrain of "armed sovereignties" across Myanmar (2019).
47. Consistent with what ethnographers of Chinese gambling have written, Chen, like Mao, is at least partly gambling to get a sense of whether his luck is changing (Chu 2010). Julie Chu sees aspiration as linked with gambling through the "struggles for practical mastery over those elusive yet powerfully pervasive forces of credit-making that exceed the visible threshold of their daily lives" (2010, 260).
48. Prices recovered in 2016 after I left but during 2015 were on a constant decline. See a Copper Prices tracker at Macrotrends, https://www.macrotrends.net/1476/copper-prices-historical-chart-data.
49. Lee and Slodkowski 2016b.
50. Mezzadra and Neilson 2019, 148.
51. Mak 2015.
52. Xinhua News 2016.
53. Rauhala 2016; Makinen 2016.
54. Makinen 2016.
55. Sun 2017, 9.
56. Sun 2017, 9.
57. Ng 2018.

5. GESTURES OF GOVERNANCE

1. Some material from this chapter has previously appeared in a journal article published in *American Ethnologist* (Ong 2020).
2. Pitchford 1937, 223.
3. Marshall and Davis 2002; Lee and Myint 2016.
4. All these figures above are derived from the 2014 Myanmar Population and Housing Census, calculated by aggregating township data and separating out government-controlled townships from the UWSA-controlled ones; census available at http://themimu.info/census-data.
5. Kramer 2007, 32–33.
6. WFP VAM 2010. The study looked at 310 households across fourteen townships in Wa Region. Food consumption scoring was based on a calculation of food diversity and availability (food insecurity). UNICEF's (2005) Multiple Indicator Cluster Survey (MICS) found Under-5 growth stunting to be at 57.7 percent and wasting at 7.3 percent.
7. Kramer 2007, xvi.
8. Renard 2013, 144.
9. Kramer 2007, 32.

10. Lee and Myint 2016.

11. Renard 2013a, 143.

12. Elsewhere in Myanmar, Chambers describes how Karen Buddhist strongmen use donation ceremonies as moral performances to mitigate criticisms of their illicitly gained wealth, leveraging on a social value of "faithfulness" (2019).

13. Scheele 2014, 44.

14. While "rebel" might be a distracting term that presupposes rebellion and antagonism toward the state, Mampilly uses it interchangeably with insurgency (2011, 3).

15. Arjona et al. 2015, 3; also Mampilly 2011; Lidow 2016; Huang 2016.

16. For instance, Florea (2020) argues that de facto states with access to lootable resources are less likely to provide governance, while those receiving external military support, possessing fixed assets, or having Marxist ideology are more likely to provide governance. He defines governance as "the entire range of political, redistributive, and extractive institutions" (2020, 1007).

17. Mampilly 2011, 16.

18. Mampilly 2011, 27; cf. Olson 1993. Olson's famous notion of the "stationary bandit" imagines the settling down of insurgents and raiders into fixed territories to extract taxes as the beginning of state formation (1993).

19. Mampilly 2011, 61.

20. For instance, Furlan writes that "rebels engage in governance in order to demonstrate their capacity and their legitimacy as rulers vis-a-vis the government, and that they do so by means of providing security, justice, and other public services to the civilian population living upon the conquered territories" (2020, 7). For her, COVID-19 provided the Taliban and Tahrir Al-Sham "an opportunity to project themselves as more reliable providers of governance . . . and score additional points in the battle for credibility, support, and legitimacy against the government" (2020, 16). Also, Florea 2020; Weinstein 2006; cf. Stewart 2020.

21. Stewart 2020. Following a series of quantitative tests, she writes that "because rebel governance does not appear to have consistently positive military consequences for the rebel group, researchers ought to question the strategic motivations undergirding some rebel groups' choices to engage in governance at all" (2020, 33).

22. For example, Terpstra and Frerks 2018 go beyond instrumental rebels' exchange of public services for civilians' compliance and examine their symbolic modes of building legitimacy. Also, Schlichte and Schneckener 2015; Terpstra 2020.

23. An alternative strand of rebel governance sees Hoffmann and Vermeijen (2018) use a framing of governmentality to decenter "rebel governance" away from rulers and institutions. They find among the Mai-Mai a pastoral form of patronage where the "father/patron is expected to provide for the well-being and security of his dependants/clients, as symbolized in his ability to 'give'" (2018, 370). For them, this is part of a governmentality that shapes the subjectivities and conduct of the ruled, operating alongside other forms of authority based in individual leaders and institutions.

24. This is the angle from which most writing on Wa Region has taken place: Ronald Renard wrote his article (2013a) reflecting on his time as the project manager of UNODC's Wa Project from 2006 to 2007, as was Jeremy Milsom before him, who contributed to an edited volume on the opium economy in Burma (2005). Sai Lone, whose master's thesis was on the political economy of opium reduction (2008), worked for UNODC in Wa Region for more than ten years in the 2000s. Tom Kramer, working with the Transnational Institute (TNI), visited Wa Region several times in 2003 and 2004 alongside the UN.

25. Sylvia Tidey (2016) argues that the juxtaposition of Weberian models of rational-legal bureaucracies against local moral economies based on reciprocity led to simplistic notions of corruption and nepotism. Tidey's own work describes how Indonesian civil

servants carefully navigate local moralities and ethical behavior in reciprocal favors and connections, complicating easy definitions of "corrupt" behavior under the rules of the good governance framework.

26. World Bank 1992; cf Grindle 2016, Weiss 2000.

27. Such concerns about "plans" in governance are also repeated in other EAO areas of Myanmar, where South and Joll identify two challenges for EAOs—governance and service delivery, and gaining recognition from state, international, and everyday people (2016, 188). South, focusing on the "hybrid governance" between the Myanmar state and the Karen National Union (KNU), argues that international organizations supporting peace must attend to both the state's institutional weakness, and develop the EAOs' capacity for "inclusive and participatory governance" (2017, 11).

28. Milsom 2005, 64.

29. Chinese administrator Chen Can, writing around 1908, cited by Fiskesjö (2010a, 257, my italics).

30. Young 2014, 28.

31. Young 2014, 36.

32. Scott and Hardiman 1900, 510. Scott's distaste for poor hygiene extended also to the Burmese.

33. Scott 1906, 138.

34. On what has been dubbed the civilizing mission of the Han Chinese in its minority areas, see Hansen 2005; Harrell 1995; and Nyiri 2006.

35. Winnington 2008, 148.

36. Winnington 2008, 130.

37. See Winnington 2008, 153. In fact, Wa resistance to newer farming techniques such as irrigation and wet rice farming can be said to have its roots not in primitive and simplistic beliefs but rather in an aversion to disturbing and rerouting waterways, and the centrality of swidden upland rice farming to religious practices and the propitiation of spirits through land management (Fiskesjö 2000, 368). Fiskesjö suggests that the Wa preferred to have irrigation through rainfall and not the canals and ditches of the wet rice terraces. Cattle ploughing and fallowing of land were practices more readily accepted by the Wa on the Chinese side of the border than on the Myanmar side (2000, 367).

38. Winnington 2008, 163. The opening epigraph to this chapter is a quotation from a Chinese cadre in Winnington's book (2008, 172).

39. Chin 2009; Jelsma et al. 2005; Chouvy 2009; Lintner and Black 2009.

40. Opium eradication campaigns in Wa Region have their roots in the CPB period, where crop-substitution programs were launched in the late 1970s (Milsom 2005, 61). The launch of three 5-year plans in November 1989 saw the announcement of the plans to eradicate opium in 1990 (Renard 2013a, 150). A UWSA drug control committee was put together in 1995 (UNODC 2006, 2). The UWSA representative Saw Lu's open proposal to the international community in 1993 was partially a plea for help to "free ourselves from slavery to an opium economy."

41. Kokang and Mongla Special Regions in Shan State had already declared their areas opium free in 2003 and 1997, respectively, providing a model for Wa to follow, but that had also meant that opium farmers moved from these areas to Wa Region.

42. Milsom 2005, 86.

43. UNODC 2006, 2; also Lone 2008, 91.

44. UNODC 2004, 7. Chin finds the US figure exaggerated (2009, 55).

45. TNI 2014.

46. Data from UNODC, collated in Berlinger 2018. TNI suggests increases in seizures may also be due to weakening relations between the Myanmar government and armed groups (2014, 33).

47. US funding for the UNODC-led Wa Project (which made up three-quarters of its funding) was cut in 2005, after three DEA agents in Myanmar received death threats. With this loss of funding, the project struggled on for two more years before closing (Renard 2013b).
48. Wa State News Media 2009, 201–11.
49. Wa News, May 22, 2016, showed 216 criminals arrested and handed over to Chinese police at the border.
50. Debate between Milsom of the UNODC and journalist Bertil Linter; see Lintner and Black 2009.
51. Chouvy 2003. Lintner, too, writes of the ease with which local informants supplied misinformation about the drug trade in exchange for cash rewards in the 1980s. Satellite imagery did not reflect the quality of poppy fields on the ground and actual production (2011, 304, 348), and the alleged routes for transportation were not always feasible.
52. As a fine example of this, one of Chin's informants suggested to him in 2008 that opium was "prohibited only in the areas along the main roads; opium is still cultivated in places far away from roads and from the view of outsiders" (2009, 242). That Chin chose to end his book with this quote suggests that such suspicions would always be taken more seriously than UWSA statements. I for one, having traveled almost all main roads through twenty-three out of twenty-four townships from 2014 to 2015, saw no poppies being grown, and years later this was no longer a point of contention. This did not mean that heroin or methamphetamines were no longer being produced.
53. *Report of the Secretary-General on Children and Armed Conflict* 2006.
54. As determined by the Office of the Special Representative of the Secretary-General for Children and Armed Conflict, from the "Paris Principles" of 2007, available at https://childrenandarmedconflict.un.org/six-grave-violations/.
55. On child soldiering in Myanmar, see Human Rights Watch 2002; Chen 2014.
56. Also serving as the "Constitution" (or Basic Law) of Wa Region, first printed in a handbook in the 2000s and republished in 2020.
57. See Steinmüller 2019 on forcible conscription in Wa Region.
58. Various scholars have examined manifestations of human rights discourses in Myanmar. For instance, Doffegnies and Wells discuss how besides being deployed in claim-making projects, human rights language is also explicitly rejected in certain political circles, while strategically avoided in others (2021).
59. Lombard 2016, 557.
60. This instance was similar to the military training that students in China go through in middle and high school. There is a distinction between these students performing partial military drills and instruction and the more regular children in the UWSA military. Videos produced and uploaded by the Wa State TV are available here: https://www.youtube.com/watch?v=OLbMdqf8HGQ&t=366s&ab_channel=UWSAWSTV.
61. See Prasse-Freeman 2019 on this pattern of authority without responsibility across Myanmar.
62. Elyachar 2010.
63. Aung-Thwin 2001.
64. UWSP 2012.
65. There was in fact a historical basis to the self-awareness of lack in the Wa hills, in comparison to the areas and groups around them. Fiskesjö records certain Wa anti-myths that provide explanatory models for why they lack writing or appear to be more impoverished than neighboring groups and suggests that these demonstrate their awareness of being "in some material sense the have-nots of the region" (2000, 107).
66. Fiskesjö 2000, 107; Fiskesjö 1999, 146. In the domain of agricultural techniques, Fiskesjö argues that "the slow progress of the expansion of fixed-field irrigated farming

is not so much the lack of capability on the part of the Wa, as in the prevailing Chinese explanation, but the weak feasibility of farming as such.... The avoidance of irrigated farming was also a matter of upholding an ideal Wa way of life" (2000, 368).

67. Kramer 2007, 29.
68. Spivak and Grosz 1990.
69. Fictitious name.

EPILOGUE

1. Lombard 2016, 114.
2. In Myanmar, Tharaphi Than argues that mobilizations of identity by the Tai Nay group in Kyaingtong (Kengtung) should be seen not as forms of nationalism but as appeals for inclusion and the recognition of diversity. Political projects of smaller peripheral groups too easily end up pigeonholed as the more recognizable form of nationalism or fundamentalism (2020).
3. Décobert 2020; Faxon et al. 2015; Harrisson and Kyed 2019; Israelsen 2019; Kyed and Thawnghmung 2019; South and Lall 2016; Thawnghmung 2017.
4. For example, Cárdenas and Olivius (2021) call for women-to-women diplomacy as an alternative grassroots model for peacebuilding.
5. Kramer 2020; Woods 2019.
6. Woods 2018, 3.
7. Woods 2018, 29.
8. Woods 2018, 24.
9. Worrall 2017, 711.
10. Davis 2009, 242.

References

Abrams, Philip. 1988. "Notes on the Difficulty of Studying the State." *Journal of Historical Sociology* 1 (1): 58–89.
ALTSEAN. 2001. *Burma: Tentative Steps, Report Card Sept.'00 ~ Jan.'01*. March 2001. Bangkok: ALTSEAN.
ALTSEAN. 2005. *Burma Briefing: Issues & Concerns Vol. 2*. Bangkok: ALTSEAN.
Anderson, Benedict. 1983. *Imagined Communities: Reflections on the Origin and Spread of Nationalism*. London: Verso.
Anzaldua, Gloria. 1987. *Borderlands / La Frontera: The New Mestiza*. San Francisco: Aunt Lute Books.
Appadurai, Arjun, ed. 1986. *The Social Life of Things: Commodities in Cultural Perspective*. Cambridge: Cambridge University Press.
Arjona, Ana, Nelson Kasfir, and Zachariah Cherian Mampilly, eds. 2015. *Rebel Governance in Civil War*. Cambridge: Cambridge University Press.
Aung-Thwin, Michael. 2001. "Parochial Universalism, Democracy Jihad and the Orientalist Image of Burma: The New Evangelism." *Pacific Affairs* 74 (4): 483–505.
Aung Zaw. 2019. "The Wa Flex Their Muscles on the Hill." *The Irrawaddy*, April 24, 2019. https://www.irrawaddy.com/opinion/commentary/the-wa-flex-their-muscles-on-the-hill.html.
Aung Zeya. 2015. "Outcome of Pang Seng Conference and the True Identity of UWSA." *Global New Light of Myanmar*, May 17, 2015.
Bakhtin, Mikhail. 1984. *Rabelais and His World*. Bloomington: Indiana University Press.
Ball, Desmond. 2003. "Security Developments in the Thailand-Burma Borderlands." Working Paper No. 9. Australia Mekong Resource Centre.
Barth, Fredrik. 1959. *Political Leadership among Swat Pathans*. London: Athlone.
Basso, Keith H. 1996. *Wisdom Sits in Places: Landscape and Language among the Western Apache*. Albuquerque, NM: University of New Mexico Press.
Baud, Michiel, and Willem van Schendel. 1997. "Toward a Comparative History of Borderlands." *Journal of World History* 8 (2): 211–42.
Bayart, Jean-Francois. 2009. *The State in Africa: the Politics of the Belly*. 2nd ed. Cambridge: Polity.
Berlinger, Joshua. 2018. "Asia's Meth Boom: How a War on Drugs Went Continentwide." *CNN*, November 5, 2018. https://edition.cnn.com/2018/11/02/asia/asia-methamphetaminegolden-triangle-intl/index.html.
Blum, Susan D. 2001. *Portraits of "Primitives": Ordering Human Kinds in the Chinese Nation*. Lanham, MD: Rowman & Littlefield.
Bonilla, Yarimar. 2017. "Unsettling Sovereignty." *Cultural Anthropology* 32 (3): 330–39.
Bourdieu, Pierre. 1979. *Outline of a Theory of Practice*. Cambridge Studies in Social and Cultural Anthropology. Cambridge: Cambridge University Press.
Brachet, Julien, and Judith Scheele. 2019. *The Value of Disorder: Autonomy, Prosperity, and Plunder in the Chadian Sahara*. Cambridge: Cambridge University Press.
Brenner, David. 2020. *Rebel Politics: A Political Sociology of Armed Struggle in Myanmar's Borderlands*. Ithaca, NY: Cornell University Southeast Asia Program Publications.
Brown, Wendy. 2010. *Walled States, Waning Sovereignty*. Cambridge, MA: MIT Press.

Buchanan, John. 2016. *Militias in Myanmar*. Asia Foundation.
Burma News International (BNI). 2017. "Deciphering Myanmar's Peace Process: A Reference Guide 2016." Burma News International.
Callahan, Mary. 2003. *Making Enemies: War and State Building in Burma*. Ithaca, NY: Cornell University Press.
Callahan, Mary. 2009. "Myanmar's Perpetual Junta: Solving the Riddle of the Tatmadaw's Long Reign." *New Left Review* 60: 26–63.
Campbell, Stephen. 2017. "State Illegibility in the Containment of Labour Unrest on the Thai-Myanmar Border." *Critique of Anthropology* 37 (3): 317–32.
Campbell, Stephen, and Elliott Prasse-Freeman. 2022. "Revisiting the Wages of Burmanness: Contradictions of Privilege in Myanmar." *Journal of Contemporary Asia*. 52 (2): 175–199.
Cárdenas, Magda Lorena, and Elisabeth Olivius. 2021. "Building Peace in the Shadow of War: Women-to-Women Diplomacy as Alternative Peacebuilding Practice in Myanmar." *Journal of Intervention and Statebuilding* 15 (3): 1–20.
Caspersen, Nina. 2012. *Unrecognized States: The Struggle for Sovereignty in the Modern International System*. Malden, MA: Polity.
Cattelino, Jessica R. 2008. *High Stakes: Florida Seminole Gaming and Sovereignty*. Durham, NC: Duke University Press.
Chambers, Justine. 2019. "Towards a Moral Understanding of Karen State's Paradoxical Buddhist Strongmen." *Sojourn: Journal of Social Issues in Southeast Asia* 34 (2): 258–89.
Chan, Debby Sze Wan. 2017. "Asymmetric Bargaining between Myanmar and China in the Myitsone Dam Controversy: Social Opposition Akin to David's Stone against Goliath." *Pacific Review* 30 (5): 674–91.
Chang, Wen-chin. 2001. "From War Refugees to Immigrants: The Case of the KMT Yunnanese Chinese in Northern Thailand." *International Migration Review* 35 (4): 1086–1105.
Chang, Wen-chin. 2002. "Identification of Leadership among the KMT Yunnanese Chinese in Northern Thailand." *Journal of Southeast Asian Studies* 33 (1): 123–46.
Chang, Wen-chin. 2006. "The Trading Culture of Jade Stones among the Yunnanese in Burma and Thailand, 1962–88." *Journal of Chinese Overseas* 2 (2): 269–93.
Chang, Wen-chin. 2009. "Venturing into 'Barbarous' Regions: Transborder Trade among Migrant Yunnanese between Thailand and Burma, 1960s–1980s." *Journal of Asian Studies* 68 (2): 543–72.
Chang, Wen-chin. 2015. "Circulations via Tangyan, a Town in the Northern Shan State of Burma." In *Asia Inside Out: Connected Places*, edited by Eric Tagliacozzo, Helen F. Siu, and Peter C. Perdue, 243–70. Cambridge, MA: Harvard University Press.
Chang, Wen-chin. 2017. "On the 'New' Burma Road: From Mule Caravans to Motorcycle Bands." *Trans-Regional and—National Studies of Southeast Asia* 5 (2): 217–42.
Charney, Michael W. 2009. *A History of Modern Burma*. Cambridge: Cambridge University Press.
Chen, Kai. 2014. *Comparative Study of Child Soldiering on Myanmar-China Border: Evolutions, Challenges and Countermeasures*. New York: Springer.
Chin, Ko-Lin. 2009. *The Golden Triangle: Inside Southeast Asia's Drug Trade*. Ithaca, NY: Cornell University Press.
Chin, Ko-Lin, and Sheldon X. Zhang. 2015. *The Chinese Heroin Trade: Cross-Border Drug Trafficking in Southeast Asia and Beyond*. New York: New York University Press.
Chouvy, Pierre-Arnaud. 2003. "Myanmar's Wa: Likely Losers in Opium War." *Asia Times*, January 24, 2003. http://geopium.org/?p=231.

Chouvy, Pierre-Arnaud. 2009. *Opium: Uncovering the Politics of the Poppy*. London: I. B. Tauris.
Christian Science Monitor. 1937. "Civilizing the Aborigines in 'No Man's Land' of Burma," November 15, 1937. From M/3/175 British Library.
Chu, Julie Y. 2010. *Cosmologies of Credit: Transnational Mobility and the Politics of Destination in China*. Durham: Duke University Press.
Clastres, Pierre. 1989. *Society against the State: Essays in Political Anthropology*. New York: Zone Books.
Clifford, James. 1997. *Routes: Travel and Translation in the Late Twentieth Century*. Cambridge, MA: Harvard University Press.
Cline, Lawrence E. 2009. "Insurgency in Amber: Ethnic Opposition Groups in Myanmar." *Small Wars & Insurgencies* 20 (3–4): 574–91.
Clunan, Anne. 2011. "State, Power, Anarchism." *Perspectives on Politics* 9 (1): 99–102.
Clymer, Kenton. 2014. "The United States and the Guomindang (KMT) Forces in Burma, 1949–1954: A Diplomatic Disaster." *Chinese Historical Review* 21 (1): 24–44.
Collier, Paul, and Anke Hoeffler. 1998. "On Economic Causes of Civil War." *Oxford Economic Papers* 50: 563–73.
Comaroff, Jean, and John L Comaroff, eds. 2006. *Law and Disorder in the Postcolony*. Chicago: University of Chicago Press.
Condominas, Georges. 1977. *We Have Eaten the Forest: The Story of a Montagnard Village in the Central Highlands of Vietnam*. New York: Hill and Wang.
Coulthard, Glen Sean. 2014. *Red Skin, White Masks: Rejecting the Colonial Politics of Recognition*. Minneapolis: University of Minnesota Press.
Cowell, Adrian. 2005. "Opium Anarchy in the Shan State of Burma." In *Trouble in the Triangle: Opium and the Conflict in Burma*, edited by Martin Jelsma, Tom Kramer, and Pietje Vervest, 1–21. Chiang Mai: Silkworm Books.
Cresswell, Tim. 2006. *On the Move: Mobility in the Modern Western World*. New York: Routledge.
Cunningham, Hilary, and Josiah Heyman. 2004. "Introduction: Mobilities and Enclosures at Borders." *Identities: Global Studies in Culture and Power* 11: 289–302.
Das, Veena, and Deborah Poole, eds. 2004. *Anthropology in the Margins of the State*. Santa Fe, NM: SAR.
Davis, Anthony. 2020. "China's Loose Arms Still Fuel Myanmar's Civil Wars." *Asia Times*, January 28, 2020. https://asiatimes.com/2020/01/chinas-loose-arms-still-fuel-myanmars-civil-wars/.
Davis, Diane E. 2009. "Non-State Armed Actors, New Imagined Communities, and Shifting Patterns of Sovereignty and Insecurity in the Modern World." *Contemporary Security Policy* 30 (2): 221–45.
Debos, Marielle. 2016. *Living by the Gun in Chad: Combatants, Impunity and State Formation*. London: Zed Books.
De Certeau, Michel. 1984. *The Practice of Everyday Life*. Berkeley: University of California Press.
Décobert, Anne. 2020. "Health as a Bridge to Peace in Myanmar's Kayin State: 'Working Encounters' for Community Development." *Third World Quarterly* 42 (2): 1–19.
Deleuze, Gilles, and Felix Guattari. 1987. *A Thousand Plateaus: Capitalism and Schizophrenia*. Minneapolis: University of Minnesota Press.
Democratic Voice of Burma. 2009. "UWSA Declares Autonomous Region." January 5, 2009.
Dennison, Jean. 2017. "Entangled Sovereignties: The Osage Nation's Interconnections with Governmental and Corporate Authorities." *American Ethnologist* 44 (4): 684–96.

Di Nunzio, Marco. 2017. "Marginality as a Politics of Limited Entitlements: Street Life and the Dilemma of Inclusion in Urban Ethiopia." *American Ethnologist* 44 (1): 91–103.

Doffegnies, Amy, and Tamas Wells. 2021. "The Vernacularization of Human Rights Discourse in Myanmar: Rejection, Hybridization and Strategic Avoidance." *Journal of Contemporary Asia*, 1–20. Published online February 1, 2021. doi.org/10.1080/00472336.2020.1865432.

Donnan, Hastings, and Thomas M. Wilson. 1999. *Borders: Frontiers of Identity, Nation and State*. London: Bloomsbury Academic.

Duffield, Mark. 2008. "On the Edge of 'No Man's Land': Chronic Emergency in Myanmar. School of Sociology, Politics, and International Studies." University of Bristol Working Paper No. 01–08.

Dunn, Elizabeth. 2018. *No Path Home: Humanitarian Camps and the Grief of Displacement*. Ithaca, NY: Cornell University Press.

E.G. 1957. "The Burma-China Frontier Dispute." *The World Today* 13 (2): 86–92.

Egreteau, Renard, and Larry Jagan. 2013. *Soldiers and Diplomacy in Burma: Understanding the Foreign Relations of the Burmese Praetorian State*. Singapore: NUS.

Elyachar, Julia. 2010. "Phatic Labor, Infrastructure, and the Question of Empowerment in Cairo." *American Ethnologist* 37 (3): 452–64.

Endres, Kirsten W. 2014. "Making Law: Small-Scale Trade and Corrupt Exceptions at the Vietnam-China Border." *American Anthropologist* 38 (1): 611–25.

Environmental Justice Atlas. 2018. "Naung Pha Dam on the Salween River, Shan State, Myanmar." Last updated on May 4, 2018. https://ejatlas.org/conflict/naung-pha-dam-on-the-salween-river-shan-state-myanmar.

Faxon, Hilary, Roisin Furlong, and May Sabe Phyu. 2015. "Reinvigorating Resilience: Violence against Women, Land Rights, and the Women's Peace Movement in Myanmar." *Gender & Development* 23 (3): 463–79.

Federal Political Negotiation and Consultative Committee (FPNCC). 2017a. "The General Principles and Specific Proposition of Revolutionary Armed Organizations of All Nationalities upon the Political Negotiation." April 19, 2017. http://fpncc.org/principles/.

Federal Political Negotiation and Consultative Committee (FPNCC). 2017b. "Provincial and Federal Peace Agreement and National Parliament-level Ceasefire Agreement." Submitted to Myanmar Tatmadaw on March 20, 2017.

Ferrie, Jared. 2015. "Burma Military Wins Rare Praise in War with Ethnic Chinese Rebels." *Reuters*, February 27, 2015. https://www.reuters.com/article/us-myanmar-clashes/myanmar-military-wins-rare-praise-in-war-with-ethnic-chinese-rebels-idUSKBN0LU0QQ20150226.

Finch, Steve. 2014. "Burma's Mong La: Debauched Haven of Drugs, Prostitution and Gambling." *Time*, March 10, 2014. http://time.com/17651/burmas-wild-east-is-a-debauched-land-of-drugs-and-vice-that-reforms-forgot/.

Fisher, Jonah. 2014. "Mong La: Myanmar's Lawless Region Where Anything Goes." *BBC News*, August 18, 2014. http://www.bbc.com/news/av/magazine-28772647/mong-la-myanmar-s-lawlessregion-where-anything-goes.

Fiskesjö, Magnus. 1999. "On the 'Raw' and the 'Cooked' Barbarians of Imperial China." *Inner Asia* 1: 139–68.

Fiskesjö, Magnus. 2000. "The Fate of Sacrifice and the Making of Wa History." PhD diss., University of Chicago.

Fiskesjö, Magnus. 2002. "The Barbarian Borderland and the Chinese Imagination: Travellers in Wa Country." *Inner Asia* 4: 81–99.

Fiskesjö, Magnus. 2010a. "Mining, History, and the Anti-State Wa: The Politics of Autonomy between Burma and China." *Journal of Global History* 5 (2): 241–64.

Fiskesjö, Magnus. 2010b. "Participant Intoxication and Self–Other Dynamics in the Wa Context." *Asia Pacific Journal of Anthropology* 11 (2): 111–27.
Fiskesjö, Magnus. 2013. "Introduction to Wa Studies." *Journal of Burma Studies* 17 (1): 1–27.
Fiskesjö, Magnus. 2017. "People First: The Wa World of Spirits and Other Enemies." *Anthropological Forum*, April 2017, 1–25.
Fiskesjö, Magnus. 2021. *Stories from an Ancient Land*. New York: Berghahn Books.
Florea, Adrian. 2020. "Rebel Governance in De Facto States." *European Journal of International Relations* 26 (4): 1004–31.
Forbes, Andrew D W. 1988. "History of Panglong, 1875–1900: A 'Panthay' (Chinese Muslim) Settlement in the Burmese Wa States." *Muslim World* 78 (1): 38–50.
Foucault, Michel. 2009. *Security, Territory, Population: Lectures at the Collège De France 1977–1978*. 1st ed. London: Picador.
Friedman, Jonathan. 1998. *System, Structure, and Contradiction in the Evolution of "Asiatic" Social Formations*. 2nd ed. Walnut Creek, CA: Altamira-Sage.
Friedman, Jonathan. 2011. "States, Hinterlands, and Governance in Southeast Asia." *Focaal* 2011 (61): 117–22.
Frontier Areas Committee of Enquiry (FACE). 1947. "Report of the Frontier Areas Committee of Enquiry." Rangoon: Government Printing and Stationery, Burma.
Fuller, Thomas. 2015. "Profits of Drug Trade Drive Economic Boom in Myanmar." *New York Times*, June 5, 2015. https://www.nytimes.com/2015/06/06/world/asia/profits-from-illicit-drugtrade-at-root-of-myanmars-boom.html.
Furlan, Marta. 2020. "Rebel Governance at the Time of Covid-19: Emergencies as Opportunities for Rebel Rulers." *Studies in Conflict & Terrorism*, 1–24. Published online September 3, 2020. https://doi.org/10.1080/1057610x.2020.1816681.
Gibson, Richard M., and Wenhua Chen. 2011. *The Secret Army: Chiang Kai-Shek and the Drug Warlords of the Golden Triangle*. John Wiley & Sons (Asia).
Giersch, C. Patterson. 2006. *Asian Borderlands: The Transformation of Qing China's Yunnan Frontier*. Cambridge, MA: Harvard University Press.
Giersch, C. Patterson. 2010. "Across Zomia with Merchants, Monks, and Musk: Process Geographies, Trade Networks, and the Inner-East–Southeast Asian Borderlands." *Journal of Global History* 5 (2): 215–39.
Global Witness. 2014. "What Future for the Rubber Industry in Myanmar?" March 2014.
Global Witness. 2015. "Jade: Myanmar's 'Big State Secret.'" October 2015.
Grindle, Merilee S. 2016. "Good Governance, R.I.P.: A Critique and an Alternative." *Governance* 30 (1): 17–22.
Guyer, Jane. 2004. *Marginal Gains*. Chicago: University of Chicago Press.
Haacke, Juergen. 2011. "The Nature and Management of Myanmar's Alignment with China: The SLORC/SPDC Years." *Journal of Current Southeast Asian Affairs* 30 (2): 105–40.
Hagmann, Tobias, and Didier Péclard. 2010. "Negotiating Statehood: Dynamics of Power and Domination in Africa." *Development and Change* 41 (4): 539–62.
Han, Enze. 2017. "Geopolitics, Ethnic Conflicts along the Border, and Chinese Foreign Policy Changes toward Myanmar." *Asian Security* 13 (1): 59–73.
Hansen, Mette Halskov. 2005. *Frontier People: Han Settlers in Minority Areas of China*. Vancouver: UBC Press.
Harrell, Stevan, ed. 1995. *Cultural Encounters on China's Ethnic Frontiers*. Seattle: University of Washington Press.
Harrisson, Annika Pohl, and Helene Maria Kyed. 2019. "Ceasefire State-Making and Justice Provision by Ethnic Armed Groups in Southeast Myanmar." *Sojourn: Journal of Social Issues in Southeast Asia* 34 (2): 290–326.

Harvey, David. 1981. "The Spatial Fix–Hegel, Von Thunen, and Marx." *Antipode* 13 (3): 1–12.

Harvey, G. E. 1933. *1932 Wa precis: A Precis Made in the Burma Secretariat of All Traceable Records Relating to the Wa States*. Rangoon: Government Printing.

Harvey, Penny, and Hannah Knox. 2012. "The Enchantments of Infrastructure." *Mobilities* 7 (4): 521–36.

Hayden, Brian, and Suzanne Villeneuve. 2011. "A Century of Feasting Studies." *Annual Review of Anthropology* 40 (1): 433–49.

Heberer, Thomas. 2014. "The Contention between Han 'Civilizers' and Yi 'Civilizees' over Environmental Governance: A Case Study of Liangshan Prefecture in Sichuan." *China Quarterly* 219: 736–59.

Hedström, Jenny. 2017. "The Political Economy of the Kachin Revolutionary Household." *Pacific Review* 30 (4): 581–95.

Herzfeld, Michael. 1987. "'As in Your Own House': Hospitality, Ethnography, and the Stereotype of Mediterranean Society." In *Honor and Shame and the Unity of the Mediterranean*, edited by D. D. Gilmore, 75–89. Washington, DC: American Anthropological Association.

Herzfeld, Michael. 2016. *Siege of the Spirits: Community and Polity in Bangkok*. Chicago: University of Chicago Press.

Herzfeld, Michael. 2019. "What Is a Polity? 2018 Lewis H. Morgan Lecture." *HAU: Journal of Ethnographic Theory* 9 (1): 23–35.

Hill, Ann Maxwell. 1998. *Merchants and Migrants: Ethnicity and Trade among Yunnanese Chinese in Southeast Asia*. New Haven, CT: Yale University Southeast Asia Studies.

Hla Oo. 2014. "War-game Anawyahtar: Burma Army's Warning to UWSA?" Blogspot.com. March 7, 2014. http://hlaoo1980.blogspot.com/2014/03/war-game-anawyahtar-burma-armys-warning.html.

Hoffman, Danny. 2011. *War Machines: Young Men and Violence in Sierra Leone and Liberia*. Durham, NC: Duke University Press.

Hoffmann, Kasper, and Judith Verweijen. 2018. "Rebel Rule: A Governmentality Perspective." *African Affairs* 118 (471): 352–74.

Horsey, Richard. 2017. "Myanmar's Peace Conference Leaves Talks on Uncertain Path." *Nikkei Asian Review*, May 31, 2017. https://asia.nikkei.com/Viewpoints/Richard-Horsey/Myanmar-s-peace-conference-leaves-talks-on-uncertain-path.

Howe, Jeff. 2013. "Murder on the Mekong." *The Atavist Magazine*, no. 30. https://magazine.atavist.com/murderonthemekong.

Htet Naing Zaw. 2019. "Military Says It Tolerated UWSA Parade for Sake of Peace." *The Irrawaddy*, June 3, 2019. https://www.irrawaddy.com/news/burma/military-says-tolerated-uwsa-parade-sake-peace.html.

Huang, Reyko. 2016. *The Wartime Origins of Democratization: Civil War, Rebel Governance, and Political Regimes*. Cambridge: Cambridge University Press.

Human Rights Watch. 2002. *"My Gun Was as Tall as Me": Child Soldiers in Burma*. October 2002.

Human Rights Watch. N.d. "Chronology of Burma's Constitutional Process." Accessed at https://www.hrw.org/sites/default/files/reports/burma0508chronology.pdf.

Humphrey, Caroline. 2004. "Sovereignty." In *A Companion to the Anthropology of Politics*, edited by David Nugent and Joan Vincent, 418–36. Malden, MA: Blackwell.

Imamura, Masao. 2015. "Rethinking Frontier and Frontier Studies." *Political Geography* 45 (2015): 96–97.

International Crisis Group (ICG). 2009. "China's Myanmar Dilemma." Asia Report No. 177. September 14, 2009. Brussels: ICG.

International Crisis Group (ICG). 2010. "China's Myanmar Strategy: Elections, Ethnic Politics and Economics." Asia Briefing No 112. September 21, 2010. Brussels: ICG.

International Crisis Group (ICG). 2016. "Myanmar's Peace Process: Getting to a Political Dialogue." Asia Briefing No 149. October 19, 2016. Brussels: ICG.

International Crisis Group (ICG). 2019. "Fire and Ice: Conflict and Drugs in Myanmar's Shan State." Asia Briefing No. 299. January 8, 2019. Brussels: ICG.

International Crisis Group (ICG). 2020. "Commerce and Conflict: Navigating Myanmar's China Relationship." Asia Briefing No 305. March 30, 2020. Brussels: ICG.

Israelsen, Shelli. 2019. "Women in War and Peace: Karen Women's Political Participation during and after the Karen–Burma Ceasefire Accords." *The Round Table* 108 (2): 175–88.

Jackson, Robert H. 1990. *Quasi-States: Sovereignty, International Relations, and the Third World*. Cambridge: Cambridge University Press.

Jagan, Larry. 2006. "Burma's Military: Purges and Coups Prevent Progress towards Democracy." In *Myanmar's Long Road to National Reconciliation*, edited by Trevor Wilson, 29–37. Singapore: ISEAS Publishing.

Jelsma, Martin, Tom Kramer, and Pietje Vervest, eds. 2005. *Trouble in the Triangle: Opium and Conflict in Burma*. Chiang Mai: Silkworm Books.

Jennings, Ronald C. 2011. "Sovereignty and Political Modernity: A Genealogy of Agamben's Critique of Sovereignty." *Anthropological Theory* 11 (1): 23–61.

Jonsson, Hjorleifur. 2012. "Paths to Freedom: Political Prospecting in the Ethnographic Record." *Critique of Anthropology* 32 (2): 158–72.

Jusionyte, Ieva. 2015. *Savage Frontier: Making News and Security on the Argentine Border*. Berkeley: University of California Press.

Jusionyte, Ieva, and Daniel M Goldstein. 2016. "In/Visible—in/Secure." *Focaal* 2016 (75): 3–13.

Kasfir, Nelson. 2015. "Rebel Governance—Constructing a Field of Inquiry: Definitions, Scope, Patterns, Order, Causes." In *Rebel Governance in Civil War*, edited by Ana Arjona, Nelson Kasfir, and Zachariah Mampilly, 21–46. Cambridge: Cambridge University Press.

Kaufman, Victor S. 2001. "Trouble in the Golden Triangle: The United States, Taiwan and the 93rd Nationalist Division." *China Quarterly* 166: 440–56.

Kaufmann, Vincent, Manfred Max Bergman, and Dominique Joye. 2004. "Motility: Mobility as Capital." *International Journal of Urban and Regional Research* 28 (4): 745–56.

Kearney, Michael. 1991. "Borders and Boundaries of State and Self at the End of Empire." *Journal of Historical Sociology* 4 (1): 52–74.

Keen, David. 2012. "Greed and Grievance in Civil War." *International Affairs* 88 (4): 757–77.

Keenan, Paul. 2013. *By Force of Arms: Armed Ethnic Groups in Burma*. Vij Books India.

Keenan, Paul. 2017. "Realising Peace in Myanmar." EBO Background Paper No. 4/2017. Euro-Burma Office Myanmar.

Kiik, Laur. 2016. "Nationalism and Anti-Ethno-Politics: Why 'Chinese Development' Failed at Myanmar's Myitsone Dam." *Eurasian Geography and Economics* 57 (3): 374–402.

Kipnis, Andrew. 1997. *Producing Guanxi: Sentiment, Self, and Subculture in a North China Village*. Durham, NC: Duke University Press.

Klein, Natalie. 2018. "A String of Fake Pearls? The Question of Chinese Port Access in the Indian Ocean." *The Diplomat*, October 25, 2018. https://thediplomat.com/2018/10/a-string-of-fake-pearls-the-question-of-chinese-port-access-in-the-indian-ocean/.

Kramer, Tom. 2007. *The United Wa State Party: Narco-Army or Ethnic Nationalist Party?* Washington DC: East-West Center Washington.

Kramer, Tom. 2020. "'Neither War nor Peace': Failed Ceasefires and Dispossession in Myanmar's Ethnic Borderlands." *Journal of Peasant Studies* 82 (2): 1–21.

Krasner, Stephen. 2011. "State, Power, Anarchism." *Perspectives on Politics* 9 (1): 79–83.

Kumbun, Joe. 2019. "Protected by China, Wa Is Now a de Facto Independent State." *The Irrawaddy*, April 23, 2019. https://www.irrawaddy.com/opinion/guest-column/protected-by-china-wa-is-now-a-de-facto-independent-state.html.

Kyaw Kha. 2017. "The Wa's Zhao Guo An: Suu Kyi Wants to Achieve Peace in Her Lifetime." *The Irrawaddy*, May 29, 2017. https://www.irrawaddy.com/in-person/zhao-guo-daw-aung-san-suu-kyi-wants-achieve-peace-lifetime.html.

Kyed, Helene Maria, and Ardeth Maung Thawnghmung. 2019. *The Significance of Everyday Access to Justice in Myanmar's Transition to Democracy*. ISEAS Trends in Southeast Asia Series. 2019 No. 9. Singapore: ISEAS Publishing.

Lahu National Development Organisation (LNDO). 2002. *Unsettling Moves: The Wa Forced Resettlement Program in Eastern Shan State (1999–2001)*. Chiang Mai, Thailand: LNDO.

Latham, Robert. 2010. "Border Formations: Security and Subjectivity at the Border." *Citizenship Studies* 14 (2): 185–201.

Lawi Weng. 2015a. "Ethnic Leaders Cite Wa Prosperity in Calls for Federalism." *The Irrawaddy*, May 11, 2015. https://www.irrawaddy.com/news/burma/ethnic-leaders-cite-wa-prosperity-in-calls-for-federalism.html.

Lawi Weng. 2015b. "'Secret Garden' that 'Leaves Much to the Imagination.'" *The Irrawaddy*, May 13, 2015. https://www.irrawaddy.com/news/burma/secret-garden-in-wa-special-region-leaves-much-to-the-imagination.html.

Lawi Weng. 2015c. "'We Have Been Subjected to International Pressure.'" *The Irrawaddy*, May 5, 2015. https://www.irrawaddy.com/in-person/interview/we-have-been-subjected-to-international-pressure.html.

Lawi Weng. 2015d. "At Panghsang Summit, Wa Leaders Urge Ethnic Unity in Post-Election Burma." *The Irrawaddy*, November 2, 2015. https://www.irrawaddy.com/election/news/at-panghsang-summit-wa-leaders-urge-ethnic-unity-in-post-election-burma.

Lawi Weng. 2015e. "At Ethnic Summit, UWSA Backs Rebels in Conflicts with Govt." *The Irrawaddy*, May 11, 2015. https://www.irrawaddy.com/news/burma/at-ethnic-summit-uwsa-backs-rebels-in-conflict-with-govt.html.

Lawi Weng. 2016a. "Wa Authorities Say Two Men Executed in Self-Ruling Region." *The Irrawaddy*, March 14, 2016. https://www.irrawaddy.com/news/burma/wa-authorities-say-two-men-executed-self-ruling-region.html.

Lawi Weng. 2016b. "UWSA Criticizes Peace Conference for 'Poor Management and Discrimination.'" *The Irrawaddy*, September 5, 2016. https://www.irrawaddy.com/news/burma/uwsa-criticizes-peace-conference-for-poor-management-and-discrimination.html.

Lawi Weng. 2017. "UWSA Steadfast in Stance on NCA Amendments." *The Irrawaddy*, May 29, 2017. https://www.irrawaddy.com/news/burma/uwsa-steadfast-stance-nca-amendments.html.

Lawi Weng. 2019. "The Cards Are in the Wa Army's Hands." *The Irrawaddy*, April 10, 2019, https://www.irrawaddy.com/opinion/commentary/145919.html.

Leach, Edmund Ronald. 1954. *Political Systems of Highland Burma: A Study of Kachin Social Structure*. London: Athlone Press.

Leach, Edmund Ronald. 1960. "The Frontiers of 'Burma.'" *Comparative Studies in Society and History* 3 (1): 49–68.

REFERENCES

Lee, Yimou, and Shwe Yee Saw Myint. 2016. "Myanmar's Strongest Ethnic Armed Group Says Drug Label 'Not Fair.'" *Reuters*, October 7, 2016. http://www.reuters.com/article/us-myanmar-wa-idUSKCN1270R3.

Lee, Yimou, and Joel Schectman. 2016. "For Apple and Others, Tin Supply Chain Has Ties to Rebel-held Myanmar Mine." *Reuters*, December 3, 2016. https://www.reuters.com/article/us-myanmar-tin-insight/for-apple-and-others-tin-supply-chain-has-ties-to-rebel-held-myanmar-mine-idUSKBN13N1VV.

Lee, Yimou, and Antoni Slodkowski. 2016a. "Through Reclusive Wa, China's Reach Extends into Suu Kyi's Myanmar." *Reuters*, December 29, 2016. https://www.reuters.com/article/us-myanmar-wa-china/through-reclusive-wa-chinas-reach-extends-into-suu-kyis-myanmar-idUSKBN14H1V8.

Lee, Yimou, and Antoni Slodkowski. 2016b. "Exclusive: Production Slowing Fast at Myanmar Mine That Rattled Tin Market." *Reuters*, October 18, 2016. http://www.reuters.com/article/us-myanmar-wa-tin-exclusive-idUSKCN12I0SI.

Lemon, Alaina. 2013. "Touching the Gap: Social Qualia and Cold War Contact." *Anthropological Theory* 13 (1–2): 67–88.

Lidow, Nicholai Hart. 2016. *Violent Order: Understanding Rebel Governance through Liberia's Civil War*. Cambridge: Cambridge University Press.

Lieberman, Victor. 2003. *Strange Parallels: Volume 1, Integration on the Mainland: Southeast Asia in Global Context, C.800–1830 (Studies in Comparative World History)*. Cambridge: Cambridge University Press.

Lieberman, Victor. 2010. "A Zone of Refuge in Southeast Asia? Reconceptualizing Interior Spaces." *Journal of Global History* 5 (2): 333–46.

Lin, Yi-Chieh Jessica. 2011. *Fake Stuff: China and the Rise of Counterfeit Goods (Routledge Series for Creative Teaching and Learning in Anthropology)*. New York: Routledge.

Lintner, Bertil. 1990. *The Rise and Fall of the Communist Party of Burma*. Ithaca, NY: Cornell University Southeast Asia Program Publications.

Lintner, Bertil. 1994. *Burma in Revolt: Opium and Insurgency Since 1948*. Boulder, CO: Westview.

Lintner, Bertil. 2011. *Land of Jade: A Journey from India through Northern Burma to China*. Bangkok: Orchid.

Lintner, Bertil. 2014. "Who Are the Wa?" *The Irrawaddy*, June. Accessed at https://www.irrawaddy.com/from-the-archive/who-are-the-wa-2.html.

Lintner, Bertil. 2017. "China Uses Carrot and Stick in Myanmar." *Asia Times*, February 28, 2017. http://www.atimes.com/article/china-uses-carrot-stick-myanmar/.

Lintner, Bertil. 2019. "Minorities, Money, and Getting It Wrong in Myanmar." *Global Asia*, March 27, 2019. https://www.globalasia.org/v14no1/feature/minorities-money-and-getting-it-wrong-in-myanmar_bertil-lintner.

Lintner, Bertil. 2021. *The Wa of Myanmar and China's Quest for Global Dominance*. Chiang Mai: Silkworm Books.

Lintner, Bertil, and Michael Black. 2009. *Merchants of Madness: The Methamphetamine Explosion in the Golden Triangle*. Chiang Mai: Silkworm Books.

Litzinger, Ralph A. 2000. *Other Chinas: The Yao and the Politics of National Belonging*. Durham, NC: Duke University Press.

Lombard, Louisa. 2016. *State of Rebellion: Violence and Intervention in the Central African Republic*. London: Zed Books.

Low, Setha, and Sally Engle Merry. 2010. "Engaged Anthropology: Diversity and Dilemmas." *Current Anthropology* 51 (supp. 2): S203–26.

Lubkemann, Stephen C. 2008. *Culture in Chaos: An Anthropology of the Social Condition in War*. Chicago: University of Chicago Press.

Lun Min Mang. 2016. "UWSA Says Not to Worry about Mongla 'Exercise.'" *Myanmar Times*, October 26, 2016. https://www.mmtimes.com/national-news/23301-uwsa-says-not-to-worry-about-mongla-exercise.html.

Lun Min Mang, and Thu Aung. 2016. "UWSA Wants China in Peace Process." *Myanmar Times*, May 2, 2016. https://www.mmtimes.com/national-news/20059-uwsa-wants-china-in-peace-process.html.

Ma, Jianxiong. 2013. "Clustered Communities and Transportation Routes: The Wa Lands Neighboring the Lahu and the Dai on the Frontier." *Journal of Burma Studies* 17 (1): 81–119.

MacLean, Ken. 2008. "Sovereignty in Burma after the Entrepreneurial Turn: Mosaics of Control, Commodified Spaces, and Regulated Violence in Contemporary Burma." In *Taking Southeast Asia to Market: Commodities, Nature, and People in the Neoliberal Age*, edited by Joseph Nevins and Nancy Lee Peluso, 140–57. Ithaca, NY: Cornell University Press.

Mak, Liz. 2015. "Funds Frozen in China P2P Cleanup." *South China Morning Post*, December 10, 2015. http://www.scmp.com/business/banking-finance/article/1889142/11-billon-yuan-frozen-funds-china-p2p-cleanup.

Makinen, Julie. 2016. "Chinese Company Lived the High Life—Until It All Came Crashing Down." *LA Times*, February 3, 2016. http://www.latimes.com/world/asia/la-fg-china-shadow-banking-20160203-story.html.

Mampilly, Zachariah Cherian. 2011. *Rebel Rulers: Insurgent Governance and Civilian Life during War*. Ithaca, NY: Cornell University Press.

Manicas, Peter. 2011. "State, Power, Anarchism." *Perspectives on Politics* 9 (1): 92–98.

Marsden, Magnus. 2012. "Fatal Embrace: Trading in Hospitality on the Frontiers of South and Central Asia." *Journal of the Royal Anthropological Institute* 18 (s1): S117–30.

Marshall, Andrew, and Anthony Davis. 2002. "Soldiers of Fortune." *Time*, December 16, 2002. http://content.time.com/time/world/article/0,8599,2056076,00.html.

Maule, Robert B. 1992. "The Opium Question in the Federated Shan States, 1931–36: British Policy Discussions and Scandal." *Journal of Southeast Asian Studies* 23 (1): 14–36.

Maule, Robert. 2002. "British Policy Discussions on the Opium Question in the Federated Shan States, 1937–1948." *Journal of Southeast Asian Studies* 33 (2): 203–24.

Maung Aung Myoe. 2009. *Building the Tatmadaw: Myanmar Armed Forces Since 1948*. Singapore: ISEAS Publishing.

Maung Aung Myoe. 2011. *In the Name of Pauk-Phaw: Myanmar's China Policy Since 1948*. Singapore: ISEAS Publishing.

Maung Aung Myoe. 2015. "Myanmar's China Policy Since 2011: Determinants and Directions." *Journal of Current Southeast Asian Affairs* 34 (2): 21–54.

Maung Pho Shoke. 1999. *Why Did U Khun Sa's MTA Exchange Arms for Peace*. Yangon: Meik Kaung Press.

Mbembe, Achille. 1992. "The Banality of Power and the Aesthetics of Vulgarity in the Postcolony." *Public Culture* 4 (2): 1–30.

McCoy, Alfred W. 1991. *The Politics of Heroin: CIA Complicity in the Global Drug Trade*. Chicago: Chicago Review Press.

McGranahan, Carole. 2018. "Refusal as Political Practice: Citizenship, Sovereignty, and Tibetan Refugee Status." *American Ethnologist* 45 (3): 367–79.

McGrath, Thomas E. 2003. A Warlord Frontier: The Yunnan-Burma Border Dispute, 1910–1937. Ohio Academy of History Proceedings, pp. 7–29.

Meehan, Patrick. 2011. "Drugs, Insurgency and State-Building in Burma: Why the Drugs Trade Is Central to Burma's Changing Political Order." *Journal of Southeast Asian Studies* 42 (03): 376–404.

Meehan, Patrick. 2015. "Fortifying or Fragmenting the State? The Political Economy of the Opium/Heroin Trade in Shan State, Myanmar, 1988–2013." *Critical Asian Studies* 47 (2): 253–82.

Meneley, Anne. 1996. *Tournaments of Value: Sociability and Hierarchy in a Yemeni Town.* Toronto: University of Toronto Press.

Mezzadra, Sandro, and Brett Neilson. 2019. *The Politics of Operations: Excavating Contemporary Capitalism.* Durham, NC: Duke University Press.

Michaud, Jean. 2006. *Historical Dictionary of the Peoples of the Southeast Asian Massif.* Lanham, MD: Scarecrow.

Milsom, Jeremy. 2005. "The Long Hard Road Out of Drugs: The Case of the Wa." In *Trouble in the Triangle: Opium and the Conflict in Burma*, edited by Martin Jelsma, Tom Kramer, and Pietje Vervest, 61–93. Chiang Mai: Silkworm Books.

Milsom, Jeremy. 2010. "Conflicting Agendas: Illicit Drugs, Development and Security in the Wa Special Region of Myanmar." PhD diss., University of Melbourne.

Mitchell, Timothy. 1991. "The Limits of the State: Beyond Statist Approaches and Their Critics." *American Political Science Review* 85 (1): 77–96.

Mol, Annemarie. 2002. *The Body Multiple: Ontology in Medical Practice.* Durham, NC: Duke University Press.

Mya Kha, and Lawi Weng. 2014. "United Wa State Army Denies Anti-Aircraft Purchase." *The Irrawaddy*, November 20, 2014. http://www.irrawaddy.com/news/burma/united-wa-state-army-denies-anti-aircraft-purchase.html.

Myint Myint Kyu. 2018. *Spaces of Exception: Shifting Strategies of the Kokang Chinese along the Myanmar/China Border.* Chiang Mai University Press.

Nader, Laura. 1972. "Up the Anthropologist—Perspectives Gained from Studying Up." In *Reinventing Anthropology*, edited by Dell Hymes, 284–311. New York: Pantheon Books.

Nang Seng Nom. 2016. "UWSA Peace Delegate: Observer Status Restrictions Made Us Uncomfortable." *The Irrawaddy*, September 2, 2016. https://www.irrawaddy.com/in-person/interview/uwsa-peace-delegate-observer-status-restrictions-made-us-uncomfortable.html.

Nan Lwin Hnint Pwint. 2019. "Confederation the Only Option for Arakanese People, AA Chief Says." *The Irrawaddy*, January 11, 2019. https://www.irrawaddy.com/news/confederation-option-arakanese-people-aa-chief-says.html.

Nathan, Laurie. 2008. "The Causes of Civil War: The False Logic of Collier and Hoeffler." *South African Review of Sociology* 39 (2): 262–75.

Newman, David, and Anssi Paasi. 1998. "Fences and neighbours in the postmodern world: boundary narratives in political geography." *Progress in Human Geography* 22 (2): 186–207.

Ng, Huiwen. 2018. "Over $27 Million Linked to Ezubao Ponzi Scheme Recovered in Singapore: Police." *Straits Times*, August 21, 2018. https://www.straitstimes.com/singapore/courts-crime/over-27-million-linked-to-ezubao-ponzi-scheme-recovered-in-singapore-police.

Nordstrom, Carolyn. 2004. *Shadows of War: Violence, Power, and International Profiteering in the Twenty-First Century.* Berkeley: University of California Press.

Norins, Martin R. 1939. "Tribal Boundaries of the Burma-Yunnan Frontier." *Pacific Affairs* 12 (1): 67–79.

Nyein Nyein. 2016. "'We Came to This Conference as Equals, but There Is Still No Equality': RCSS." *The Irrawaddy*, September 2, 2016. https://www.irrawaddy.com/in-person/interview/we-came-to-this-conference-as-equals-but-there-is-still-no-equality-rcss.html.

Nyiri, Pal. 2006. "The Yellow Man's Burden: Chinese Migrants on a Civilizing Mission." *China Journal* 56: 83–106.

Nyiri, Pal. 2012. "Enclaves of Improvement: Sovereignty and Developmentalism in the Special Zones of the China-Lao Borderlands." *Comparative Studies in Society and History* 54 (3): 533–62.

Olson, Mancur. 1993. "Dictatorship, Democracy, and Development." *The American Political Science Review.* 87 (3): 567–76.

Ong, Aihwa. 1999. *Flexible Citizenship: The Cultural Logics of Transnationality.* Durham, NC: Duke University Press.

Ong, Aihwa. 2000. "Graduated Sovereignty in South-East Asia." *Theory, Culture & Society* 17 (4): 55–75.

Ong, Andrew. 2018. "Producing Intransigence: (Mis) Understanding the United Wa State Army in Myanmar." *Contemporary Southeast Asia* 40 (3): 449–74.

Ong, Andrew. 2020. "Tactical Dissonance: Insurgent Autonomy on the Myanmar-China Border." *American Ethnologist* 47 (4): 369–86.

Ong, Andrew, and Hans Steinmüller. 2020. "Communities of Care: Public Donations, Development Assistance, and Independent Philanthropy in the Wa State of Myanmar." *Critique of Anthropology* 41 (1): 65–87.

Osburg, John. 2013. *Anxious Wealth: Money and Morality among China's New Rich.* Palo Alto, CA: Stanford University Press.

Peel, Michael, and Henry Sanderson. 2016. "Mystery Myanmar Mines Shake Up World Tin Market." *Financial Times*, August 29, 2016. https://www.ft.com/content/808c277a-6b53-11e6-a0b1-d87a9fea034f.

Phoenix New Media. 2009. The World Today program, "The Quandary Facing Myanmar's Militia," aired on September 7, 2009. https://www.youtube.com/watch?v=uTCBeRmJ07A.

Pitchford, V. C. 1937. "The Wild Wa States and Lake Nawngkhio." *Geographical Journal* 90 (3): 223–32.

Prager Nyein, Susanne. 2009. "Expanding Military, Shrinking Citizenry and the New Constitution in Burma." *Journal of Contemporary Asia* 39 (4): 638–48.

Prasse-Freeman, Elliott. 2012. "Power, Civil Society, and an Inchoate Politics of the Daily in Burma/Myanmar." *Journal of Asian Studies* 71 (2): 371–97.

Prasse-Freeman, Elliott. 2019. "Of Punishment, Protest, and Press Conferences: Contentious Politics amid Despotic Decision in Contemporary Burmese Courtrooms." In *Criminal Legalities in the Global South: Cultural Dynamics, Political Tensions, and Institutional Practices*, edited by George Radics and Pablo Leandro, 124–42. New York: Routledge.

Prasse-Freeman, Elliott. 2021. "Necroeconomics: Dispossession, Extraction, and Indispensable/Expendable Laborers in Contemporary Myanmar." *Journal of Peasant Studies* (2021): 1–31. Published online July 27, 2021. doi.org/10.1080/03066150.2021.1943366.

Prasse-Freeman, Elliott. 2022. "Resistance/Refusal: Politics of Manoeuvre under Diffuse Regimes of Governmentality." *Anthropological Theory.* 22 (1): 102–27.

Pye, Daniel, and Saw Yan Naing. 2013. "Wa Rebels Caught Up in Regional Chessmatch." *The Irrawaddy*, May 2, 2013. https://www.irrawaddy.com/opinion/wa-rebels-caught-up-in-regional-chess-match.html.

Rath, Robert. 2016. "Why Cops Are Raiding Arcades over a Fishing Game." *Waypoint*, November 24, 2016. https://www.vice.com/en_us/article/znm8zx/why-cops-are-raiding-arcade-over-a-fishing-game.

Rauhala, Emily. 2016. "How a Huge Chinese 'Ponzi Scheme' Lured Investors." *Washington Post*, February 8, 2016. https://www.washingtonpost.com/world/asia_pacific

/how-a-huge-chinese-ponzi-scheme-lured-investors/2016/02/08/fcbae776-ca9c-11e5-b9ab-26591104bb19_story.html?utm_term=.83ec9fa32e23.
Reeves, Madeleine. 2014. *Border Work: Spatial Lives of the State in Rural Central Asia*. Ithaca, NY: Cornell University Press.
Reid, Anthony. 1995. *Southeast Asia in the Age of Commerce, 1450–1680*. Vol. 2, *Expansion and Crisis*. New Haven, CT: Yale University Press.
Renard, Ronald D. 2013a. "The Wa Authority and Good Governance, 1989–2007." *Journal of Burma Studies* 17 (1): 141–80.
Renard, Ronald D. 2013b. "Bertil Lintner and Michael Black. Merchants of Madness: The Methamphetamine Explosion in the Golden Triangle." (Book Review). *Southeast Asian Studies* 2 (1): 204–10.
Reno, William. 2000. "Shadow States and the Political Economy of Civil Wars." In *Greed and Grievance: Economic Agendas in Civil Wars*, edited by Mats Berdal and David Malone, 43–68. Ottawa: IDRC.
Report of the Secretary-General on Children and Armed Conflict. October 26, 2006, A/61/529–S/2006/826. https://undocs.org/S/2006/826.
Risse, Thomas, ed. 2011. *Governance without a State? Policies and Politics in Areas of Limited Statehood*. New York: Columbia University Press.
Roitman, Janet. 2005. *Fiscal Disobedience: An Anthropology of Economic Regulation in Central Africa*. Princeton, NJ: Princeton University Press.
Rosaldo, Renato. 1993. *Culture & Truth: The Remaking of Social Analysis*. Boston: Beacon.
Sai Aung Tun. 2009. *History of the Shan State: From Its Origins to 1962*. Chiang Mai: Silkworm Books.
Sai Lone. 2008. "The Political Economy of Opium Reduction in Burma: Local Perspectives from the Wa Region." MA thesis, Chulalongkorn University.
Sai Wansai. 2015. "Ethnic Armed Resistance Leadership: Constitutional Amendment Key to Ethnic Conflict Resolution." *Shan Herald Agency for News*, May 12, 2015. https://english.shannews.org/archives/12403.
Sai Wansai. 2019. "The Founding of UWSA 30th Anniversary and Bao Youxiang's Wa State Aspirations." *BNI Online*. https://www.bnionline.net/en/news/founding-uwsa-30th-anniversary-and-bao-youxiangs-wa-state-aspirations.
Satyawadhna, Cholthira. 1991. "The Dispossessed: An Anthropological Reconstruction of Lawa Ethnohistory in the Light of Their Relationship with the Tai." PhD diss., Australian National University.
Saw Lu. 1993. "The Bondage of Opium: The Agony of the Wa People, a Proposal and a Plea." https://www.burmalibrary.org/en/the-bondage-of-opium-the-agony-of-the-wa-people.
Saw Yan Naing. 2010. "Tension Rises Further as BGF Deadline Passes." *The Irrawaddy*, March 15, 2010. http://www2.irrawaddy.com/article.php?art_id=18042.
Saw Yan Naing. 2011. "Naypyidaw, UWSA Hold Talks on Development." *The Irrawaddy*, December 27, 2011. http://www2.irrawaddy.com/article.php?art_id=22734.
Scheele, Judith. 2014. "The Values of 'Anarchy': Moral Autonomy among Tubu-Speakers in Northern Chad." *Journal of the Royal Anthropological Institute* 21 (1): 32–48.
Schein, Louisa. 2000. *Minority Rules: The Miao and the Feminine in China's Cultural Politics*. Durham, NC: Duke University Press.
Schlichte, Klaus, and Ulrich Schneckener. 2016. "Armed Groups and the Politics of Legitimacy." *Civil Wars* 17 (4): 409–24.
Scott, James C. 1972. "The Erosion of Patron-Client Bonds and Social Change in Rural Southeast Asia." *Journal of Asian Studies* 32 (1): 5–37.
Scott, James C. 1998. *Seeing Like a State: How Certain Schemes to Improve the Human Condition Have Failed*. New Haven, CT: Yale University Press.

Scott, James C. 2009. *The Art of Not Being Governed: An Anarchist History of Upland Southeast Asia*. New Haven, CT: Yale University Press.
Scott, James G. 1906. *Burma: A Handbook of Practical Information*. London: De La More Press.
Scott, James G., and J. P. Hardiman. 1900. *Gazetteer of Upper Burma and the Shan States*. Rangoon: Government Printing, 1900–01.
Selth, Andrew. 2002. *Burma's Armed Forces: Power without Glory*. Norwalk, CT: East Bridge.
Selth, Andrew. 2010. "Modern Burma Studies: A Survey of the Field." *Modern Asian Studies* 44 (2): 401–40.
Selth, Andrew. 2019. *Secrets and Power in Myanmar: Intelligence and the Fall of General Khin Nyunt*. Singapore: ISEAS Publishing.
Shan Herald Agency for News (SHAN). 2007. "Shan Drug Watch Newsletter," Issue 1 (June 2007).
Shan Herald Agency for News (SHAN). 2015. "The Panghsang Summit: Excerpts from a Journal." Shan Herald Agency for News, May 20, 2015. https://english.shannews.org/archives/12432.
Shan Herald Agency for News (SHAN). 2016. "Burmese Military Orders UWSA to Withdraw from Mongla." Shan Herald Agency for News, October 24, 2016. https://www.bnionline.net/en/news/shan-state/item/2435-burmese-military-orders-uwsa-to-withdraw-from-mongla.html.
Shenzhen Wutong Broadcasting Corporation. 2004. *"Wabang Shuangxiong,"* from the "Chinatown" series.
Shryock, Andrew. 2012. "Breaking Hospitality Apart: Bad Hosts, Bad Guests, and the Problem of Sovereignty." *Journal of the Royal Anthropological Institute* 18 (s1): S20–S33.
Silverstein, Josef. 1980. *Burmese Politics: The Dilemma of National Unity*. New Brunswick, NJ: Rutgers University Press.
Simpson, Audra. 2014. *Mohawk Interruptus*. Durham, NC: Duke University Press.
Sino-British Joint Commission for the Investigation of the Undelimited Southern Section of the Yunnan-Burma Frontier. 1937. *Volume VI: Report of the British Commissioners on the Work of the Sino-British Boundary Commission 1935–7* (Confidential). Rangoon: Superintendent, Government Printing and Stationery. British Library Asia and Africa Collections M/3/175.
Slaughter, Anne-Marie. 2004. "Disaggregated Sovereignty: Towards the Public Accountability of Global Government Networks." *Government and Opposition* 39 (2): 159–90.
Smith, Martin. 1999. *Burma: Insurgency and the Politics of Ethnic Conflict*. 2nd ed. London: Zed Books.
South, Ashley, and Christopher M. Joll. 2016. "From Rebels to Rulers: The Challenges of Transition for Non-State Armed Groups in Mindanao and Myanmar." *Critical Asian Studies* 48 (2): 168–92.
South, Ashley, and Marie Lall. 2016. "Language, Education and the Peace Process in Myanmar." *Contemporary Southeast Asia* 38 (1): 128–53.
South, Ashley. 2017. "'Hybrid Governance' and the Politics of Legitimacy in the Myanmar Peace Process." *Journal of Contemporary Asia* 48 (1): 50–66.
Spivak, Gayatri C., and E. Grosz. 1990. "Criticism, Feminism, and the Institution." In *The Postcolonial Critic: Interviews, Strategies, Dialogues*, edited by S. Harasym, 1–16. New York: Routledge.
Steinberg, David I. 2001. *Burma: The State of Myanmar*. Washington, DC: Georgetown University Press.
Steinberg, David I., and Hongwei Fan. 2012. *Modern China-Myanmar Relations: Dilemmas of Mutual Dependence*. Copenhagen: NIAS Press.

Steinmüller, Hans. 2019. "Conscription by Capture in the Wa State of Myanmar: Acquaintances, Anonymity, Patronage, and the Rejection of Mutuality." *Comparative Studies in Society and History* 61 (3): 508–34.
Stewart, Megan A. 2020. "Rebel Governance: Military Boon or Military Bust?" *Conflict Management and Peace Science* 37 (1): 16–38.
Strangio, Sebastian. 2014. "Dirty Old Town." *Foreign Policy*, July 30, 2014. https://foreignpolicy.com/2014/07/30/dirty-old-town/.
Su, Xiaobo. 2016. "Repositioning Yunnan: Security and China's Geoeconomic Engagement with Myanmar." *Area Development and Policy* 1 (2): 178–94.
Sun, Yun. 2017. "China and Myanmar's Peace Process." *United States Institute of Peace Special Report 401*. Washington DC: USIP.
Sun, Yun. 2019a. "Why China Is Sceptical about the Peace Process." *Frontier*, October 3, 2019. https://frontiermyanmar.net/en/why-china-is-sceptical-about-the-peace-process.
Sun, Yun. 2019b. "China Walks Political Tightrope in Myanmar." *Nikkei Asia*, October 8, 2019. https://asia.nikkei.com/Opinion/China-walks-political-tightrope-in-Myanmar.
Sunday Express. 1937. "Secrets of Sacred Lake Worshipped as God by Natives." October 24, 1937. From M/3/175 British Library.
Swancutt, Katherine. 2012. "The Captive Guest: Spider Webs of Hospitality among the Nuosu of Southwest China." *Journal of the Royal Anthropological Institute* 18: S103–16.
Tagliacozzo, Eric. 2009. *Secret Trades, Porous Borders: Smuggling and States along a Southeast Asian Frontier, 1865–1915*. New Haven, CT: Yale University Press.
Takano, Hideyuki. 2002. *The Shore beyond Good and Evil: A Report from inside Burma's Opium Kingdom*. Reno, NV: Kotan Publishing.
Tambiah, Stanley J. 1977. "The Galactic Polity: The Structure of Traditional Kingdoms in Southeast Asia." *Annals of the New York Academy of Sciences* 293 (1): 69–97.
Taylor, Robert H. 2009. *The State in Myanmar*. Singapore: NUS Press.
Taylor, Robert H. 2015. *The Armed Forces in Myanmar Politics: A Terminating Role?* Trends in Southeast Asia 2015 No. 2. Singapore: ISEAS Publishing.
Terpstra, Niels. 2020. "Rebel Governance, Rebel Legitimacy, and External Intervention: Assessing Three Phases of Taliban Rule in Afghanistan." *Small Wars & Insurgencies* 31 (6): 1–31.
Terpstra, Niels, and Georg Frerks. 2018. "Rebel Governance and Legitimacy: Understanding the Impact of Rebel Legitimation on Civilian Compliance with the LTTE Rule." *Civil Wars* 19 (3): 279–307.
Thaler, Kai M. 2021. "Reflexivity and Temporality in Researching Violent Settings: Problems with the Replicability and Transparency Regime." *Geopolitics* 26 (1): 1–27.
Tharaphi Than. 2016. "Mongla and the Borderland Politics of Myanmar." *Asian Anthropology* 15 (2): 152–68.
Tharaphi Than. 2020. "Nationalism: The Wrong Framework for Understanding Local Activism in Myanmar." ISEAS Perspectives, 2020 No. 45. Singapore: ISEAS Publishing.
Thawnghmung, Ardeth Maung. 2017. "Signs of Life in Myanmar's Nationwide Ceasefire Agreement? Finding a Way Forward." *Critical Asian Studies* 49 (3): 379–95.
Thein Swe, and Paul Chambers. 2011. *Cashing in across the Golden Triangle: Thailand's Northern Border Trade with China, Laos, and Myanmar*. Chiang Mai: Silkworm Books.
Tidey, Sylvia. 2016. "Between the Ethical and the Right Thing: How (Not) to Be Corrupt in Indonesian Bureaucracy in an Age of Good Governance." *American Ethnologist* 43 (4): 663–76.

REFERENCES

Ting Xiao. 2001. "A Report on the Support and Assistance to Myanmar's Special Region No. 2 (Wa State) for the Development of its Drug Eradication Program." Unpublished.

Tinker, Hugh. 1956. "Burma's Northeast Borderland Problems." *Pacific Affairs* 29 (4): 324–46.

Tooker, Deborah. 1996. "Putting the Mandala in Its Place: a Practice-Based Approach to the Spatialization of Power on the Southeast Asian 'Periphery'—the Case of the Akha." *Journal of Asian Studies* 55 (2): 323–58.

Transnational Institute (TNI). 2012. "Financing Dispossession: China's Opium Substitution Programme in Northern Burma." February 2012. Amsterdam: TNI.

Transnational Institute (TNI). 2013. "Developing Disparity: Regional Investment in Burma's Borderlands." February 2013. Amsterdam: TNI.

Transnational Institute (TNI). 2014. "Bouncing Back: Relapse in the Golden Triangle." May 2014. Amsterdam: TNI.

Transnational Institute (TNI). 2016. "China's Engagement in Myanmar: From Malacca Dilemma to Transition Dilemma." Myanmar Policy Briefing 19. July 2016. Amsterdam: TNI.

Transnational Institute (TNI). 2017. "Beyond Panglong: Myanmar's National Peace and Reform Dilemma." Myanmar Policy Briefing 21. July 2017. Amsterdam: TNI.

Transnational Institute (TNI). 2019. "Selling the Silk Road Spirit: China's Belt and Road Initiative in Myanmar." Myanmar Policy Briefing 22. Amsterdam: TNI.

Trouillot, Michel-Rolph. 2001. "The Anthropology of the State in the Age of Globalization: Close Encounters of the Deceptive Kind." *Current Anthropology* 42 (1): 125–38.

Tsing, Anna Lowenhaupt. 1993. *In the Realm of the Diamond Queen: Marginality in an Out-of-the-Way Place*. Princeton, NJ: Princeton University Press.

Tsing, Anna Lowenhaupt. 2005. *Friction: An Ethnography of Global Connection*. Princeton, NJ: Princeton University Press.

Turner, Frederick Jackson. 1920. *The Frontier in American History*. New York: Holt.

UNICEF. 2005. Multiple Indicator Cluster Survey (MICS) 2005. Myanmar, 2005.United Nations Office on Drugs and Crime (UNODC). 2004. *Myanmar Opium Survey 2004*.

United Nations Office on Drugs and Crime (UNODC). 2005. *Myanmar Opium Survey 2005*.

United Nations Office on Drugs and Crime (UNODC). 2006. *Life in the Wa Hills: Towards Sustainable Development*. September 2006.

United States Department of the Treasury. 2005. "Treasury Action Targets Southeast Asian Narcotics Traffickers." March 11, 2005. https://www.treasury.gov/press-center/press-releases/Pages/js3009.aspx.

United States Department of the Treasury. 2008. "Treasury Action Targets Burmese Drug Cartel." Press release, November 13, 2008. https://www.treasury.gov/press-center/press-releases/Pages/hp1268.aspx.

United States Institute of Peace (USIP). 2018. "China's Role in Myanmar's Internal Conflicts." Washington, DC: USIP.

United States Institute of Peace (USIP). 2020. "Myanmar's Casino Cities: The Role of China and Transnational Criminal Networks." Special Report No. 471. July 2020. Washington, DC: USIP.

United Wa State Army (UWSA). 2017. *"Process of Wa State's Consultation and Negotiation with the Government of Myanmar on Modification of Nationwide Ceasefire Agreement,"* April 30, 2017.

United Wa State Party (UWSP). 2012. "Instructions Regarding the April 2012 to April 2019 Workplan." Pangkham, March 16, 2012.

Uretsky, Elanah. 2016. *Occupational Hazards: Business, Sex, and HIV in Post-Mao China*. Palo Alto, CA: Stanford University Press.

Urry, John. 2007. *Mobilities*. London: Polity Press.

van Schendel, Willem, and Itty Abraham. 2005. *Illicit Flows and Criminal Things: States, Borders, and the Other Side of Globalization*. Bloomington: Indiana University Press.

Vrieze, Paul. 2015. "Inside Mong La: The Myanmar Town Where You Can Buy Drugs, Sex, and Endangered Animals." *Vice News*, December 14, 2015. https://www.vice.com/en_us/article/avyq3g/inside-mong-la-the-myanmar-town-where-you-can-buy-drugs-sex-and-endangered-animals.

Wa Gazetteer Editorial Committee. 2004. *Wa State Gazetteer*. April 2004. Hong Kong: Tianma Publishing Company.

Wa Historical Committee. 2017. Wa History (*Num Riah Dee Kaoh Pui Ceu Vax [Wa]*), or *wabang lishi*. Chinese version, 2nd ed. Panghsang: Wa Historical Committee.

Wa State News Media. 2009. Commemorative Yearbook of the "Twentieth Anniversary of the Establishment of Peace." Wa State Authority.

Walker, Andrew. 1999. *The Legend of the Golden Boat: Regulation, Trade and Traders in the Borderlands of Laos, Thailand, China, and Burma*. Honolulu: University of Hawaii Press.

Walton, Matthew. 2008. "Ethnicity, Conflict, and History in Burma: The Myths of Panglong." *Asian Survey* 48 (6): 889–910.

Wang, Ningsheng. 2010. "Changes in Ethnic Identity among Han Immigrants in the Wa Hills from the Seventeenth to Nineteenth Centuries." *Asia Pacific Journal of Anthropology* 11 (2): 128–41.

Watkins, Justin. 2014. *Dictionary of Wa: With Translations into English, Burmese and Chinese*. Leiden: BRILL.

Weber, Cynthia. 1995. *Simulating Sovereignty: Intervention, the State and Symbolic Exchange*. Cambridge: Cambridge University Press.

Wee, Sui-Lee. 2015. "Myanmar Official Accuses China of Meddling in Rebel Peace Talks." *Reuters*, October 9, 2015. https://www.reuters.com/article/us-myanmar-china/myanmar-official-accuses-china-of-meddling-in-rebel-peace-talks-idUSKCN0S22VT20151008.

Weinstein, Jeremy M. 2006. *Inside Rebellion: The Politics of Insurgent Violence*. Cambridge: Cambridge University Press.

Weiss, Thomas G. 2000. "Governance, Good Governance and Global Governance: Conceptual and Actual Challenges." *Third World Quarterly* 21 (5): 795–814.

Welker, Marina. 2014. *Enacting the Corporation: An American Mining Firm in Post-Authoritarian Indonesia*. Berkeley: University of California Press.

Wikileaks. 2009. "A Heart-to-Heart with the Wa." October 22, 2009, Rangoon. https://wikileaks.org/plusd/cables/09RANGOON704_a.html.

Winichakul, Thongchai. 1994. *Siam Mapped: A History of the Geo-Body of a Nation*. Honolulu: University of Hawaii Press.

Winnington, Alan. 2008. *The Slaves of the Cool Mountains: Travels among Head-Hunters and Slave-Owners in South-West China*. London: Serif.

Wolters, Oliver W. 1999. *History, Culture & Region in Southeast Asian Perspectives (Studies on Southeast Asia, Vol 26)*. Ithaca, NY: Cornell University Southeast Asia Program Publications.

Woodman, Dorothy. 1962. *The Making of Burma*. London: Cresset.

Woods, Kevin. 2011. "Ceasefire Capitalism: Military–Private Partnerships, Resource Concessions and Military–State Building in the Burma–China Borderlands." *Journal of Peasant Studies* 38 (4): 747–70.

Woods, Kevin. 2018. "The Conflict Resource Economy and Pathways to Peace in Burma." Washington, DC: USIP.

Woods, Kevin. 2019. "Rubber out of the Ashes: Locating Chinese Agribusiness Investments in 'Armed Sovereignties' in the Myanmar–China Borderlands." *Territory, Politics, Governance* 7 (1): 79–95.

World Bank. 1992. "Governance and Development." Washington, DC: The World Bank.

World Food Programme, Vulnerability Analysis and Mapping (WFP VAM). 2010. "An Analysis of the Food Security Situation in Selected Areas across Wa." June 2010. Unpublished.

Worrall, James. 2017. "(Re-)Emergent Orders: Understanding the Negotiation(S) of Rebel Governance." *Small Wars & Insurgencies* 28 (4–5): 709–33.

Xiang, Biao, and Johan Lindquist. 2014. "Migration Infrastructure." *International Migration Review* 48 (S1): S122–48.

Xinhua News. 2016. "Online P2P Lender Suspected of $US 7.6 Billion Fraud." *Xinhua Insight*, February 1, 2016. http://www.xinhuanet.com/english/2016-02/01/c_135065022.htm.

Yang, Li. 1997. *The House of Yang: Guardians of an Unknown Frontier*. Bookpress.

Yang, Mayfair Mei-Hui. 1989. "The Gift Economy and State Power in China." *Comparative Studies in Society and History* 31 (1): 25–54.

Yawnghwe, Chao Tzang. 2010. *The Shan of Burma: Memoirs of a Shan Exile*. Singapore: ISEAS Publishing.

Ying, Duan. 2008. "Kuomintang Soldiers and Their Descendants in Northern Thailand: An Ethnographic Study." *Journal of Chinese Overseas* 4 (2): 238–57.

Young, Harold Mason. 2014. *Burma Headhunters: The History and Culture of the Ancient Wa, a Mountain Tribal People*. Xlibris Corporation.

Young, Iris Marion. 2005. "Self-Determination as Non-Domination." *Ethnicities* 5 (2): 139–59.

Zhongguo Shenghuo. 2011. "zoujin wabang: quanqiuhua shidai de shanzhai shehui (Entering Wa Region, copycat society in the age of globalization)." *Lifeweek*, October 28, 2011. http://www.lifeweek.com.cn/2011/1028/35453.shtml.

Index

Accumulation, 5, 8, 27, 41, 130–131, 155, 161, 224
Action Plan, 179–180, 182
Afghanistan, 60
Ai Cheng Free Trade Zone, 131, 161
Allies, 18, 20, 52, 76, 84, 121, 124, 127–128, 151, 223
American economy, 94
annexation of Upper Burma, 72
antagonist characteristics, 136
anti-Chinese, 105, 135, 137, 225
Anti-Fascist People's Freedom League (AFPFL), 214n43, 218n28
anti-gambling operations, 52
Art of Not Being Governed, 11
Asian colony, 72
Asia World, 209n2
Asset Creation programs, 193
Aung Myint, 98
Aung San Suu Kyi, 18, 125–126, 137, 149, 223
Aung-Thwin, Michael, 186
autonomous polity, 1, 8, 12, 22, 37, 134, 199, 201, 206
Autonomy, visions of, 66

bad governance, 15, 172, 190, 192
Bamar leadership, 105
Banhong Incident, 73
Bao Youxiang, 2, 4, 6, 16–18, 115, 117, 121–122, 218–219
Bayart, Francois, 86
Belt and Road Initiative (BRI), 18, 20, 94, 132, 134–136, 144, 160
bin Laden, Osama, 4
Border Guard Force (BGF), 117, 120, 125, 218n29, 222n90, 223
borderlanders, 36, 209
Brachet, Julian, 71, 213, 216; British colonial project, 72; brotherhood, 84
Brown, Wendy, 12
Burma Act, 73
Burma-China, 73, 102–103
Burma-China Boundary Demarcation Joint Commission, 73
Burma Democratic Solidarity Party, 220n62

Burma Independence Army, 218n28
Burma Nationalities Democratic Solidarity Party, 109; Burma Nationalities Democratic United Army, 112; Burma Road of World War II, 20
Burma National United Army, 220n62
Burmese areas, 94, 106, 110, 152, 219

Callahan, Mary, 72
Cangyuan, 13, 44, 60–61, 108, 207
capacity-building, 172, 200
ceasefire capitalism, 20, 201
Central African Republic, 8, 28, 112, 181
Chang Wen-Chin, 31, 107, 111, 140, 149, 209n16
Chen, Kai, 102–104, 108, 110–111, 129, 154–159
Children and Armed Conflict 2006, 229n53
China-Burma border, 13, 74
China Central Television (CCTV), 37, 160, 224
China-Myanmar relationship, 207n37, 224n4
China's People's Liberation Army, 136
China-Vietnam border, 209n9
Chinese: Border Police, 34, 135, 140; influence, 94; Muslim, 49, 211; nationals, 102, 139, 151, 177, 210–211
Chinese border, the, 39, 52, 63, 104–105, 140, 219
Chinese currency (CNY), 3, 33, 39, 49–53, 152–159
Chinese Provincial Level Crossing Point, 35
Chin Ko-lin, 78
Chu, Julie, 37, 226
circulations, 22, 36, 42, 63; circumscription, 213n20; citational practice, 67
Civil society, 122, 167, 172, 200, 225
Clifford, James, 29, 36
Colombia, 60
colonialism, 113, 206
common knowledge, 152
Communist Party of Burma (CPB), 3, 6, 13, 114, 116, 121, 217–221, 225, 228
Communist Rule, 106
complexity, 11, 143, 200
Condominas, 208n52

249

INDEX

confidence-building measure, 120
contradictions, 11, 125, 128, 186, 206
conventionalization, 27, 112–113, 199
conventionalization of rebellion, 112
corrupt exception, 209n9
cosmopolitanism, 1, 29, 31–39, 55, 57, 59, 61, 63, 209
cross-boundary relations, 12, 133, 201
cultural heartlands, 207n30
Cultural Revolution, 108

Davis, Anthony, 205, 207n46, 215, 222n102, 226n3
Debos, Marielle, 69, 196
democracy jihad, 186
democratic transition, 134
Dennison, Jean, 206n23
Department of the Treasury, US, 215n61
Diaoyu Islands, 148
discrepant cosmopolitanisms, 36
disorder, 8–9, 20–21, 27, 71, 135, 199–202, 212
"divide and rule" strategies, 100, 113
drug abuse, 54; US Drug Enforcement Agency (DEA), 115, 229
dwelling-in-traveling, 29, 39–40, 48, 111

Eastern District Court of New York, 67
economy of appearances, 146–147, 160
Elyachar, Julia, 94, 186
enactment, 9, 21, 95, 208
entangled sovereignties, 206n23
erroneous behavior, 190
Ethnic Armed Organizations (EAOs), 17–18, 24, 128, 135, 137, 200–201, 222–223
ethnic Chinese, 40–41, 48, 78–79, 82, 102–103, 139–140
ethnic minorities, 45, 106, 109, 113, 125–126, 210, 214, 222, 224
ethnonationalism, 22, 112–114, 199
ethnonationalists, 5, 19, 205

face-to-face quality, 94
Failed Generosities, 118
farmer fortresses, 69
Federal Political Negotiation and Consultative Committee (FPNCC), 127–129, 223–224
Ferghana Valley, 8, 206
financing dispossession, 56
Fiskesjö, Magnus, 13, 25, 55, 57, 210–217, 225, 228–229
Flexible Citizenship, 51
food consumption score, 183
Forced Mobilities, 54

Foreign Narcotics Kingpin Designation Act, US, 78
freedom, 22, 24, 31, 37, 39, 45, 71, 103, 141, 218
friction of terrain, 5, 11
Frontier Areas Committee of Enquiry (FACE), 6, 16, 50, 74, 120, 128, 137, 139, 158
Frontier Areas into Ministerial Burma, 73

Gayatri Spivak, 192, 230n68
Generosity, 27, 69, 83–85, 88, 95, 100, 149, 205
Ghosts, 96
Global New Light of Myanmar, 135
Global Witness, 208, 215n45, 219n52, 226n46
Golden Triangle, 4, 20, 46, 115, 138, 141, 173–174, 218
good governance, 28, 89, 167, 170–172, 183, 200, 216, 228
Governance, Gestures of, 162–163, 165, 179–195, 226
grassroots participation, 122
Guizhou veterans, 220n57

Hans Steinmüller, 208, 210n26, 229n57
harsh enforcement, 54
Harvey, David, 130, 145
Headquarters of the Military Directorate of the United Army, 112
Hedström, Jenny, 209n67
Herzfeld, Michael, 208n56
Hezbollah, 19, 205n1
high-energy biscuits (HEB), 196–197;
highland autonomy, 11, 20, 63, 77, 213;
Hoeffler, Anke, 205n5
Hoffman, Danny, 64, 77
Hong Pang company, 75, 154, 215n60
Hopang, 103–104, 106, 108, 110, 214, 217, 219, 221
hospitality, 7, 24, 27, 69, 120, 129, 169, 205, 215–216
Human Capital, 45, 48, 191
human rights discourse, 180, 229

illegibility, 146
illicit: flows, 36; trafficking, 54; wealth, 63, 78
illiteracy, 166
Imamura, Masao, 133
incongruities, 53, 98–99, 101, 121–127
Indian Ocean, 17, 20, 134, 224
Indonesia, 21
inequality, 28, 48, 89, 167, 172
INGOs, 170–171, 179, 182–183
inhabitants, 8–9, 26, 33, 36–37, 73, 85, 102, 120
intermittence, 15, 101, 125

INDEX

Internal Critiques, 190
International Day, 54
intimacies of tyranny, 89

Joint Monitoring Committee (JMC), 223n114
Jonsson, Hjorleifur, 11, 206n16
Jusionyte, Ieva, 208n65

Kachin Independence Organization (KIO), 42, 128, 209n67, 223n108, 224n129
Kachin State, 9, 19, 21, 108, 113, 134, 151, 185, 189
Ka Laung Pa, 57–58
kamajor, 79
Karen Buddhist, 227n12
Karen National Union (KNU), 223n108, 228n27
Khin Nyunt, 20, 54–55, 61, 114–116, 122, 125, 186, 221–222
Khun Sa's surrender, 211n42
Kokang, 49, 63, 174, 185, 209, 211, 218, 221–223; defense force, 104; region, 103–104, 107, 116, 221
Kramer, Tom, 162, 205, 208, 215–216, 219–220, 225–227
Kunma, 13, 60, 73, 75–76, 82, 90, 207, 219
Kunming (China), 12–13, 209–212, 222–225
Kuomintang (KMT), 13, 20, 66, 71, 80, 103–106, 209, 217–220

lack of capacity, 190
laissez-faire 1990s, 186
language of Wa Region, 47
laoguai, 91, 216
Lashio, 59–60, 184, 194, 209, 212, 217, 219
Lawi Weng, 211n40, 217, 222–224
leadership qualities, 81
leadership styles, 172
legibility, 4, 15, 62, 121, 138, 146, 168–169
Liberation Tigers of Tamil Eelam (LTTE), 205n1
Lintner, Bertil, 17–18, 107, 137, 215, 217–225, 228–229
local political culture, 8–9, 28, 170, 200
logics of authority, 1, 26–28, 74, 81, 168, 170, 198, 200
Lo Hsing-Han, 209n2, 221n79
Longtan, 73, 162–166, 168
lowland Myanmar, stability of, 185
Luxury homes, 131

MacLean, Ken, 20
management of relations, 69

Mandalay (Myanmar), 1–21, 78, 88, 91, 110, 207–212, 215, 219–230
Manicas, Peter, 206n17
Man Maw, 147–148, 150, 154–155, 157–159
Man Xiang, 33, 43, 47, 57–59, 139, 158, 209, 219
Marshall, Andrew, 205, 207, 215, 226
Maung Pho Shoke, 211n42, 221, 223n106
Menglian Port Joint Inspection Station, 35
Mengmao, 60–61, 106–107, 154, 164, 188, 214, 217, 219
Meung Vax, 3, 112
Milsom, Jeremy, 172, 208, 210, 215, 221–229
Min Aung Hlaing, 18, 126, 129
Ministerial Burma, 72–73
mobilities turn, 37, 209
mobility, 13, 15, 21, 26, 48–54, 148, 209
Mong Kar, 54
Mong Phen, 40, 54, 187–188, 222
Mong Tai Army (MTA), 54, 115, 221–223
Mong Tai Army's Khun Sa, 54
Mon-Khmer group, 12
most-favored nation, 18
motility, 209n12
Multiple Indicator Cluster Survey (MICS), 183, 226n6
mutiny, 13, 75, 82, 106, 109, 114
Myanmar: China highlands, 20; delegation, 18; government, 18, 24, 31, 40, 47–49; Immigration, 32, 35, 49, 118–119, 135, 207; military (Tatmadaw), 9, 214–225, 227, 229; National Convention, 68, 112–113, 223; reputation, 20, 22, 48, 54, 70, 146, 152, 165, 177, 197, 215
Myanmar Peace Centre (MPC), 223n114

Nam Hka Rivers, 73, 104
Nam Rai River, 57
National Democratic Alliance Army (NDAA), 52–53, 121, 220–221, 225
National Democratic Front (NDF), 100, 220
nationalisms, 113
National League for Democracy (NLD), 18, 101, 125, 136–137, 207, 223
Nationwide Ceasefire Agreement, 18, 101, 200
Nationwide Census, 117, 121
Naung Pha dam on the Salween River, 225n31
Navigating Histories, 102
Nawd Kham, 212n1
nepotism, 157, 172, 199, 227
New Harvest Festival, 42, 163, 166
non-domination, 12

nongovernmental organizations (NGOs), 23, 28, 183, 185, 189–190, 192, 198, 226
nonsecession, 16–18, 101
Norins, Martin R., 213–214
Northern Chad, 69, 71, 168, 212

One Blood, 112
One Leads Ten, 79–80
oppression, 11–12, 105, 107
orphan army, 217n24
oscillations, 9, 15, 27, 98–105, 117–129, 217

Pangkham, 59–61, 64–67, 211–212, 221–222
Pang Yao, 210n25
Parasitic Accumulation, 138, 142, 199
Paris Principles, 229n54; Patterson Giersch, 208n54; Peng Jiasheng, 116, 221
People's Liberation Army (PLA), 135–137, 224
People's Park field, 175
phatic labor, 94, 186, 190
Ping Fu-chang, 162
Politburo, 6, 18, 40, 76, 82, 86–88, 188–189
Political dialogue, 99–100, 127
political situation, 28, 190, 197
politics of knowledge, 24, 150
politics of the belly, 86
poor governance, 191
poor management, 81
porosity, 8, 26, 31, 35–37, 39–40, 50, 63
porous borders, 36
Porsche Cayenne, 76
predatory periphery, 13, 151
primitiveness, 4, 28, 191
process geographies, 21, 208n54
promissory politics, 181
proxy, 13, 105, 134–138, 151, 154, 207, 225
Public Security, 135

rebel governance, 22, 169–170, 227
rebellion, 19, 22, 112–114, 199, 211, 224, 227
rebels, 4–5, 20, 67, 111–112, 169–170, 207, 227
Reform, Spectacles of, 173
Region-making, 1, 7, 9, 22, 26, 36, 111, 199
Relational Autonomy, 8–9, 12, 15, 101, 121, 199–202
Renard, Ron, 45
Report on Children and Armed Conflict, 179
resourcefulness, 133, 145, 155
road collapse, 34, 145
Ruptures, 96

Sai Lone, 208n47, 210n31, 211, 218n33, 227n24
Scheele, Judith, 71, 168, 212–213, 216, 227

Scott, James G., 70–71, 73, 94, 206, 210n30
second-generation leaders, 82
"Secret Garden," 98
Self-Administered Areas (SAAs), 221n75
self-reliance, 1, 9, 26, 39, 48, 69–70, 72, 75, 77, 81, 97, 122, 168
Selth, Andrew, 25
Sentosa Cove of Singapore, 161
separatism, 112, 199
serfs of the army, 166
shadow economies, 1, 13, 36, 53, 77, 201–202
Shan militia, 39, 42, 108, 212
Shan State Army, 221n85, 222n102
Sierra Leone, 79
Singapore, 43, 46, 161, 212
South Asian heritage, 43
Southeast Asia (SEA), 4, 16, 22, 115, 130–131, 134–135, 143, 209
Spatial Imaginaries, 134
Special Region, 60, 112, 114, 119, 218–219, 228
Spectacular Accumulations, 146
stability, 9, 20–21, 27, 53, 199, 201, 224
state evaders, 11
state evasion, 4, 9, 11–12
State Law and Order Restoration Council (SLORC), 110, 220
Stories from an Ancient Land, 57
storytelling, 26
strategic essentialism, 192; String of Pearls, 134, 224n7; strong leadership, 84
Sun Guoxiang, 17, 128, 137
sustainable development, 189
Swiss colonel Frederic Iselin, 73

tactical dissonance, 9, 15, 72, 100–101, 198
Taiwan Ministry of Defence, 217n15
Tamil Tigers, 19
Tar Gaw Et Bridge, 32, 114, 184
Tatmadaw, 5, 121–129, 135, 137, 172, 207, 218–223
Tatmadaw's isolation of Wa Region, 185
Tenth Anniversary Commemoration, 175
10th Anniversary of Wa Region's Eradication of Opium, 175
Thailand, 4, 10, 40, 55, 107, 115–116, 120–121
Tharaphi Than, 211n36, 230n2
Thein Sein, 101, 115, 124, 134, 223
Third Army of General Li Wen-huan, 218n24
Third Panglong Conference, 128
the Thirtieth Anniversary Celebration, 16–17, 115, 202
Toyota Hilux, 29, 154

Transnational Institute (TNI), 56, 212, 216, 223–228
traveling-in-dwelling, 29, 39–40, 48
travel permits, 105
Treasury Department, US, 4, 67
tribesman, 77, 136
Tsing, Anna, 133, 146
Turner, Frederick Jackson, 133
2014 Myanmar Population and Housing Census, the, 222n99, 226n4

United Myanmar National Democratic Army, 220n62
United Nationalities Federal Council (UNFC), 100, 123–124, 128, 223n108
United Wa State Army (UWSA), 170–180
United Wa State Party, 6, 162, 205n9
UNODC, 47, 167, 172, 174, 185, 208, 227–229
Unratified Mobilities, 48
Uretsky, Elanah, 216n86
U Thein Swe, 207n40
UWSA leadership, 4, 27, 37, 89, 105, 172, 198, 225
UWSA officials, 19, 22–25, 28, 56, 171, 185, 188

Value, Tournaments of, 85, 93; village of Yaong Soi, 56–57; village stockades, 69
violence, 11, 70–71, 84–85
virtue-signaling narrative, 94

Wa authorities, 23, 58, 60, 111, 118–121, 143, 147–148, 221–222; government, 2–4, 67–69, 75, 77, 120–128, 132, 216–228; guerrilla groups, 76–77, 82, 106; Health Department, 135, 166; hills, 1–2, 5, 7, 9, 76–77, 102–108, 111–114, 128, 165, 218–219, 229; Historical Committee, 214n42, 217n13, 217n20, 219n35; polity's struggle, 5; Region, 1–5, 7–15, 20–37, 101–107, 203, 205, 207–222, 225–229; Region's political culture, 7, 198; State, 18, 112–113, 130, 199, 205, 207, 212–214; village, 3, 104, 106, 188, 217; World, 72

wabang, 4, 9, 35, 112, 205, 216
Wa Democratic Party (WDP), 221n75
Wa National Army (WNA), 106, 220
Wa National Organization (WNO), 211n46, 220n56
Wa Region Gazetteer, 113
warlordism, 112
warlords, 4–5, 22, 200
War Machine, 64, 69, 71, 76–77, 85
Wa Self-Administered Division, 114
Wa Temporary Residence Permit, 49
weak capacity, 167, 191
wealth, 17, 97, 115–116, 132, 139, 141, 221
Weber, Cynthia, 67
Wein Kao, 42, 54, 106, 205
Wei Xuegang, 78, 84, 122, 215, 220
Welker, Marina, 21, 208
wheel of fortune, 65
Winnington, Alan, 104, 173
Woodman, Dorothy, 213–214
Woods, Kevin, 20, 207–208, 226n46, 230
World Food Programme (WFP), 1, 5, 166–167, 185, 188, 193–197
World War II, 20, 73–74, 103, 214n42, 218n28

Xi Jinping, 96, 160
Ximeng, 60, 162, 164, 207
Xinjiang Uighurs, 94
X-ray Fluorescence (XRF), 155

Yaong Kraox, 192–194
Yaong Soi, 56–60
Yawd Serk, 221n85
Yin Phan (Vingngun), 104, 106, 211, 214, 217, 219–220
Young, Harold Mason, 2, 5–6, 65–66, 76, 79, 205–206, 228
Young, Iris Marion, 12
Yucheng Group, 131, 143–145, 160
Yunnan-Burma Frontier, 214n33

Zhang Chengyu, 213n14
Zomia, 11, 206
zones of refuge, 11–12

Milton Keynes UK
Ingram Content Group UK Ltd.
UKHW010714271023
431431UK00008B/414